MW01470614

Kennesaw State University: The First Fifty Years,

1963–2013

Kennesaw State University: The First Fifty Years,

1963–2013

Por Guissela Patricia

Tom Scott

Thomas Allan Scott

Kennesaw State University Press

The Kennesaw State University Press
Kennesaw State University
www.kennesaw.edu/ksupress

Author: Thomas Allan Scott

Editor: Cathleen Salsburg-Pfund
Cover and Book Design: Holly S. Miller

Library of Congress Cataloging-in-Publication Data

Scott, Thomas Allan.
  Kennesaw State University : the first fifty years, 1963-2013 / Thomas Allan Scott.
    pages cm
  Includes bibliographical references and index.
  ISBN 978-1-933483-29-0 (hardcover with jacket : alk. paper) -- ISBN 978-1-933483-30-6 (softcover : alk. paper)
  1. Kennesaw State University--History. I. Title.
  LD2755.S36 2013
  378.758'245--dc23

Printed in the United States of America
10 9 8 7 6 5 4 3 2 1

Contents

Acknowledgments   vii

Preface   ix

Chapter 1   Democratization of Higher Education and Creation of   1
             Kennesaw Junior College

Chapter 2   Junior-College Years, 1965–1976   23

Chapter 3   "Four Years Now": The Conversion to Senior-College   65
             Status

Chapter 4   A New President and a View of the Future   99

Chapter 5   Building the College of the Future   133

Chapter 6   Transforming the Identity and Culture of a Maturing   179
             Public College

Chapter 7   Weathering the Storms of a Troubled Era   219

Chapter 8   Becoming a University, 1996–2006   249

Chapter 9   New President, New Era   297

Chapter 10   Kennesaw at Age Fifty   341

Epiloque   387

Endnotes   391

Index   435

Acknowledgments

This book is dedicated to all the Kennesaw family (students, alumni, faculty, staff, retirees, trustees, and community friends). I especially want to thank President Daniel S. Papp and his executive assistant, Lynda K. Johnson, for their support from the beginning. President Papp read the manuscript and offered a number of helpful suggestions. I owe the largest debt of gratitude to my wife, Kathleen S. Scott, an alumna of Kennesaw Junior College and former Student Government Association and Alumni Association president. Her advice and support over the years have been priceless. We have lived the history of Kennesaw State University together for the last four decades, and I could not have produced this work without her. I also much appreciate the encouragement of Catherine Lewis, Tamara Livingston, Anne Graham, Heather Oswald, Vera Gargano, Beth Holahan, and everyone in the Department of Museums, Archives, and Rare Books, who have been great colleagues since my retirement in 2011. They provided me with an office, supplies, and a key to the archives, and helped me find all the documents and photographs that I needed.

Former vice president for academic affairs, Edwin A. Rugg, was my first reader as each chapter was finished. After he left the vice presidency, he moved to the Department of Enterprise Information Management, and continued to serve the university by overseeing institutional research. His perspectives on the accomplishments of the Siegel and Papp years greatly enriched my understanding, and he helped improve the manuscript stylistically as well as substantively. After I made the corrections that Ed suggested, I asked professor emerita of English, Dede Yow, to be my second reader. Over the years, she helped conduct a number of interviews for the KSU Oral History Series. I have been blessed to have Ed's vice-presidential and Dede's faculty perspectives. Where their memories differed, I have learned from both and, hopefully, produced a more balanced account as a result.

One of my goals for the fiftieth anniversary history was to distance myself from campus politics and focus on faculty, staff, and student achievement. I am grateful to all the members of the campus community who allowed me to interview them, or have answered my e-mail requests for information. Those interviews and e-mails have provided important primary source material. I will be forever thankful to Bill Hill and the Center for Excellence in Teaching and Learning (CETL) for providing financial support and a location to conduct interviews with the faculty award recipients. The College of Humanities and Social Sciences, the KSU Foundation, the Center for Regional History and Culture, and the KSU Archives have also paid some of the transcribing and binding costs. Additionally, a number of students from my oral history classes did important interviews with longtime members of the faculty and staff. Their work is acknowledged in the endnotes.

Even in a relatively long book, I have not been able to include all who made important contributions to the growth of the university. I hope they will forgive my omissions. I urge readers who want to know more about faculty accomplishments to go online through the KSU Archives and CETL for transcripts of the interviews in the KSU Series. Finally, I want to thank all the students who took my classes during a forty-three-year teaching career, and my colleagues across campus who, from the beginning, made me feel that this was where I was meant to be.

From our first discussion, President Papp and I agreed that we needed at least two external reviewers. I think we chose the best available in the University System of Georgia. Thomas G. Dyer's accomplishments at the University of Georgia are almost too many to list. He is university professor emeritus, vice president for instruction emeritus, and the author of *The University of Georgia: A Bicentennial History, 1785–1985*. August W. (Gus) Giebelhaus is the founding director of Georgia Tech's School of History, Technology, and Society and a coauthor of *Engineering the New South: Georgia Tech, 1885–1985*. Their critiques of the manuscript were positive and insightful, and their many detailed suggestions have helped produce a better book. Needless to say, I take total responsibility for this volume's remaining deficiencies.

Preface

Who would have guessed fifty years ago that a small campus at the intersection of Chastain and Frey Roads in rural Cobb County would become home to one of the University System of Georgia's fastest-growing, comprehensive, doctoral degree-granting universities? The last half-century of progress began with a group of politically savvy visionaries of the early 1960s who understood the importance of higher education in meeting the needs of a growing population. In the 1962 gubernatorial campaign, the successful candidate, Carl Sanders, promised to build a junior college in neighboring Cartersville rather than Cobb County. But leaders from the Marietta-Cobb area had other ideas, and their superior arguments and political clout won over the Board of Regents of the University System of Georgia and led to the creation of Kennesaw Junior College.

Local boosters were not acting in a vacuum. Similar stories can be found throughout the nation as an expanding economy, the GI Bill, and a baby boom fueled grand expectations in the generation following World War II. Especially in the Sun Belt, a proliferation of public colleges made higher education affordable and accessible. Neither before nor since has Georgia experienced a time like the 1960s when new institutions seemed to spring up everywhere. In the year 1963 alone, the regents chartered three new junior colleges (including Kennesaw) and converted two older junior colleges into four-year schools.

Of the junior colleges created in Georgia during the thirty years after World War II, none advanced quite as rapidly as Kennesaw. Since the enrollment of the first 1,014 students in the fall of 1966, the institution has grown into a metropolitan university of almost 25,000 students, with a projected enrollment by 2016 (the fiftieth anniversary of the first class) of about 30,000. At least once a decade, Kennesaw has advanced to a higher level. From 1966 to 1976 it was a two-year school. In April of 1976, the Board of Regents authorized its conversion into a senior college. Nine years later, in 1985, Kennesaw enrolled its first masters' students. In 1996, the regents awarded university status. In 2007, Kennesaw State University started its first doctoral program.

During the first fifty years, Kennesaw had only three presidents, each a good fit for a particular developmental stage. The charter president, Dr. Horace W. Sturgis

(1965–1980), led with a sense of dignity that won community support for the start-up junior college. In his fifteen years of service, Kennesaw established a solid reputation for exemplary teaching, was elevated into a senior college, and in the spring of 1980 granted its first baccalaureate degrees. Dr. Betty L. Siegel (1981–2006) was the first woman to serve as president of any unit of the University System of Georgia. Her entrepreneurial, visionary leadership and oratorical and friend-making abilities brought Kennesaw onto a national stage as a dynamic, inviting college of the future.

Along with the KSU Foundation, President Siegel played a central role in the establishment of residence halls in 2002, an event that almost immediately transformed the campus culture. The current president, Dr. Daniel S. Papp (2006–present), has employed his strategic vision and extraordinary managerial talents to accelerate the institution's remarkable expansion. Progress in the last seven years has been particularly apparent in the awarding of the first doctoral degrees; the increased focus on applied research, global initiatives, and community service; rising retention and graduation rates; and the expansion of student housing and recreational facilities.

I joined the faculty in the fall of 1968 in time for the third year of classes. On my first visit to campus, I was struck by the beauty of the buildings and grounds and by the excitement that everyone displayed over the college's future. The faculty was young and inexperienced, but dedicated to teaching, and as fine a group of scholars as one could hope to encounter. We were tiny in number—few enough to hold faculty meetings in a modest seminar room in the library. The student body was equally small—1,368 when I arrived—but they were highly talented and hard-working. From the beginning, Kennesaw specialized in serving the needs of over-the-traditional-age students, as well as younger scholars, many of whom were nontraditional in the sense of being gainfully employed or married with children. They typically had the intellectual gifts to go to college anywhere, but chose Kennesaw because of family or economic circumstances or because Kennesaw was small enough for everyone to know their names.

Although relatively few of the "long-marchers" (President Siegel's name for those who joined the faculty and staff in the 1960s or 1970s), held doctorates when they arrived on campus, they had the opportunity to mature intellectually along with the college. As they completed their degrees, they did not need to look elsewhere for bigger and better challenges because Kennesaw kept growing with them. I have had the great fortune of being part of Kennesaw's development for most of its first fifty years. But I must confess to being a bit envious of those who are just now at the beginning of their careers, because they will have a chance to observe the university's expansion over the next half-century. I am sure it will continue to grow in stature and significance as it serves the needs of north Georgia—and the rest of the state and nation. President Siegel always liked to say that if you see a turtle on a post, you know it didn't get there by itself. My wish is that the author of the centennial history will be just as proud of KSU (or whatever its name may be by that time) as I have been, and that he or she will recognize that the successes of the second half-century were greatly facilitated by the hard work and accomplishments of the people in the pages that follow.

Democratization of Higher Education and Creation of Kennesaw Junior College

On a gorgeous early October day in 1963, the Board of Regents of the University System of Georgia gathered in Carrollton for its monthly meeting. The members awakened to temperatures in the low fifties that would rise to about eighty under an afternoon sun. They met on the West Georgia College campus so they could dedicate a new science building in memory of Cason J. Callaway, an heir to a textile-mill fortune and agricultural reformer who founded, with his wife Virginia, the Callaway Gardens in Pine Mountain. In 1963, his son, Howard (Bo) Callaway, held his father's old seat on the Board of Regents.[1]

The regents began their October 9, 1963, meeting with a report from West Georgia College president James E. Boyd on his school's history. A case study of a poor state's struggles to provide adequate educational opportunities, West Georgia had opened in 1908 as the Fourth Congressional District's A&M high school. In 1933 the Carrollton institution joined the recently-created University System of Georgia as a junior college, and did not offer its first bachelor's degree (in elementary education) until 1957. However, in the six years since then, student enrollment had more than doubled from 576 to 1,268.[2]

After thanking President Boyd,[3] the regents devoted much of the meeting to the routine work of property transactions and faculty appointments. The agenda item that received the greatest press coverage was the establishment of a new junior college in the Cobb County area. Although the vote was unanimous, the selection was not without controversy, and the *Atlanta Constitution* reported a "spirited contest" among several north Georgia communities. In addition to Cobb, the regents received bids from Cartersville in neighboring Bartow County and Rome in Floyd County. During the 1962 gubernatorial campaign, the eventual winner, Carl Sanders, had campaigned on placing a public college within commuting distance of all but the most isolated Georgians. At the time, the only public college in northwest

Mayor Charles Cowan of Cartersville

Georgia's Seventh Congressional District was Southern Technical Institute in Marietta, and its curriculum was focused on architecture and engineering.

As a candidate, Sanders promised Mayor Charles Cowan and the people of Cartersville that any new junior college in the Seventh District would go to their city. As a result, Mayor Cowan began accumulating a tract of land for a potential campus site. At the same time, the leadership of Cobb County launched its own initiative. When the final decision was made, Mayor Cowan was gracious in defeat, congratulating Cobb and telling the press that his city and county had received a fair hearing. He added, "I am naturally disappointed in our great loss. We feel very much like Adlai Stevenson did on losing the Presidential election when he said, 'We are too big to cry, and it hurts too bad to laugh.'" The regents perhaps made amends to the mayor a few months later by placing the new college in north Cobb near the Bartow County line and by appointing his brother-in-law as the charter president.[4]

How Cobb County persuaded Governor Sanders and the Board of Regents to locate the school in the Kennesaw area remains a matter of local pride that will be explained later. A broader set of questions is how and why the post–World War II generation of Georgians became committed to major improvements in higher education. In the three decades following World War II Georgia made major strides in raising professors' salaries and upgrading established colleges and universities. Further, as table 1 reveals, the university system between 1958 and 1976 added thirteen brand new junior colleges, and absorbed three more two-year schools that had been locally created. Two other institutions, today's Southern Polytechnic State University and Georgia Perimeter State College, were also products of the postwar era, although they were not independent units of the University System at the time.[5] These eighteen schools made up a majority of Georgia's public colleges and universities. Growth of this magnitude had not happened in Georgia before and has not happened since. But, Georgia was not acting alone. Throughout the nation a revolutionary change took place in the thirty years after World War II that affected virtually all colleges and made access to higher education more widespread than ever before.

TABLE 1	Junior Colleges that were Created or Joined the University System of Georgia, 1958–1976		
Institution	Date of Charter or Authorization	Year Opened for Classes
Augusta	1958	1925
Columbus	1958	1958
Armstrong	1958	1935
Brunswick (Coastal Georgia)	1961	1964
Albany (Darton)	1963 (April)	1966
Dalton	1963 (July)	1967
▶ Kennesaw	1963 (October)	1966
Gainesville	1964 (April)	1966
Macon	1965	1968
Clayton	1965	1969
Atlanta Metropolitan	1965	1974
Floyd (Georgia Highlands)	1968	1970
Bainbridge	1970	1973
Emanuel County (East Georgia)	1970	1973
Waycross	1970	1976
Gordon	1972	—

Note: Gordon College started before the Civil War as a private high school. By 1928 it offered a junior college as well as a high school curriculum. From the time of World War I, the school operated a military program. Due to financial difficulties in the 1960s, the trustees of Gordon Military College asked the Board of Regents to assume ownership. On July 2, 1972, the transfer took place under the new name of Gordon Junior College.

Sources: New Georgia Encyclopedia; official campus websites of schools listed in this table.

Impact of World War II on Higher Education

In many respects, the decades following World War II were a golden age for American higher education with everyone seemingly benefiting from enlightened policies at federal, state, and local levels. The elite research universities and, in time, the flagship state institutions profited from a tremendous expansion of federal grant opportunities following the academic science community's important role in helping to win the war. From his post as director of the Office of Scientific Research and Development, Vannevar Bush oversaw the wartime Manhattan Project and otherwise brought scores of college professors into direct service to the American military. In July of 1945 he presented President Harry Truman with a report titled *Science, the Endless Frontier* that provided the blueprint for competitive, peer-approved grants to college scientists through agencies such as the National Science Foundation, the National Institutes of Health, and the Defense Department. Between 1940 and 1960 federal grant dollars flowing to American universities increased one hundred fold, and grantsmanship and "soft money" became a way of life for many faculties. In the 1950s a few "federal grant universities" monopolized the government largesse — six elite universities received 57 percent of all federal grant funding and the top twenty received 79 percent. For those schools, the US government was hugely important, accounting for anywhere between 20 and 80 percent of their operating budgets.[6]

No university in Georgia, public or private, ranked in the top twenty. Cameron Fincher argues that at the beginning of the postwar era none of the university system schools even "deserved status as a full-fledged university."[7] In time, however, federal dollars began flowing more freely to flagship schools and turned institutions such as the University of Georgia and Georgia Tech into true research universities. In his bicentennial history of the University of Georgia, Thomas G. Dyer finds a fair amount of research on campus throughout the postwar years, but notes a significant expansion after the completion of a multimillion-dollar science center in 1960. By the 1970s UGA was appearing in top fifty lists of research universities. Between 1945 and 1985, spending on research rose from a mere $168,000 to $75 million.[8]

Current KSU president Daniel S. Papp, formerly USG senior vice chancellor for academics and fiscal affairs, arrived as a young assistant professor at Georgia Tech in 1973 and was immediately caught up in the spirit of change that emanated from President Joseph M. Pettit.[9] Robert C. McMath Jr. and his fellow authors of *Engineering the New South* vividly describe Georgia Tech's scholarly limitations before Pettit left a deanship at Stanford in 1972 to head the Atlanta campus. On the eve of World War II, only 31 of Tech's 165 faculty members possessed doctorates, and most were assigned fifteen-hour teaching loads, leaving little time for scholarship. Tech's wartime contract work was minimal, compared to the great research universities of the north and west. Nonetheless, Tech's Engineering Experiment Station and its Guggenheim School of Aeronautics led the way in attracting external funding for vital defense projects. After the war, physics professor James Boyd engaged in significant electronics work at the Experiment Station. His contracts in the 1950s and early 1960s with the Office of Naval Research were an important foundation for the tremendous growth in Tech's defense contracting in later years.[10]

Joseph Pettit was a protégé of Frederick E. Terman, a Stanford engineering professor and giant voice in the development of the modern research university. After Pettit completed his doctorate in electrical engineering at Stanford in 1942, he moved with his mentor to the Radio Research Laboratory at Harvard University, where Terman and his crew did pioneering radar research for the military during World War II. After the conflict, when Terman returned to Stanford as dean of engineering and later as provost, Pettit became part of Terman's faculty and ultimately replaced him as dean.

Over the next several decades Terman, Pettit, and a host of their students and colleagues set the standard for the academic world in aggressively pursuing military contracts for high-technology research and development. They also encouraged their graduate students to form their own technology companies. Under their guidance, northern California's Silicon Valley became the center of the nation's high-tech electronics industries. During the age of student protest in the late 1960s, Stanford's applied-research ties to the military became controversial. Nonetheless, it was quite a coup when Georgia Tech persuaded Pettit to move to the Southeast. It would not have happened if the Board of Regents had not made clear its desire to elevate scholarship in the university system. McMath and his colleagues note that Pettit's strengths were precisely in areas where Tech was weak. In his first interview after accepting the Tech appointment, Pettit issued a wake-up call to Georgians by describing his new university as merely a "first class undergraduate school," adding that it would be a major challenge to strengthen the graduate programs.[11]

Applied-research connections between academia and industry, however, were something that fit well into Tech's mission. As McMath maintains, "the translation of scientific and technological knowledge into regional economic uplift was an objective equally at home in the Silicon Valley of Terman and Pettit and the New South of Henry Grady and his spiritual heirs." While Tech's progress in the Pettit years (1972–1986) was not as great as he may have hoped, sponsored research income increased fivefold in a decade, and in the twenty-first century Tech has consistently maintained a top-ten ranking in research expenditures among universities lacking a medical school. Dan Papp notes that the university system is sometimes criticized for not producing more nationally-recognized scholarship, yet it yearly ranks at, or near, the top ten nationally as a generator of academic research. This is a remarkable accomplishment, Papp claims, given the university system's brief history in this highly competitive arena.[12]

A Baby Boom of New Colleges

At the other end of the higher educational spectrum, the post–World War II era saw a remarkable expansion of junior and community colleges, allowing millions of working Americans to live at home and attend college at nontraditional ages. There were at least three major causes of this transformation, of which the most important was the growth of American affluence. In the aftermath of the Second World War, the economies of most Old World countries were in shambles, and American industry had no rivals. Following a decade and a half of depression and war, America's pent-up demand for housing, automobiles, and consumer goods was tremendous. Moreover, the Cold War kept military spending high.

Despite inflationary worries, jobs were plentiful, and most Americans had an optimistic faith that things would continue, indefinitely, to get better. By 1960 the purchasing power of the median American family was 30 percent greater than just a decade earlier. The 1960s were even more prosperous with per capita income growing during the decade by some 41 percent. In his magisterial history of the postwar generation, James T. Patterson speaks of the American people's "grand expectations" that the economic expansion would go on indefinitely, that wise federal programs would and should create equal rights and opportunities for previously disadvantaged groups, and that access to higher education was an essential element in creating an equal-opportunity society.[13]

While all regions experienced unprecedented prosperity, no section grew faster than the South. In Georgia, for example, per capita income in 1940 was only 57 percent of the national average. But by 1950 it had risen to 70 percent, and by 1970 to 84 percent.[14] Cobb County, Georgia, is a case study of how the South advanced out of poverty. A middle-sized, rural county with just 38,272 people in 1940, Cobb County used Civil Aeronautics Administration funds in 1941 to build a commercial airport. Shortly after Pearl Harbor, the United States Army Air Corps took over the airstrip for a military base, and on adjacent lands the Corps of Engineers and Atlanta-based Robert & Company began constructing a manufacturing plant for the Bell Aircraft Company. By February of 1945 Bell's Marietta plant employed 28,158 workers, the vast majority native Georgians, who delivered to the military some 663 long-range B-29 bombers. The plant did more than provide temporary employment. Workers with little previous industrial experience took advantage of the company's extensive training programs to learn new skills. Those who became supervisors attended classes that taught them managerial principles, helping many of them to start their own businesses after the war.

The plant closed almost immediately after the Japanese surrender, but reopened under the management of the Lockheed Corporation about five years later in January of 1951 when the Korean War created a new demand for military aircraft. At first Lockheed's Georgia Division refurbished B-29s, then built B-47 jets, before gaining the contract for a new transport plane, the C-130 Hercules, which has been the mainstay of the Marietta plant for well over a half century. Originally an operation that assembled planes designed elsewhere, Marietta's United States Air Force Plant 6 became home to teams of engineers who completed the production design work on the C-130, then did all the design work in-house for the next major plane, the C-141 Starlifter, awarded to Lockheed-Georgia in 1961. One cannot overestimate the importance of the defense industry for the local economy and culture, as a suddenly affluent and suburban population demanded a host of amenities from better roads to parks, libraries, schools, and colleges.[15]

If James Patterson is correct that prosperity was the central force behind post-war America's expanding rights consciousness, and if the opportunity to attend college was one of those rights to which Americans felt entitled, the major single event that opened college doors to working-class families was the 1944 passage of the Servicemen's Readjustment Act, popularly known as the GI Bill. Described by Patterson as "the most significant development in the modern history of American education," this popular bill started out more as an unemployment plan than an educational measure. Once victory in the war seemed likely, President Roosevelt and Congress began thinking of how to incorporate the millions of veterans back into civil society. A major fear of postwar planners was that the servicemen would flood the job market, causing a return of Depression-era high unemployment. At first, the federal government imagined a bill that would provide unemployment benefits to veterans until industry had time fully to convert to peacetime produc-tion. Planners also wanted funds to help veterans buy homes or start businesses.

Lobbying by the American Legion, the American Council on Education, and others led to the addition of educational benefits. At the time, few people seemed to have grand expectations for the educational component. The prevailing wisdom was that men and women who had given up years of their lives to fight the Nazis and the Japanese would not want to sacrifice more years by returning to school. Even the bill's advocates thought that a maximum of 10 percent of the veterans would apply for the college-level educational benefits. Both friends and foes, however, underestimated the bill's appeal. Before the program's termination in 1956 some 2.2 million veterans enrolled in college (approximately 16 percent of those eligible), while another 3.5 million matriculated in non-college technical schools, and 0.7 million took advantage of on-the-farm agricultural training.

The federal government directly paid colleges up to $500 a year to cover each veteran's tuition, fees, books, and supplies for a maximum of four years. The veteran also received a modest stipend (originally, ninety dollars a month for those with dependents and sixty-five a month for those who were single) to help with housing and other expenses. One of the popular features of the bill was that the subsidies were portable, following the veteran who transferred from one school to another.

During the bill's twelve-year run the government paid some $14.5 billion to colleges, technical schools, and other educational institutions, a huge entitlement for its day.[16]

Thomas Dyer notes the dramatic impact of the GI Bill on the University of Georgia. As soon as the bill became law, Chancellor Steadman V. Sanford began warning university system administrators to prepare for an influx of a new type of students who were likely to be more diligent in their studies and more demanding in the classroom, expecting professors to know their subjects and to present stimulating, relevant information. Sanford also anticipated the need to give veterans credit for what they had learned in the military, allowing them to exempt some classes. UGA president Harmon Caldwell joined the chancellor in warning policymakers of a crisis in classroom space and housing if appropriations for higher education did not increase substantially. Caldwell hoped to capitalize on the urgency of the moment to build an institution with greatly expanded teaching, research, and public service roles. Enrollment had declined from around 3,800 hundred students on the eve of the war to 1,836 students in 1944. Caldwell predicted that the GI Bill might fuel an increase to more than five thousand. In reality, his estimate was quite conservative; enrollment in the fall of 1946 reached 6,643, and in fall of 1947 some 7,532. In the latter year veteran enrollment was an all-time high of 4,340 (57.6 percent of the student body).

The rapid growth in student population put pressure on all campus resources, but perhaps none more so than housing. As early as August 1945 five hundred veterans engaged in a mass protest over the inadequacy of the situation. The university responded by moving one hundred trailers in early 1946 onto "Ag Hill" to create for the veterans and their families a shanty town that was accessible by dirt roads that were dusty in dry season and almost impassably muddy during rainstorms. In time, several hundred more units were added to "Trailertown," as the veterans dubbed their makeshift community.

Georgia Tech experienced a similar growth in enrollment accompanied by a housing crisis. Fortunately, the Atlanta area was better prepared than Athens to accommodate the surplus students. Some of the married veterans commuted from Marietta Place, a public housing project built during the war for Bell Aircraft employees. Tech placed others at Lawson General Hospital next to the Naval Air Station in Chamblee. Like the UGA veterans, Tech's nontraditional students were no-nonsense individuals who were not shy about letting their feelings be known. For instance, a threatened veteran-led sit-down strike during the 1946 Tech-Navy football game was averted only when the Athletic Association agreed to better student seating.[17]

While the future Georgia State University was much smaller at the time than UGA or Tech, it also benefited from the GI Bill, although in ways that were sometimes ethically questionable. Merl Reed describes how the downtown Atlanta institution operated from 1913 to 1933 as an evening school for Georgia Tech, then struggled independently through the Depression and war years as the University System of Georgia Evening School. Despite limited degree offerings and a lack of accreditation, the Evening School was the university system's third largest college in 1941 with 1,602 students. That number declined during the war, but rose again to 2,174 in 1945. The promise of the GI Bill helped administrators make the case for improved facilities.

A 1947 merger with the University of Georgia gave the newly-designated Atlanta Division the right to offer the BBA degree and the chance to gain accreditation. Prior to the merger, the Atlanta school received much-needed cash from the Veterans Administration in a sweetheart deal that became controversial when it was exposed to the light of day. For reasons that are somewhat murky, the VA paid out-of-state tuition for all veterans at the Atlanta Division, even if they were permanent Georgia residents. After UGA officials in Athens blew the whistle on this questionable practice, the VA stopped paying nonresident tuition for anyone. By that time, muckraking national reporter Drew Pearson had been tipped off that the Atlanta Division was charging veterans more per credit hour than non-veterans, billing the federal GI Bill program for the higher rate. The elimination of these practices caused the school to suffer public embarrassment and the loss of about $300,000 a year in expected revenues.[18]

Despite such problems, the GI Bill helped the former servicemen attend college and whetted the public's appetite for more educational opportunities. President Truman responded by appointing a twenty-eight-member Commission on Higher Education, chaired by the president of the American Council on Education, George F. Zook, and containing such well-known dignitaries as historian Douglas Southall Freeman, Vassar president Sarah Gibson Blanding, and Kansas State University president Milton S. Eisenhower, the brother of World War II hero, General Dwight D. Eisenhower. Between December 1947 and February 1948 the commission issued a six-volume report titled *Higher Education for American Democracy*. It's central assumption was that American colleges and universities could "no longer consider themselves merely the instrument for producing an intellectual elite," but should "become the means by which every citizen, youth, and adult is enabled and encouraged to carry his education, formal and informal, as far as his native capacities permit."

To accomplish this objective, the commission called on the states to provide tuition-free community colleges as part of their public school systems; advocated legislation that outlawed racial and religious discrimination in admissions; and urged the federal government to provide grants to colleges for new construction, scholarships "for at least 20 percent of all undergraduate non-veteran students," and fellowships for graduate students. The commission's liberal vision angered fiscal conservatives who objected to the cost, white southerners who resented its attack on segregation, and private school administrators who objected to granting federal aid only to public colleges. Given the political climate of the late 1940s, the plan had no chance of passing through Congress. Yet, much of what it advocated became a blueprint for the future, with the states taking the lead in expanding their networks of community and junior colleges.[19]

As a healthy economy, the GI Bill, and rising public expectations fueled college enrollment growth, the force that made the 1960s the pivotal decade in the postwar history of higher education was the baby boom. With the return of soldiers and sailors from overseas, the birth rate rose dramatically in 1946 and remained high for the next decade and a half. The first of the baby boomers turned eighteen (college age) in 1964. In the early 1950s, communities throughout the nation scrambled to build more classrooms to meet the K–12 demand. By the end of the decade, the states were beginning similar preparations on the college level. In Georgia, Governor Marvin Griffin and the General Assembly decided in 1957 to create a Junior College Study Committee, which, according to Chairman Frank Cheatham, was charged with studying whether the state should support two-year colleges in Savannah, Augusta, Columbus, and possibly other communities. The Junior College of Augusta had operated under the Richmond County Board of Education since 1925, and Armstrong College in Savannah had been a city-run junior college since 1935. Meanwhile, Columbus boosters had been working since the late 1940s to raise sufficient funds to build a campus in their community. All three cities hoped to receive state aid while maintaining local control.

The primary opposition came from established colleges that feared the dilution of state revenues if the funds had to be split in more directions. University of Georgia president O.C. Aderhold argued that his institution could handle the increased demand if the regents would build more dormitories in Athens and expand the network of UGA off-campus centers to additional communities around the state. When the legislature adopted the Junior College Act of 1958, it gave the proponents the main thing they wanted: state aid for an expanded network of junior colleges that had the option of operating under local control or applying for admission to the university system. However, the final bill reflected the critics' concerns by requiring recipients of state funds to comply with all university system policies and standards and ordering the Board of Regents to certify annually that the disbursement of funds under the Junior College Act would not affect the efficient operation of any unit of the university system.

Under the circumstances, Columbus and Augusta decided it would be simpler to be part of the state system than try to exist independently. They applied for admission and were accepted by the Board of Regents in April 1958. Savannah held out a little longer, but found itself in a fight it could not win. When the Junior College Study Committee began its work in 1957, the USG's director of plant and business operations, Hubert Dewberry, conducted a facilities study of the Armstrong campus. He concluded that the school needed to make about a half million dollars of improvements to meet minimum university system standards before becoming eligible for state assistance. Ultimately, the city and the regents negotiated a deal where Savannah would have four years to pay $495,000 for the building upgrades, and the regents would take control immediately. In October of 1958 the regents voted to admit Armstrong to the system, and the city signed the final paperwork the following February.[20]

While the Junior College Act of 1958 proved vital in bringing Columbus, Augusta, and Armstrong into the university system, only one local jurisdiction created and operated its own junior college under the act's provisions. In the spirit of President Truman's Commission on Higher Education, DeKalb County school superintendent Jim Cherry envisioned a community college with open admissions for all graduates of the county's high schools. The first campus opened in Clarkston in 1964. By the second year of operation, enrollment exceeded two thousand, and the first group of students graduated in the spring of 1966.

In 1972 DeKalb College's second campus opened just outside Decatur. That same year, students were afforded the opportunity to enroll jointly at DeKalb Area Technical School in Clarkston. For the next fourteen years the combined institutions operated under the name of DeKalb Community College. As the college grew, it opened multiple campuses around DeKalb County and beyond, including a Dunwoody campus in Fulton County in 1979. However, the DeKalb County School Board separated the technical and liberal arts aspects of the school in 1986 and turned the latter over to the university system. In 1997 the name changed to Georgia Perimeter College and then in 2012 to Georgia Perimeter State College, reflecting the beginning of baccalaureate programs. The five campuses in Clarkston, Decatur, Dunwoody, Alpharetta, and Covington together enrolled about twenty-seven thousand students, making it the third-largest college in the university system.[21]

Higher Education in Cobb County before 1963

The home of a major defense industry, Cobb County tripled in population between 1940 and 1960, growing from 38,272 people to 114,174. By the latter date it was the largest county in Georgia without a junior or senior college. In 1951 the University of Georgia had established an off-campus Marietta Center, one of ten around the state. But local leaders wanted more than a branch campus that lacked its own identity. In the late 1950s Commissioner Herbert McCollum, the Cobb legislative delegation, and the Marietta Kiwanis Club set to work to bring to the area either a liberal arts or a technical college. In the end they got both.

UGA's Marietta Center never had a campus of its own. For the first six years it was exclusively an evening program, operating out of offices and classrooms at

Marietta High School. When it began offering day classes in 1957, it obtained four designated classrooms from the Marietta School District at the underutilized Banberry School, east of what is currently US 41, then known colloquially as the Four Lane Highway. With four hundred students by 1958, the Marietta Center received additional rooms at Pine Forest Elementary School.[22]

The director of the Marietta Center, Dr. Archie S. Rushton, met in 1957 with the Marietta Kiwanis Club's Public and Business Affairs Committee and made the case for better facilities. Chaired by newspaperman Bill Kinney, this powerful committee included powerbrokers such as Representative Harold Willingham, Lockheed general manager Carl Kotchian, and Judge James T. Manning. The Kiwanians asked for and received the enthusiastic support of Cobb's Commissioner of Roads and Revenues, Herbert McCollum, who informed them that the county planned to sell the old almshouse on Fairground Street and that the Marietta Center could have the eight-acre site. Moreover, forty acres of county-owned land behind the almshouse were available for future expansion.[23]

With architectural drawings of the Marietta Center building in hand, a local delegation visited Governor Griffin. At the time he was not willing to pledge any state funds, but gave his support in principle, saying it was a step in the direction of what his Junior College Committee was advocating. Fortunately, one of the Kiwanis Public and Business Affairs Committee members, John King, happened to be the governor's personal pilot, and he told his colleagues how to gain a financial commitment. He had observed the governor horse trading with legislators around the state to gain support for a rural roads bill. Cobb may not have needed rural roads, but King suggested they offer their support in exchange for a Marietta Center building.[24]

Shortly afterward, the governor invited to his office Harold Willingham, Raymond Reed, and Gene Holcombe, Cobb's three lower-house representatives. Griffin told them that he needed their support for his roads bill. After some bargaining, he agreed to find $600,000 for the new building. The governor was willing to be generous because his rural roads bill faced stiff opposition from Lt. Governor Ernest Vandiver, the Atlanta newspapers, and most urban legislators, including Cobb's lone senator, Fred Bentley. Griffin was nearing the end of his term, and Vandiver had already emerged as heir apparent. The future governor denounced the bill as "pork-barrel" legislation that would force a tax increase. Despite the support of the three Cobb representatives, the bill went down to defeat in the House, 106-95.[25]

The Griffin administration ended in scandal due to corruption in the Highway Department and other agencies. Nonetheless, the governor kept his word to Cobb's legislators, although he switched the funds from the off-campus center to another educational project. A few days after the rural roads vote, Representative Willingham received an invitation from Freeman Strickland, the vice chairman of the Board of Regents. At a Capitol Club luncheon in downtown Atlanta, Strickland related the university system's fear that all the other UGA centers would lobby for new buildings if Marietta received one. Instead, the regents wanted to move Southern Technical Institute to Cobb County. In an address to the Marietta Kiwanis Club on March 20, 1958, Governor Griffin announced that the promised $600,000 would be used to accomplish that purpose.[26]

Since 1948, Southern Tech had offered classes in World War II military barracks at the old Atlanta Naval Air Station in Chamblee. The state created the two-year school to train engineering technicians to translate the plans made by research and design engineers into practical instructions for assembly line workers. Under the supervision of Georgia Tech, STI filled a vital niche in Georgia's booming, postwar industrial economy. Unfortunately, the old barracks were not designed to handle the weight of numerous students and heavy shop and lab equipment. As maintenance costs rose, director Lawrence V. Johnson began seeking a new campus. When the DeKalb County government seemed reluctant to provide an upgraded facility, Johnson and the university system began looking elsewhere.[27]

In April of 1958 a delegation from the Board of Regents visited Cobb and expressed a preference for a Clay Street (present South Marietta Parkway) site close to US 41 and only about a mile from the Lockheed plant, where Southern Tech students were likely to co-op and seek employment. Commissioner McCollum immediately went to work to acquire the ninety-three-acre tract. The Marietta Housing Authority already had an option to buy, but it was more interested in owning nearby Marietta Place, where temporary housing had been constructed in the 1940s for Bell Aircraft workers and had been used after World War II by Georgia Tech students. The county owned Marietta Place and was presently leasing it to the city for public housing. On May 6, 1958, the county and the Marietta Housing Authority swapped real estate. With the property exchange, the county bought the campus site and offered it free of charge to the Board of Regents.[28]

Realizing they were about to lose their college, the DeKalb County government put together a 108-page brochure, explaining why the regents should leave the campus near Chamblee. Afraid they might be outbid, the Cobb legislative delegation, along with Lockheed general manager Carl Kotchian, went back to Governor Griffin and persuaded him to give Cobb more money. In a generous mood, the governor released to the university system $2 million from his contingency fund with the provision that the revenues could only be spent to build a campus for Southern Tech in Cobb County.

The governor's grant went toward the construction of classroom and administrative buildings. In addition, the Cobb County government graded and paved the streets and parking lots, the City of Marietta provided curbs and sidewalks, the Cobb County-Marietta Water Authority put in water lines, and the Marietta Board of Lights and Water provided electricity and sewerage. Finally, the Marietta Housing Authority agreed to furnish dormitory rooms. With the complete plan in place, Harold Willingham sent a detailed letter to Hubert Dewberry at the Board of Regents, which became the "Bible" for all future college development, setting the precedent for local communities providing the campuses, all site improvements, and utilities. On June 11, 1958, the Board of Regents voted unanimously to move Southern Tech to Marietta.[29]

The Chancellor chose local architect Bill Tapp to design the campus. The groundbreaking ceremony occurred on a chilly day in December of 1958. Marvin Griffin took the controls of a bulldozer and turned a small amount of turf. That night the Kiwanis committee held an appreciation program for the Board of Regents at the Larry Bell Center. Griffin got up and told the gathering that he once told Cobb's representatives, "I am not used to paying $200,000 a piece for votes upstairs [in the legislative chambers], but damned if it didn't cost me $666,666 each before I got through." In July 1959, Larry Johnson became director of Georgia Tech's engineering extension division. At the same time, Hoyt L. McClure, a Southern Tech faculty member since 1951, became acting director. Two years later he became permanent director, in time for the opening of the Marietta campus on October 2, 1961. The initial enrollment for the two-year school was 894. Since STI classes took place mainly in the daytime, the institution was able to designate four classrooms at night for the UGA off-campus branch. So the Marietta Center received a new campus after all, although still not one it could call its own.[30]

Southern Tech became the first public college in the Seventh Congressional District. Almost simultaneously Cobb County gained a new vocational institution, officially chartered as the Marietta-Cobb Area Vocational-Technical School in April 1961. The Marietta School District had already agreed to designate classroom and office space at Banberry School, and in September of 1961 the first three programs (electronics, electricity, and drafting) got under way. During the next two years, the Vo-Tech school constructed a permanent campus at 980 South Cobb Drive, south of Marietta, not far from the Lockheed plant. By the time the original building opened on September 3, 1963, the school had grown to twelve programs and 120 students. In the spring of 1964 Marietta-Cobb Area Vocational-Technical School held its first commencement for thirty-one graduates. Thus, Cobb County, by the early 1960s had met local needs with a technical two-year branch of Georgia Tech that would grow eventually into Southern Polytechnic State University and a vocational facility that would become, in time, Chattahoochee Technical College. However, the county still lacked a liberal arts junior college. Filling that gap became the next major objective of local leaders.[31]

Origin of Kennesaw Junior College

The campaign to create Kennesaw Junior College demonstrates the same degree of civic involvement and aggressiveness that was displayed in the Southern Tech fight. In the decade following World War II, the Board of Regents relied on off-campus centers of the University of Georgia to spread higher education into growing communities. After the passage of the Junior College Act of 1958, the board began to favor separate colleges headed by presidents who could communicate directly with the chancellor's staff. Anxious to phase out the off-campus centers, the board, in the fall of 1959, ruled that students graduating from the University of Georgia could earn no more than a fourth of their credits at one of the branches.[32]

Harold Willingham attended the dedication of the new junior college chartered in 1961 in Brunswick. While there he lobbied the regents on Cobb County's behalf. Despite the efforts of Willingham and others, Governor Ernest Vandiver seemingly had little interest in a new school north of the Chattahoochee. When Carl Sanders ran for governor in 1962, he was far more open to the idea. However, he originally favored Cartersville as the site for the next college in the Seventh Congressional District. Willingham supported Sanders's opponent, former governor Marvin Griffin. After the election, when he visited the victorious Sanders, he found him still strongly committed to Bartow.

Although Willingham had tremendous influence as a Talmadge/Griffin loyalist and as attorney for the Cobb County School District, he represented only one wing of local politics. A leader of the moderate/liberal wing was Fred D. Bentley Sr. a veteran legislator and attorney, who served in 1962 as Carl Sanders's Cobb campaign manager. In 1963 he was president of the Cobb Chamber of Commerce. The chamber played a major role in the junior-college fight by sending the Board of Regents' Committee on Education an abundance of data to document Cobb's need for a liberal arts school. Armed with this information, Bentley journeyed to the Capitol early in 1963 to convince the new governor. In years to come the two would joke about that day—the governor recalling that Bentley "parked in his outer office until he [Sanders] finally caved in" and put money in the state budget to make it happen.[33]

Fortunately, by that time, Sanders was coming to realize that the rapidly growing Cobb was a better location for a new school than Bartow. In the campaign of persuasion, Bentley credited the central role of Senator Edward S. Kendrick and a twenty-eight-person steering committee, chaired by *Marietta Daily Journal* editor and Cobb County native Robert Dobbs Fowler. The citizens' group contained some of the most important names among Cobb's educational, political, and civic leadership.[34] Having learned their lesson well in the Southern Tech fight, they lobbied the governor and Board of Regents aggressively.

On April 3, 1963, County Commissioner McCollum and the school boards of Marietta and Cobb submitted to the Board their formal application for a new college. In this document they argued that Cobb was one of the largest counties in the state without a liberal arts school. They promised to donate the land for the campus, sell bonds to construct the buildings, pay for the landscaping, and provide roads and all utilities. In the Southern Tech fight a few years earlier, the local leadership had relied on Governor Griffin to provide the funds for building construction. This time they pledged local revenues. Wanting a liberal arts school badly, Cobb volunteered more than any community had offered before.[35]

During the next half year the need for new junior colleges became a major subject of discussion, first by the chancellor's staff, then by a special task force, and finally in the summer of 1963 by Governor Sanders's Commission to Improve Education. Cameron Fincher calls the governor's commission the first comprehensive study ever conducted of education in Georgia, both academic and vocational, from the elementary grades through college.[36] Recognizing Cobb's rapid population growth, the commission recommended acceptance of its application. In the late summer Hubert Dewberry of the chancellor's staff held several meetings with Bob Fowler and his steering committee to make sure they understood what the regents expected of them. Dewberry was apparently satisfied with their response, as Chancellor Harmon Caldwell joined in recommending acceptance of the request from Marietta and Cobb County. When the Cartersville and Bartow County schools seemed slow in offering a counter proposal, the Board of Regents decided on October 9, 1963, to go along with the chancellor and the commission's recommendation, voting to create a junior college in Cobb County at a site to be approved later.[37]

A few weeks afterward, Dewberry began meeting with the steering committee and conducting appraisals of the possible site. By early 1964 he had narrowed the list to six properties: a tract east of Marietta owned by O. C. Hubert and others; the Jordan and Frey properties, both north of Marietta on the Four Lane Highway (US 41); the Vaughn property at the intersection of Old and New US 41; the County Farm property southwest of Marietta on Callaway Road; and a tract northeast of Marietta that was bordered on the east by Steve Frey Road and on the west by Frey Lake Road. The last option was owned by Pinetree Corporation and included part of the 321-acre farm formerly owned by Steve Frey and his family, along with several smaller tracts adjacent to the Frey farm.

To the west of the potential campus site, Pinetree Corporation owned additional acreage that contained a country club, golf course, and swimming pool. The Frey farm originally ran from east of Steve Frey Road to just west of the Pinetree clubhouse. The entire Pinetree Corporation holding appears in Board of Regents documents as the Recreation Center site. The Chairman of the Board of Regents, James A. Dunlap, had originally argued for a property in Marietta next to Southern Tech, but changed his mind after learning that STI administrators objected to another college located so close. On February 12, 1964, Dunlap and six other regents joined

16

with Dewberry and a local delegation for a tour of the various sites. By the end of the day, Dewberry and the regents' committee agreed that the Recreation Center site was their first choice.[38]

In later years Commissioner Herbert McCollum recalled the local delegation taking the regents to lunch at the Gold House Restaurant on the Four Lane Highway (US 41). Afterwards, they escorted them to the Frey farm where they got "full of red bugs and mosquitoes." Harold Willingham pushed hard for this location. The delegation stopped at the five-way McCollum Parkway-Ben King-Big Shanty entrance to Pinetree Country Club, just west of the proposed site. He remembered Hubert Dewberry asking where all the roads went. Willingham responded that one led to Kennesaw and Dallas, a second to Acworth and Cartersville, a third to Roswell and Alpharetta, a fourth to Marietta and Atlanta, and the last to Canton and Ellijay. Dewberry turned to the chair of the steering committee, Bob Fowler, and asked, "Bob, is that right? Do all those roads go to all those places Harold said?" Fowler thought for a while, then responded, "I guess you could get where he said on all of them."[39]

The old Frey farm had a number of advantages. The land was affordable, and it was located almost half-way between Marietta and Cartersville, so Governor Sanders could tell disappointed constituents in Bartow County that he at least built a junior college within commuting distance.[40] On the other hand, the Recreation Center and Pinetree Corporation had been scalded in the *Atlanta Journal* and by a Cobb County grand jury just a little over a year earlier for an ethically questionable deal that involved a number of prominent and powerful individuals. In the late 1950s the Cobb County Recreation Authority had bought the property for a public golf course and swimming pool to be surrounded by a county-developed subdivision. The largest tracts had been owned by the Frey family and by real estate developer Robert Bozeman.

With Bozeman as chairman of the Recreation Authority and Willingham as its attorney, the authority built a clubhouse, a golf course that met Professional Golfers Association (PGA) standards, and an Olympic-size pool, all sources of pride to the people of Cobb County. It also began dividing adjacent lands into residential lots, and, on nearby Bozeman Lake, planned boat docks and picnic facilities. The City of Kennesaw and Cobb County partnered to provide water and sewerage to the clubhouse and new homes. The Rural Electrification Administration put in streetlights, and the State of Georgia paved the streets.

For several years the Recreation Center site and new subdivision seemed an unqualified asset to the county. The white public enjoyed using the segregated pool and golf course, and the state and county benefited from increased tax revenues as suburban lots were developed. Then, in November of 1962, the authority, without public notice, sold everything to Pinetree Corporation of Atlanta. At the

time, Willingham told the surprised local citizenry that the authority had to do it because the US Supreme Court had ordered Atlanta in 1955 to integrate its public golf courses, and it was only a matter of time until someone sued Cobb County for access to the Recreation Center facilities. He claimed that Cobb "couldn't sell high-priced lots if just anybody could chase golf balls around your yard."

However, the Recreation Authority had purchased and developed the site after the Supreme Court ruling in the Atlanta case, and a number of people suspected an even more tainted explanation for the authority's haste in selling. One authority member, architect William R. Tapp Jr., objected at the time and had the foresight to include his reservations in the authority's November 6, 1962, minutes. While he did not publicly name anyone, he suspected that certain parties were using the sale for private gain. A Cobb County Grand Jury agreed with Tapp's conclusions. The grand jury report for the January–February 1963 term concluded that, "While no criminal statute has been violated, it is the forceful opinion of the Grand Jury that the intent of the law has been twisted and circumvented in violation of all reasonable moral conduct in these transactions."[41]

If the stench of corruption over the country club was not bad enough, a further complication was that one of the three owners of Pinetree Corporation, Jesse Draper, was a member of the Board of Regents. However, Hubert Dewberry insisted that he made his choice before asking who owned the property. Moreover, Draper immediately made known his conflict of interest and abstained from all discussion and voting on the property deal. Pinetree Corporation originally offered only about one hundred acres at a price of $100,000. Hubert Dewberry insisted on an additional fifty to sixty acres at the same price. Thanks to his foresight, Kennesaw Junior College received 152 acres, enough to handle the growth of the next quarter century. The chancellor's office required Cobb County to do all clearing and grading, build a parking lot for twelve hundred cars, zone adjacent properties to guard against undesirable developments, pave Shiloh Road (about a half mile north of campus), repave parts of Big Shanty, and extend McCollum Parkway from Old US 41 to the new Four Lane Highway.[42]

The steering committee had one more task to perform. The governments of Cobb County and Marietta decided to pay for the new college by selling bonds, of which $425,000 would be issued by the City of Marietta and $1,925,000 by the Cobb County Board of Education. Before they could increase indebtedness, they had to submit the question to the voters in a referendum. So, the steering committee went to work to persuade the electorate. The issue was decided on April 22,

(Opposite Page) Groundbreaking Ceremony — Herbert McCollum holding the umbrella and Governor Carl Sanders at the podium.

1964. With no organized opposition and overwhelming public support, the bonds were easily approved. Combining the city and county totals, a lopsided 88 percent voted in the affirmative (6,305 for to only 871 against). Every Marietta ward and county election district supported the issue.[43]

The groundbreaking ceremony occurred at three o'clock on the cold, drizzly afternoon of November 18, 1964, in a pasture just off Frey Lake Road, approximately where the first administration building would be located. Governor Sanders arrived a little late, claiming he got stuck in traffic. Dr. W. C. Mitchell, the president of the Cobb County Board of Education, acted as master of ceremonies, while greetings were offered by Bob Fowler, Hubert Dewberry, and Acting Chancellor S. Walter Martin. Board of Regents chairman James Dunlap introduced the governor. Sanders made a nice speech in which he paid tribute to Cobb's leadership, remarking, "The example set by the local citizens here in laying the groundwork for this college should and, I am sure, will be followed by those in other areas of Georgia.… In order for a community to receive state help in creating a junior college, they must put up at least $1 million in locally subscribed funds. Cobb and Marietta, however, voluntarily doubled this amount in local financial outlay—a feat not equaled by any other community in Georgia."

Commissioner Herbert McCollum and Marietta School Board chairman Dempsey Medford presided over the actual ground breaking. They distributed forty chrome-plated ceremonial shovels to the governor, the steering committee, and other dignitaries. After the local leaders turned their spades of earth, Rev. Joseph T. Walker of St. James Episcopal Church in Marietta offered the benediction. And thus a still to be named junior college was born. Even before the ground breaking, local power brokers had begun to dream not just of a two-year school, but an eventual senior college. But, work had to be done first in establishing a proper foundation.[44]

(Opposite Page) The new campus under construction

Chapter 2

Junior-College Years, 1965–1976

About a month after the groundbreaking ceremony, a middle-aged Atlanta couple drove out to Cobb County to find the site of the new college. It was a cold December day, and while they were on their way, snow began to fall. As the man drove further and further into a largely undeveloped part of Cobb County, his wife began to "sigh as she was not sure that [they] ought to be in this sort of thing." After several stops to ask directions, they found Frey Lake Road and then a hillside, thick with trees, where they spotted a little eighteen-inch sign that said, "Future Site of Junior College." Someone had erected the sign for the groundbreaking ceremony just in front of where the college's administrative offices would be housed. As the couple looked around, they saw cattle grazing nearby in the pasture. In this manner Dr. Horace Wilbur Sturgis and his wife, Sue, had their first encounter with Kennesaw Junior College.[45]

President Horace Sturgis

In 1912, Horace Sturgis was born in the small community of Grand Valley, Pennsylvania, and spent most of his childhood beside the Great Lakes in the Erie suburb of Wesleyville. He finished high school just at the start of the Great Depression, and the experience of hard economic times made him security conscious. So, he decided upon science education as a career where there would always be plenty of jobs. Both his father and mother had taught school at one time and were determined to send their son to college. A member of their church was a graduate of Piedmont College in Demorest, Georgia, and used his chemistry degree to land a depression-secure job with General Electric. Young Horace followed his advice, journeying to the mountains of north Georgia to major in chemistry. Tuition costs

(Opposite Page) President Horace W. Sturgis

were cheaper in the South, and, despite the distance, he could travel for free since his father worked as an engineer for the New York Central Railroad.[46]

Piedmont College turned out to be an excellent choice. The school had a strong Congregational church influence, and a number of faculty members were natives of New England who brought the region's high academic standards to Georgia. As one of only two students from north of the Mason-Dixon Line, he was something of an oddity, but by living and working on campus he quickly made lifelong friends and enjoyed southern life so much that he became a permanent Georgia transplant. One of his closest classmates was Phil Landrum, a future Georgia congressman. Dr. Sturgis would recruit Phil's younger brother, James (Spec) Landrum, to be Kennesaw College's coordinator of development and alumni relations. Later, Spec became Kennesaw's first athletic director.[47]

Sturgis received a BS in 1935 with a major in chemistry and minor in mathematics. Degree in hand, he accepted a job at the high school in Fayetteville, just south of Atlanta, where he served as principal, taught a full load of math and science, and coached basketball and track. After a few years, the school system in Eatonton in central Georgia recruited him away and there his basketball team won a state championship. In Eatonton he met and married a popular teacher named Sue Cowan. In his spare time, he completed a master's in education at the University of Georgia, where he was a student of the legendary dean of the College of Education, Walter Cocking.[48] For his master's thesis he did a statistical study of his students in Eatonton, documenting that they learned just as much under a simple pass/fail policy as they did under a standard grading system.

In 1940, Sturgis moved to North Fulton High School in the Buckhead area of Atlanta. In the evenings he took several engineering and science courses at Georgia Tech. After the United States entered World War II, a Tech physics professor, Lawrence V. Johnson, recruited Sturgis to teach in the Civilian Pilot Ground School Program sponsored by Tech and Southern Airways. In time, Sturgis went with Johnson to UGA to run a similar program, then followed him back to Tech where Johnson became acting director of the School of Aeronautics, and Sturgis taught Johnson's undergraduate physics classes. Although Sturgis claims that he "was not a physicist by any stretch of the imagination," he benefited from the lack of professors during wartime. The Physics Department chair, Dr. Joseph Herman Howey, hired him first as an instructor and then promoted him to assistant professor. He also worked part-time in the registrar's office. Although he was engaged in essential wartime employment, he became increasingly uncomfortable with his deferred status and joined the United States Navy, serving a tour of duty before returning to Tech after the war as assistant registrar.[49]

While working at Tech, Sturgis took advantage of the GI Bill and a liberal vacation policy to attend graduate classes for seven straight summers at New York

University. Never taking a vacation, and spending many evenings researching and writing in his campus office, he completed his PhD in higher education administration in 1958 with a dissertation on "The Relationship of the Teacher's Knowledge of the Student's Background to the Effectiveness of Teaching." In the meantime, he was promoted to associate registrar. One of his proudest moments came during the McCarthy era in early 1954. As president of the Tech chapter of the Georgia Education Association, he helped lead the fight against a state-mandated security questionnaire that asked each faculty member to vouch that neither he nor any member of his extended family was a communist. Through the efforts of Sturgis and others, the attorney general dropped the requirement that faculty members answer questions about their relatives.[50]

Even before he finished his doctorate, Sturgis began receiving administrative job offers from other Georgia colleges. He turned down an invitation from President O. C. Aderhold to be dean of students at the University of Georgia, largely because he feared he would never finish his dissertation if he accepted such a time-consuming assignment. In the fall of 1964 Sturgis received a call from Harry S. Downs, the University System of Georgia's assistant vice chancellor. Downs asked Sturgis if he was interested in becoming president of one of the newly chartered junior colleges. He learned later that his old friend Larry Johnson had recommended him. Johnson had been the first director of what today is Southern Polytechnic State University, while it was still in DeKalb County. After the technical institute moved to Marietta, Johnson continued to exercise oversight as director of Georgia Tech's Extension Division. During these years, Johnson called on Sturgis frequently to recommend former high school colleagues who might be good technical college faculty members or administrators.

In pre-affirmative action days, when cronyism prevailed throughout academia, Sturgis benefited from a time-honored system where trustworthiness and loyalty to one's friends and employers carried significant weight. Sturgis, of course, also profited from the fact that the college population was growing nationwide at an unprecedented rate, creating the most favorable job climate in academic circles of any time in the twentieth century. In later years, Sturgis was the first to admit that only in the 1960s would an associate registrar be considered for a college presidency. When Harry Downs contacted him, Sturgis responded that he was happy at Georgia Tech, but would be willing to consider other opportunities. So, early in 1965, he received an invitation from the Board of Regents' Committee on Education to come for an interview.

After Sturgis talked about his experiences, the chairman of the board, James A. Dunlap, mentioned that the regents planned to open three new junior colleges in the fall of 1966 in Gainesville, Albany, and Cobb County, and he wondered if Sturgis had a preference. His response was that he would only be interested in the

Marietta area, because he already had a close relationship with Southern Tech. He thought better of telling the regents that he was attracted to Cobb County because it already had a vocational-technical school and a technical college, so the new junior college could focus almost exclusively on liberal arts transfer programs, and not try to offer everything for everybody as most community colleges did. If he was going to leave Georgia Tech, he wanted to lead a school where it was possible to establish high academic standards and have a serious liberal arts focus from the beginning.

After hearing nothing for several months, Sturgis received a second invitation to the chancellor's office in late April or early May. The purpose was to let some of the regents have a second opportunity to meet him and to introduce him to the incoming chancellor, George L. Simpson Jr., who had already been selected, but would not take office until the middle of July. The two chatted briefly—apparently long enough for Simpson to be satisfied that Sturgis was acceptable. Several days later, Harry Downs called Sturgis to tell him that the board was prepared to elect him as president of the college in Cobb County. At the board meeting on May 12, 1965, it became official. In making his recommendation, Acting Chancellor S. Walter Martin indicated that several candidates had met with the Committee on Education and that, after conferring with several persons, he and Dr. Downs, the coordinator of junior colleges, agreed that Sturgis was the best man for the job. Despite the fact that he was officially recommended by Martin, Sturgis had reason to believe that he was actually the first president approved by Chancellor-elect Simpson.[51]

The College Naming Controversy

On July 1, 1965, Sturgis assumed his duties at a college lacking faculty, students, books, and buildings. For fiscal year 1965–66 the regents gave him a modest operating budget of $70,000. Southern Tech graciously provided office space in its administration building, and Sturgis received visitors there for his first six months on the job. When he began, his embryonic institution did not even have a name. Local people referred to it as the Cobb County Junior College, Cobb-Marietta College, or Kennesaw Mountain Junior College, and at least one local resident proposed Richard Russell College after Georgia's senior senator, but the regents had not yet made an official choice. While ordering stationery, Sturgis decided to put "Marietta College" on the letterhead, reasoning that system institutions such as Columbus College and Augusta College were named after nearby cities. It occurred to him that people outside the area might never have heard of Cobb County, but perhaps knew of Marietta as the home of Lockheed. An outsider to local turf battles, he innocently assumed that all citizens of Cobb identified with the county seat. Such proved not to be the case.[52]

Mayor John Adams of Kennesaw was incensed by the proposed name, along with the Kennesaw Junior Chamber of Commerce that adopted a resolution calling for a title that reflected "the exact vicinity of the college or the area it is to serve." The *North Cobb News* printed a strong editorial against President Sturgis's action. John and Nina Frey, whose family once owned the campus property, were part of a group of unhappy local citizens who took their protest to the governor.

Soon a delegation of officials from throughout the county descended upon the president's office. One of the mayors, Mary B. McCall of Acworth, told Sturgis, "I don't know where you came from, but I don't like what you're doing." A person of strong opinions, she took exception to the name Marietta when the whole county had approved bonds to build the school. At first, Sturgis told his critics that he could not change the name because he had already paid for the stationery. They responded that they would be glad to donate the money to pay for new letterhead. Confronted by an unhappy delegation, Sturgis realized that the only way to dispel tension was to reconsider his position.

Mary McCall told him, "Well, we've got to choose a name," then asked, "What do you suggest?" Sturgis did not like the name Cobb Junior College, and he thought Kennesaw Mountain Junior College was too wordy. But the mountain, a site of an important Civil War battle, seemed the one prominent landmark that everyone in the county claimed. He responded that he favored Kennesaw College, leaving out "mountain" and "junior." That name satisfied McCall and the others and Sturgis made that proposal to the board. However, he continued to use a Marietta mailing address, thinking that the Marietta Post Office was better equipped to handle a large volume of mail than the tiny facility in the City of Kennesaw.[53]

By this time, Chancellor Simpson had taken office. He did not object to the name "Kennesaw," but he did object to the omission of "junior." Brunswick College had opened the previous year, and its name apparently caused some people to think it was a four-year school. Simpson thought that an institution's title should be an accurate reflection of its mission. In addition to Kennesaw, the chancellor's office was considering names for the new schools in Albany, Gainesville, and Dalton. So Simpson proposed at the August 11, 1965, Board of Regents meeting that "junior" be added to Brunswick's title and that Kennesaw and the other three have "junior" in their name from the start. The board concurred, and on that date the designation Kennesaw Junior College (KJC) became official.[54]

Building a New Campus

Back in June of 1964 the Board of Regents selected Bothwell and Associates of Marietta as the architectural firm that would draw up the preliminary plans and specifications for the campus buildings. Upon its approval of those plans the following February, the board gave Bothwell and Associates a contract for the final plans and specifications.[55] On September 15, 1965, the regents awarded Thompson and Street Company the contract to construct the original eight buildings. The

President Sturgis observing the construction of the original library.

Atlanta firm's low bid of $2,497,700 was almost $30,000 less than the nearest competitor, but was almost a half million dollars more than the City of Marietta and the Cobb Board of Education had provided for campus construction the previous year. Fortunately, the regents had just received a $993,586 construction grant for the Kennesaw campus from the Higher Education Facilities Commission of the United States Department of Education. So the university system had sufficient funds to pay Thompson and Street and was able to keep part of the Cobb and Marietta donation in reserve.[56]

The Cobb County Commission could have used a similar grant to finance campus grading, paving, and electrical, water, and sewer work. Unfortunately, the authors of the April 1964 bond referendum underestimated infrastructure costs, and the quarter million dollars they designated for such expenses were exhausted by grading alone. Commission chairman Ernest Barrett took office in January 1965 after the bond referendum, and was not happy when he realized that campus improvements were likely to cost an additional $400,000. On March 2, 1966, he visited the Board of Regents to complain that the state should be picking up the bill, but the chancellor's staff told him they had a binding contract and not to expect any help from them. Years later, Dr. Sturgis recalled that the commission chairman "didn't understand why he had to have this responsibility." Yet, "he mellowed as time went on, and he was as proud of the college as anybody."[57]

Campus construction was marred by one labor dispute after another. Strikes between September 1965 and November 1966 kept all laborers idle for eleven weeks and slowed work for thirteen more. The first to strike were the ironworkers. Until they won a contract with better wages and benefits, they held up projects throughout the Atlanta area for sixty-seven days from September to November 1965. During the work stoppage, Sturgis told a reporter that the grading had been done and the buildings staked out, but the foundations could not be laid until the ironworkers came back on the job.[58]

A major cause of unrest was that Thompson and Street, the primary contractor, hired union labor to construct the buildings, while Cobb County used nonunion subcontractors to put in roads, sewers, and utilities. In February 1966 the Plumbers and Steamfitters Local 72 AFL-CIO set up a picket line after the county hired the nonunion W. S. Pruitt Construction Company to put in sewers. For the next month Thompson and Street's workforce and subcontractors came on campus only on days when Pruitt did not. Historically, labor unions in Georgia have been weak, and, except for an occasional strike at Lockheed, picket lines were a novelty in Cobb County. Nonetheless, the *Marietta Daily Journal* editorialized on March 13, that

(Opposite Page) The new campus under construction

30

the work stoppage was "a graphic reminder right here at home of the tremendous power wielded today by labor unions" and that the students who planned to enroll in the fall would "suffer most from a prolonged delay." A few days later the *Smyrna Herald* opined that the prospective students should picket the unions.[59]

In defense of the county, Chairman Barrett argued that Cobb was required by law to contract with the low bidder, union or nonunion. Nonetheless, President Sturgis and Hubert Dewberry, who oversaw the project for the Board of Regents, were tired of the frequent work stoppages and relieved that Barrett chose to bypass a nonunion low bidder for the electrical contract in favor of Marable-Pirkle, a company that employed only union labor. The final major delay came in the summer of 1966 when carpenters and sheet metal workers struck for over a month. By that time the building exteriors were almost finished, but much work remained on the interiors. The work stoppages prevented Kennesaw from opening on schedule in September 1966. Still, KJC benefited financially from the construction slowdowns.

President Horace W. Sturgis and wife, Sue, at home.

Until contractors and subcontractors completed their tasks, they were not paid. Thus, the bond money stayed in the bank longer, drawing thousands of dollars of interest. This unexpected windfall was used to purchase library books, audio-visual supplies, and state-of-the-art microscopes and other equipment.[60]

By the time that President Sturgis took office, the chancellor's staff had approved architectural drawings, but Sturgis from time to time sought the advice of Georgia Tech engineers on minor changes. One day he was watching workers put the steel door and combination lock on the vault in the Administration Building when a laborer remarked: "I don't know what they're putting that iron door on there for, because it's just cinder block; and all you have to do is take a sledge hammer and knock a hole in the side of the wall." It turned out that no one had thought to put steel reinforcements in the walls. So, Sturgis was able to correct that shortcoming. From the original approval of the construction contract in September 1965 to the completion of the project in December 1967, the Board of Regents approved seven change orders for minor alterations, raising the amount paid to Thompson and Street by about $27,000 and bringing the final total for the original buildings to $2,524,995. In addition, Cobb County had spent approximately three-quarters of a million dollars to buy the land, grade it, and provide utilities. So the entire project was completed for around $3.25 million, not a bad price for a facility designed for about 2,500 students.[61]

On many occasions, Horace and Sue Sturgis drove to campus after hours and on weekends to see how things were progressing. Not long before the grand opening, on a cold winter day, they went inside the almost complete Science Building and found themselves in the second floor physics lab. The building was unheated, so they did not plan to stay long. But when they started to leave, they discovered, to their horror, that they were locked inside. Somehow, the door handle had not been properly attached and did not work from the inside. They could look out the window on a deserted parking lot and feared they might have to spend the night there. Fortunately, at that moment a Cobb County patrol car drove by, and Mrs. Sturgis waved her scarf out the window. After the officer was able to rescue them, he told them that he did not normally drive through the campus, but for some reason had decided to do so on that occasion. Thus, the charter president and his wife avoided freezing to death before the first students set foot on campus.[62]

Recruiting Faculty and Administrators

While the campus was under construction, Sturgis built an administrative team. The first to join him, Derrell Clayton Roberts, reported to work as dean of the college at the start of January 1966. On the day that Roberts arrived, Kennesaw's headquarters moved from Southern Tech to Banberry Elementary School, where President Sturgis was given the principal's office and Dr. Roberts occupied the clinic. Located just east of US 41, this Marietta city school had been built in an unfortunate location and never had enough students to fill the building.[63] Its principal headed two schools and never used the Banberry office, so the Marietta system was delighted to let a startup junior college make temporary use of the facility.[64]

Since the president's background was in math and science, he wanted an academic dean from the humanities or social sciences. Roberts received a PhD in history from the University of Georgia in 1958 with a dissertation on "Joseph E. Brown and the New South." While finishing his degree, he taught introductory history classes at Georgia State College of Business Administration. In 1958 he accepted his first full-time college position at Florida Southern College, where he became chair of the History Department just two years later. From there he moved to Mobile College, a brand new Baptist institution, where, prior to coming to Kennesaw, he was professor of history and the school's first chair of the Social Sciences Division. One of his assets as Kennesaw's charter academic dean was his experience with a beginning institution.[65]

For several months Sturgis and Roberts did all the interviewing and hiring of prospective faculty members and administrators. Most of the interviews were conducted at Banberry, but Roberts and, occasionally, Sturgis traveled to recruitment fairs held on university campuses throughout the Southeast. In a 1998 interview, Roberts recalled how hard it was to recruit faculty members in the 1960s when new colleges were popping up all over the nation. He wrote everyone he knew to ask them for recommendations of people who possibly would be interested in working at a new college. In a "faculty member's market," Kennesaw found it necessary to recruit a large number of high school teachers who were good in the classroom, but had no intentions of completing doctorates. The alternative was to hire graduate students, who were more likely to acquire a terminal degree, but lacked much teaching experience. The first Kennesaw Junior College catalog (1966–1968) lists eight administrators who held earned doctorates, but just three out of forty-two of the full-time teaching faculty (7 percent) did so. In the latter group, twenty-eight (67 percent) were non-tenure-track instructors, and the rest were assistant professors.[66]

Still, Kennesaw had competitive advantages that rival junior colleges lacked. The metropolitan Atlanta location was as asset. The northern suburbs were growing, and there was no doubt that the college would expand along with them. Both Sturgis and Roberts were encouraged by the fact that Cobb County already had a vocational-technical school and a technical college, so, as Roberts said, "We did not need to become a community college. We recognized that from the beginning and set up the curriculum along that line.… The first Southern Association [of Colleges and Schools] visiting team…accused us of having a two-year university."[67]

Kennesaw's administration received strong community support for its vision of becoming a senior college. In fact, President Sturgis discovered that the public was way ahead of him. He first met with community leaders when Acting Chancellor Martin and junior college coordinator Downs took him to a meeting at the board room of the Cobb County School System. After Sturgis made a short speech about building a quality institution, the first question he received was, "When are we going to be a four-year college?" His answer at the time was that Kennesaw first had to be a good junior college.[68]

From the start, Sturgis and Roberts told candidates coming for interviews that Kennesaw would probably become a senior college, and they tried to hire people who could make the transition to four-year status. The first member of the teaching faculty that they hired was George Henry Beggs, whose contract was approved by the Board of Regents in February 1966. Two months later the regents also authorized his appointment as chairman of the Division of Social Sciences. Beggs and Roberts went back a long way together. When Roberts was a young teacher at

(Opposite Page) George H. Beggs

Tifton (Georgia) High School, George Beggs and Beggs's future wife, Rosemary, were two of his students. After Beggs finished his coursework for a doctorate at the University of Arizona, he called Roberts and told him he was looking for a full-time job, and Roberts invited him to join the faculty at Mobile College.

As a political scientist, Beggs visited Atlanta often for professional meetings and to study local politics. On one of his trips, he heard that a new junior college was about to be built in Cobb County, and he came out to tour the campus site. Convinced that the school was in an excellent location, he encouraged Roberts to apply for the deanship. When Beggs came for his job interview, he asked President Sturgis how long he thought it would be before Kennesaw became a four-year college. Sturgis told him "ten years." Decades later, Beggs remarked that "we hit it right on the mark. Ten years. So we always had that senior institution in mind."[69]

All three of the original division chairs were finishing their dissertations when they were hired. Beggs completed his doctorate just before classes began in September 1966, but had to wait until the following February to receive the degree. The chair of the Humanities Division, John C. Greider, had to take a six-week leave of absence in the middle of fall quarter to return to England to defend his dissertation. While he was gone, two assistant professors, Virginia C. Hinton and James F. Whitnel, covered his classes. Greider had a BD from New Orleans Baptist Theological Seminary (1955) and an MA from George Peabody College (1956), as well as the PhD from the University of Liverpool that he completed in 1966. For the Division of Natural Science and Mathematics, Sturgis decided to hire a biologist, since the introductory biology course was likely to be students' favorite science elective. His choice was Wesley C. Walraven, who was about finished with his dissertation at the University of Georgia. The degree was officially awarded at UGA's spring commencement on June 3, 1967. In 1970, Walraven became the academic dean of Floyd Junior College, and was replaced at Kennesaw by Herbert L. Davis.[70]

If college jobs were abundant in the affluent 1960s, the opposite was true in the following decade, when problems of unemployment and inflation plagued American society. Universities had responded to good times by expanding their graduate programs, producing in the 1970s a surplus of newly minted PhDs. Suddenly, the buyer's market became a seller's market, and Kennesaw found it much easier to recruit people with PhDs. When Bowman Davis joined the KJC faculty in the fall of 1970, he had completed all the work for a doctorate in parasitology at Emory University, but could not find a senior-college job in his field. That year there were only two or three openings for parasitologists in the entire nation. One of them

(Opposite Page) Bowman O. Davis Jr.

Robert J. Greene

was in upstate New York, and when he discovered that the ranch houses had tin roofs because shingles would not survive the spring thaws, he decided that any job in the South was superior to one in such a cold climate.

Davis thought, at first, that he would stay at Kennesaw only until something better came along. However, once he arrived, he never left, in large part because he found his colleagues across campus to be so congenial. The price he paid for remaining at Kennesaw was that he lost touch with the discipline of parasitology, since even at the time of his retirement in 2002, Kennesaw lacked adequate laboratory facilities to allow him to keep up with his field. Instead, he devoted his efforts to the classroom, for which he received Kennesaw's Distinguished Teaching Award in 1988, and to service, helping especially to develop the First-Year Seminar (currently KSU 1101) that oriented new students to college life.[71]

By the 1975–76 school year—the year in which the regents approved KJC's conversion to four-year status—thirty-two members of the full-time teaching faculty possessed doctorates (42 percent) and only twenty-three (29 percent) had less than a year beyond a master's. Meanwhile, ten faculty members were writing their dissertations and another sixteen were doing graduate coursework. According to George Beggs, "We began to develop a faculty that was the envy of much of the University System at that time…. We were very competitive, because of the great location and a great community support." He added that Dr. Sturgis deserved much credit "because the community had learned to love him literally from the very beginning."[72]

Opening the College

With the north Cobb campus not completed on time, Kennesaw opened in fall quarter, 1966, at Southern Tech, using the four classrooms previously designated for the off-campus center. KJC's registrar and director of admissions, Cecil L. Jackson, was headquartered at Southern Tech, but most administrative offices were located at Banberry. Dean of student affairs Mark E. (Gene) Meadows, director of guidance Carol L. Martin, and counselor Inez P. Morgan met with students in classroom 1, while tabulating supervisor James W. Woods ran a punch-card operation in classroom 2. Controller Toney W. Bryant and Librarian Robert J. Greene occupied classroom 3. Greene recalls purchasing the same thirty-cent lunches in the Banberry cafeteria that the school children ate.

Kennesaw students could use the Southern Tech library, but could not check out books. The Cobb County branch library in the Marietta Place housing project, just west of the Southern Tech campus, assisted KJC instructors by placing books on reserve for their classes. Before becoming head librarian at Kennesaw, Greene had been the science librarian in Georgia Tech's Science and Technology Library. He had talked to Dr. Sturgis on occasion, but did not know him well until one day Sturgis asked him if he would be interested in starting up a junior-college library. In lieu of a master's thesis at Florida State University, Greene had written a paper on science resources needed in new junior-college libraries. So he knew something about creating a collection from scratch and jumped at the opportunity. Much of his time during the first several months was devoted to ordering books. By the time the campus opened, the collection had grown to about six thousand. The first book was a donation from the Cobb County Public Library of Sarah Temple's *First Hundred Years: A Short History of Cobb County, in Georgia.*[73]

The initial registration occurred at the Marietta Place Recreation Center. A total of 1,014 students enrolled—not quite as many as expected, but a respectable number for a school that lacked its own campus. Southern Tech proved to be an ideal host, yet space was tight. One of the charter members of the staff, Madeline Miles, worked as secretary for two division chairs (humanities and social sciences) in a room at Southern Tech that they shared with the registrar and his secretary. The developmental studies staff[74] was housed in the Marietta Place Recreation Center, but most faculty members lacked offices. Despite the cramped quarters, English professor David Jones enjoyed the camaraderie that came from knowing many of the students and everyone on the faculty and staff. Lacking an office, he held conferences with students in

David M. Jones Jr.

Early *Sentinel* **staff meeting. Students meeting with President Sturgis, Dean Mark E. (Gene) Meadows, and English professor and** *Sentinel* **advisor Mary H. Swain.**

his automobile. The Shoney's restaurant on the Four Lane Highway (US 41) near Southern Tech was a favorite spot for meetings with colleagues. Jones spent much of his time at Shoney's, drinking coffee and grading papers. The first official gathering of the English faculty was a lunch meeting at the Plantation Restaurant, another institution along US 41.[75]

The campus colors and mascots were largely administrative decisions, with some student involvement. According to President Sturgis, the colors came from the gold of Georgia Tech and the black of the University of Georgia. The owl became the mascot to emphasize academics, as in the "wise owl." Sturgis noted that universities that had the owl as a mascot, such as Rice and Temple, tended to be highly respected. The original college seal was designed by art professor

M. Thomson Salter III. He used the Georgia state seal with its symbolic depiction of the Constitution as an arch supported by the three pillars of Wisdom, Justice, and Moderation. He made slight alterations in the sentinel standing guard and added a line drawing of Kennesaw Mountain in the background. The constitutional arch of Salter's seal was encircled by the words, "Kennesaw Junior College" at the top, and "University System of Georgia" at the bottom. The charter date, 1963, was placed just to the left of the arch.[76]

Students made the most of the cramped facilities at Southern Tech and Banberry. By October 3, 1966, they had produced the first issue of the campus newspaper, with Robert McDearmid serving as the charter editor in chief. A news article explained that interested students began meeting with President Sturgis and Dean Meadows to plan the newspaper several weeks before the fall quarter began. The original staff, consisting of six writers and two photographers, came up with a list of possible names for the paper and submitted them to the Advisory Council for final approval. The inspiration for the title, the *Sentinel*, was the guard, sword in hand and "ready for action," on the college seal.

The first issue's editorial cartoon showed a rocket bearing the name of Kennesaw Junior College blasting off into a sky labeled "Future." The exhaust fumes said, "Hopes," "Dreams," and "Plans," while "Venture into the Unknown" was written off to the side. The second issue on October 31 carried a cartoon about the problems of student parking on the Southern Tech campus. The third issue contained the first student-written letter to the editor, criticizing the military draft (along with a rebuttal letter supportive of the draft). By the end of the spring quarter the newspaper staff had put out eight issues, with Ronnie Bennett becoming editor in chief in the winter of 1967.

A commuter junior college with a preponderance of nontraditional students, KJC was never a hotbed of student activism, and the *Sentinel* was almost always respectful of authority and supportive of the administration. Nonetheless, the college attracted, from the start, a handful of nonconformists who felt more at home on a small campus and who were attuned to the spirit of protest engulfing academia in the late 1960s. Many of their spirited discussions took place over coffee in the Student Activities Building, not far from the offices of the Student Government Association and the *Sentinel*.[77]

As late as the December 1 issue, President Sturgis expressed concerns that all the construction delays would make it impossible to open the Kennesaw campus by the start of winter quarter. However, work crews made sufficient progress during December for Sturgis to change his mind. At the time, noted Georgia humorist Roy Blount Jr. was a young writer for the *Atlanta Journal and Constitution*. He visited the campus just before it opened and obviously liked what he saw. His story on January 8, 1967 starts: "On the crest of a hill near Kennesaw Mountain, overlooking a lake and acres of rolling wooded ground, stands a nearly finished junior college.... Despite the unacademic flavor lent by cement mixers and aluminum tool sheds, the campus is handsome.... The long, low buff-brick buildings…look crisp and permanent."[78]

The campus was still not landscaped, but the Board of Regents in its January meeting accepted a recommendation from President Sturgis that Symmes Nursery's low bid of $43,494 be accepted. They would plant trees, flowers, and shrubbery according to a plan proposed by the Atlanta landscape architectural firm of H. Boyer Marks and Associates. A few years later, charter English professor (and former Marietta High School principal) Mary Swain reflected on the change in

(Above) Donald J. Fay teaching an English class on the quadrangle.
(Opposite Page) View from the quadrangle, looking south toward
the Student Services Building.

appearance from before the site was graded to when the landscaping was completed: "My husband and I would ride up to where the college was going to be placed; and it was beautiful rolling land with pine trees and everything. And the bulldozers came in there and leveled it and graded it off with all that red dirt. I thought, 'Oh, this is going to be the ugliest place on earth.' But when they built the buildings and spent [money] on landscaping, it became a beautiful place."[79]

Classes began on the new campus on January 9, 1967, just two days behind the scheduled start. The administration announced two Saturday make-up days toward the end of the quarter to maintain the required number of contact hours. On opening day the Science, Humanities, and Student Services Buildings were entirely finished, with the Administration Building completed four days later. Prior to the move to Frey Lake Road, the Department of Plant Operations and the various

Overhead view of Campus Green

contractors made use of the main office of the Humanities Building. When humanities secretary Madeline Miles first arrived, the office reeked of cigar and cigarette smoke. Despite the cold winter weather, she opened the window and brought in deodorizers to drive out the smell. The Maintenance Service Building (later remodeled to house the music offices and classrooms) was completed on January 18. Until the first of February, when the Social Sciences Building was ready, historians and social scientists taught their classes in the Student Services Building.

The Library Building was not ready until March 16, but its small collection fitted nicely into the physics laboratory during the winter quarter. The gymnasium would not be finished until June 10, at the end of the 1966–67 academic year. So physical education classes were held at first in the Student Services Building and then, after it opened, in the Social Sciences Building. Charter faculty member C. Grady Palmer recalls teaching tumbling in one of the larger lecture rooms (designed eventually to hold about eighty desks) on the first floor of the Social Sciences Building, with mats stretched throughout the room and with students beginning their approaches from the hallway. Another classroom was converted into a weight room, while tennis was taught at the Pinetree Country Club. Classes tended to be noisy — sometimes a disruption for nearby academic courses — and students had nowhere to take showers after workouts. Nonetheless, Palmer asserted that students and faculty were good-natured about the situation.[80]

Faculty, Staff, and Students

The employees of the 1960s seemed immensely proud of the college they helped to birth. Madeline Miles claimed they were the happiest people on earth when they had a chance to move to the new campus. In a 1992 interview she rattled off the names of a number of original students and colleagues and claimed that she knew by name everyone on the faculty and staff and about half the students. She noted that all were well-groomed and courteous.[81]

J. B. Tate was one of the early faculty members who came from the high school ranks. He actually was offered a job at Kennesaw in 1966, but turned it down because he was enjoying teaching at Milton High School in Alpharetta. The next year, however, he experienced "crop failure" at Milton and applied to Kennesaw again. When President Sturgis offered him a job for the 1967–68 school year, he admonished that there would not be a third offer. The chairman of the Social Sciences Division, George Beggs, impressed upon Tate the administration's commitment to high academic standards and told him not to worry about the "body count" if he found it necessary to flunk a large number of students.

Kennesaw had virtually open admissions, but provided developmental (remedial) classes in English and math for students who did not score high enough on placement tests to enroll in the required introductory courses. The faculty and administrators were sensitive to the fact that four-year schools often looked on junior colleges as little more than another two years of high school. They were determined that Kennesaw overcome that prejudice, regardless of the attrition rate.

J. B. Tate, history faculty

Some courses, such as Composition, were notorious for the number of Fs that students received. Tate remembers walking around the classroom one day while monitoring a test and seeing etched into a wooden desk the following student's lament: "Transferred to Saigon University because of a god damned comma splice," which Tate interpreted as meaning he was about to be expelled, drafted, and sent to Vietnam because "the English department nailed him." In defense of the English faculty, students who passed KJC's Composition classes were well prepared for the Regents' Test, a system-wide examination of basic reading and writing skills. Kennesaw prided itself on being at or near the top year after year in the percentage of students passing on the first try.[82]

In time Kennesaw's poor student retention rate was viewed as a problem. The first institutional self-study in 1972 noted that the college lost an average of 32 percent of its students from fall to winter quarter and from winter to spring quarter. Nonetheless, those who transferred tended to hold their own at the receiving institutions. As the following table from the self-study reveals, students transferring from Kennesaw Junior College during the academic year of 1969–70 saw their grade point averages rise significantly if they transferred to West Georgia College, go up modestly at the University of Georgia, remain about the same at Georgia State University, and fall slightly at Georgia Tech:[83]

TABLE 2	Comparison of Average Grade Received at KJC and Average Grade Received at other Institutions by Transfers from KJC, 1969–1970		
Number of Students	Receiving Institution	Mean GPA Sent	Mean GPA Received
19	Georgia Tech	2.86	2.53
91	Georgia State University	2.50	2.45
44	University of Georgia	2.38	2.55
50	West Georgia College	2.20	2.70

Despite the focus on standards, many instructors had a virtually open-door policy where students could drop by their offices most any time. As a result, they devoted many hours to helping students learn. Tate, for example, told students that he designed the course so they could make a C with a little effort or whatever grade they wanted as long as they were willing to work. When asked once by a student how many he had failed the previous quarter, he responded, "As many as wanted to"—in other words, as many as were unwilling to attend class regularly or do the readings necessary for success.[84] A remarkably popular instructor, Tate made teaching and learning fun. He spent hours preparing for class ("keeping ahead of the posse," as he liked to say), produced lectures full of humor that he delivered without notes, and enjoyed students' company outside as well as in class.

Stephen E. Scherer was another faculty member in the junior-college era with a reputation for being tough, but caring about his students. Having received a PhD in mathematics from Georgia Tech in 1974, he turned down an offer of a university job because he wanted to work in a public institution that placed major emphases on teaching and service. He quickly gained a reputation as someone who enjoyed teaching developmental courses and freshman algebra to the nonmajors. Students in these classes often needed encouragement to overcome math anxiety. When slower learners had trouble comprehending basic concepts, he encouraged them to attend after-class study sessions where he promised to stay as long as they wanted. It became his practice to spend as much time with students outside class as inside. In 1982 he became the first recipient of Kennesaw's Distinguished Teaching Award, in part because of stories such as the following:

> I had one lady who still teaches kindergarten not far from where I live…. At the time she was probably in her fifties. She came to me and explained that she had already failed the course once, and she was petrified of it. I said, "Okay, I'm pleased that you told me, but do me a favor, keep an open mind and do what I ask you to do. Come to our problem sessions." I used to give problem sessions on the weekends, in the afternoons, whenever we could get time. I don't think she ever missed one. That was the one year that I actually taught the entire sequence back to back…. She ended up making an A in all three of them, and she was so delighted when she finished. It just made it worthwhile.[85]

Scherer enjoyed what he described as a "big family" at Kennesaw, where he knew faculty members across campus and even students who had not taken his classes. One of his math colleagues, Elaine Hubbard, experienced the same friendly atmosphere from the perspective of a student as well as faculty member. The first person to receive a Kennesaw degree, then go on to earn a PhD and return to Kennesaw to

(Opposite Page) Stephen E. Scherer

Elaine M. Hubbard

teach, Hubbard enrolled at KJC in the fall of 1968, straight out of high school. Two or three weeks into the first quarter, she was in the Student Center one day when President Sturgis sat down at her table and ate doughnuts with her. It became a tradition throughout the rest of her two years at Kennesaw for President Sturgis to meet her in the Student Center for doughnuts almost every week.

They were often accompanied by Kennesaw's lone physics professor, Charley G. Dobson, a Georgia Tech graduate, and the two of them constantly encouraged her to go to Tech after she graduated from Kennesaw. Math instructor Micah Y. Chan was a third faculty member who began almost immediately urging her to go to Tech for a PhD in math. Even after she left Kennesaw, he continued to call her to encourage her in her studies. Hubbard received an associate of science diploma from KJC in 1970, and then three Georgia Tech degrees (a BS in 1972, an MS in 1974, and a PhD in 1980). In the meantime she joined the KJC faculty as a full-time instructor in 1975 and made a career at Kennesaw. She won the Distinguished Teaching Award in 2001.[86]

Stories abound about the mentoring that Micah Chan provided for students in the early years of the college. A native of the Portuguese colony of Macao, Chan began his teaching career before he gained US citizenship, requiring Kennesaw to inform the Board of Regents annually that it could not find an American as qualified to teach his classes. Chan had a master's degree from the University of Tennessee when he joined the KSU faculty and would eventually complete his PhD in 1982 at the University of Georgia. He was one of the rare faculty members who worked as well with developmental studies students as he did with star students such as Elaine Hubbard.[87]

(Opposite Page) Faculty socializing in the Student Services Building — Charley G. Dobson Jr., Roger E. Hopkins, unknown, Donald J. Sparks, and Herbert L. Davis Jr.

One of the people who took his Mathematics 099 developmental class was Kathy Sherlock [Scott], a nontraditional student who enrolled at Kennesaw in 1972 after almost a decade outside academia. Many nontraditional students needed a refresher course in either English or math to restore the skills they once possessed. Based on her score on KJC's math placement test, Sherlock had to take Micah Chan's Mathematics 099. Her central memory of the class was Chan taking all the blame on himself whenever students failed to grasp the concepts he tried to teach. Turning red in the face, he would exclaim, "Why am I so stupid that I can't explain it to her in the way that she will understand!" And then he would patiently go back to the board and start over to make sure that everyone grasped what he was saying.

Just out of high school, Kathy Sherlock had attended Shorter College before signing up in 1964 for Governor Terry Sanford's North Carolina Volunteers, a pilot program for Volunteers in Service to America (VISTA), one of Lyndon Johnson's Great Society initiatives. After her tour of duty in the US Navy was cut short by health issues, she enrolled at KJC in 1972 and instantly became involved in student government, serving as the Student Government Association's (SGA) president from the fall of 1972 to March 1974, and chairing the Academic Improvement Committee of the system-wide Student Advisory Council during the 1973–74 academic

Aerial view of campus

(Above) Students of the 1970s
(Opposite Page) Campus parking area near the old Science Building

year. In the latter capacity, she presented a Student Advisory Council resolution to the Board of Regents in March of 1974 calling on every institution to develop a campus-wide system of faculty evaluation by students. While the Regents did not adopt the plan immediately, the board's Committee on Education agreed to begin studying an idea that eventually would be implemented throughout the state.[88]

Many students merely attended classes and did not participate in the full life of the college, but those who did found numerous opportunities for service. Lynnda Bernard [Eagle], for instance, was an entering freshman in the fall of 1966 when KJC first opened for business on the Southern Tech campus. From the start, she was involved in a host of campus activities. A recipient of a prestigious regents' scholarship, she said she chose KJC over the University of Georgia and Georgia State because she "like[d] new things" and wanted to stay close to her Austell home, where she trained horses to take to horse shows. An education major, Bernard was on the *Sentinel* staff, the Student Activities Committee, and the Student Constitution Committee, and represented KJC at meetings of the Southern University Student Government Association in Atlanta and in Mobile, Alabama.

Lynnda Bernard Eagle later earned an MEd from Georgia State and an education specialist degree from West Georgia. A career educator in Cobb County, Eagle served at various times as teacher, supervisor for gifted education, principal, and director for leadership management. After retiring, she ran for a seat on the Board of Education and represented Post 1 in northwest Cobb from 2009–2012, including one year as school board chair.[89]

Another former student, Stevan Crew, transferred from West Georgia College in time for the first quarter on the new campus in the winter of 1967. He graduated in the spring of 1968 and went on to receive a bachelor's degree at UGA in insurance and risk management. However, his primary loyalty was to Kennesaw, where he later served as a trustee of the KSU Foundation. In reflecting on his college days, he argued that standards at Kennesaw were higher than those at West Georgia and probably higher than those at UGA outside his major concentration. His favorite instructor was John Greider, whom he described as a marvelous teacher who brought literature alive.

Stella Merritt and other students
enjoying the music at KJC Day, 1970.

According to Crew, students were divided into two groups: traditional-aged students like him who were in college to enjoy life, and the nontraditional students who were more serious and who had a positive influence on their younger peers. He notes that "we were so blessed to be around those folks because they helped us mature rather than hanging out with a bunch of people that were here just to party." After he received his bachelor's degree, he joined the United States Army, where he won a number of awards, volunteered three times for the Vietnam war, but ended up instead in Germany. After his tour of duty, he went on a personal grand tour of Europe, then returned home to Paulding County, where he became a highly successful businessman and public servant, chairing the Paulding County Chamber of Commerce and serving as a member of the Paulding County School Board, trustee of the KSU Foundation, and chairman of the board of Chattahoochee Technical College.[90]

Ralph W. Walker III is another KSU Foundation trustee who graduated from Kennesaw Junior College. A young man in a hurry, Walker received an associate's degree in pre-law from Kennesaw in 1975, a bachelor's degree in psychology from Georgia State in 1976, and a law degree from Woodrow Wilson College of Law in 1977, all while holding down two jobs on the side. By the time he received his law

degree, he had already passed the bar exam and opened a practice in north Georgia. He started his academic career at KJC because he had heard good things about the school, academically, and because he could save money by living at home. In a 2007 interview, he reflected that, "I have for many years told many people that, far and away, not even closely, far and away the best education I got, what I learned the most, what I took the most from, was the two years here at Kennesaw. I felt like the professors — they were smaller classes for me, they were more attentive, the professors were. It was a better fit for me."[91]

Former alumni president Melonie J. Wallace had a similar experience. Her relationship to Kennesaw Junior College began in November 1964, when her mother took her, as a fourth grader, to the groundbreaking ceremonies. Her most vivid memories were standing in a clearing surrounded by many trees, being impressed with all the dignitaries, and obtaining an autograph from Governor Sanders. When she graduated from high school in 1973, she enrolled in KJC, where she found instructors such as Virginia Hinton and S. Frederick Roach to be challenging and helpful whenever she had a problem.

After receiving her associate's degree, she attended the University of Alabama, but grew homesick and returned to Cobb County. When Kennesaw began offering upper-level classes, she reenrolled and graduated with the first four-year class in 1980. Again, she found the faculty and staff to be helpful. She enjoyed being a pioneer, taking classes offered for the first time at Kennesaw. Some years later she recalled, "The classes were small. I did take some night courses, and you really were all in the same boat then, people that were working and taking classes. You did get to know each other and get to bond with each other. There were a lot of study sessions in the library and coffee sessions at the Student Center, or at the Cracker Barrel."[92]

Students by no means spent all their time studying. KJC was several years behind the rest of the country in experiencing the counterculture of the 1960s, but by the 1970s hippie culture and hippie habits were clearly apparent. At the time, Kennesaw offered fifty-minute classes five times a week from eight o'clock to noon and from one o'clock until around half past ten. To encourage students to stay on campus for something other than classes, the college set aside the hour between twelve and one o'clock for clubs and committee meetings. J. B. Tate recalled that not all students used the break for these purposes. At about a quarter past twelve he used to see students pop the trunks of their automobiles, take out their dope, and head for a wooded area on a hill approximately where the Wilson Building and parking lot now stand. The smoke rising through the pine trees was so thick that Tate wondered why no one called the fire department.

(Opposite Page) The old junior college library

Kennesaw also experienced the streaking phenomenon during the 1970s. Tate recollected that when the word circulated that students planned to streak around the quadrangle:

> People must have been twenty deep all the way around.... We waited and waited and...then around the old Student Center a big noise erupted...and suddenly two or three, maybe four or five—these all looked like football players, you know jocks. They were all naked, and they ran out at the flag pole and danced around...and took off in the other direction. They had a car waiting for them. So people waited and waited and said, "Well, I guess it's all over," and then suddenly noise went up again. It was a girl this time, and she had on a ski mask as the boys did. So she ran out to the flag pole, and you could hear around the quadrangle, "Oh, my God, it's Eleanor!" She was the only red head we had on campus; the ski mask didn't matter; we all knew each other.... So Eleanor, she went in and flashed Dr. Sturgis, a hyper-conservative guy. I'm sure he hyperventilated.[93]

Streakers and hippies were products of their time, but the typical Kennesaw students remained serious, pragmatic, and hard working, often holding down a job or two while attending school, and frequently supporting a family as well. By the fall of 1975, 32 percent of the students were married and 18 percent were veterans. When the college started, more than two-thirds of the students were male (77 percent in fall 1967), but that number was falling as more and more nontraditional-aged women enrolled in the daytime programs. By the fall of 1975 a gender balance was beginning to emerge with 55 percent male and 45 percent female. The numbers for the faculty were similar. Of the 116 people listed in the faculty section of the 1975–76 catalog, 50 were female (43 percent).[94]

The young faculty members of the junior-college years devoted practically all their professional time to teaching classes and completing doctorates. Instructors had few service obligations, and they were not required to do much scholarship beyond the completion of their PhD dissertations. Nonetheless, Kennesaw Junior College was involved in one major community project—the Cobb County Symposium—that brought it positive attention. In 1966 the Cobb County Medical Society, Judicial Bar Association, and Ministerial Association began holding an annual symposium to which they invited internationally prominent speakers. The first was Father Noah Mailleoux, a Jesuit priest from Montreal, who was a

(Opposite Page) The Cobb County Symposium, 1979

world-renowned criminologist. When the Cobb County Symposium expanded in 1968 into a two-day event with multiple speakers, the directors approached President Sturgis about a shared sponsorship.

Sturgis jumped at the opportunity, opening the campus to the community by offering the new gymnasium as a meeting site for the various sessions. At a time before cable television or the Internet, the symposium was a major cultural event in Cobb County, offering local people the opportunity to interact with such world-famous intellectuals as Margaret Mead, Elisabeth Kubler-Ross, William Pollard, Max Lerner, Joseph Fletcher, Mary Calderone, Norman Cousins, and Richard Leakey. Kennesaw students swelled the audiences, as the administration encouraged faculty members to take their classes to hear the speakers. The annual Cobb Symposia were well attended throughout the 1960s and 1970s. In time, they lost their uniqueness and significance, but they had a quarter-century run before being totally abandoned.

President Sturgis wrote for one of the symposia publications in the late 1970s that "to us, controversy can be constructive and well-meaning—and a part of what education is all about." He added that, "The image of our college came to the forefront through our participation in the symposia and this has helped us to gain recognition and support for us to become a four-year institution."[95] As the 1970s progressed, campus and community pressures grew to elevate Kennesaw to senior-college stature. But first, local and campus leaders had to overcome opposition from the chancellor's office and sister institutions in the university system.

Chapter 3

"Four Years Now": The Conversion to Senior-College Status

From its opening in 1966, Kennesaw Junior College worked quietly to achieve senior-college status. Hiring and promotion policies favored advanced degrees over teaching experience, and by the early 1970s the faculty seemed qualified to teach upper-level courses. The campus community bought into the notion that Kennesaw would earn its way up the academic ladder by maintaining high academic standards, regardless of the drop-out rate. Most programs of study prepared students to transfer to senior colleges and universities. To meet a critical need in north Georgia, Nursing, the main "terminal" associate degree program, gained Board of Regents approval in December 1967 and its first students enrolled the following fall.[96]

While Jimmy Carter was governor (1971–1975), state officials seemed to favor the community college concept where two-year schools would offer vocational as well as transfer programs. In December 1971, the Board of Regents approved a plan whereby junior colleges would offer vocational courses funded partly by the State Board for Vocational Education. By 1974, Brunswick, Dalton, and Bainbridge Junior Colleges had Vocational-Technical Education Divisions. To counter pressures to move in that direction, Kennesaw developed a limited number of cooperative programs with the Marietta-Cobb Area Vocational-Technical School. Secretarial science, for instance, allowed students to receive an associate's degree after taking a year of typing and similar courses at the Vo-Tech School and a year of academic classes at KJC. However, the college kept such programs to a minimum.[97]

President Sturgis and his leadership team had to be careful what they said in public, because Chancellor George L. Simpson and the Board of Regents envisioned Kennesaw as a permanent feeder institution for Georgia State University. The chancellor's long-range plan was for junior colleges in metro Atlanta to surround Georgia State from the northwest (Kennesaw), northeast (Gainesville), south (Clayton), east (DeKalb) and west (today's Atlanta Metropolitan College). Their two-year graduates were expected to come together for upper-level classes in Georgia State University's more diverse, cosmopolitan atmosphere. President Sturgis thought that this concept was plausible in principle, but not very practical, due to the immense amount of congestion on all roads leading to downtown Atlanta.[98]

His perspective was prophetic. The nontraditional adult students, who comprised a large segment of the enrollees at suburban two-year colleges, were often resistant to continuing their educations downtown. They and their unmet educational needs were instrumental in the conversion of Kennesaw into a four-year institution. In turn, the decision to grant Kennesaw four-year status forced the Chancellor to come up with a new plan for the metropolitan Atlanta area. Harry Downs, the president of Clayton Junior College, was quick to see that Kennesaw's transformation held promise for his institution.

Downs had coordinated the junior colleges for the regents in the 1960s and had helped forge the old plan of metropolitan feeder schools. Shortly after the regents announced Kennesaw's conversion, he told a reporter that Georgia needed a new plan, with a new tier of metropolitan junior and senior colleges. His institution would be the next to add upper-level courses, although Clayton had to wait until 1985 before it happened. As table 3 reveals, the expanded vision for higher education

led, in time, to the development of four-year programs at the older two-year schools and the creation of a new four-year college in Gwinnett County.[99]

TABLE 3	University System of Georgia Institutions Elevated to Senior-College Status, 1955–2008		
Institution	First Year in USG	4-Year Approval	University Status
Georgia State	1933	1955	1969
West Georgia	1933	1957	1996
Armstrong (Atlantic)	1958	1963	1996
Augusta	1958	1963	1996
Georgia Southwestern	1932	1964	1996
Columbus	1958	1966	1996
Southern Tech (Poly)	1948	1970	1996
▶ Kennesaw	1963	1976	1996
Clayton	1965	1985	1996
Macon	1965	1996	—
Dalton	1963	1998	—
Gainesville	1964	2005	—
Georgia Gwinnett	2005	2005	—
Gordon	1972	2007	—
Brunswick (Coastal Georgia)	1961	2008	—

In KJC's first decade, two obstacles to four-year conversion stand out. One was Cobb County's lack of racial diversity at a time when the regents were under pressure from the federal courts to desegregate the university system. Kennesaw's successes in the early 1970s in attracting African American students turned out to be crucial to the case for conversion. The other obstacle was the political opposition from nearby senior colleges and their representatives. Campus and Cobb community leaders had to engage in persistent lobbying over a period of several years to convince the chancellor and the Board of Regents that a four-year college in

(Opposite Page) A pinning ceremony
for new nursing graduates

northwest Georgia was needed and justified. The regents' plan for KJC to remain a feeder school to Georgia State University had to change, and that plan was well entrenched, politically.

The Higher Education Achievement Program and the Changing Campus Culture

Building a racially diverse student body, faculty, and staff was a major challenge everywhere in Georgia in the 1970s. In the aftermath of the civil rights movement, however, colleges that wanted to grow realized they had to change with the times. By the 1970s the population of Atlanta was majority black, while the surrounding suburbs were almost entirely white. Percentage-wise, the African American portion of Cobb County's population had dropped throughout the twentieth century, reaching a low point of about 3 percent in the middle of the 1970s before rising back to 4 percent at the time of the 1980 census. The University System of Georgia had been slow in developing affirmative action guidelines, but was under pressure from the courts and the federal Department of Health, Education, and Welfare (HEW) to do a better job of integrating its college and universities. So it was necessary for KJC to make the case that a four-year school in the northern part of Cobb County would not undermine the system's efforts at diversity.

During its first five years of operation (1966–1971), Kennesaw had one Asian instructor, no African American faculty members or secretaries, and very few black students—only 10 in the fall quarter of 1970, out of a total enrollment of 1,570 (0.6 percent). According to a 1972 report, edited by English instructor Belita M. Kuzmits, KJC had "gained a reputation in the community as an institution with narrow purposes and with a white, relatively well-to-do student population." Efforts to recruit African Americans and low-income white students were often frustrated by the common perception that KJC provided few options beyond the liberal arts and was a "difficult institution" with few support networks for minorities and others with special needs.[100]

As early as August 13, 1968, President Sturgis told the members of his Administrative Council that KJC needed to recruit qualified black faculty members.[101] But affirmative action was not a high priority, and Kennesaw's first successful effort to diversify the faculty and student body began not in the president's office but in that of dean of the college Robert H. Akerman, who replaced KJC's first academic dean, Derrell Roberts, in the fall of 1970.[102] Akerman held a PhD in history and political science from American University. At age forty-two, he was a veteran journalist and educator. In the mid-1950s, he had served as associate editor of the *Florida Times-Union*. In 1958 he joined the faculty of Florida Southern College in Orlando, and rose to the chairmanship of the Social Sciences Division by 1967, the year in which he earned his doctorate. He would serve as Kennesaw's academic dean for only three years before returning to the newspaper business as editorial associate of the *Atlanta Journal*, where his columns appeared daily on the editorial page.[103]

About the time he arrived at KJC, Akerman heard about a unique project designed to improve educational opportunities for low-income and minority students at southern junior and community colleges. The US Office of Education was in the process of starting a Higher Education Achievement Program (HEAP) and had selected the Southern Association of Colleges and Schools (SACS) to assist in developing and administering it. In the fall of 1970, Akerman filled out the grant application to bring the program to campus. Toward the end of that academic year, on April 27, 1971, he received word from the Office of Education that Kennesaw had been awarded a $113,000 grant to implement HEAP during the 1971–72 academic year, with the understanding that the grant could be renewed for two additional years.

HEAP began operations in 1971 with a consortium of nine schools, public and private, stretching from North Carolina to the Florida Keys to Laredo, Texas.[104] Each institution was expected to recruit and provide special counseling and skills instruction each year for approximately one hundred high-risk students. SACS already was involved in a similar experiment at fifteen historically black institutions called the College Education Achievement Project (CEAP). If these pilot programs succeeded in removing class and racial barriers to higher education, then they hopefully would be the model followed by higher education systems throughout the South.[105]

The Office of Education's announcement exposed a serious lack of communication (and possible lack of trust), as Dean Akerman had not informed President Sturgis about the application before the official letter arrived. In later years Sturgis said he was delighted when he found out. Regardless of his feelings at the time, the president later found HEAP useful in making the case to the Board of Regents that Kennesaw was taking diversity seriously and would not undermine the system's desegregation plans if it became a four-year school.[106]

Dean Akerman had from April to September to find a coordinator, two counselors, and an instructor for each of the HEAP subject areas of mathematics, reading, speaking-listening, reaction writing, and reaction ideas (the study of current and controversial issues). He discovered the resume of the first coordinator, Stewart G. Phillips, in a list of potential administrators circulated by the chancellor's office. Akerman attempted to recruit minority faculty by asking SACS to provide referrals of CEAP professors from the black colleges. When it became obvious that none of them wanted to work at Kennesaw, Akerman went through the stack of letters he had received from applicants making general inquiries about job openings at Kennesaw. Whenever he found minority candidates or anyone with successful experience working with at-risk students, he sent a brief description of HEAP along with a request that they consider applying for vacant positions.[107]

Akerman initially wanted to offer the coordinator job to an African American candidate from Minnesota. However, KJC was unable to meet his salary demands. The grant from the Office of Education funded a salary of only $14,000, some $4,000 less than this individual was earning already. Thus, the dean had no choice but to offer the coordinator opening to the most qualified white applicant. He had more success in filling the two counselor posts, for which several African Americans applied. Ultimately, he selected a white male, James E. Conley, and a black male, Bobby L. Olive, the first African American professional on the KJC faculty or staff.

To Akerman's chagrin, the candidate pool for the teaching positions contained no African Americans with the required master's degree in the teaching field. None-theless, he managed to fill the posts with talented, young, white idealists. Ronald D. Carlisle, for instance, was offered the job as math instructor at age twenty-nine, based on his background as a PhD candidate in mathematics at Emory University, two years as a Peace Corps volunteer in the Philippines, and experience as an associate director of a summer institute that prepared math teachers to work with disadvantaged youth. He would receive his PhD in 1972. Similarly, the speech instructor, Elaine M. Amerson, at age twenty-seven was an EdD candidate at the University of Kentucky, had worked in a day camp in Harlem, and had taught in the Pan American Institute of the Republic of Panama. She would be awarded her doctorate in the spring of 1974. Of the original eight HEAP professionals, four were male and four female; two were in their early thirties and the rest in their twenties.[108]

The HEAP coordinator and one of the counselors spent the summer recruiting one hundred students who probably would not have been accepted at KJC otherwise. Much of their time was spent contacting metropolitan area principals and school counselors, seeking referrals. They tried to achieve a balance of African Americans, rural whites, and high-risk students, regardless of income. To reach the goal of one hundred, the last group was essential because Kennesaw, in 1971, offered little financial aid and had few work-study positions.

KJC's Office of Administration and Records helped by giving Coordinator Phillips the names of applicants that did not qualify for the regular program because their projected grade point averages were less than 1.6 on a scale of 4.0. By enrolling some of these students, HEAP effectively turned Kennesaw into an open-door college. The initial class consisted of forty-three blacks, fifty-six whites, and one Asian American. Reflecting the student body as a whole, males outnumbered females about two to one.[109]

Many of the HEAP students came from downtown Atlanta. For those of limited income, transportation was a major problem. Cobb County lacked public transit at the time, and I-75 would not reach the campus for several more years. So the campus seemed remote to those traveling from Atlanta. Fortunately, the HEAP faculty was able to contract with a bus service to transport students from the inner city in the morning and back to downtown in the afternoon. While President Sturgis vetoed the idea of KJC operating its own bus, he allowed the Student Activities Committee to subsidize the bus rides through the student activities fee. The Southern Education Foundation, several inner-city agencies, and private donors contributed as well. Meanwhile, a prominent Marietta couple, M. J. and Kathryn Woods, donated a car for the students to use. The system worked well until the bus company tripled its rates in March 1974, forcing HEAP to operate on a three-day-a week schedule for the last quarter of its existence.[110]

HEAP operated as a separate division reporting directly to the academic dean. Prior to the Board of Regents' approval of faculty statutes in December 1972, Kennesaw had a hierarchical, top-down administrative style with relatively little faculty involvement in decision making.[111] HEAP operated outside that model, creating a team concept that included students as well as faculty in planning and evaluation. Throughout the academic year, the faculty and four elected student representatives met for staff meetings at least once and often two or three times a week. Anyone was free to put items on the agenda, and all important program decisions resulted from these discussions. From a staff perspective, the system worked well, at least for the first two years of the program.

HEAP's final report noted that student participation in time-consuming staff meetings fell off in the last year after policies had already been well established. By that time, however, HEAP students had become integrated into the life of the college in other ways. Eddie Jackson, for instance, became KJC's first African American student elected to an executive office in the Student Government Association when he served as vice president during the 1973–74 academic year. Jackson also became involved in the system-wide Student Advisory Council as the chairman of the Junior College Committee.[112]

Kennesaw's stated purposes had always included serving the needs of the community through developmental, as well as transfer and terminal degree programs. Prior to 1971, however, the Special Studies Program operated primarily in the summer quarter and was limited to sixty students per year. While students could take developmental math, English, and psychology-orientation courses in the summertime, only the math class was offered during the academic year. The first annual HEAP report noted that a 1972 institutional self-study described the developmental program as a "token effort of what is needed." Stimulated in part by HEAP's example, KJC began in 1972 to expand its remedial offerings during the academic year.[113]

After Stewart Phillips headed the program for its first two years, he accepted a position as the SACS coordinator of the region-wide HEAP consortium. Ron Carlisle became his replacement at KJC. In the final annual report in 1974, Carlisle argued that HEAP "represented a major attempt of the college to be more nearly what it had professed" to be. He asserted that HEAP had helped students overcome "motivational and academic barriers to success" and had started to change the campus culture by creating a more inviting atmosphere and converting at least some of the regular faculty to a sense "that the many and not merely the few could profitably attend college."[114]

As the program wound down, the HEAP staff grew increasingly pessimistic about their accomplishments. The 1974 annual report concludes that while HEAP had a number of success stories, "objective measures of student success [had] not revealed spectacular results," and the achievement gap did not seem to close significantly between HEAP and regular admission students. The report praised Kennesaw for seeking the advice of the HEAP faculty in planning a Special Studies Program for 1974–75, but expressed doubt that Special Studies would receive sufficient backing in the absence of federal funding. It also noted that none of the HEAP staff was asked to work in the new program. Most of them took their expertise to other colleges in metropolitan Atlanta, particularly Georgia State University and the newly-opening Atlanta Junior College (today's Atlanta Metropolitan College). Their loss was particularly unfortunate because three years of work in a pilot program had given them a wealth of experience in dealing with high-risk students. By 1974 they shared a sense that three years were not enough to accomplish all their program goals and that they were just beginning to learn which teaching and motivational techniques worked best.[115]

An independent evaluation was conducted during the final year by a team headed by Robert Stolz of the Atlanta office of the College Entrance Examination Board, and including a SACS staff member, George Rolle, and Kennesaw HEAP instructor Elaine Amerson. The evaluators credited HEAP with improving students' self-esteem and helping students adopt realistic goals. The team seemed to suggest that if HEAP could attract and retain minority and disadvantaged students at Kennesaw, "with its history, image and location," then similar programs could succeed anywhere. The evaluators gave HEAP credit for transforming "the campus image from an all-white rather elite institution to an integrated institution with a broad service interest."[116]

Unlike HEAP, Special Studies had few faculty members other than reading instructors dedicated to that program alone. From 1973 to 1979 Morgan L. Stapleton served as coordinator of the Special Studies Program, while continuing to teach and be evaluated in the Division of Natural Sciences and Mathematics. Until 1978 he lacked a clear role in the administrative hierarchy, and Special Studies struggled for respect and recognition. A number of instructors were outstanding teachers and genuinely cared about developmental students, but others were less interested and less successful.

On January 5, 1978, President Sturgis received a letter from an exasperated vice chancellor, John W. Hooper, who described Kennesaw's Special Studies Program as "inadequate and unacceptable." He reminded Sturgis that staff from the central office had expressed their concerns to him a number of times. Hooper asked the president to appoint, by spring quarter 1978, a coordinator who reported directly to the academic dean, and to set up by fall quarter 1978 a department with "at least a minimum 'core' faculty."[117]

Stapleton coordinated the program for one more year before becoming the academic dean at Brunswick Junior College. Before he left, he persuaded English professor Mary Zoghby to take his place. She would serve six years (1979–1985), the first four as coordinator and the last two as chair of the Department of Developmental Studies. Throughout her tenure, the Special (or Developmental) Studies Department had its own budget and a small core faculty, supplemented by many others borrowed from English and math.

When Mary Zoghby first accepted the position, her office was in the Administration Building next to Dean Eugene R. Huck. She was the first woman to serve as a department head and one of only two women on the dean's staff (along with Assistant Dean Betty J. Youngblood). On the college Tenure and Promotion Committee, she would be the only woman meeting with Huck and the various division chairmen. It did not take her long to realize that students were reluctant to drop into her office in the Administration Building, so she asked to move to the top floor of the new library, where there was also room for math, English, and reading labs. A number of instructors volunteered their time to help students in the labs. They were uncompensated for their efforts, but Zoghby was able to pay a few top math students to serve as tutors. For a number of years after Kennesaw became a senior college, the Developmental Studies Program played a vital, if underappreciated, role.[118]

The Developmental Studies Program was particularly valuable in helping Kennesaw's nontraditional students adjust to college life. Many of them had been out of school for years and needed a refresher course or two to put them on an equal footing with their younger classmates. While Kennesaw had no intentions of abandoning that clientele, its mission would change after it became a senior college, and in the late 1980s it would self-impose higher freshman admission standards to curb the enrollment of under-prepared traditional-aged students, diverting them instead to area junior colleges.

A perception existed on more elite campuses that Kennesaw used the Developmental Studies Program in the 1980s to grow its enrollment and gain greater formula funding from the Board of Regents. Table 4 argues the opposite. At the start of the 1980s, some 18 percent of all Kennesaw students took developmental studies courses, a percentage typical of Georgia junior colleges. By the end of the decade, the percentage had dropped to just 7.2 percent, a proportion well below the senior-college average. The de-emphasizing of developmental studies coincided with Kennesaw's maturing into a full-fledged metropolitan college. Yet, the original emphasis of HEAP on diversifying the campus culture would never stop being a major institutional goal.[119]

TABLE 4	Developmental Studies (DS) Program Enrollment, University System of Georgia, as Percentage of Total Headcount (HC) Enrollment, 1980–1989											
	Kennesaw			Universities			Senior Colleges			Junior Colleges		
Year	DS	HC	%	DS	HC	%	DS	HC	%	DS	HC	%
1980	703	3,903	18.0	1,061	57,374	1.8	5,434	47,411	11.5	4,301	22,022	19.5
1981	704	4,195	16.8	1,216	60,203	2.0	5,589	49,197	11.4	4,556	22,774	20.0
1982	800	4,779	16.7	1,152	61,002	1.9	5,799	51,412	11.3	4,763	24,398	19.5
1983	845	5,385	15.7	1,219	59,853	2.0	5,491	53,405	10.3	4,305	24,485	17.6
1984	880	5,821	15.1	1,217	59,874	2.0	5,545	52,815	10.5	3,894	22,452	17.3
1985	1,102	6,866	16.1	1,290	60,418	2.1	5,615	54,201	10.4	3,631	21,345	17.0
1986	907	7,296	12.4	1,251	61,383	2.0	5,973	58,705	10.2	5,755	27,420	21.0
1987	1,027	7,946	12.9	1,487	62,696	2.4	6,953	62,621	11.1	6,417	28,335	22.6
1988	902	8,614	10.5	1,554	63,587	2.4	8,139	66,242	12.3	7,597	31,954	23.8
1989	656	9,140	7.2	1,685	64,963	2.6	8,915	71,518	12.5	9,129	35,709	25.6

Additional Efforts at Diversity and at Making Higher Education Affordable

There is little question that the campus was never quite the same after the HEAP experience. Minority enrollment remained low, but not quite as low as it once was. In fall quarter 1975, for instance, 59 African American students constituted about 2 percent of the overall campus enrollment of 3,098. This number was considerably above the 10 (less than 1 percent) enrolled in the fall of 1970, but below the 79 (4

(Opposite Page) Terri Thomas Arnold

percent) enrolled in the fall of 1972, during HEAP's middle year. Of course, African Americans were extremely underrepresented in most other units of the university system with the exception of the historically black colleges. By way of comparison, Georgia Tech's African American enrollment in 1969–1970 was under 1 percent, and Georgia State University's in the fall of 1974 was just 12 percent (2,101 of 17,510) in a city with a population that was majority black.[120]

During this era, Kennesaw made a few significant efforts to integrate the workplace as well as the student body. In January 1971 Charles Williams became only the second black employee and first in a management position as food services supervisor. The first African American secretary, Terri Ferguson [Arnold], was hired in June 1971. Her father, Charles Ferguson, started working in 1951 at the Lockheed plant in Marietta and by the 1960s had become one of the first blacks at Lockheed to move into management. Her uncle, Lewis Scott, was a history teacher at Lemon Street High School, which Terri attended until 1967, when the city school system fully integrated. After graduating from Marietta High School in the class of 1969, she attended Morris Brown College for a year. She then worked in Atlanta for six months before hearing from a family friend that Kennesaw Junior College was seeking minority applicants for a secretarial job with HEAP. At the time, she had no idea where the college was located and had always assumed that "they don't want us any more than we want to go there." Nonetheless, she decided she had nothing to lose by applying.[121]

While she was on campus for her HEAP interview, the dean of student affairs, Carol L. Martin, told her he was losing his secretary and asked if she would interview with him. Since he could pay her a higher salary than HEAP offered, she went to work in his office. Thus began a career at Kennesaw that lasted over forty years, first in the Office of Student Affairs, then as an administrative assistant for Controller (later vice president) Roger E. Hopkins and his replacement B. Earle Holley, and finally in a post-retirement part-time job as a manager in Arlethia Perry-Johnson's Office of External Affairs. Her entire career would be spent in the old Administration Building and Kennesaw Hall where she recalls that she never had to work her way up. Except for an unhappy two years at Marietta High School, she had never spent much time around white people, and she admits that she was as curious about them as they were about her. She recalls that everyone was extremely nice and greeted her with open arms, and another secretary in the Administration Building, Barbara Blackwell, quickly became her "best buddy."[122]

A number of additional African American hires followed. Betty Jackson was employed as HEAP secretary in July 1971, but left shortly afterwards and was replaced by Phyllis Baker. Paulette Long was hired as secretary for the Social Sciences Division in September 1971. The first two African American members of the teaching faculty, Karen Maples in Biology and Ruth Rundles in Economics, started in September 1972. HEAP added a clerk-typist, Karen Bullock, in October 1973 the first three black custodians, William Johnson, George J. Milton Sr., and George J. Milton Jr., and the first black groundskeeper, James L. Echols, began work in 1973. Including HEAP counselor Bobby Olive, KJC, over a three-year period, succeeded in adding thirteen African Americans to the faculty and staff. In the absence of support networks, Kennesaw had a difficult time retaining black employees in what must have seemed a sea of whiteness. Only Terri Arnold stayed for an entire career. Nonetheless, the modest increase in African American students, faculty, and staff allowed the administration to claim that blacks would feel less conspicuous and isolated in the future and that the number of African American students and employees should continue to grow.[123]

All colleges and universities found it easier to attract minority and disadvantaged students after Congress, in 1972, amended the Higher Education Act of 1965 to create Basic Educational Opportunity Grants, renamed Pell Grants in 1980 in honor of their chief sponsor, Rhode Island Senator Claiborne Pell.[124] President Truman's Commission on Higher Education called for affordable tuition as far back as 1947, but the federal government only now put massive amounts of money into student aid. Historian John R. Thelin credits a cadre of little known student lobbyists in prodding Congress into action, much to the displeasure of the Association of American Universities and the American Council on Education. In the *Great Transformation in Higher Education*, Clark Kerr noted that such mainline organizations wanted federal subsidies to go directly to member schools and were lukewarm about portable financial aid that followed students to any accredited institution they chose to attend.

Since World War II, federal support of higher education had come primarily through grants for competitive research and capital expenditures of the type that the Higher Education Facilities Commission gave the university system to construct KJC's original buildings. After the campus turmoil of the 1960s, public faith in universities diminished, and members of Congress saw little political gain in putting money in the hands of college administrators to spend as they saw fit. Nonetheless, congressmen saw immense political advantage in making students and parents happy through grants that went directly to pay tuition bills and other college expenses.

The Basic Educational Opportunity Grants (BEOG) had the virtue of being democratic—they were available to all full-time students from low-income families as long as they were in good academic standing at any accredited college. It did not matter whether they enrolled at an elite university or a junior college because the amount of the grant varied depending on how expensive it was to attend a particular school. Thelin notes that the program "helped promote the appeal of 'going to college' to a new generation of students at a time when colleges needed this boost."[125]

Tuition and fees were low at junior colleges in the University System of Georgia; so the Pell Grants, arguably, were less important in attracting students to KJC than to more expensive institutions. At the time, tuition at KJC was only $85 a quarter for in-state and $205 for non-resident students. The student services fee was ten dollars a quarter, and the parking fee was four dollars a year. Nonetheless, starting in 1974–1975, the official campus catalogs consistently list the Basic Educational Opportunity Grants as an attractive form of financial aid. According to the catalogs, BEOG was a federal program that helped with tuition, books, and other college expenses, less the amount that the student and his family could pay, based on income. In the fiscal year 1974 (July 1, 1973 through June 30, 1974) Kennesaw enrolled its first thirty-three students on Basic Educational Opportunity Grants. They received an average award of $240.30, about enough to cover tuition for a year. By fiscal year 1977 the numbers had risen to 142 students (about 4 percent of the student body) and the average grant to $568.11. In the latter year Kennesaw awarded 391 grants, loans, or work-study opportunities (roughly one per every eight students) totaling $200,623—a small amount compared to future years, but still highly significant for the students most in need.[126]

Along with BEOG grants, Supplemental Educational Opportunity Grants provided $200 to $1,000 to students of exceptional financial need who would otherwise be unable to remain in college. These were just two of a number of government grants and loans that originated in this era to help students with college costs. According to the KJC catalog for 1974–75, the Georgia Higher Education Assistance Corporation (GHEAC) allowed students to go to a bank and borrow up to $1,200 a year with GHEAC paying the interest on the loan while the individual was still in school. National Direct Student Loans and Nursing Student Loans enabled students to borrow up to $2,500 for the first two years at 3 percent interest. The National Direct Student Loans were provided jointly by the federal government and KJC through matching funds provided by the KJC Foundation and various civic groups.[127]

In early 1969, President Sturgis invited a few civic leaders to help create a KJC Foundation to raise funds for such things as student scholarships. One of the first people he approached was Superior Court judge G. Conley Ingram, who had just completed a four-year term on the bench and was back in private practice. He would later serve on the Georgia Supreme Court. Ingram attended at least two small gatherings that winter, the first at the home of his next-door neighbor, Marietta businessman R. Steve Tumlin; the second at the residence of a local dentist and past Kiwanis International president, Dr. R. Glenn Reed Jr. Others involved in those initial meetings included Dr. William H. Dunaway, a pharmacist who owned a chain of north Georgia drugstores; and Robert T. Garrison, the recently retired president of the Arrow Shirt Company. Ingram volunteered to prepare and file the

Charter members of the KJC Foundation

incorporation papers with the Georgia secretary of state. Since Garrison had more free time than his colleagues, he agreed to become the first chairman of the board.[128]

Once the legal paperwork was completed, the first official meeting of the KJC Foundation took place on April 17, 1969. By that time, the group of charter trustees had grown to twenty-three. Ingram recruited one non-Cobb County trustee, Judge William A. (Bud) Foster Jr. a superior court judge in Paulding County. Soon afterwards, State Representative (and future governor) Joe Frank Harris provided a Bartow County presence. At the April meeting, Garrison appointed a fundraising committee to conduct the first annual campaign. It was chaired by Marietta businessman Sidney Clotfelter, and included Campbell Dasher, Howard Ector, and Ed Massey.[129] In the junior-college years, a typical campaign raised only about $20,000 to $30,000 a year, but it was a start in adding to the funds available for student scholarships, aiding faculty members with the costs of completing their dissertations, and supplementing administrative salaries, among other projects.[130]

Probably the most conspicuous beneficiaries of government financial aid programs in the 1970s were the police officers who enrolled in criminal justice and attended class in their uniforms. The Justice Department's Law Enforcement

79

Educational Grants (LEEG) paid tuition and books for any police officer wanting to attend college. When these grants first became available, Kennesaw Junior College lacked a criminal justice faculty, but operated a program with instructors provided by Georgia State University. The college asked Professor J. B. Tate to be their on-site advisor and contact person. According to Tate, the officers intimidated faculty and students when they walked into the classroom with guns strapped to their waists, but, in fact, the officers themselves were terrified to be in a college environment. Most were first-generation college students, and the campus seemed an alien place. So they clung to Tate "like a security blanket" and took every history class he taught.

One of Tate's vivid memories is of an encounter one night between his policemen and the guests of KJC's lone psychology instructor. That instructor had been hired in part for his apparent respectability. He was an ordained clergyman as well as a psychologist. What the administration apparently did not know was that his ministry was on Fourteenth Street when that was the center of Atlanta's hippie culture. The instructor thought his students would benefit from actually meeting some hippies, so he asked several to come to campus. As Tate recalled:

> All these guys came rolling up on motorcycles, and they had turbans, naked from the belt up except for little halter tops, with big earrings.... I didn't see them come in. I heard all those motorcycles, but I had already started my class. [The psychology professor] gives them a break at the same time I give my policemen a break, and they converged out there on the hall.... That was the longest ten minutes of my life. They were cussing each other, and you can imagine the epithets going back and forth. The policemen didn't really like the idea of being called pig and particularly when you add a few more adjectives to go with it. So I finally got my policemen back in the classroom, and they are hot. They are hot! You know, somebody could have gotten killed out there real easy. It took me twenty or thirty minutes to get them settled down enough that we could get the class going again. Well needless to say [the psychology instructor's] days are numbered.[131]

By making higher education more affordable, Pell Grants, LEEG grants, and similar types of aid probably did as much to diversify student bodies throughout the nation as all the conscious efforts at affirmative action. Until the mid-1970s,

(Opposite Page) Charter foundation members R. Sidney Clotfelter
and W. Wyman Pilcher

the police officers taking advantage of LEEG grants were all white, but most of them came from a social class and nontraditional age group that had not gone to college in the past. On October 27, 1976, President Sturgis submitted to the Board of Regents an *Impact Study on the Proposed Conversion of Kennesaw Junior College to Senior College Status*. In it he argued that the main impact of conversion would be the expansion of educational opportunities to a large number of north Georgians who otherwise would be denied the opportunity to pursue a bachelor's degree. The report particularly emphasized nontraditional students—not only the older students, but the 62 percent of the student body who held full- or part-time jobs and the third, roughly, who were married. Such students, he maintained, could not easily give up their jobs or leave their families to go off to residential colleges.

Sturgis argued that suburban Cobb's median family income in 1970 may have been fairly high, but the nearby rural counties of Bartow, Cherokee, and Paulding were below the state average.[132] Since the Seventh Congressional District of northwest Georgia lacked a public, senior college, the people of the area would especially benefit from an affordable school in commuting distance. Moreover, he noted that minority enrollment in several area school districts was quite significant (for the 1975–76 school year 12.8 percent in Bartow County, 20 percent in Cartersville City, and 7.3 percent in Paulding). While enrollment in the Cobb County School District was only 3.2 percent black, that of Marietta City Schools was 27.8 percent. These data, he maintained, gave one "reason to believe that the conversion will be attractive to minority students in the service area."[133]

The Politics of Conversion

Diversity was just one of the challenges that four-year advocates had to overcome in making their case. Perhaps the greatest problem was alleviating the fears of Georgia State, West Georgia, Columbus, and other public institutions that a senior college in Cobb County would take away their students and vital funding. In addition, downtown business leaders appeared concerned that the core of Atlanta would crumble if the suburbs were dotted with dynamic four-year schools that pulled students away from Georgia State and economic development from the central city. They wanted Georgia State to be "the" metropolitan university around which the region revolved. Chancellor George Simpson shared their vision and feared the possible domino effect if he let any more junior colleges (especially those in metro Atlanta) advance to four-year status.[134]

In the 1960s the Board of Regents had created a number of four-year schools across the middle and southern parts of the state. Three of them (Augusta, Armstrong, and Columbus) were nonresident, commuter schools of a model that Kennesaw hoped to adopt. KJC's service area by the 1970s was much larger than that of any of the three, and there were no public senior colleges anywhere in northwest Georgia's

Seventh Congressional District. Therefore, the task for President Sturgis was to show that population growth in an underserved area made a new senior college essential, and that Kennesaw's elevation would not adversely affect anyone in other parts of the state. Meanwhile, local powerbrokers realized they would have to use their considerable political skills to outmaneuver a chancellor, other area colleges and universities, and the Atlanta business elite. The story of how they did so is at least as dramatic as that of the previous decade when some of the same leaders managed to take Southern Technical Institute from DeKalb County and Kennesaw Junior College from Bartow.

The legislative delegation, Cobb Chamber of Commerce, and local educators were committed from the beginning to turning Cobb's two-year schools into senior colleges. Southern Tech gained the right to offer upper-level courses in 1970 (although it had to wait ten more years before gaining independence from its founder, Georgia Tech). Whenever President Sturgis spoke to civic groups, he invariably fielded questions about when Kennesaw would become a four-year college. In public, he was always careful to remember his loyalties to the chancellor. His standard response was that the decision would be made by the Board of Regents when Kennesaw could justify the need for a four-year liberal arts college in northwest Georgia.

Much of Sturgis's role in the four-year campaign was in writing research reports on the impact that conversion would have on the region and other university system institutions. While these internal reports were for the chancellor and board, he quietly circulated them to local leaders such as Representatives Joe Mack Wilson and Joe Frank Harris, attorney Harold Willingham, charter KJC Foundation president Robert T. Garrison, and newspaperman Bill Kinney, telling them he was sure they would be interested in the findings. When these individuals spoke subsequently in public, they took their talking points straight from the president's reports.[135]

Three local delegations addressed the Board of Regents without success. The first made its presentation on January 13, 1971. Its spokesperson was Senator Cy Chapman. Others present were Hubert Black of the Cobb Chamber and virtually the entire legislative delegation: State Senator Jack Henderson and Representatives Hugh Lee McDaniel, Howard (Red) Atherton, A. L. Burruss, Bob Howard, Gene Housley, George Kreeger, and Joe Mack Wilson. Chapman argued that Cobb's tremendous population growth and economic progress justified the conversion and that Cobb Countians were united in their support. Board of Regents chairman T. Hiram Stanley thanked the delegation and promised the matter would be considered carefully. But, while the board was polite, it took no action, and, for all practical purposes, the matter went no further.[136]

A second delegation, headed by Senator Jack Henderson, made its appeal to the board on October 10, 1973. This time the delegation included a broad group of political, educational, and business leaders, including the press. Henderson introduced Harold Willingham who used the same arguments that Cy Chapman had employed almost three years earlier, along with a new point that the planned construction of I-75 by the campus would increase accessibility and demand for higher education in north Cobb County. Again, board chairman William S. Morris III thanked the group and promised that the regents would study the issue, and, again, the board took no further action.[137]

Before another delegation addressed the regents, Joe Mack Wilson and his colleagues in the legislature pursued another approach. In January 1974 they pushed through both houses of the Georgia General Assembly resolutions calling on the Board of Regents to elevate Kennesaw Junior College to senior-college status.[138] When the resolutions proved insufficient to catch the regents' attention, Wilson and a united local leadership played politics expertly in the 1974 gubernatorial election. With Governor Jimmy Carter about to leave office, three major contenders vied for the nomination of the Democratic Party: Calhoun banker and state highway director, Bert Lance, a close friend of Governor Carter; Lieutenant Governor (and former governor) Lester Maddox; and Georgia House majority leader George Busbee of Albany.

As Busbee campaigned in Cobb County, he met privately with Wilson, Burruss, Willingham, and others, and asked what he needed to do to gain their endorsement. His strength was in south Georgia, and he was not well known outside that region. So he was willing to offer a lot to gain some north Georgia support. Wilson and Burruss, of course, had served with him for a long time in the Georgia House. They asked for three things: the conversion of KJC to senior status, the governor's support in persuading the federal government to complete the last segment of I-75 from North Marietta Parkway to Cartersville (and by the Kennesaw campus), and the construction of a Western and Atlantic Railroad bridge over what would become South Marietta Parkway, so that traffic could move freely during rush hour from west Marietta to US 41 and I-75. Busbee gave his support to all three projects, and in exchange the local power elite went all out to help elect him. Just before the general election, the *Marietta Daily Journal* threw its support to Busbee, calling him the best man for the job and citing his endorsement of the three local improvement projects.[139]

Roy E. Barnes was a young politician at the time, running his first race for the state senate. He was not part of the meeting with Busbee, but heard about it immediately and recalls how remarkable it was that all major factions of Cobb's Democratic Party came together in support of one candidate and one set of issues. In a 1976 article journalist Bill Kinney made a similar observation, arguing that not since the Southern Tech fight fifteen years earlier had there been such "unanimous and determined" local support as there was for Kennesaw's conversion. In the final years of the Democratic Party's domination in Cobb County, before the Republican Party's takeover, the old guard scored one of its last major victories in electing Busbee and holding him to his campaign promises.[140]

A. L. Burruss managed the Busbee campaign in Cobb County and for the next eight years would be Cobb County's "ear" in the governor's office. In the months following his election, Busbee continued to assert his support for Kennesaw Junior College. In December 1974 he told a *Marietta Daily Journal* reporter that KJC would be the "next junior college in the state to be elevated" to four-year status. In February 1975 he told a local delegation that Kennesaw's conversion would have little impact on other institutions, and that "we should have four-year colleges where the students are." The fight, however, was not going to be easy. In the weeks following the general election, the *Atlanta Constitution* editorialized against those who tried to exert political influence over the university system and threw its support behind Charles A. Harris, the chairman of the Board of Regents, who had come out against the conversion of junior colleges into senior institutions. Harris said that the university system had just begun to "work as we had planned," and did not see any possibility in the next few years that Georgia would create more four-year institutions. Instead, he wanted to direct resources to the existing upper-level and graduate programs. The board chairman was also on record as saying that the state and national economies were too weak at the time to think about diverting precious resources to junior-college conversions.[141]

In early 1975 the Cobb Chamber of Commerce formed a select committee, chaired by former Arrow Shirt president Bob Garrison, to make the case to the Board of Regents that the county needed a nondormitory, four-year school. Harold Willingham served as vice chair, and other members included Cobb Commission chairman Ernest Barrett, Marietta mayor Dana Eastham, chamber president Stan St. John, and the entire Cobb legislative delegation. Using information fed to them by Horace Sturgis, Garrison sent a letter to the regents, noting that Cobb County

**Charter foundation chairman
Robert T. Garrison**

had grown from about 62,000 in 1950 to an estimated 260,000 in 1974, and that 55,000 pupils were enrolled in Cobb County schools in the current academic year.

Garrison noted that there were only three non-resident senior colleges in the university system — Augusta, Columbus, and Armstrong — and that Cobb was larger and growing faster than the counties of Richmond, Muscogee, and Chatham, where those institutions were based. Further, he argued that conversion would cost the university system very little, because Kennesaw's facilities were adequate to handle the initial expected enrollments and because operating funds would be the same whether KJC's associate's degree graduates finished their upper-level work in Cobb County or elsewhere in the university system. According to Garrison, the main cost would be in providing access to upper-level degree programs for students who otherwise could not afford to complete their education.[142]

On March 12, 1975, the chamber's select committee made Cobb's third presentation to the Board of Regents. Garrison introduced Harold Willingham who did most of the talking, repeating the arguments made by earlier delegations and Garrison's letter. Three Kennesaw Student Government Association leaders (President Howell Swain, Secretary Pat Loyd, and Senator June Rowland) accompanied the committee. Prior to the meeting, the Student Government Association had gone out to Cumberland Mall and other shopping centers and asked people to sign a petition supporting Kennesaw's elevation to senior-college status. Now, Swain presented the petition with nine thousand signatures. Described as a "clean-cut" young man who held down a full-time job while going to school, Swain lamented that he could not afford to go into Atlanta to Georgia State and would have to drop out if Kennesaw did not go to four-year status. However, as before, the delegation received only a polite "thank you" from Chairman Charles Harris, who told them that the regents would take the matter under advisement.[143]

Meanwhile, Joe Mack Wilson, A. L. Burruss, and Joe Frank Harris tried another strategy, putting funds in the state budget to pay for the conversion. Future governor Harris was chairman of the House Appropriations Committee, on which Wilson also served. They made up two of the five members of the powerful "green door" group that largely wrote the appropriations bills that came out of the House. Originally, they designated $350,000 as a line item for the Board of Regents that could be used only for the conversion of Kennesaw to four-year status. Although the amount was later reduced to $250,000, they, according to one reporter, cleared "more hurdles than an Olympic sprinter" in keeping the funds in the final budget.[144]

(Opposite Page) Governor George Busbee and President Sturgis at the dedication of the Carmichael Student Center.

The regents chose not to spend the quarter million dollars during the 1975–76 school year, but Wilson and his colleagues resolved to keep the money in the budget until they came around. Meanwhile, President Sturgis's correspondence makes clear that he was taking a more aggressive role, perhaps under prodding from Wilson and others. In addition to his private letters to a variety of policymakers, he was becoming more assertive in his discussions with the chancellor. George Simpson could seem overbearing at times, and it took some courage to stand up to him. By August 7, 1975, however, Sturgis wrote to him stating that while there might be some logic to his argument that the system should not take on new projects during a recession, yet, "I believe we must be very much concerned about the number of individuals in our geographic locality who, under present conditions, are being denied educational opportunities because they cannot afford the cost of attending another institution in the System." The president went on to say that the cost of conversion would be "nominal" as the data in his enclosed *Profile* proved. He concluded that

Student Government Association officers: June Rowland [Krise], president; Randy Krise, vice president; Winifred Seay, treasurer; and Nancy Mitchell, secretary.

he understood all junior colleges could not be converted, but the data supported "an affirmative decision" in the case of KJC.[145]

Two months later, pressure on the chancellor and board increased when state leaders gathered in Cobb County for the dedication of the James V. Carmichael Student Center. Carmichael was one of the outstanding statesmen and business leaders of twentieth-century Georgia. He played a central role in bringing the Bell Aircraft plant to Marietta during World War II and was its general manager at the end of the conflict. He also served as the first general manager when Lockheed reopened the plant in 1951 and was president for over a decade of the Atlanta-based Scripto pen company. In 1946 he was the progressive candidate for governor against Eugene Talmadge, winning the popular vote, but losing in the antiquated county-unit system, by which ballots in the Democratic primaries were counted at the time. He was also involved in a host of community organizations.

Carmichael was perhaps most admired for his tremendous courage, having come close to death as a teenager in 1926 when he was hit by a speeding motorist on the Dixie Highway in front of his parents' general store. His back was broken and the spinal cord all but severed. He spent a year recovering, first at Crawford Long Hospital, and then at home, with his mother staying constantly by his side, reading and singing with him sometimes all night while Jimmie learned to endure the intense pain that would never leave him. The next several years were marked by minor victories, advancing from a wheelchair to crutches and then to a cane by 1933 when he earned an Emory University law degree.[146]

He returned home to a successful legal career, two terms in the legislature, and tenure as county attorney before his role in the aircraft industry. Appointed to the

Board of Regents by Governor Carl Sanders, he helped direct the university system until his death in 1972. In declining health, he performed one last service for Kennesaw Junior College in May 1971 when the Board of Regents met on campus to consider whether the growing school needed a new student center. According to President Sturgis:

> He was very, very instrumental in the college getting a Student Center, influencing the members of the Board…. The man was just a brave, brave person…. They had the Board meeting, and then the next morning they had a breakfast on campus here for the Board of Regents. Mr. Carmichael was in front of the Library, and he said he didn't know whether he could make it—it took him three hours to dress in the morning. He was just terribly in pain. But who would be the first one at that breakfast next morning? Mr. James V. Carmichael. It was really a great, great effort.

When the thirty-six-thousand-square-foot Student Center was completed, the board voted unanimously to name it for Carmichael. It became the first building on campus to be named for an individual. The dedication was scheduled for October 2, 1975 on what would have been his sixty-fifth birthday. Governor Busbee came to deliver the major address, and Carmichael's widow and children, the chancellor and the Board of Regents, the legislative delegation, and many other dignitaries were invited. Prior to the official half past nine opening, Governor Busbee addressed an early-bird breakfast of the Cobb Chamber where he asserted, "Without any doubt, we believe we will have a four-year college at Kennesaw." Chairman Charles Harris of Ocilla, in south Georgia, skipped the early-bird meal, but responded to a reporter's question that Kennesaw was playing a fine role as a junior college, and since the system had Georgia State and West Georgia, it did not need more four-year schools in this area; therefore, the regents, he claimed, intended to devote their limited resources in a down economy to professors' salaries.[147]

At the actual dedication, the governor did not mention four-year conversion. However, shortly after his address, the matter came up unexpectedly. June Rowland [Krise] was sitting on stage in her capacity as Student Government Association president to present a plaque to Mrs. Carmichael; so she was in an excellent position to see what happened. Behind the audience, on the balcony of the Student Center, a number of students had gathered. As the program neared its end, Randy Krise (June's future brother-in-law), Wayne Carter, and roughly a half-dozen others, unfurled a huge banner that read, "Four Years Now." Some of the people on stage began clapping, and then the audience turned and erupted in applause. Rowland noted that Governor Busbee smiled sheepishly and nodded, and Joe Mack Wilson looked very proud.

Students releasing the Four Years Now banner at the Student Center dedication.

President Sturgis had worried that students might try to disrupt the program with some type of demonstration and he met with the SGA ahead of time to urge them not to "embarrass the college or the community or the governor." He had no idea what the students planned to do, but he quickly realized that, without saying a word, they had made the perfect appeal, demonstrating to state leaders that Kennesaw students were solidly behind the four-year effort. He noted that the students were "just great," that it "broke up the meeting," and that Governor Busbee seemed as happy as anyone. Immediately afterwards, he wrote a note to June Rowland saying, "I could not have been more proud of you and our students than I was this morning during the dedication of our James V. Carmichael Student Center."[148]

In January 1976, as V. Fred Aiken was sworn in as Cobb Chamber president, he asserted that his top priority was four-year status for KJC. At the ceremony, he recognized Chancellor Simpson in the audience and told him, "We will not give up until four year status for KJC has become a reality."[149] Governor Busbee held a press conference in February where he presented a two-page report on why Kennesaw needed a senior college. At the conference he revealed that he was talking directly with Chancellor Simpson, urging him to support the project "in the interest of better education." He also indicated that if the general assembly put another quarter million dollars in the budget for Kennesaw's conversion, he would not exercise a line-item veto. Using data that originated with President Sturgis, he noted that one of the big issues was 62 percent of KJC students were working people who needed educational opportunities closer to home, and that the cost of conversion would be "very nominal." Moreover, he asserted, traffic on I-75 and US 41 had made commuting into Georgia State "almost impossible."[150]

With clear support from the governor, Joe Mack Wilson, A. L. Burruss, and Joe Frank Harris beat back attempts in the House to strip the $250,000 for conversion from the fiscal year 1977 budget. After heated debate, an amendment to strike the item lost, 104-56. A few weeks later, Representatives Wilson, Burruss, and George Kreeger escorted four Kennesaw student leaders into the governor's office. Their main spokesperson, Richard Krise, a twenty-five-year-old Woodstock resident and KJC graduate, told Busbee, "I may have to quit school because it just costs too much to travel downtown, pay for food and parking, and go to classes at Georgia State." The future high school principal remarked that if Kennesaw offered upper-level courses, he would definitely transfer back.

Joining Krise were incoming SGA president Pat Ashcraft and outgoing president June Rowland, along with Larry Croft, a twenty-eight-year-old night student from Acworth, who said he could not afford to drive downtown for classes. Rowland added, "I know there are a lot of housewives who can afford to go to Kennesaw because it's close to their homes, and they can take their children there to sit in the back of the classroom. Those women won't go on to Georgia State simply because it's too far and not convenient."[151]

Political pundits credit the second $250,000 appropriation as the tipping point in bringing influence-makers on board. For instance, the Seventh Congressional District regent, Judge James D. Maddox of Rome, had stayed largely on the sidelines until this point, but now he became active. An ardent Jimmy Carter supporter, he began lobbying fellow regents who had also been Carter appointees. In Cobb County, Judge Luther Hames suddenly got on the bandwagon, working through his long-time friend Lester Maddox to sway a vote. Governor Busbee also called his four board appointees, asking for their support.[152]

Bob Garrison had been working for some time on two regents, especially a good friend from Albany, Charles T. Oxford, with whom he went bird hunting. Horace Sturgis also lobbied Oxford. After receiving one of Sturgis's *Annual Reports*, Oxford wrote the president that Kennesaw had a good chance of gaining senior-college status, and "I hope this can be accomplished." Garrison claimed to make a personal call on another board member, apparently Lamar Plunkett, a clothing manufacturer from Bowdon, in Carroll County, near West Georgia College. This individual, he said, had a practical reason to oppose Kennesaw's conversion, yet he spoke up at the crucial board meeting, saying, "What Garrison tells you is the truth." According to a newspaper account, Plunkett entered the April 1976 board meeting with "reservations," but after hearing a report on KJC's many accomplishments, was convinced that Kennesaw would "make a good senior college."[153]

Joe Mack Wilson was always proud of his role in orchestrating contacts with regents and legislators. He persuaded President Sturgis to make a phone call to Clarence Vaughn of Conyers, the majority leader in the House and a friend for many years of Horace and Sue Sturgis. DeKalb Junior College was in his district, and it was important to make sure that Vaughn did not raise an objection to a four-year public college going into Cobb before DeKalb County received one. Sturgis and Wilson hoped to persuade Vaughn to say a good word about Kennesaw to Regent John R. Richardson, who was also from Conyers. In addition, Wilson involved *Marietta Daily Journal* editor Bill Kinney and his wife Alberta in the campaign. Mrs. Kinney was originally from Madison, and newspaper editor Carey Williams Sr., of nearby Greensboro, was a regent. So, Wilson claimed, "we sent her home" to talk to him. Meanwhile, Regent John R. Robinson of Americus was approached by fellow physician Alfred Colquitt of Marietta, who wrote him that KJC was a "wonderful cultural asset," due to the nationally-acclaimed Cobb County Symposium, held each year on the Kennesaw campus. He told his friend "Bud" Robinson that "the people of the area interested in quality education are behind [the four-year conversion] 100%."[154]

The Vote on Four-Year Status and the Ending of an Era

With the issue coming to a head, President Sturgis journeyed to Rome before the April 1976 board meeting to talk personally to Regent Maddox. After discussing a number of institutional needs, he brought up the four-year issue and suggested that it was time to give Kennesaw's supporters an answer. He did not ask that the item be placed on the agenda, but that was the crucial final step to force a vote. No decision could be made without first placing the question on the agenda. Maddox agreed that it was time, and promised to have the matter added. When the first agenda was circulated among college presidents a few days before the meeting, Sturgis noted with alarm that the four-year question was not there. So he placed a frantic call to Maddox, who said he would handle it. When the revised agenda came out, the Kennesaw question was included.[155]

At the April 14, 1976, meeting, Bob Garrison again headed the local delegation. After Chairman Charles Harris said that the Kennesaw matter had been studied in detail by the chancellor's staff, he recognized Garrison, who spoke a few words about the growth in number of college-age students in north Georgia and the "pressing need" of a senior college at Kennesaw. Next, Representative A. L. Burruss argued that the financial recession was reason to take action rather than delay, and that upper-level classes were needed hopefully as early as the fall. Appropriations Committee chairman, Joe Frank Harris, followed with a few remarks about state funding, offering assurances that revenues would be available to meet the expenses of all operations of the university system, including the upgrading of Kennesaw Junior College.

The regents discussed the matter for two hours. Lamar Plunkett asked about the potential impact on enrollment at other university system colleges. Plunkett and Milton Jones of Columbus urged that the proposed change be reported to HEW to determine whether the federal government would approve Kennesaw's change in status. Regent Erwin A. Friedman asked Chancellor Simpson to review his office's planning principles for the five-county Atlanta metropolitan area. After reporting the old plan of feeder junior colleges supporting Georgia State University and emphasizing that any change would have serious implications, Simpson, surprisingly, made a case for conversion.

The chancellor conceded that the Cobb County area was quite capable of supporting a senior college, that the board had always tried to place institutions where they were needed, and that northwest Georgia had not been fully served. He concluded that the real question was whether a new four-year school should go in Kennesaw or somewhere further north. After further discussion, Regent Maddox made the motion to approve Kennesaw's change of status, effective fall quarter, 1978. The reason for the two-year delay, apparently, was so HEW would have time to comment on whether the change would have an impact on the system's desegregation plan. After receiving a second from Regent John Richardson, the motion passed, 11-2. The two negative votes were cast by David H. Tisinger of Carrollton, who feared the impact on West Georgia College, and Milton Jones of Columbus, who, according to the *Marietta Daily Journal*, launched "a vicious attack" on what he considered an "ill-advised," unnecessary proposal. Interestingly, neither of the African American members voted against the plan. Elridge W. McMillan was absent, and Jesse Hill Jr. voted yes.[156]

Howls of protest emanated almost immediately from Central Atlanta Progress,[157] the Georgia State University student newspaper, the *Signal*, and the Georgia State Conference of the National Association for the Advancement of Colored People (NAACP). GSU students wondered why the regents could find new revenues for Kennesaw, but apparently could not find sufficient funds to start Georgia State's promised law school. The NAACP asked how the regents could find resources for Cobb County, when they were dragging their feet in complying with a court order to upgrade the historically black Fort Valley State College. The critics wondered whether anyone had looked at the needs of the rest of the state.[158]

President Sturgis prepared an *Impact Study on the Proposed Conversion* that the Board of Regents accepted in November and forwarded to the Department of Health, Education, and Welfare. When, after almost a year, that agency had neither approved nor disapproved, the university system took its inaction as evidence that Kennesaw's change in status had passed federal inspection. None of the protests lasted long or went very far. As one of the regents explained, "The wheels were already well-greased," and the governor had the votes.[159]

For the next two years the Kennesaw faculty worked to prepare senior-level courses and programs. President Sturgis invited several consultants to campus, such as Jack Anderson, an academic dean at Columbus College, who gave advice on how his institution handled the transition a decade earlier. As a junior college, Kennesaw hired faculty to teach core curriculum courses, with especially high demands in areas such as English, history, music, mathematics, biology, and business administration. Not surprisingly, these became the original baccalaureate programs, joined quickly by education and political science. Recognizing that business administration and education would be popular fields of study, Kennesaw created two new divisions and began hiring faculty under the direction of original chairpersons William P. Thompson (business administration) and Robert L. Driscoll (education).[160]

It was an ideal time to be a Kennesaw College professor. The various disciplines caucused and democratically developed upper-level course proposals. Since no one had been hired to teach narrow specialties, it was not always clear who had the inside track to teach a particular junior or senior class. Among historians, the standard practice was to let individuals volunteer to teach what they wanted, and if two or more expressed interest in the same course, they taught it in rotation. For some professors, this liberal policy provided an opportunity to develop new specialties or hone old ones.

Possible institutional name changes were discussed in faculty meetings, and President Sturgis asked the advice of foundation trustees, alumni, students, and the Cobb Chamber. His preference was simply to drop "junior." He never liked "state" in the name of an institution, remembering a time when "state" implied a teacher's college or agricultural and mechanical school. So he was happy when a consensus emerged around Kennesaw College (KC). In September 1977 the regents approved the name change, in time to order new stationery and ask the state to change the road signs.[161]

A final step in the conversion process was to elevate salaries to a senior-college level. When Southern Tech became a four-year school, the faculty had to wait three or four years before salaries came up to par with other senior institutions. President Sturgis did not want Kennesaw's professors to have to wait that long. So he met with Regent Maddox and wrote a letter to the Chancellor, arguing that if students were paying senior-college fees, faculty should receive senior-college salaries. Once again, he was successful, and 1978–79 proved to be a banner year, with professors enjoying the opportunity to teach upper-level classes and to receive the largest percentage raise of their careers.[162]

Junior-level courses began in fall quarter, 1978, with senior classes initiated the following year. The first bachelors' degrees were awarded in June 1980. Having overseen Kennesaw's transition, Horace Sturgis announced his retirement, effective December 31, 1980. The institution had just completed a successful accreditation visit from the Southern Association of Colleges and Schools. The new library (eventually named for Dr. Sturgis) was almost complete. After forty-six years in education, he felt the time was right to bow out. In looking back on his accomplishments, the president took greatest pride not in individual achievements, but in the growth of the college he was privileged to head—particularly the growth in quality of faculty and students that made the four-year conversion possible. As he said when announcing his retirement, "We set out to build a quality institution and I think we have done that." Thus, the first major era of Kennesaw's history came to a close. Sturgis was clearly the right person to lead the institution through its junior-college years and the conversion to a four-year school. But now faculty and students yearned to move in different directions, and they soon would have a dynamic new president with an expansive vision of how far the college might go.[163]

(Opposite Page) Mike Goldberg, the first campus resident who lived in the woods before being discovered.

Chapter 4

A New President and a View of the Future

Kennesaw's accomplishments in the Sturgis era were impressive. But they paled in comparison to the growth of the college under the next president. When administrations change, colleges have an opportunity to seek and secure presidents who bring different visions, talents, and leadership styles. In some cases, they make one-hundred-eighty-degree turns. That was certainly true when Betty L. Siegel became the University System of Georgia's first woman president. Soon afterwards, the pent-up energies and ideas of KCs talented faculty and staff, liberated by Siegel's invitational leadership, produced a new view for the future that changed the course of Kennesaw's history in positive and rewarding ways.

A History-Making Search

Horace Sturgis's retirement gave the campus an opportunity to reflect on its progress from junior to senior college and its hopes for the future. In many ways, Sturgis's top-down style of administration had served the young institution well. In the early days, when most of the teaching faculty lacked doctorates and instructors outnumbered tenured professors, no other approach was perhaps practical. By 1980, however, the growing four-year school was a much different place than it had been just a decade before. The faculty had matured with the college and demanded a greater role in decision making. It also yearned for a president with solid academic credentials and national reputation who could spread the word about Kennesaw College beyond its immediate service area.

Despite the charter president's solid record of outreach to Cobb County, he was virtually unknown beyond Atlanta, and the same could be said for the faculty and the institution as a whole. The quality of Kennesaw College's programs seemed a well-kept secret even in greater Atlanta. While some students and professors took pride in calling Kennesaw a "Little Harvard in the Pines," others perceived that the college was too cloistered and hoped the next president would champion a broader vision of faculty involvement beyond the yellow brick walls of an insular campus.

Chancellor Vernon Crawford made a visit to Kennesaw early in the fall of 1980 to listen to anyone who wanted to share an opinion on the qualities needed in a new president and how the search should be conducted. A number of students and professors took advantage of the opportunity, and Crawford's calendar was booked solidly for two days with fifteen-to-twenty-minute appointments. Afterwards, he selected a nineteen-member search committee that, surprisingly, was not headed by a high-ranking administrator. The sessions apparently made Crawford aware of a growing chasm of distrust between administrators and the teaching faculty, and that the campus community would be deeply suspicious of any committee moderated by a dean or division head.

Crawford's choice as chairman was S. Frederick Roach Jr., a history professor, who had served on the faculty since 1968. While teaching a full load, Roach had managed to complete his dissertation at the University of Oklahoma in 1972, writing on the humorist Will Rogers under the supervision of the noted western and agricultural historian, Gilbert C. Fite. After earning his degree, Roach had taken on some administrative responsibilities in the Social Sciences Division, helping the chairman, George Beggs, with class scheduling, book orders, and other details, but continuing to teach a full load and never exercising a supervisory role over other faculty.[164]

The search committee's vice chairperson was charter faculty member and Business Division chair, William P. Thompson, a retired US Army major and an accountant with a PhD from Georgia State University. His fellow committee members were fortunate to have a detail-oriented person of his background, because most of them had never served on a search committee of any type. In the past, the administration had filled academic slots with little input from the teaching faculty. Consequently, the committee members had little experience in developing procedures, forms, and questionnaires that would stand legal challenge. Thompson took the leadership in these areas. Meanwhile, Roach took responsibility for meeting with committee members individually in their offices or at local restaurants to listen to their concerns and try to build esprit de corps.[165]

One appointee to the committee, alumni president June Krise, met with Roach at a McDonald's a few miles from campus. When Roach asked her how she would describe the perfect college president, she responded that she wanted someone well grounded like Dr. Sturgis, but also good looking, charismatic, and "on fire." Since the university system had never had a woman president, she described her ideal male candidate. Later, Krise concluded that the search produced precisely

(Opposite Page) S. Frederick Roach Jr.

the type of person she envisioned, although she had the gender wrong. During his meetings with faculty members, Roach heard again and again from the women of the search committee that they resented the lack of females in high places. He, therefore, suspected from the beginning that, everything being equal, at least one female would make the final list.

Like the chancellor, Roach was impressed by the degree of faculty distrust of the current administration and the likelihood that the committee would reject internal candidates and seek outsiders with new ideas and a strong record on shared governance. As the years went by, Sturgis and his administrative team had become more open to bottom-up leadership from students and faculty. After 1972, when the regents approved Kennesaw's first set of statutes, the top administrators usually took the advice of the Academic and Student Affairs Councils, on which elected faculty members and student government officers had major voices. But the circle around the former president consisted of white males who tended to be "old school" in their preferences and resented the lack of respect for authority of many young scholars who were products of the rebellious 1960s.[166]

One of the reasons for faculty distrust was the total power that the administration held over tenure and promotion decisions. The campus Tenure and Promotion

Committee had no elected members. The academic dean presided over unannounced, closed meetings where the only ones in attendance were the five division chairs and the chair of the Developmental Studies Department. Faculty members had no formal way to initiate a request for tenure or promotion and did not always know they were under consideration until after the fact. Political science professor Helen S. Ridley remembered the process:

> George Beggs came by to see me one day and said, "Dr. Ridley, we're not going to tenure you this year." I had prepared nothing—you prepared nothing [at that time].... I said, "Okay. Is there a particular reason?" He said, "Some think you have a bad attitude, and you need to correct it." *Who, me?* I said, "Okay, give me some examples so that I'll know what to correct." He said, "I've never seen it, and your colleagues have never seen it; but, nevertheless, you have to correct it." I said, "Well, rest assured I will".... In any event, about a week later he came back and said, "Dr. Ridley, we've realized that if we don't tenure you, we can't keep you." I said, "Well, that's a relief." So I got tenured. And that was the way the decisions were made.[167]

Thanks largely to Chancellor Crawford, the 1980–81 presidential search was remarkably open and democratic. The search committee reported only to the chancellor and included faculty from a variety of disciplines; three chief administrators; and student, staff, alumni, and community representatives. Allowed to develop its operating procedures, the committee spent the fall getting organized and agreeing on the language of the job announcement. The deadline for submitting applications was February 27, 1981. An unusually large number of individuals applied—including one resident of a psychiatric hospital in a nearby state. After many hours of labor and often heated discussions, the committee winnowed the original 147 applicants down to about a dozen semifinalists, nine of whom visited campus for interviews during May and early June. At that stage, faculty, staff, and students were given the opportunity to meet the candidates and provide input.[168]

Faculty members packed a lecture hall in the new Humanities Building for their chance to interact with the candidates. Several of the semifinalists were already presidents of sister institutions; the rest were deans or chief academic officers. Most of the sessions were informative, but not terribly exciting. All the candidates were qualified, but few articulated an inspiring vision of what Kennesaw could become.

(Opposite Page) President Sturgis with Dean Eugene R. Huck and his wife, Marie Huck

The one exception was Betty Lentz Siegel, Dean of the School of Education and Psychology at Western Carolina University, who made her visit to campus in early June. Her meeting with the faculty quickly became spirited and interactive as candidate and audience engaged in a lively discussion. Siegel remembered that: "I loved your questions. I really loved the people. I think I was so smitten that I really wanted the job. I had been at other interviews at which I had been half-heartedly interested. I might be interested; I might not. But I remember saying to my husband afterwards, 'Oh, this is wonderful. Those people are wonderful.' It's people that make the difference. I've always been blessed by liking the people with whom I find myself. I really thought [the interview at Kennesaw] was great. It was marvelous."[169]

Siegel seemed to make a good first impression on everyone she encountered. James D. (Spec) Landrum was serving at the time as Coordinator of Development and Alumni Affairs, having come to Kennesaw after a successful career as a college football coach and president of the Georgia Conservancy. His wife, Mildred, was a professor of Business Education and a member of the search committee. Spec had agreed to let the presidential candidates use his office in the Administration Building if they needed a work space during the breaks in their schedules. He volunteered his services to take candidates on campus tours and, in general, to make them feel at home. Most of the visitors were polite, but did not take advantage of his offer. The exception was Siegel. When she arrived, Landrum told her:

> "Dr. Siegel, here's my office, and it's yours. Anything I can do for you, let me know. I'll be outside or somewhere in the building if you need me for anything…." And I started out the door. She [said], "Wait a minute. I want to talk to you." I'd gotten back in my chair behind my desk, and I got up, and I went around to get in another chair, so she could sit at her own desk if she wanted to. She said, "No, you stay over there." So she sat down and she quizzed me about Marietta, everything you can imagine.[170]

Along with two full days of meetings, each applicant experienced a major social event, a dinner with the committee and friends of the college at such popular Atlanta restaurants as Ray's on the River. Bill Thompson's wife, Mary, accompanied her husband to a number of the dinners. She later recalled that she became so bored with the conversations that she begged out of the one where Siegel was the honored guest. Instead, she asked Bill to take his secretary, Barbara Blackwell. When they

(Opposite Page) Dr. Betty L. Siegel

104

came back to the house raving about Betty Siegel, Mary realized she probably had missed an opportunity to meet Kennesaw's next president.[171]

Siegel managed to dominate every meeting she attended, including the critical exchange with the search committee in the late afternoon of the second day. According to Chairman Roach, committee members had become experts at asking probing questions that stripped candidates of their pretensions and got to the heart of what they believed and what type of temperament they had. Siegel, however, seized the initiative before anyone had a chance to start grilling her. As Roach recalled,

> She said, "Before we get started, let me tell you what's happened to me…. [Just before this meeting], I went down to the bookstore, and there were two students…so I went up to one of them and said, 'Why did you choose to come to Kennesaw?' And they told me because they were a business administration major and that Kennesaw had the best Business Administration Department in the state." Well, the assistant chair of the search committee was the [chairman] of the Business [Division]. And then she went over and talked to the other student and said, "Why did you come to Kennesaw? What's your major?" And she said, "I'm a history major, and I came to Kennesaw because Kennesaw's got the best History Department in the system." So she took the lead in the interview away from us on that last day.[172]

After all the candidates had left town, the committee decided upon three finalists: Siegel, President John Pilecki of Westfield (Massachusetts) State College, and Acting President Richard Carl Meyer of Texas A&I University. On June 19, 1981, those names were submitted to the chancellor. Crawford and his staff then spent the next month conducting their own interviews and background checks. The process took so long that Betty Siegel had about concluded she was out of the running.

On July 29, 1981, Betty and her husband Joel were vacationing at their beachside condominium. They arose early to view the televised wedding of Charles, Prince of Wales, and Lady Diana Spencer. Afterwards, they went for a walk on the beach. Betty remembers confiding in Joel: "I guess I didn't get the job…[but] I don't define myself in terms of this job. I want it, but I don't think it was meant to be. It's okay…we have such a good life at Western, such a happy place and the jobs are so good. The children are happy. It's okay. It's wonderful." As they returned to the condominium, she heard the phone ringing. It was the chancellor. He said, "Betty, we want you to take the job." She instantly responded, "Yes!" She later remarked, "I didn't ask what it paid. I took the job, just like that. So in the space of one hour I'd gone from thinking that my life was absolutely fine and that I didn't define myself in terms of that job. On that day, I remember, that's what happened."[173]

The board and chancellor's office kept the appointment a well-guarded secret. The only person notified on the Kennesaw campus was the chairman of the search committee, Fred Roach, and he was instructed not to tell anyone. The publisher of the *Marietta Daily Journal* (*MDJ*), Otis A. Brumby Jr., was determined to print the name of the new president before the chancellor made the official announcement. Roach received numerous calls from reporters, but neither Roach nor anyone else in Georgia talked. So Brumby told his staff, regardless of cost, to call the campuses of all the finalists to see if any of them had talked to anyone or submitted their resignations or had plans to be in Atlanta for the board meeting on August 19.[174]

The *MDJ* broke the story on August 18, 1981, with a front page headline, "Woman to be Named Kennesaw President." Reporter Donna Espy reached Betty Siegel at her Western Carolina office. While Siegel would neither confirm nor deny her selection, she admitted that she expected to be in Atlanta the following day. She also volunteered that she had enjoyed her campus interviews and that she would enjoy serving as president. After the article appeared, the usually affable Crawford phoned Roach to chastise him for divulging the secret. Roach, however, denied that he was the source, and by the next day Crawford had calmed down, realizing that his search committee chair was telling the truth.[175]

The appointment became official at the monthly meeting of the Board of Regents on August 19, 1981. The chancellor introduced Roach, who gave a brief report on the process by which the search committee made its choices. Then Crawford explained how he reached his decision to recommend Siegel. He said her selection was a "milestone" for the university system. The meeting was a mere formality, and with virtually no discussion, the board voted unanimously for the first woman president in the history of the university system. Fittingly, the board in 1981 was headed by its first female chair, Marie W. Dodd of Roswell, a vice president of the Ivan Allen Company. Later, Siegel said that the opportunity to be the first woman president was "very significant to me," but she looked forward to the day when such appointments would not be considered unusual.[176]

At age fifty, Siegel had already had a remarkable career. She grew up in eastern Kentucky, where her father went to work out of high school shoveling coal in a local mine. Through hard work and determination, he saved his money, bought a saw mill and then a coal mine, and continued accumulating other small mills and mines. The women in her family were strong role models. Her maternal great-grandmother was a Republican Party chairperson and the owner of a large farm. Her grandmothers were shrewd businesswomen, one running several family farms and the other a boarding house. At the same time, they engaged in many community services and supported the local schools.[177]

Siegel's introduction to higher education came at Cumberland College in Williamsburg, Kentucky, where her great-great-uncle, Lloyd Creech, had just retired

Betty Lentz [Siegel] at her high school graduation.

as president. Cumberland had a liberal curriculum that allowed her to take anything she wanted, so she concentrated on English and history. After receiving an associate's degree in 1950, she enrolled at Wake Forest, where she received a BA in 1952 with a dual major in those two areas. The following year, she earned a MEd at the University of North Carolina. After teaching high school for three years and then college at Lenoir-Rhyne in Hickory, North Carolina, she took a leave of absence for two years to complete a PhD at Florida State University.

By this time her interest had shifted to developmental psychology. Her major professor, Herman Frick, played a prominent role in helping Florida school systems develop desegregation plans in accordance with the Supreme Court's *Brown* decision. She recalls that she learned from him that academics have an obligation to help society see "what is the righteous, good thing to do." As Frick's assistant, she traveled with him on Southern Association of Colleges and Schools accreditation visits and learned the importance of group thinking and long-range planning.[178]

After earning her doctorate in 1961, Siegel returned to Lenoir-Rhyne for three years, then went to Indiana University for a postdoctorate where she gained child psychology clinical experience and worked with Boyd McCandless on intervention strategies that were effective in the psycho-social development of culturally and economically disadvantaged children. She also was able to teach as a visiting professor in the Indiana University Graduate Program.

In 1967 she was offered a job teaching psychological foundations at the University of Florida (UF) in a department that was otherwise all male. She had met her husband, Joel, at Indiana University and showed up in Gainesville, Florida for the start of her first fall quarter six months pregnant. She recalls that the men in the department were all panicky, but she told them not to worry and that it would not interfere with her teaching. On the last day of exams, she went to the hospital, had her first child, and graded the student papers while still recovering. Joel ran them back to the department office before any of her colleagues had graded their finals. When classes began again in January, she was back in the classroom and did not miss a single day. Among the University of Florida's 3,500 professors, her reputation spread quickly as "that woman." Despite having given birth over fifteen months to two children, she became, in 1969, one of the first three recipients of UF's Outstanding Teacher Awards.[179]

In 1972 she was invited to become dean of academic affairs for continuing education, the first woman dean in the history of the University of Florida. Soon, President E. T. York gave her the task of heading the committee that wrote the institution's first affirmative action plan. She recalls that it was the hardest year of her life, but President York and federal officials in Washington approved the plan that set Florida's flagship institution in the direction of greater diversity. York became a significant role model, teaching her that a university can be a force for social change. She later recalled that, "what I learned from that job and from him was that an institution that is cloistered would not be an institution of the future. I give him the credit for being a significant moving force in my life and leading me to see a deeper, more inclusive way of looking at higher education rather than being exclusive."[180]

In 1976 Western Carolina University asked Siegel to head its School of Education and Psychology. Excited by the opportunity to be an academic dean in her research and teaching field, she accepted the offer. A believer in the Clark Kerr admonition that "if you're not heard outside your institution, you're not heard inside," she used her new position as a vehicle to engage in outreach throughout North Carolina and beyond, speaking to any group that invited her and becoming an educational consultant in several southern states, New Mexico, and Washington.[181]

As her reputation spread nationally, she was soon being nominated for a number of presidencies and was a finalist at Valdosta State College. She, therefore, knew that Georgia had an outstanding university system. Someone nominated her for the opening at Kennesaw, and the committee sent her a letter asking her to consider applying. She had never heard of Kennesaw College and left the letter in a stack on her desk. One day she heard a colleague at Western Carolina raving about a trip she had just taken to Marietta and to a wonderful little college there. Siegel began thinking, "Marietta, Georgia, where have I heard of it?" A quick search of her desk located the job advertisement, but the deadline to apply was that day. So she called Chairman Roach and asked if their phone conversation would suffice to

President Betty L. Siegel

initiate her candidacy. He agreed, and by this fortunate circumstance she was able to submit her application papers.[182]

By the time she came for her interview, she had done her homework. According to Siegel, the literature on up-and-coming colleges described the institution of the future as a college in the Sunbelt, in a major population area, along a major economic thoroughfare, that catered to nontraditional students. She began thinking that Kennesaw College fit that description exactly. Recognizing Kennesaw as a prototype of the college of the future, she arrived on campus excited by the opportunity to help shape its growth. Thus, a developing college and a developmental psychologist found in 1981 their perfect match.[183]

View of the Future

With her extensive background at a variety of research and teaching institutions, Betty Siegel came to Kennesaw College with a clear vision of what needed to be done for the relatively new school to reach its full potential. She knew, however, that some of her mentors had alienated people by being too "hard-hitting" in trying to impose their vision on others. Her goal was to invite faculty and staff to participate in forging a plan for the future that would have broad support. While her detractors believed that real leaders rule with iron fists, she perceived the campus community was more likely to follow her direction if everyone thought they had a chance to participate in shaping policy.[184]

Siegel spent the first year of her presidency meeting with students and faculty and talking to some 161 different civic groups. From these numerous conversations,

she reached several major conclusions. One was that local people were proud of their college, but wanted to see it more community-engaged, with faculty offering their expertise in meeting the needs of metro Atlanta and rural northwest Georgia. A second was that the emphasis of the junior-college era on high academic standards had created a culture where low retention rates were the norm and where too few programs helped students succeed. Siegel wanted to create a climate where teaching was personalized and invitational, and student retention and graduation were the expectations.

Another conclusion was that Kennesaw gave students few reasons to stay on campus for purposes other than attending class. Siegel believed that Kennesaw could create a residential campus feel, even while it continued to be a commuter college. But to do so, it had to focus more on campus life and the unique problems of target audiences such as first-year and nontraditional students. Finally, the president realized she had a talented, young faculty, but one burdened with heavy teaching loads and little support for scholarship. There was probably little she could do at that time about teaching loads, but to build faculty morale and unleash creative abilities, she believed that the administration needed to find innovative ways of facilitating faculty development.185

The 1981 academic year began with a faculty retreat at Unicoi State Park where President Siegel announced the establishment of an annual distinguished teaching award, given to one faculty member each year, based on student nominations and the input of a special awards committee.[186] About a month later, on October 15, 1981, President Siegel asked Dr. Helen S. Ridley to head a major ad hoc committee called the View of the Future that would involve the total faculty in a year-long institutional study.

Ridley was in her seventh year at Kennesaw College, having joined the faculty in 1975, shortly after receiving her PhD from Emory University. A political scientist, she was an expert on constitutional law; her dissertation had been on plea bargaining in Fulton County. Not long after joining the faculty, she became the parliamentarian for monthly faculty meetings until she started making rulings that President Sturgis did not like. As she recalled, she was removed from her post for insisting on *Robert's Rules of Order* rather than "*Horace's Rules.*" A reputation as an "uppity woman" was not a good thing under the old regime, but apparently was more socially acceptable after Betty Siegel's arrival. When Siegel came for her job interview, Ridley had the opportunity to meet her and serve as her guide, taking her to various places on campus. After one of the sessions, Siegel followed Ridley to her office, and they had a chance to engage in casual conversation. They established a rapport that carried over to the View of the Future study.[187]

Siegel charged the committee to be a conduit through which faculty concerns and perceptions were channeled to the president and her leadership team. The final report was to include both short-term and long-term recommendations that the president promised to study and implement. Siegel and Ridley worked together in choosing a committee composed of four associate professors, four assistant professors, and three members of the staff.[188] All five academic divisions were represented, along with the library, counseling, and personnel.[189]

(Opposite Page) Chancellor Vernon D. Crawford leads Dr. Siegel to her inauguration as the second president of Kennesaw College.

Throughout the 1981–82 year, the View of the Future Committee investigated four major topics that President Siegel asked it to study. The first was the quality of professional life at Kennesaw College; the second was the publics served by Kennesaw; the third was the mission of the institution; and the fourth was personalized teaching and learning. The first two topics were divided into a variety of subcategories to be studied by task forces of up to ten people, each appointed by President Siegel and chaired by a View of the Future Committee member. Task forces were charged with producing written reports on their particular subjects.[190]

The regularly-scheduled monthly faculty meetings became forums in which the entire professoriate gave input into the various task force topics. In the first general faculty meeting, a few top administrators dominated the discussion in ways that intimidated some people. When Ridley brought the problem to the president's attention, Siegel agreed to exclude from future forums the president's staff (the dean of the college, dean of students, controller, and director of development and public service). However, Siegel and the committee thought that division chairs needed to hear what the faculty thought. They were allowed to participate, with the admonition that they be on their best behavior.[191]

The Task Force on Missions had the assignment of envisioning a more democratic, inviting campus culture for faculty and students. The group was headed by View of the Future Committee members Judy Mitchell and Pamela J. Rhyne. While the specific language of their recommendation was never officially adopted, the statement seemed to catch President Siegel's spirit of interactive leadership, sprinkling expressions such as "mutual respect and trust" and "collegial environment" throughout the brief document. The most specific change embedded in the proposed mission statement was a shift in focus to "instruction in career and professional areas to prepare students for their life work." In explaining this emphasis, the task force conceded the need for a liberal arts foundation in all programs, but argued that Kennesaw had to expand the number of courses and majors in business, education, and nursing to meet both student and community demand. The report also advocated an increased emphasis on internships and cooperative programs and on career counseling and placement.[192]

The proposed mission statement was significant in promoting a greater sense of community for students and faculty. To meet that end, it called for more personnel and improvement of facilities that could help improve school spirit. Specifically, it recommended the establishment of fraternities and sororities and, at least, hinted at intercollegiate athletics. It also advocated increased interaction between students and professors, increased services and activities for evening students, and support for a strong Student Government Association.[193]

The various tasks forces were often quite specific in listing improved ways of meeting faculty needs. For example, the Faculty Development-Research Task Force, chaired by Duane Shuttlesworth, went to the heart of faculty members' concerns over lack of support for research. Eight years before Ernest L. Boyer's landmark study, *Scholarship Reconsidered: Priorities of the Professoriate*, the group noted that virtually everyone on campus was teaching heavy fifteen-hour loads. With multiple class preparations, papers to grade, and students to mentor, and with growing service expectations, faculty members had little or no time for traditional scholarship. Shuttlesworth's discussion group noted that the professoriate was further hindered by inadequate secretarial support, travel funds, and assistance in applying for grants. Moreover, the science faculty had to operate without adequate research labs.

Given the budget constraints under which state colleges functioned, the task force called for a broad definition of research as "creative behavior leading to scholarly

excellence." Such a definition would allow one to receive tenure and promotion credit for activities other than publications and presentations. Recognizing that Kennesaw's primary mission was teaching, the group suggested that Kennesaw's definition of research include something as basic as mathematicians retooling to teach computer science. It also suggested that one should be given scholarship credit for such service activities as assisting community agencies in writing grants or doing contract work for businesses.

Among its short-term recommendations were flexible scheduling and reduced teaching loads, awarded on a competitive basis. It also called for the hiring of a grants officer, internal faculty development grants, and lowered service expectations for those with tangible research achievements.[194] A Faculty Development-Skills and Techniques Task Force, headed by Associate Librarian Marty Giles, seconded the idea of an Office of Campus Development, staffed by a full-time director who would be responsible for seeking funds for faculty development and assisting professors in writing grants. This group also suggested that the director serve as a confidential advisor to those seeking assistance in improving their teaching evaluations. These proposals seemed to point the way to the eventual establishment of an Office of Sponsored Programs and a Center for Excellence in Teaching and Learning.[195]

The idea of flexible scheduling was championed by a special Scheduling Task Force that called on the campus to abandon daily-fifty-minute classes for a longer time period that would allow classes to meet only two or three days a week. The idea appealed to students as well as faculty. It would help the parking problem if all the students did not have to be on campus every day. They could make use of their class-free days to work off campus to help pay for their education. For faculty, the main advantage was blocked times on non-teaching days to conduct research or engage in community service.[196]

The View of the Future found that academic freedom was generally well-respected on campus, but problems existed in a few divisions where rigid rules, designed to govern a handful of irresponsible instructors, limited faculty members' rights in textbook selection and testing. The Academic Freedom Task Force recommended that faculty members be free to determine the number of tests appropriate to their style of teaching and when they would be given. With regard to textbooks, the book store had an ironclad rule against changing books in the middle of the school year. The task force noted that such a rigid policy prevented instructors from abandoning texts that proved ineffective. Further, the task force called upon the divisions to remove obstacles in the way of instructors who wanted to experiment with different materials and teaching techniques.[197]

There were no students on the View of the Future Committee or any of the task forces, so it should not be surprising that the reports were far more specific on faculty concerns than student needs. However, President Siegel was an advocate of personalized, invitational education long before she arrived at Kennesaw and in the summer of 1982 founded, with her former University of Florida colleague, William W. Purkey, and other American and Canadian educators, the International Alliance for Invitational Education. Siegel's interest was reflected to some degree in the task force's Personalized Teaching and Learning Reports.

The Personalized Teaching and Learning Task Force, headed by Duane Shuttlesworth, and including Ed Bostick, Gail Walker, Diane Willey, and Nancy Zumoff, stopped short of calling for radically new styles of teaching, but it made several recommendations that would ultimately be adopted. Most importantly, it called for an instructional resources facility, similar to that proposed by the Skills and Techniques group, that became one of the inspirations for Kennesaw's Center for Excellence in Teaching and Learning. The task force envisioned a full-time director who would organize workshops and forums to help faculty improve their teaching methodologies. The group also championed an Honors Program, flexible scheduling for experimental courses, and travel support to teaching conferences.[198]

At about the same time, the Board of Regents mandated a statewide needs assessment study to chart the course of higher education in Georgia. In his history of the university system, Cameron Fincher describes the final report, *The Eighties and Beyond: A Commitment to Excellence*, as the "most relevant statement on public higher education since the 1963 Governor's Commission to Improve Education." Vice chancellor for research and planning, Haskin R. Pounds, directed the research staff that put together the final report, with the help of the colleges and universities, each of which produced its own needs assessment report. Kennesaw's study was headed by a sociologist, Vassilis C. Economopoulos, assisted by fellow sociology professor B. Edward Hale, history professor Linda M. Papageorge, and a very busy Helen Ridley. The institutional report supplemented the conclusions of the View of the Future Committee.[199]

Economopoulos and his committee provided sociological data on the steady rise in student population as a byproduct of the increased number of people living in Cobb and neighboring counties. They described Kennesaw College as unique because: it was growing at a time when other schools in the university system were experiencing retrenchment; it was a commuter school without any students living on campus; and it catered to nontraditional students, as seen in the fact that 62 percent were age twenty-three or older, 75 percent worked while going to school, and about 33 percent were married.

Noting the large number of students majoring in professional areas, the researchers found the most critical instructional need to be additional faculty slots in Division of Business Administration. They found classroom and conference space to be totally inadequate. At the time, Kennesaw ranked thirty-second out of thirty-three university system institutions in square feet per equivalent full-time student. The

Aerial view of campus, early 1980s

Aerial view of campus after the completion of the new library.

greatest shortages in classroom space were in business, science, math, and nursing. The report also found critical staffing deficiencies in the library, counseling, and placement and noted "an urgent need to move into the world of computers."[200]

Haskin Pounds's *The Eighties and Beyond* recommended that all colleges "utilize fully" the results of its institutional needs assessment. The conclusions and statistical data of the Kennesaw study complemented the findings of the View of the Future Committee and fit nicely with President Siegel's vision for Kennesaw. In later years, she reflected, "That bright faculty, that very, very wonderful group of long-marchers, were the architects for the new view. You didn't need an outside voice to do that. It was here, just waiting to be orchestrated. I felt my role as president was to point the way."[201]

In late May 1982, Siegel took her staff, the division chairs, and the View of the Future Committee on a two-day retreat to discuss its recommendations. Half of the twenty-two invitees were committee members, the other half were the president's staff, the assistant dean, and the division chairs. The minutes of the retreat provide a

lesson in leadership for anyone trying to break recalcitrant senior administrators of old habits. One can see in the minutes that not everyone was on board the first day, but by the end, a positive faculty-administrative consensus seemed to have developed.

Years later Siegel reflected on the opposition she received from her presidential staff—most of them holdovers from the previous administration—especially after she excluded them from faculty meetings during the school year while the View of the Future was being discussed. She recalled that they considered her interactive style naive and questioned her abilities, asking, "Are you out of your mind? You've opened up a can of worms. Isn't this just like a woman?" The president reflected:

> I wasn't really operating as a woman. I was operating as a psychologist, as a person who's comfortable with that. I mean, I was a dean ten years before I became a president. People think I just emerged out of the classroom and then became president. I was a dean at a major university—University of Florida…and dean of a college [Western Carolina]. So I know what it's like to run a school. And our school was stellar, I thought. So it wasn't that I came in foolish or naive. But they really thought, "Oh, you're asking for it. You're going to get it." Then when suggestions came out of the faculty…. "Ah, they don't know what they're talking about!"[202]

Noting that the View of the Future Committee championed many of the things she would have recommended, she added:

> When I think in terms of the View of the Future, I think that it was a fantastic clarion call and that it was implemented. If you were to go back and look at the View of the Future—and I do that periodically—I am just amazed at how well y'all did. To see what you all prompted; it was easy for me to sell. I said, "Hey, this came from all over the college. How can we as deans and administrators not be listening to this? How can we not be more facilitative? We have no choice."[203]

The president opened the retreat by talking about the importance of the process in bringing together faculty and administrators and faculty and faculty. She called it an "exercise in understanding" that showed how faculty could facilitate learning and the administration could facilitate teaching. She then took on a role as group facilitator for everything that happened over the next two days. As the task force chairs presented their reports, she asked the attendees to listen in silence without questions or comments. After the first set of reports, she assigned people to five different groups and told them what she wanted them to discuss.[204]

challenges similar to those that led to Peabody's merger into Vanderbilt. So, Rugg began looking for other opportunities.

By chance, he heard from a former Peabody colleague about a dynamic college president in metropolitan Atlanta, Betty Siegel. The friend had just become a dean at Kent State University and had invited Siegel to speak to her college faculty. During casual conversation, she learned that Siegel was trying to fill a new position for an assistant to the president. The dean told Siegel that she knew of someone from her Peabody days who would be an ideal candidate. Knowing that Ed's wife, Sharon, was from Rome, Georgia, the Kent State dean called him and suggested that he consider applying. Based on that phone call, Rugg submitted his application, as one of nearly two hundred candidates.

The search committee was impressed with Rugg's qualifications and invited him for a job interview on Memorial Day 1982. On the Sunday afternoon before the interview, Ed and Sharon decided to drive around the campus. They came away disappointed. Compared to the grand campus of the University of Mississippi, Kennesaw College appeared architecturally unimpressive and still looked very much like a small junior college. Consequently, Rugg's first comment to Sharon after parking the car in front of the old administration building was, "I don't think so, sweetheart."

However, Rugg's initial impression changed the following day after meeting President Siegel and the search committee. He later remarked, "There was an energy here. There was an optimism about the future. There really was opportunity to grow and develop as an institution." His previous experiences had been at established institutions that were set in their ways, stagnant in their growth, and increasingly unable to compete for nontraditional students. In contrast, Kennesaw was "a place that hadn't developed much history yet and could make choices and choose to be a contemporary place." So, when given the opportunity, he jumped at the chance to work for Betty Siegel. He soon was involved in helping to implement a host of changes growing out of the View of the Future.[210]

Memories have grown murky over the years as to exactly what initiatives came directly from the View of the Future. When asked a quarter century later for specifics, Helen Ridley had to pause to think and then proposed, "A different style of governance. I think it helped [Siegel] realize that some drastic changes were going to have to be made if she was going to have the successful tenure that she wanted."[211] The two major governance changes of the era were the development of an elaborate tenure and promotion policy and the creation of a Kennesaw College Senate to replace the older system of Administrative, Academic, and Student Affairs Councils.

Not long after the *View of the Future* report, the faculty worked out detailed guidelines for tenure and promotion, specifying what to include in a portfolio, when one could be eligible for tenure or promotion, and what the expectations were at each rank. Under the new plan, the process began at the departmental level with

State representative and foundation trustee Joe Mack Wilson
with President Siegel

independent evaluations by the chair and by an elected department committee. Then the portfolio went to a school committee composed of department chairs and two elected faculty members from each department. Next, the school dean issued a fourth written assessment. If opinion was divided at these levels, the portfolio went to an appellate college-wide committee, consisting of deans and elected faculty members. Then the vice president for academic affairs and the president made the final decision and submitted a recommendation to the chancellor's office. Compared to the old system, where the administrators acted in virtual secrecy, the new tenure and promotion policy was remarkably democratic.[212]

In the late 1980s, the faculty revised the Statutes, placing campus governance in one body, the Kennesaw College Senate. The senate's virtue was that it brought all constituencies (faculty, staff, administrators, and students) together in advising the president on policy matters. Its weakness was that it contained more than seventy members, making it unwieldy at times. Forty-two seats on the senate went to the teaching faculty (one elected member per department plus at-large tenured, untenured, and graduate faculty representatives). Fourteen members came from the administrative faculty (the dean of each school, one elected department chair per school, and various other administrators). The staff had eight elected representatives (two from each administrative unit: academic, business affairs, student affairs, and college advancement). The students had six seats (the SGA president and five other representatives). Finally, the president, vice president for academic affairs, vice president for business and finance, vice president for student affairs, and chief college advancement officer attended as ex officio members.

To facilitate the decision-making process on issues primarily affecting the faculty, the Statutes permitted the faculty representatives to convene as a Teaching Faculty Caucus and the staff delegates as a Staff Caucus. Recommendations from the two caucuses were then forwarded to the full senate. In the late 1990s, the names were changed to Teaching Faculty Council and Staff Council, and the total representation on the senate was reduced slightly, but remaining above sixty voting members. At the very end of the Siegel era in 2006, the senate would be replaced by a smaller University Council that could assign issues to four senates (faculty, staff, university administrators, and the SGA, respectively). But for a long while, the governance system growing out of the View of the Future seemed to provide an adequate vehicle for the expression of campus opinion.[213]

In a 1993 interview, President Siegel made the following observation about the work of the faculty in creating the View of the Future:

> I give our people, all of our people in 1982, a great deal of the credit because it was they who explored tough questions. And look how visionary they were! Think about that! Think about that! They weren't schooled in colleges. Many of them, their first-time college experience was here. But you all came up with it. To me, all along the way, those first four or five years afterwards—remember the View of the Future? You all said that you wanted a CAPS Center.... You wanted a hearty ten-year process. You wanted to offer graduate school. You wanted to teach in your discipline. You didn't want to be just a generic teacher. Remember those things? Okay, now, you've got to do that.... It was a wonderful time because it was a small college. I felt so intimately involved in the life of the college.[214]

Siegel's vision and the faculty effort led, during the 1980s, to a remarkable number of initiatives including: the establishment of departments and schools; expanded professional programs in business, education, and nursing; intercollegiate athletics; the computerization of the campus; and such innovative programs as CAPS (Counseling, Advisement, and Placement Services), CETL (Center for Excellence in Teaching and Learning), the Kennesaw College Freshman Seminar (KC 101), and a chair of private enterprise, one of just fifty in the nation. Such initiatives and

President Siegel's leadership abilities received national recognition when Kennesaw was featured in a 1986 book, *Searching for Academic Excellence: Twenty Colleges and Universities on the Move and Their Leaders.*

Published for the American Council on Education, *Searching for Academic Excellence* highlighted Siegel's role in achieving a more inviting campus atmosphere. The authors, J. Wade Gilley, Kenneth A. Fulmer, and Sally J. Reithlingshoefer, argued that Kennesaw's strategic location in an affluent growth area and its catering to career-oriented, nontraditional students were the primary reasons for its unprecedented ability to become "a model contemporary college." They noted that the excellence of its academic programs could be measured by such outcomes as a five-year 98 percent passing rate for teacher education graduates on the Georgia certification test, a 95–100 percent annual pass rate for nursing graduates on the state board examinations, and a high success rate for KC graduates in gaining admission to graduate and professional schools.

Siegel told the book's interviewers that Kennesaw could have assumed "the posture that had served us well in a less demanding time or we could aspire to become a contemporary college in a contemporary setting for contemporary students." She expressed her desire to "recruit talented, inviting, caring teachers and help them to create a nurturing, stimulating environment that exemplifies college-wide commitment to excellence in teaching." Siegel concluded, "As someone who has been excited by what is happening here at Kennesaw College, I sincerely hope that this institution will never lose its dynamic qualities, its spirit of adventure, and its can-do attitude." The president spent the next decade attempting to translate the institution's "dynamic qualities" and "can-do attitude" into specific programs, departments, and centers designed to help Kennesaw reach its lofty goals.[215]

Chapter 5

Building the College
of the Future

Kennesaw made remarkable progress in the 1980s in developing the necessary infrastructure for an emerging metropolitan college. The View of the Future inspirited the campus with a vision of what could be accomplished when everyone worked together. Much of the creative energy of the Siegel administration's first decade went into building new schools and departments, expanding upper-division offerings, computerizing the campus, starting intercollegiate athletics, and implementing such innovative ideas as a chair of private enterprise; CAPS (Counseling, Advisement, and Placement Services); Kennesaw College 101 (KC 101, the core course of the First-Year Experience); and CETL (the Center for Excellence in Teaching and Learning). These changes made Kennesaw a more inviting place to work and study and allowed the college to do a better job of meeting community needs.

Only a vibrant institution could have made so much progress at a time of severe budget challenges. When the Siegel administration began, the fall 1981 student headcount was 4,195. Over the next decade, enrollment increased by 6–18 percent per year. In the fall of 1990 it reached 10,030, breaking ten thousand for the first time in school history. Throughout the decade, the administration told the Board of Regents again and again that Kennesaw was an exceptional, rapidly expanding, institution, but one that might fall short of its promise if new sources of revenue were not found to overcome its woeful lack of resources.

On February 12, 1983, President Siegel sent the chancellor a report titled *Critical Needs for Additional Funding at Kennesaw College*. She argued that Kennesaw deserved special consideration because all its programs were expanding at a time when many Georgia colleges faced retrenchment. The college needed at least twenty-four new faculty slots to provide all the classes that students needed to fulfill their degree requirements on schedule. The problem was particularly acute at the upper level where some required courses could be offered only once a year at most. Not

only did Kennesaw trail all the other senior colleges in state funding per equivalent full-time student (EFT) but, Kennesaw's fiscal year 1983 appropriation was almost $2 million short of the junior-college average per EFT![216]

Despite the appeal, Kennesaw fell even further behind in fiscal year 1984, provoking the president to describe as "alarming" the growing gap between what Kennesaw needed and what it received from the state. In the academic year of 1983–84, the college's quarter credit hour production grew by 11 percent, but the operating budget for "new workload" grew by only 5 percent. She questioned whether the college could continue to serve the public and maintain its reputation for academic excellence. In a February 1984 appeal, she suggested that the lack of funding was putting "in serious jeopardy" Kennesaw's reaccreditation by the Southern Association in 1986.

In fiscal year 1985, the regents finally heeded Siegel's pleas, providing a 15 percent increase in the operating budget for new workload, slightly more than enough to cover the 11 percent increase in quarter credit hour production. However, Siegel noted that while Kennesaw had stopped falling further behind, the increase was not sufficient to raise the college from its position near the bottom of the thirty-three University System of Georgia institutions.[217] Former vice president for academic affairs Ed Rugg recollected that in those years and, indeed, for most of the Siegel era, Kennesaw "rarely had two nickels to rub together" anywhere on campus. The beauty of the Kennesaw story, he maintained, is that the faculty achieved so much despite the budgetary challenges. The secret to success was that the campus community was "excited about doing something and willing to put the sweat equity into getting it done."[218]

A host of oral histories with veteran Kennesaw faculty members demonstrate the truth of Rugg's observations. Again and again, the interviewees reflected on the Kennesaw spirit and the joy of working at a young institution, where even assistant professors could create programs and centers without someone telling them that it had never been done that way before. A story told by Helen Ridley illustrates that the freedom to do things one's own way remained a selling point in faculty recruitment at least as late as 1998. As chair of the Political Science Department, she hired Mark W. Patterson that year to start up a Geographic Information Systems (GIS) Program. He had just received his doctorate, had been offered a teaching position at one of the California state universities, and made Kennesaw wait for his decision while he interviewed at a research university with a GIS Department.

(Opposite Page) Dr. Siegel at the Georgia State Capitol with Governor Joe Frank Harris.

Ridley recalled telling him at the time, "You go there [and] you're going to be carrying somebody's water and books for a long, long time. You come here—you get to design the whole smash." Years earlier, Dean George Beggs had told her, "You've got to take it out of your hide first. But if you take it out of your hide and you get it going, then you get support." Patterson liked the Atlanta weather and the faculty he met during his job interview. So he decided to take the job despite the lack of a GIS lab. As he later recalled, "We were sharing a computer lab with the College of Science and Math, and at any given time you could walk into the lab and someone may have deleted the file to start the software that we needed, so it was a little bit frustrating to begin with. One of the first things I had to do was to find money to put together a lab. So I submitted a grant proposal to the National Science Foundation, which was funded, and we put together a GIS lab."[219]

The 1991 Distinguished Teaching Award winner, E. Howard Shealy Jr., told a related story about Kennesaw's devotion to quality teaching, despite its historic lack of resources. He remembered:

> We've always been short of faculty, short of money, short of classroom space, and the student body keeps growing faster than we can build those things…. The workload for everybody…has continued to grow. It never seems to lessen. All those committee positions have to be filled. One thing I am pretty sure we've kept within our college [of Humanities and Social Sciences]…is the emphasis on teaching and on students, the notion that students matter…. [As chair of the Department of History and Philosophy] I've had a chance to interview a number of our alumni who have come back to apply for part-time teaching positions…. I always ask them why they want to come here, when there are other places in the metro area they could teach part-time…. Everyone has given me some version of the same answer, which was, "I want to come back to Kennesaw to give another generation of students the experience I had as an undergraduate."[220]

The recipient of the 1992 Distinguished Teaching Award, Jo Allen Bradham, had a long career teaching eighteenth-century literature at Agnes Scott College before coming to Kennesaw. She recalled Betty Siegel asking her to compare teaching at the two institutions. Her reply was, "One thing I like about Kennesaw is that it has no past and all future. Agnes Scott has a very rich past." At Agnes Scott,

(Opposite Page) Howard Shealy

she felt an expectation to "do things the way they had always been done"—not a bad thing, given Agnes Scott's history of quality teaching, but still stifling. For example, her predecessor, Ellen Douglas Leyburn, had always taught the Eighteenth-Century Literature course at half past eight in the morning. When Bradham asked to teach it later in the day, she was "looked upon as if this were a dangerous, dangerous suggestion."

At Kennesaw, Bradham set out to "find openings and avenues in which I could build." One of her early projects was BioFest, a yearlong conference celebrating biography. She recalled:

> I was able to get [a] grant from the Georgia Humanities Council. The College Foundation under the leadership of Norman McCrummen [director of development] got behind BioFest.... In the course of the year, we brought in six major speakers who had published important books and biographies.... In addition to these major speakers, we had regular informal coffee discussions with local biographers, including Zell Miller. There was a third level...there were regular meetings in the [Bentley Rare Book Gallery] in which faculty members talked about favorite people. I talked about Lady Mary Wortley Montagu. Dr. [David N.] Bennett in Nursing talked about Florence Nightingale. Fred Roach talked about [Will Rogers].... George Beggs talked about Thomas Jefferson. So this was easy, informal; it wasn't demanding...but it showed people interested in people in the good way and people talking about people.[221]

Jo Allen Bradham was just one of the talented, innovative faculty members of the 1980s who experienced the joy of building a senior college from the ground up.

Creation of Schools, Departments, and Endowed Chairs

While Kennesaw College spent the years 1976–78 preparing to offer baccalaureate programs, it did so without any thought of administrative reorganization. President Sturgis was nearing retirement and wanted to leave that decision to his successor. In 1982, the View of the Future Committee argued strongly for the elimination of academic divisions and the establishment of vice presidents, school deans, and instructional department chairs, as well as faculty distinguished chair-holders. By this time, no senior college the size of Kennesaw in the university system maintained a divisional structure. As the faculty grew, the division chairpersons were

(Opposite Page) Jo Allen Bradham

overwhelmed by the number of people they had to supervise and by the difficulty of evaluating quality research in disciplines other than their own. For promotion and tenure decisions and group cohesiveness, it made sense to create separate departments for the various disciplines. Similar organizational problems plagued the nonacademic services on campus.

In the fall of 1982 President Siegel sent to the chancellor a report titled, *Proposed Consolidation and Realignment of the Organizational Structure of Kennesaw College.* The Board of Regents approved the academic reorganization plan in February 1983. Under the new structure, four units (academic affairs, business and finance, student development, and public relations and development) reported directly to the president. The senior member of the President's administrative team, Roger Hopkins, had been the chief business officer for the last fifteen years. Now, he took on a new title as vice president for business and finance.

On the academic side, four schools and seventeen departments replaced the old divisions. The regents, however, stipulated that Kennesaw had to hire school deans and department chairs without any increase in the operational budget and no additional released time for administrative responsibilities. Consequently, almost all of the administrative searches were internal. The president's office circulated an anonymous questionnaire, asking faculty members to indicate their preference for department chair, dean, and academic vice president. Practically everyone on campus responded. Executive assistant Ed Rugg summarized the results, and the president used them in making her decisions.[222]

The position of vice president for academic affairs was one of the few administrative posts filled through a national search. Eugene R. Huck had been dean of the college for about a decade, but in December of 1982, he concluded he had served long enough and did not want to be considered for the new vice presidency. President Siegel persuaded him to stay a little longer. Nonetheless, in the spring of 1983, he submitted his resignation again, and that time she deferred to his wishes. After a national search, James W. Kolka was chosen for the new position. Huck returned to the classroom as a Distinguished Professor of History and International Affairs. In 1989, the year before his retirement, he received Kennesaw's Distinguished Teaching Award.[223]

Kolka's tenure as vice president for academic affairs was rather brief, and in 1986, President Siegel asked Ed Rugg to take on the responsibilities of acting chief academic officer. Rugg had come to Kennesaw with a fair amount of administrative experience from his time at Peabody and the University of Mississippi. Having played a major role as Betty Siegel's executive assistant in implementing the View of the Future, Rugg shared the president's vision of developing a college of the future. His interim title lasted two years until he was selected to the permanent position in a national search completed in 1988. He would remain vice president for academic affairs another fourteen years until 2002, serving through Kennesaw's transition from a fledgling baccalaureate college into a comprehensive, master's-level university.

The other top administrator selected by a national search was the dean of business administration. Along with Gene Huck, the first chairperson of the Division of Business Administration, Bill Thompson, stepped down in 1983 at the time of the administrative reorganization. After his retirement, Faye H. Rodgers served as acting chair for a few months until the new plan took effect. Then S. Alan Schlact served as acting dean while a national search was conducted. Harry J. Lasher became the first permanent dean of the School of Business on January 15, 1984. The holder of a 1970 PhD from Syracuse University, Lasher had taught and served as assistant dean for the College of Business at Bowling Green University. The Kennesaw search committee was impressed that he also had ten years of practical business experience in banking and with the international corporation, Celanese, where he managed training and development worldwide.

Lasher would serve as dean from 1984 until 1990, during which a general business administration degree was transformed into multiple bachelor of business administration (BBA) diplomas in the various business fields. Among his achievements was the development of Kennesaw's first graduate program, the MBA, launched in 1985. Near the end of his tenure, he presided over the designing, funding, and construction of a new one-hundred-thousand-square-foot business building (the Burruss Building, named in memory of Georgia legislator A. L. Burruss). While Lasher was dean, the number of business faculty members with doctorates quadrupled. His real-world business experience proved invaluable in guiding the faculty into a greater service role in the local business community.[224]

Harry J. Lasher

Herbert L. Davis Jr.

Two of the internal dean searches were relatively easy choices. The longtime chair of the Natural Sciences and Mathematics Division, Herbert L. Davis Jr., became the new dean of the School of Science and Allied Health. The chair of the Education Division, Robert L. Driscoll, became the first dean of the School of Education. A more difficult problem was the selection of the remaining academic dean. Since the Board of Regents allowed Kennesaw only four schools, it became necessary to combine the arts, humanities, and social sciences into a relatively large School of Arts and Behavioral Sciences. President Siegel decided to select as dean, the former chair of the Social Sciences Division, George H. Beggs, over the erstwhile chair of the Humanities Division, John C. Greider. The latter became chairperson of the school's largest department, English.[225]

The first person hired in 1966 as a full-time member of the teaching faculty, George Beggs had devoted his professional career to Kennesaw. On occasion, his military bearing (he was an officer in the US Army Reserves) and his

(Left) George H. Beggs and his wife, Rosemary; (Opposite Page) Robert L. Driscoll

old-school attitude toward proper dress intimidated young professors. One of his successors, Dean Linda M. Noble, recalled her interview for a job in the Psychology Department:

> I had spent my last dime on a navy blue business suit, skirt, jacket, and high collared lace blouse. It was very uncharacteristic of my style from graduate school, but I knew I had to have something more professional. As a graduate student at UGA I was teaching classes in jeans and tennis shorts. It was much more laid back there.… I sat down across the desk from Dr. Beggs, and he spent the first five to ten minutes of the interview talking about how it was imperative that faculty at Kennesaw State dress professionally. I remember almost beginning to perspire. I thought to myself, if this is not professional enough, I can't work here because this is about as good as it gets for me. But at the end of that talk he said, "But I can tell by looking at you that we won't have to worry about that with you." So that's how he started the interview process, and I remember being very panicked thinking I don't know how I could dress more professionally than I was that day.[226]

When his colleagues knew him better, they realized that Beggs cared passionately about students, the institution, and the community. Believing that people dress up for the significant events in their lives, he saw professional attire as a means by which academics tell students that what transpires in the classroom is important. Those who worked for him learned quickly to respect students, respect their colleagues, and never forget the taxpayers and tuition payers who made their jobs possible.

Dean Beggs was determined to use the taxpayers' money wisely and to run his school with honesty and integrity. What he promised in private was what he delivered in public. Once he gave his support for a project, he considered it a matter of honor to fight for it and for his faculty until a final decision was made. He further backed his faculty and students by spending a considerable amount of time attending every concert, conference, art or museum opening put on by members of his school. Even after his retirement, one could always count on his presence at college-sponsored events.

A strong believer in community service, Beggs encouraged faculty to take their expertise beyond the campus borders. For example, he supported faculty members who engaged in public history projects. In annual reviews and in many other ways,

Beggs voiced his appreciation for those who spent time in the community doing oral histories and speaking to schools and civic clubs. Deeply involved in community service himself, Beggs saw public engagement as central to the mission of a tax-supported college.

In the 1980s a spirit of service, applied scholarship, and creative activity increasingly pervaded the campus culture. The faculty in the Music and Visual Arts

(Opposite Page) Wayne Gibson directing the Kennesaw Junior College Chorus. (Right) Wayne Gibson advising a student during registration. (Below) Joseph D. Meeks working with a student at the piano.

Programs had been putting on public performances and shows since the junior-college days. R. Wayne Gibson joined the music faculty in 1972 and Joseph D. Meeks in 1975. Together they built the Music Program, starting with one big studio room on the bottom floor of the Humanities Building (today's Willingham Hall), where Meeks played the piano and Gibson conducted a choir of about eighty students. Gradually, the program was rewarded with a second room, then a third, and then a fourth. Meeks recalled:

> We started designing curriculum. Wayne and I would leave here every day—he'd make dinner, and we would write until two and three in the morning. We did that night after night to start designing the music program. Then, all of a sudden, the students were just coming from everywhere, and I had more piano students than I could possibly handle. My theory classes were just full, thirty or so students. We could have just had them packed in like sardines. We were doing concerts; we started a concert series; and I was playing a lot; and we were having guest artists come out.[227]

In April 1980 the music faculty gained a facility of its own after a half million dollars of renovations to the old Maintenance Building. To recruit students, the Music Program used its small size as an advantage, advertising that even the introductory courses such as Music Theory would be offered by experienced teachers and performers, as opposed to the graduate assistants or adjuncts who handled such entry-level courses at many universities. As a teaching, as opposed to a research, institution, Kennesaw could claim accurately that its professors were in the classroom because they wanted to be there. The strength of the program was its success in giving students individual mentoring, enabling them to reach their full potential as performers. In 1984, just a year after gaining department status, the Music Program achieved accreditation by the National Association of Schools of Music, one of only four colleges to do so that year out of fifty applicants.[228]

The Visual Arts Program had a similar history of starting with limited resources and gradually developing outstanding programs through the efforts of a handful of talented professors. For a number of years, M. Thomson (Tom) Salter was the one-man art faculty. Salter was passionately committed to teaching art appreciation to nonmajors and reaching out to the general public with art shows. Through his efforts, the program had a fair degree of visibility from the earliest days of the college. A colleague, Roberta T. Griffin, remembered that "Tom's legacy was all of the art in the KSU Permanent Collection. In his very quiet way, he very graciously accepted all this artwork, donations of wonderful nineteenth-century art, from Fred Bentley, Alan Sellars, Noah Meadows, and some other people. So we had this great base

Roberta T. Griffin

of nineteenth-century paintings." However, when the administrative reorganization occurred, Kennesaw lacked enough art professors to support an independent
department. So, along with foreign languages, philosophy, and other disciplines, the
art faculty became part of the catch-all Department of Liberal Studies, headed by
English professor David M. Jones Jr.[229]

The growth of the student population justified additional art professors, with
Barbara J. Swindell arriving in 1978, Patrick L. Taylor in 1982, and Roberta Griffin in

Barbara J. Swindell

1983. Pat Taylor was the only one with a doctorate (PhD from UGA, 1982), and he emerged as the leader of the group. Taylor would recall in later years how shocked he was at the small size of the campus and the lack of developed programs when he first arrived. Fortunately, Kennesaw had just opened a new Humanities Building in 1981. Thanks to Tom Salter's lobbying, the facility included four nice art studios on the first floor.

Art was not an original major when Kennesaw became a senior college, but, almost as soon as he joined the faculty, Taylor was put in charge of developing one. It was approved by the Board of Regents in May 1985 and went into operation in the fall quarter. From the start, the Visual Arts Program had over thirty majors and grew to fifty within three years. Many were nontraditional scholars, including several IBM retirees, who brought a degree of dedication and commitment rarely seen in the traditional-aged students. All the art professors were popular with students, perhaps none more so than Barbara Swindell, who received Kennesaw State's Distinguished Teaching Award in 1993.[230]

In 1987, the art faculty was large enough to form a department, with Taylor as the first chair. Roberta Griffin described him as "a great chair of the department; he had visions, too, to do things. We started the art major together. It was so much fun." Pat Taylor recalled that class enrollments were usually too large, and there were never enough resources. When he became chair, he did not have a secretary; then when he hired Caroline Gibbs, he did not have a separate office for her. Instead, she shared his office. But the quality of the faculty and staff made up for the deficiencies in facilities.[231]

(Opposite Page) Patrick L. Taylor

Taylor recalled that originally, graphic design had only a few drafting tables and computers, making it difficult to attract and hold talented faculty members. But the program produced outstanding students, most notably a 1990 graduate, Andres (Andy) Azula, who became a nationally-known advertising executive. His clients included Microsoft, BMW, Budweiser, and, most famously, United Parcel Company, for whom he appeared in television commercials. His drawings with a marker on a whiteboard became so popular with the viewing public that they were parodied on *Saturday Night Live*.[232]

Before coming to Kennesaw, Griffin had directed the art gallery at Miami-Dade Community College's downtown campus. Betty Siegel had dreams in the early 1980s of developing a Center for the Arts, and Griffin was hired not only to teach, but to raise money and help design the center. It failed to materialize at the time, but Griffin was able to place quality shows in the Sturgis Library (opened in 1981) and the Joe Mack Wilson Performing Arts Building (completed in 1989). During her career, she curated more than eighty major exhibitions. She also took students on museum tours. On occasion, Griffin and Taylor accompanied thirty or more students on weekend trips to the museums of New York City. For her efforts, Griffin won Kennesaw's Distinguished Service Award in 2001.[233]

During the late 1980s, the School of Business equaled the School of Arts and Behavioral Sciences in public service and applied scholarship. It had not always been that way. Before Harry Lasher became dean in 1984, the school was comparatively small and just beginning to play a significant role in the community. In the fall of 1984 less than a quarter of KC's full-time faculty worked in the School of Business, but business majors made up half the student body. In fiscal year 1984, some 64 percent of all recipients of bachelors' degrees were business majors. Of the business professors listed in the 1984–85 catalog, only ten held doctorates, and some were teaching outside their area of expertise. The program had to grow in size and quality before it could offer much to the campus or community.

Ed Rugg recalls that in the spring of 1983, as part of the administrative reorganization, "we all agreed that we had to build business, and I remember one decision that was made that spring…[was that] several of the former division heads, now school heads, gave back positions that had been allocated to them, so that we could feed the building of a business school." Those administrators recognized that Kennesaw College could not become a leading four-year institution in metropolitan Atlanta without a strong School of Business. Gradually, the school expanded in size and stature, and, along with the School of Education, was able to start masters' programs in 1985.[234]

(Opposite Page) Kennesaw State College
graduate Andres (Andy) Azula

151

Craig E. Aronoff

One of the most innovative aspects of the School of Business was the chair of private enterprise, created in 1982 by a gift from the Georgia International Life Insurance Company and the Cobb County Bankers' Association. For the first year, a retired Southern Bell vice president, Jasper Dorsey, held the seat while a national search was conducted. Out of an applicant pool of about one hundred candidates, the committee chose Craig E. Aronoff, an Atlanta native on the faculty of Georgia State University, where he worked for Michael H. (Mike) Mescon, the chairperson of the Management Department and holder of the nation's first chair of private enterprise.[235]

When he was a promising graduate student in the Annenberg School for Communication at the University of Pennsylvania, Aronoff had an encounter with a star professor who said there were only twenty people in the world he considered his peers and with whom he cared to talk. He told Craig that if he applied himself, he might aspire to rise into that elite company. Aronoff claims that the conversation induced an epiphany. Later, in his dormitory room, he thought, "I don't want to live in a world with twenty people." Instead, he wanted to be part of a world where he could serve society in a direct way. He already knew Mike Mescon, who told him business schools needed academics that specialized in communication. So, Aronoff gave up his Ivy League pretensions and transferred to the University of Texas, where he earned his PhD in 1975. Mescon quickly hired him, and, at age twenty-four, he became an assistant professor of management at Georgia State.[236]

After moving to Marietta, Aronoff immediately joined the Cobb Chamber of Commerce and the Marietta Kiwanis Club, where he was mentored by local business leaders such as Joe Daniell, Mack Henderson, and Campbell Dasher. Henderson took him to lunch at the Georgian Club and told him,

> Your position is very important. Thirteen banks and our biggest insurance company have put money behind your position. We think Kennesaw College is an extremely important part of the overall community. We want a good business school, and we want a business school that is focused on real business in a practical way. Don't be Harvard in the Pines. You need to find some way that will distinguish the business school. So relate to local businesses; don't be overly academic or intellectual. Keep it practical and applied, and find a way that we can distinguish ourselves.[237]

That advice fit nicely into Kennesaw's evolving mission in the 1980s, and President Siegel gave her enthusiastic support when Congressman Buddy Darden asked Aronoff to chair his economic advisory task force and the chamber invited him to serve on a blue-ribbon transportation committee. As vicechair of the chamber committee, Aronoff played a major role in developing a public bus system, Cobb Community Transit, approved in a special referendum on June 9, 1987. A little over a decade earlier, Cobb Countians had voted against joining MARTA. In a series of public meetings, Aronoff made the case that Cobb could meet the demands of business and special needs people by operating its own system for about a tenth of the cost of joining MARTA. He was quoted at the time that Cobb had done something unique in developing a publicly owned, privately operated, system that would be "a model for the nation, for Gwinnett and for the other counties."[238]

As Aronoff delivered speeches around the country to chamber and civic groups, he was impressed by the number of people who came up to him to ask for advice about their family businesses. Realizing that the standard business curriculum did not address the problems that result from mixing family and business, he started a Family Business Forum that companies could pay to join. In 1987, he took the lead in creating the Cox Family Enterprise Center for the research, education, and recognition of family businesses. In 1992, the center began an annual dinner to announce the winners of its Georgia Family Business of the Year Awards.

The Family Business Forum did something else to enhance Kennesaw's reputation. One of the forum's advisory board members, Jack Dinos, owned, with his brother Tony, the Southern Tea Company. When they sold the company, they endowed two distinguished faculty chairs at Kennesaw. Aronoff's chair became the Mary and Jack Dinos Distinguished Chair in Private Enterprise. The other was the Tony and Jack Dinos Eminent Scholar Chair of Entrepreneurial Management, originally held by Dean Timothy S. Mescon. Finally, the sale of Southern Tea to

Tetley Inc. led to a generous endowment from Tetley's CEO, Hank McInerney, that established Kennesaw's Tetley Distinguished Leader Lecture Series and brought to campus a number of outstanding national leaders who lectured and interacted with students, faculty, and the community.[239]

Aligning Upper-Division Baccalaureate Programs with Student Demand

Reorganizing the faculty was vitally important to Kennesaw's success as a four-year college, but aligning baccalaureate program offerings to current and potential student interests and community needs was also key to the college's continued growth. The nontraditional nature of KC's student body explains why so many gravitated toward undergraduate majors in applied professional fields such as business, teacher education, and nursing. To meet student demand, Kennesaw also created applied programs in the 1980s in computer science, information systems, communication, human services, psychology, and art. Virtually all areas of baccalaureate study at Kennesaw grew in the 1980s, but professionally-oriented programs expanded the quickest and accounted for most of the declared majors and degrees conferred.

As indicated in the *Kennesaw College 1988–1989 Fact Book*, prepared by Deborah J. Head and Ed Rugg, upper-division enrollment in business fields boomed in the mid-1980s after the BS degrees in business administration and secretarial science were discontinued to be replaced with BBAs in specific areas. Interest in business fields was on the rise nationally, but the trend appeared especially pronounced at KC among older students. Upper-division enrollments in the School of Business nearly doubled from fall 1984 to fall 1988, growing from 603 to 1,187 declared majors. By the latter date, business led the campus in the number of upper-division declared majors, headed by management (341), accounting (271), and marketing (243). Not surprisingly, Kennesaw College's first graduate program was the MBA, building firmly on this undergraduate base.[240]

During that same period, upper-division enrollment in the School of Education almost tripled, growing from 144 in fall 1984 to 388 in fall 1988. The K–4 Elementary Education Program was the most popular teacher education field, attracting 138 declared juniors and seniors. Kennesaw was typical of comprehensive, public, four-year universities in attracting large numbers of education and business students. Accordingly, the second graduate-degree program launched at KC was the MEd.[241]

Nursing was another popular field of study—the largest upper-division major in the School of Science and Allied Health in fall 1988 (144 declared majors). Two relatively new and fast-growing bachelors' programs in computer science and information systems had a combined total of 127 declared majors that year, followed by biology (66 majors). Despite limited science lab, nursing lab, and computer lab facilities,

The first two recipients of the Distinguished Teaching Award,
Thomas B. Roper Jr. and Stephen E. Scherer, with President Siegel
and vice president for academic affairs James W. Kolka.

upper-division enrollment in this school grew from 112 in fall 1984 to 418 in fall 1988, a 273 percent increase and the largest gain of the four schools for the period.[242]

Several fast-growing programs recently established or added in the 1980s within the School of Arts and Behavioral Sciences contributed to that school's tripling of declared upper-division majors, growing from 167 in fall 1984 to 508 in fall 1988. Psychology led the way with 149 majors, followed by a three-year-old program in communication at 74 majors, and four-year-old programs in public and social services (48 majors) and art (50 majors).[243]

During this period, the college's long-standing commitment to the instruction of freshmen and sophomores continued. As late as the fall of 1988, some 60 percent of all undergraduates were at the lower level. However, as one would expect at a four-year metropolitan college, upper-division enrollment grew each year, with the number of juniors increasing by 94 percent and the number of seniors by 222 percent from fall 1984 to fall 1988. A key to that impressive trend was the aligning of undergraduate degree programs with student interest.[244]

Nancy S. King

The CAPS and CETL Centers

When the Board of Regents approved Kennesaw's 1983 reorganization, a newly created CAPS (Counseling, Advisement and Placement Services) Center fell under both academic affairs and student development. The CAPS director reported primarily to the vice president for academic affairs, but also advised and consulted with the dean of student development. President Siegel brought from Western Carolina University the concept that became the genesis of CAPS. The first director, G. Ruth Hepler, also chaired the Psychology Department. Housed in a new suite of offices on the second floor of the old library (Pilcher Building), CAPS advised students without declared majors. The center also provided professional counseling and testing, placement services, a career resource library, and an innovative new course titled Kennesaw College 101 (KC 101).[245] The View of the Future Committee had called for a personalized style of teaching that replaced the traditional professor-centered lecture with a student-centered approach to help students discover their own truths. The View of the Future also called for a more effective means of orienting newcomers to the campus culture. The KC 101 course was designed to accomplish precisely those objectives.

Betty Siegel was an admirer of John N. Gardner and his work with the First-Year Experience at the University of South Carolina. As a young faculty member in 1972, Gardner developed USC's University 101 course to improve the skills of incoming students in areas such as time management, study techniques, and career planning. Under Gardner's leadership as executive director from 1974 to 1999, Carolina's First-Year Program significantly improved student self-esteem, retention, and graduation rates; as a result, Gardner and the University of South Carolina became international leaders for their work with undergraduates.[246]

Shortly after her arrival at Kennesaw, President Siegel persuaded Ruth Hepler and an English professor, Carol L. (Cary) Turner, to go to one of Gardner's workshops. They came back excited by what they had learned and determined to involve the entire faculty. The result was a Gardner-led weekend-long seminar at Kennesaw. A young English instructor, Nancy S. King, recalled the experience as so life-changing that she thought she had landed in a whole new world of thinking about teaching. Over a two-year period about 125 individuals (the majority of the faculty) participated in at least one Gardner-led event. Even those who never taught the new KC 101 course claimed to benefit from their exposure to innovative teaching techniques.[247]

Ten volunteer faculty members, on loan from their various departments, taught the first sections of KC 101 to about one hundred students in the fall of 1983. Nancy King and biology professor Bowman Davis became the program coordinators, a function that Davis continued for the rest of the decade. Davis described KC 101 as an extended orientation course that taught study skills, but, more importantly, built student-faculty relationships, so that students had someone to whom they could talk whenever problems arose during their academic careers. In a 1987 campus publication, he claimed that a comparison of students who took KC 101 to those with similar SAT scores who had not taken the course provided evidence that it was successful in increasing retention and academic performance.

In the early days, the biggest problem for the coordinators was to keep faculty members teaching in the program. Davis noted that they lacked sufficient funds to compensate the academic departments for the lost sections that KC 101 professors did not teach in their disciplines. Consequently, the chairs were reluctant to release their faculty members too often. Moreover, the courses were time-consuming when taught properly and not always rewarded in tenure and promotion decisions.[248] Despite these difficulties, Kennesaw never lost its commitment to the First-Year Experience. The funding for the program was vastly increased toward the end of the Siegel administration, and it found a home in University College where a 1989 Kennesaw graduate, Keisha L. Hoerrner, headed the Department of First-Year Programs.[249]

From almost the beginning, CAPS tied KC 101 to an improved student advisement program. In February 1986, Nancy King received a call to come to a Friday afternoon meeting with Betty Siegel. Apparently impressed with King's teaching and her commitment to KC 101, Siegel asked her to move to CAPS part time to create an advisement program for undeclared students. King recalls telling the president that her passion was teaching, but Siegel would not take "no" for an answer and invited her to come back on Monday morning. At that time, she persuaded her that administration could be a different venue for teaching.

King worked with one of the counselors, Charles L. (Chuck) Goodrum Jr., on an advisement program that President Siegel wanted in place within six months. In response to King's protest that she knew too little about advisement to implement a program that quickly, Siegel invited a consultant to campus, President Robert E. Glennen of Emporia State University, whose research area was advisement. In addition, Siegel sent King and Goodrum to Kansas City for the annual conference of the National Association for Academic Advising (NACADA), and from there to nearby Emporia State to view its advising center firsthand. That trip was profitable in more ways than one. Kennesaw's CAPS Center was modeled to a large degree on the Emporia State center; and, by the time King left the NACADA meeting, she had been elected to the board as a public college representative. A decade later, 1997–1999, she would serve two years as president of the almost ten-thousand-member NACADA, where she was able to make Kennesaw's name well known nationally in advisement circles.[250]

King and Goodrum were determined to do more than help students work out a course schedule. Playing on Arthur W. Chickering's concept of developmental advising, they created a program where advisors and students worked in partnership to explore career and personal goals and how they related to potential academic majors. In time, the program came to see advising as a type of teaching, helping students see connections among the various courses in a general education curriculum and helping them "get outside themselves" and think about the wider local and global communities.[251]

King was soon playing a larger role in CAPS. In 1985 Ruth Hepler gave up the directorship and concentrated on her other job as chair of the Psychology Department. Her successor served about a year and a half and then departed suddenly, creating a need for a temporary replacement. The administration asked Nancy King to become acting director while a national search took place. She took on that assignment, thinking that she could soon return to teaching and part-time work with CAPS. During the search, however, her colleagues in CAPS told the President, "Things are going really well; why don't you just let Nancy stay?" So President Siegel met with her and said, "You've started some really good initiatives over there, and I just want you to stay and carry this out." She would be CAPS director until 1995, when, in another administrative reorganization, she would become vice president for student success and enrollment services.[252]

From its origin, Kennesaw prided itself on the quality of classroom instruction. The 1986 SACS self-study documented a number of examples of academic success: the best record of any college in Georgia, public or private, in the percentage of students passing the teacher certification test in 1984; a virtually 100 percent success rate in placing nursing graduates in jobs in their field; a remarkable record of about fifty percent of all science graduates gaining admission to medical, dental, or other graduate programs; a superior performance on the Georgia Certified Public Accountant exam, with one student receiving the highest score in the state; and national accreditation for the music program.[253]

The *View of the Future* report recommended a continued commitment to teaching excellence through the creation of a center to provide faculty development workshops and allow for the exchange of ideas on effective teaching methods. As part of the 1983 administrative reorganization, Kennesaw created the Center for Excellence in Teaching and Learning (CETL), one of the first of its kind in the state or nation. Initially, an associate professor of education, Diane L. Willey, served as part-time acting director. By 1985–86, the center received its first substantial budget to allow it to fulfill its mission. While CETL's directors served only part time before 2002, they played a valuable role on campus. During her short tenure as director, Janis Coombs Epps, began in 1987 a quarterly publication titled *Reaching through Teaching* that provided numerous faculty-authored articles about effective teaching.[254]

In the opening issue, interim vice president for academic affairs Ed Rugg justified CETL as a means of preserving quality teaching as Kennesaw's number one priority. Citing Ernest L. Boyer's book, *College*, Rugg argued that the best schools are those that "care about teaching, know their students, have a spirit of community on the campus, and can document student achievement." Support for CETL, he claimed, was a way to show the public that Kennesaw took "teaching seriously."

President Siegel said much the same. She asserted in the same issue that "to deny the centrality of teaching in our lives, and in the life of the university…can only be paralyzing." In addition to the obvious task of knowing their subject matter, teachers, she believed, needed "the most accurate understanding available about others, and a concern with people and their reactions." She saw CETL as a useful tool in moving professors beyond the authoritarian, mechanistic model of the past and molding them into facilitators of learning who saw their role as "freeing, rather than restricting" and involving "the learner in the personal meaning of the subject matter."[255]

In addition to *Reaching through Teaching* and other publications, under the leadership of Donald W. Forrester, CETL began in 1993 an annual Georgia Conference on College and University Teaching. Despite limited staff and limited funding, the center coordinated a variety of campus activities that facilitated faculty development. Still, CETL would not reach its full potential before the early twenty-first century, when its budget increased and G. William (Bill) Hill IV became the first full-time director.[256]

Computerization of the Kennesaw Campus

When Ed Rugg arrived on the Kennesaw campus in the fall of 1982, one of his main tasks as executive assistant to the president was to upgrade Kennesaw's primitive

Randall Goltz

computer operation. Former president Sturgis and President Siegel had both expressed concern that the founding director of data processing had failed to keep up with changes in the field and needed to retool or move on. It became Rugg's job to see that one of those options was pursued. By spring 1983, Rugg had accepted the director's resignation. For years, Kennesaw's administrative data processing had relied on outdated keypunch machines and a fifteen-year-old Honeywell 200 computer that typically ran an hour or two a week. Data Processing had a modern minicomputer with distributed data management capabilities, but its terminals sat next to the keypunch machines, and data was formatted in the familiar 80-character record of the outdated IBM punch card. Contemporary computing technology was woefully absent across the entire campus. The lone staff person with more than a high school degree in the Data Processing Department, Randall C. Goltz, seemed to have angered the director by daring to go back to school for a relevant two-year degree.[257]

Shortly after Rugg's arrival, Kennesaw invited a consulting team from the University System Computer Network (USCN) to conduct a six-month evaluation of the college's shortcomings. One of the recommendations was to merge academic and administrative activities into one service-oriented department with joint heads reporting to Rugg. Steve Scherer became the coordinator for academic computing and Randy Goltz became the director for administrative computing. Scherer also became the USCN campus coordinator. For a number of years Rugg, Scherer, and Goltz worked harmoniously in maintaining and developing campus computer services.[258]

On the administrative side, Rugg and Goltz directed the transition from the old keypunch operation to interactive online systems. They replaced the old Honeywell 200 with a TI-990 Model 12 computer with considerably more storage space. With growing demand, however, the original TI-990 reached its capacity by the end of 1984 and "crashed" as often as ten times a day. The college was forced to acquire a second one in January 1985, giving them enough capacity for the next several years. For the first time, the college made full use of the free technical support and applications software that the University System Computer Network provided. Prior to this time, data entry took place essentially in one central location. Under the reorganization, Goltz's staff provided technical support, while data entry and file maintenance were decentralized into the different user departments. By the 1984–85 school year, Rugg and Goltz were able to distribute forty used word processors around campus for administrative use and they placed computer terminals and printers in the library, the Division of Continuing Education, and various administrative locations.[259]

When Steve Scherer joined the faculty in 1974 as a young mathematics professor, students and faculty had access to a grand total of three "dumb" Teletype computer terminals connected by telephone lines to a CYBER at the University of Georgia and operating at the incredibly slow speed of 110 bytes per second. Scherer's division chair, Herb Davis, asked whether he had used a computer in working on his dissertation. To an affirmative response, Davis exclaimed, "Good, you're the computer coordinator!" In that informal manner, Scherer took on a function that consumed much of his time for several decades.[260]

Prior to the 1983 reorganization, Scherer carried out his responsibilities with a minimum of administrative support. Gradually the number of Teletype terminals grew until they filled a classroom downstairs in the old Humanities Building (Willingham Hall). By 1983 Scherer was able to place a few Apple computers with memory in an adjoining room. Several faculty members made use of them for research projects or dissertations, among them a future KSU vice president, Nancy King, who utilized a word processing program to write her dissertation on Charles Dickens for the English Department at Georgia State.

Unfortunately, her document grew in size until it exceeded the storage capacity of the early Apple files. When a message popped up on the screen saying she could add no more, she closed that file and started a new one. Not understanding what she was doing, she gave the new file the same name as the old, and then saved it, thereby erasing all the previous work. When King realized what she had done, she let out a "blood-curdling scream" so loud that Scherer heard it from his office on the upper floor. He ran downstairs and tried to help, but had to tell her that her material was permanently lost. King had to go back to work, recall the lost text as best she could, and save it properly the second time. She finally completed the dissertation and earned her doctorate in 1984.[261]

In April 1983 the Board of Regents approved a BS in computer science. A year later, the instructional computer lab moved to the second floor of the old library,

renamed the W. Wyman Pilcher Public Service Building, after a prominent Marietta banker who served on the presidential search committee that brought Betty Siegel to Kennesaw. Scherer was now aided by an academic computing facilitator, Michael Carroll, and a number of student lab assistants. Despite the limited personnel, they managed to hold frequent faculty and staff development workshops and provide individual assistance during eighty-eight hours of open lab time each week.[262]

Soon after moving to the Pilcher Building, Scherer began constructing a campus computer network, starting by stringing wire to the Social Sciences Building (later renamed University College), where the Mathematics Department occupied much of the second floor. The computer science instructors had the greatest need for a computer network, so Scherer thought he would test it out on them. Originally, he strung the wire from the bottom side of the roofs of the covered walkway that ran around the quadrangle. He soon discovered that the campus occupied a relatively high elevation and was lightning-prone. The wiring became a giant antenna that blew out the network on a regular basis. Learning from that flawed network installation, he turned to a series of tunnels below the campus where conduits carried electrical and telephone lines.

Some of the four-inch-wide conduits were empty, and Scherer gained permission to use them to pull his fiber optic cables. From manholes located throughout the campus, one could go down into tunnels that were about six feet wide and eight feet deep. All were muddy and sometimes contained as much as six feet of water. Even the telephone cables were buried in water. After plant operations workers pumped out the water, Scherer, lacking funds to contract the job out, personally descended into the tunnels to pull the cables through the conduits.

The biggest challenge was to go from the Pilcher Building to the old Social Sciences Building. Even though the two structures were just a few feet apart, the tunnels did not run directly between them. So he had to go down a manhole on the southeastern side of the Pilcher Building, near the Sturgis Library, and follow a tunnel westward toward the Administration Building (currently the home of the Department of Public Safety). From there, he picked up another tunnel running north until he hit a manhole from which he could start eastward past the Social Sciences Building. Then he made a one-hundred-eighty-degree turn that led back to his destination. Somewhere along the journey, he discovered that even the conduit was filled with mud, complicating the process of pulling cables. Through this extraordinary effort, he gained a perspective on campus construction that few faculty and staff have enjoyed.[263]

For a couple of years in the 1980s, Rugg increased the supply of dedicated word processors on campus by purchasing used, but relatively new, Lanier Easy-Ones that Georgia Tech planned to surplus. Fortunately, personal computer prices dropped significantly during the decade, and Kennesaw eventually bought new multipurpose desktop computers for what the college had been paying for used. With personal computers becoming a necessity for busy professors, Rugg and Scherer set out in the early 1990s on an ambitious multiyear goal of placing computers in virtually every faculty office. According to Scherer, the English faculty at first was the most resistant to new technology, but in time the professors realized the immense instructional possibilities of word processing.

For several years, Kennesaw jumped from one software package to another before eventually settling on Microsoft as the company that provided the best support. The complaints from secretaries were loud when, having just learned Word Perfect, they had to retool and master Microsoft Word. Scherer had to make a special exception for one staff member who adamantly refused to make the change until the day she retired.[264]

One of the most enthusiastic users of the new technology was the Sturgis Library. The first library director, Robert J. Greene, did away with the old card catalog, replacing it with microfilm machines and an online database. His replacement, Robert B. Williams, built on that beginning, going beyond an exclusive emphasis on print materials and opening up a variety of electronic possibilities. Betty Siegel played the central role in bringing Bob Williams to Kennesaw. Two years before he became director, Williams met Siegel at Cumberland College in Kentucky, where he headed the library and she served as a member of the alumni board.

Williams was just beginning some modern technological changes at Cumberland, and Siegel was impressed enough to invite him to Cobb County to prepare an evaluation report of the Kennesaw College library. After writing a positive assessment of Bob Greene's operation, he returned to Cumberland College with no thoughts of a career move. But Siegel had other ideas. When Greene retired in 1986, she invited Williams to campus for another consulting visit. When he came, she asked him to apply for the job.[265]

Despite the real progress of the 1980s, technology was inadequately funded. The arrival of the Internet made computerization central to the college's teaching mission. By the mid-1990s Tina H. Straley, a former chair of the Mathematics Department, became associate vice president for academic affairs and dean of graduate studies. In this role, she supervised both the library and computer operations and became a major advocate for state-of-the-art technology. Rugg and Straley came up with the idea of a technology fee to meet Kennesaw's instructional- and student-support needs, one of the first such mandatory technology fees in the University System of Georgia.[266]

(Opposite Page) Robert B. Williams

For the 1997–98 school year, the Board of Regents approved a twenty-five dollars per semester fee. The following year it went up to thirty-eight dollars and then jumped to fifty dollars in 2006. In the first year, the fee generated about $1 million of additional revenues for student technology support, allowing Scherer to upgrade and add more computer labs across campus with expanded network capabilities. The final step in Kennesaw's technological upgrade came when Rugg and Straley drafted a job description and gained President Siegel's approval to conduct a national search for a new cabinet-level position of chief information officer. The slot was filled in 1998 by Randy C. Hinds.[267]

Intercollegiate Athletics

President Siegel came to Kennesaw with a belief that intercollegiate athletics play a major role in creating an inviting campus atmosphere for students and the general public. Throughout the junior-college years, her predecessor had steadfastly resisted pressures to build competitive sports teams. As a young teacher at Eatonton (Georgia) High School, Horace Sturgis had been a highly successful basketball coach, winning the Class B state championship in 1939.[268] However, as president, he did not support intercollegiate athletics for two reasons: the cost to students and his preference to put limited resources into an active intramural program. A fiscal conservative, Sturgis opposed charging students more than the bare minimum to finance their educations. During his presidency, the student activities fee was a mere ten dollars, and Kennesaw did not even charge a diploma fee. Sturgis reasoned that Kennesaw was not a traditional, residential college, but instead had large numbers of working, older students, who were not interested in staying on campus to watch sporting events.[269]

The former president believed that the fledgling junior college lacked the funds to support quality sports teams, so he preferred not to settle for mediocrity. According to Kennesaw's first athletic director, James Davis (Spec) Landrum, the president was not against athletics on principle, but he "knew we didn't have enough money. He knew from being at Tech. He knew that if you didn't have the money that you were going to have to go outside to get the money, and then your athletic

program was going to be ruled somewhere else besides the president's office and the campus." Despite his reservations, Sturgis in his retirement supported Landrum as the charter athletic director, writing him a letter that began, "Dear Spec, you know that I never really [wanted] athletics to come to Kennesaw. However, the way that it's been handled is a compliment to you and the president. I just want you to know that."[270]

By the 1980s the college was in a better position to fund winning teams, and Betty Siegel thought that intercollegiate sports were worth the price if they increased school spirit and bonded students and alumni to the institution. Landrum, at the time, was a development officer and the alumni coordinator, and Siegel solicited his help in gaining introductions to prominent people in Georgia. He quickly arranged meetings for the president with the head of the Woodruff Foundation and similar organizations. Landrum and Siegel became well acquainted as he drove her

James (Spec) D. Landrum

to various events. One of the trips took them to Macon where Siegel delivered a noonday speech at his old alma mater, Mercer University, and then to Athens for an evening speech at the University of Georgia. On the way, they talked for the first time about athletics at Kennesaw.[271]

Landrum remembered that the president was grateful for his opinions, but she made no commitment at that moment. In a later meeting, however, she said, "Well, we've got to get on this." That decision was apparently reached as the two drove around campus. According to President Siegel:

> One of the things that I found that is elusive is how you create a sense of community on a campus that is a commuter campus. I was riding around with Spec Landrum who was my Development officer then, and had a very fine athletic career in his own right. I said, "Ah, Spec, it grieves me sometimes to see all these beautiful fields on the campus; and nobody's ever on them. It's sad to me that I don't see people out playing sports and, you know, really involved. What I really need is an athletic program."[272]

President Siegel claimed that she determined on the spot to ask Landrum to be her athletic director. Landrum's recollection was slightly more convoluted. He recalled that she asked him to recommend an athletic director, and he told her, "I don't think you know anybody that can do as good a job as I can do." She laughed and asked, "Are you serious?" He responded, "Betty, the reason that I left college athletics was that I wasn't headed in the direction that I really wanted to be, and that was an athletic director." Landrum recalls, "In, I guess, less than a month she had made a decision and asked me to be athletic director. I was so very happy."[273]

During the 1982–83 school year, Kennesaw College competed as an independent school—unaffiliated with any conference or national organization. A student athletics fee of $6 a quarter generated $103,000—the total Athletic Department budget. Relying on volunteer coaches in some sports, Kennesaw fielded nine sports teams (women's basketball; men's soccer and golf; and men's and women's cross country, track, and tennis). Coached by Luis Sastoque, the men's soccer team finished the 1982 season with a record of 8-6, while Gary Wisener's women's basketball

(Opposite Page) Members of the cross country team. Pictured in the first row (L-R): Kathy McDonald, Carolyn Oswalt, Dawn Arnett, Suzanne Hall, and Coach Tom Roper. Second row (L-R): Larry Kraska, Mark Olah, Sam Boothe, David Bond, Dave Heglton, Paul Okerberg, and Coach Dave L. Morgan.

team ended the 1983 season 9-13. Win-loss records from the 1982–83 seasons are incomplete or nonexistent for the other sports. Two faculty members, Dave Morgan (mathematics) and Tom Roper (business law), coached the initial cross country teams, while history professor Gird Romer served as golf coach. Landrum went off-campus to find part-time coaches for the other sports (Mary Quadfasel in women's tennis, Paul Riggins in men's tennis, and Roscoe Googe in track).[274]

After a year of experimentation, Landrum and the Intercollegiate Athletic Committee recommended that Kennesaw join the National Association of Intercollegiate Athletics (NAIA) and affiliate with the Georgia Intercollegiate Athletic Conference (GIAC). According to Landrum, the decision to join the NAIA rather than the National Collegiate Athletic Association (NCAA) was largely a question of money. The NCAA required more sports than Kennesaw wanted to field in the 1980s and required significantly more compliance rules. Moreover, the potential NCAA rivals were located further away than a host of NAIA schools, so travel would have been a huge expense. In the NAIA, Kennesaw could compete against a number of nearby colleges such as North Georgia, Berry, Shorter, and Southern Tech, all of whom asked Kennesaw to join them in the GIAC and NAIA. Created in 1936, the NAIA consisted of several hundred schools nationwide, mostly small colleges, and seemed a suitable home for a startup program with a small athletic budget.[275]

According to Landrum, President Siegel made it clear that she wanted winning teams, but she wanted even more for Kennesaw to be a place where academics came first. From the start, Landrum worked with an Intercollegiate Athletic Committee that included people such as the vice president for business and finance, Roger Hopkins, and the dean of the School of Science and Mathematics, Herb Davis. Landrum recalls that Hopkins was "a wonderful, wonderful help, and Davis took on the responsibility of ensuring that athletes were academically eligible and that the program complied with all NAIA rules and regulations."[276]

During the 1983–84 school year, baseball (under the direction of former major league pitcher Jim Nash and, for the last part of the season, Frank Fillman) became the tenth sport, and in 1985 men's basketball (coached by Phil Zenoni) became the eleventh. The year before Zenoni's arrival, I. David Harris, a physical education professor and former department head, invited students to try out for a club sports team. According to Landrum, Harris was "one of the better coaches in the whole state of Georgia." Unfortunately, he was expected to teach a full load while he was coaching. Since he also had family obligations, he had no time to recruit or do all the other things a successful coach needed to do. Consequently, he knew he could not compete with other programs and had to relinquish his responsibilities when men's basketball became an official intercollegiate sport.[277]

Even in the early years, the sports teams had some notable successes. In 1986, Jon Hough won the NAIA individual championship in golf while the team finished tenth. That year, the women's track team, led by an outstanding triple jumper and

(Opposite Page) Members of the 1982–83 women's basketball team, Beth Horne (45) and Christie Alexamder (31).

171

hurdler named Jenifer Turner, brought home Kennesaw's first team championship at the NAIA district outdoor meet. However, Dave Harris's dilemma points out a fundamental problem of trying to offer a full complement of sports. Although the Board of Regents agreed to raise the student athletic fee in the fall of 1987 to $17, even that amount supported an athletic budget of only a modest $431,500. Few of the student athletes received more than tuition, fees, and books, making it almost an accident when Kennesaw attracted star high school players. The college simply lacked the money to offer full scholarships or hire full-time coaches in most sports.

Consequently, in the spring of 1987, Siegel, Landrum, and the athletic board made the decision to reduce the number of sports to men's and women's basketball, baseball, and slow pitch softball, the last little more than a club sport since neither the NAIA nor the NCAA held a national championship. As President Siegel recalls, "Rather than doing all of those sports…we began to narrow it down and say, 'These are the things we can make a difference in—softball, baseball, basketball.'"[278]

Spec Landrum retired that year and was replaced in July 1987 by Dr. David L. Waples, the commissioner of the NCAA Division I Gulf Star Conference (in Louisiana and Texas) and former coach at Valdosta State. Waples was one of many new employees of the 1980s that was attracted to Kennesaw not by its well-established programs, but by its dynamic leadership and vision of what the college could become. Waples remembered:

> We had a president, Dr. Betty Siegel, who understood what athletics could do for this university. She had this grandiose plan of taking this little old commuter school and making it nationally known. I know there were people on campus that said, "It's a waste of money. Why doesn't she stay on campus? We're a commuter school. We're serving this little quadrant. Let's just leave it at that." Well, that wasn't Dr. Siegel, so she knew what athletics could do. She said to me, "I brought you here to take athletics the same way that this university is going. I don't know anything about athletics. I'm trusting you to do it."[279]

During Waples's first five years as athletic director, the basketball, baseball, and softball programs did remarkably well. The women's basketball team, coached by Ron Walker, won the 1988 GIAC championship and NAIA district tournament. By 1989–90 the Athletic Department was sufficiently funded to offer the maximum ten full scholarships in men's and women's basketball. During the 1990–91 school

(Opposite Page) David L Waples

172

year, the college signed a lease with College Quarters, a private apartment complex just north of campus, to house student athletes. At the same time, it reestablished the men's golf program and started fast pitch softball. In the first year, Coach Scott Whitlock's softball team recorded a 41-11 record and finished fourth in the NAIA national tournament, thanks in large part to a phenomenal pitcher from Canada named Dyan Mueller. Meanwhile, the baseball team was the GIAC champion in both 1988 and 1990.[280]

As early as November 1988, Waples entered into discussions with other athletic directors and schools about a possible jump to NCAA Division II. As the athletics budget increased and Kennesaw added more sports, such a move became more feasible. In 1991, the commissioner of the Division II Peach Belt Conference, Marvin Vanover, made frequent visits to campus to persuade and prepare the college to join his organization. The Peach Belt seemed a good fit because it included such Georgia peer institutions as Armstrong State, Augusta, Columbus, and Georgia College, along with similar colleges in South Carolina.

With the Peach Belt's endorsement, Kennesaw applied and was accepted by the NCAA in August 1992, with the understanding that the school would complete a two-year transition period before gaining full membership in the 1994–95 season. The only downside to the decision was that President Siegel had served two terms on the NAIA Executive Committee and was in line to chair the organization if Kennesaw had stayed there a little longer. She had found the NAIA experience helpful, claiming that "it gave me an opportunity to really see the importance of athletics and how you govern athletics. I have a great respect for athletics as a consequence of my association."

The change from the small-school NAIA to the larger NCAA Division II seemed to make little difference in the success of Kennesaw's athletic teams. To meet the Division II minimum requirements, Kennesaw added women's tennis and men's and women's cross country. Starting in 1994, Coach Stan Sims's cross country teams won both the men's and women's Peach Belt titles for six years in a row. Under Coach Mike Sansing, the baseball team won the NAIA national tournament in 1994 and the Division II national tournament in 1996; and, in its first two years of eligibility, softball won the 1995 and 1996 Division II national championships. Thus, Kennesaw made the transition to Division II look easy.[281]

National Recognition and Erikson's Stages of Development

Kennesaw's progress in the 1980s caught the eye of the rest of the nation. As the first decade of the Siegel era drew to a close, *U.S. News & World Report* recognized Kennesaw in 1989 as one of only five southern institutions in the category of "Up-and-Coming Regional Colleges and Universities." The following year, Kennesaw and George Mason University were singled out as among the "best up-and-coming colleges" in the South. Then, in 1991, the news magazine identified Kennesaw as a "rising star."

In a 1992 interview, President Siegel used developmental psychologist Erik Erikson's "Eight Stages of Life" to place Kennesaw at the stage of "identity" as it moved through adolescence toward young maturity. Adolescence, of course, is a time when individuals are obsessed with what others think of them. One sees that obsession in the early 1980s when the campus community smarted at the perceived failure of the larger community to realize the school was no longer a junior college. Siegel presided over a well-publicized bonfire in which students burned signs containing the words "junior college" and asserted that Kennesaw should be called "junior" no more. By the late 1980s the college's anxieties had "matured" into a concern with local and national recognition.

Erikson saw adolescence as a time of "identity crisis" where what one has become is at odds with what society expects one to be. That was certainly true of Kennesaw in the 1980s and for many years afterwards. Kennesaw, as a commuter college, was at its best when it recognized that its clientele was the nontraditional student, but many of the faculty, educated in traditional ways, worried whether a school without residence halls or a football team could be a "real college." The faculty felt the tension of changing expectations, as service and scholarship rivaled teaching in importance, and as the sense of camaraderie across campus diminished as the college increased in size. Meanwhile, young professors, coming straight from graduate schools, fretted over the lack of time and support at a state college for the types of scholarship they were trained to produce. The college was growing up, but not fast enough for some and too fast for others.

In time for the college's twenty-fifth anniversary in 1988 the word "state" was inserted in Kennesaw College's name. The change was made to eliminate two sources of confusion. After the Board of Regents allowed two-year schools to drop "junior" from their names, Kennesaw needed a title that clearly implied senior college. It also needed a name that did not sound like a small, private school. Kennesaw State College connoted both "public" and "four-year" standing. The name remained KSC until June 12, 1996, when the Board of Regents granted university status to most of the state's senior institutions. By that time, Kennesaw was positioned to build on the gains of the early Siegel era and move far beyond its modest beginnings into a new type college that would be modern, nontraditional, learner centered, and community focused.

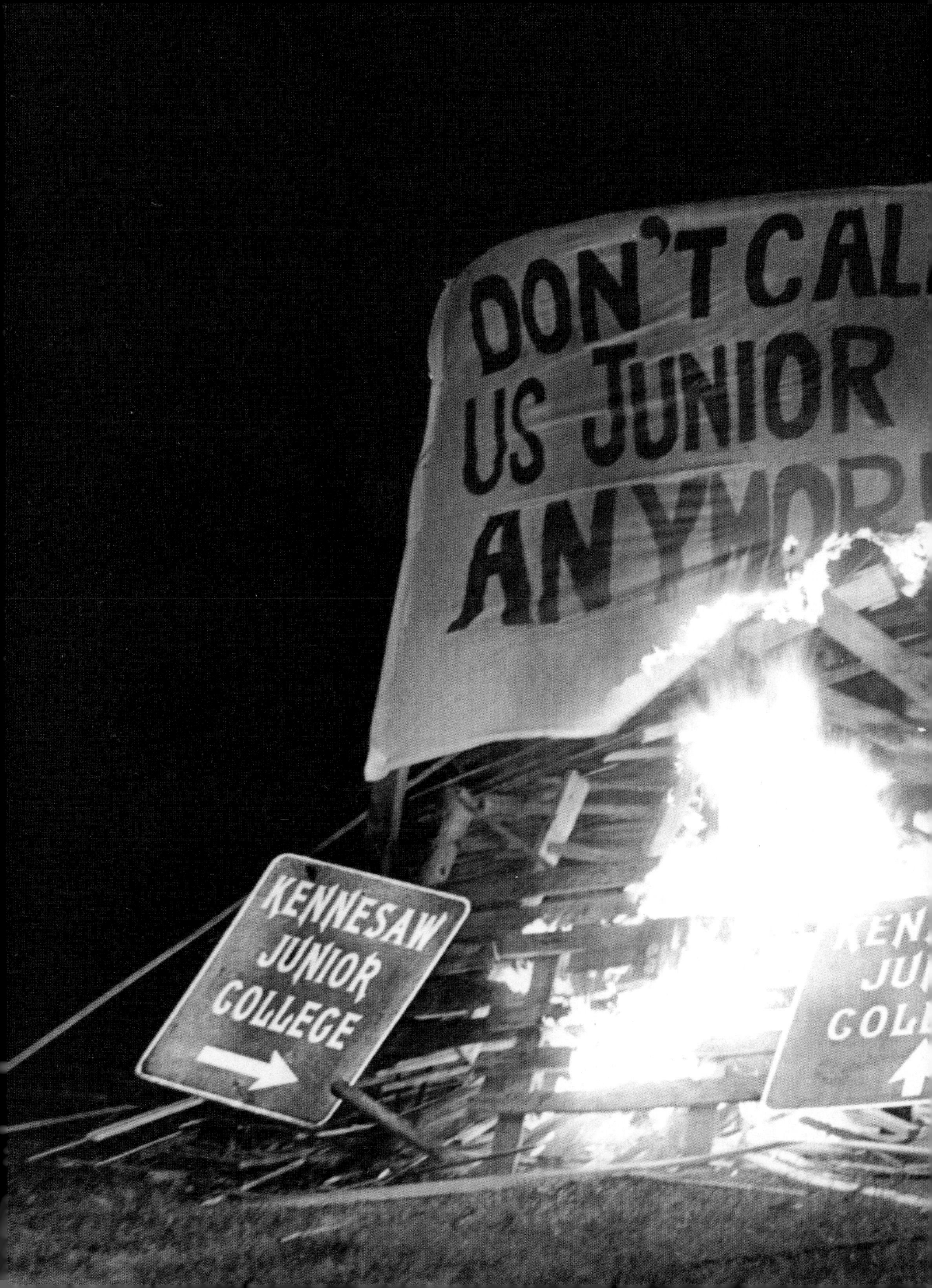
DON'T
US JUNIOR
KENNESAW
JUNIOR
COLLEGE

Kennesaw College student-led bonfire held to
eradicate all references to "junior."

Chapter 6

Transforming the Identity and Culture of a Maturing Public College

In 1985 Kennesaw College revised its mission and goals to reflect the Siegel administration's thinking that a progressive, public college should possess "an inviting campus environment" that displays a "genuine concern for all people and for their personal development." From the beginning, excellence in teaching had been central to the college's mission, and remained so, but now service was placed on an equal footing. Presentations and publications remained tertiary concerns, but KC's revised purpose statement encouraged applied research that supported teaching and service. In time, the college would live up to its mission and goals statements, becoming an institution with a proven commitment to diversity, community service, and globally and locally based scholarship. In the early days of the Siegel presidency, however, the college struggled to put its stated objectives into practice.[283]

Although they were exceptionally few in number for most of the 1980s, African American students and employees made their voices heard, as they questioned the depth of the administration's commitment to black students. Gradually, the north Atlanta suburbs and the campus became more diverse. By 1990, African Americans made up 10 percent of Cobb County's population, and by the end of the century, 19 percent. Kennesaw College was not that diverse; yet, the rise in number of black students in the 1980s and 1990s was substantial. In fall 1985, some 223 African Americans made up a little over 3 percent of the student body. Five years later (fall 1990) the numbers had increased to 424 (more than 4 percent). With the passing of another half decade (fall 1995) the number of African American students rose to 832 (almost 7 percent); and at the close of the millennium enrollment reached 1,303—just under 10 percent.[284]

Removing the Barriers to Campus Diversity

As part of its desegregation plan, the University System of Georgia issued directives in the early 1980s requiring all institutions to hire minority student recruiters to increase black enrollment. While Kennesaw College did so, it was disappointed in the results. It was apparent that African Americans would not enroll in large numbers until KC created a supportive campus culture, but that would not be easy on an overwhelmingly white campus in a county that was only 4.5 percent black at the start of the Siegel era. Without proper support groups and a "critical mass" of African American faculty, staff, and students, blacks were destined to feel uncomfortable no matter how many welcoming statements the administration issued. When KSU's current vice president for student success, Jerome Ratchford, joined the faculty in 1988 as coordinator of minority student retention, he found only 275 African American students with whom to work. In a 2011 interview, he argued that if inclusion means being welcoming and inviting, then Kennesaw deserved a low grade when he arrived, because that was not yet the case.[285]

According to a 1985 desegregation report written for the chancellor by executive assistant to the president Ed Rugg, morale among African American faculty, students, and staff reached a low point in the 1982–83 school year. Several professors and staff members resigned or requested leaves without pay as the desegregation progress seemed stalled. African American campus leaders approached President Siegel with their concerns. Rugg recalled them telling her: "You've been here two years; you've talked about inclusiveness and the importance of engaging all; and we're not seeing the connection with the minority community. We're not seeing much progress; we're not seeing much focus here. We're seeing a lot of good things happening, but we don't see this particular agenda being addressed yet. What are we going to do differently in that area? Is it really an institution that serves the broader community?"

The delegation had respect for President Siegel because they knew of her own struggles in breaking glass ceilings and her role earlier in her career in writing the first affirmative action plan for the University of Florida. So they thought her heart was in the right place. But she conceded that the criticism was warranted—that she had not yet put as much energy into diversity as she had into other things. To make amends, she asked Dr. Joseph H. (Pete) Silver in the summer of 1983 to serve as her coordinator of minority affairs—with responsibilities that went beyond those of an EEO officer.[286]

A political scientist, Pete Silver had joined the faculty in 1977 at age twenty-two, shortly after receiving his master's degree from Atlanta University. He completed his

(Opposite Page) Josephy (Pete) H. Silver Sr. with the Black Student Alliance, 1984

PhD from the same institution in 1980 with a dissertation on the use of discretion in administering bail in Fulton County, Georgia. Before putting his credibility with black colleagues on the line, he sought assurances that Siegel and her administration were sincere in their commitment to diversity. Once convinced, he threw himself into the new role of minority affairs coordinator. During the next few years, Silver had to fight for everything he achieved, yet he stayed the course, making contacts with historically black churches, the Cobb County branch of the National Organization for the Advancement of Colored People (NAACP), and other organizations. In his almost weekly speeches to community groups, he conveyed a message that everyone was welcome on campus, and that a new day was dawning at Kennesaw College.[287]

Following Silver's advice, President Siegel appointed an African American advisory board consisting of such prominent people as Rev. Robert L. Johnson, pastor of Marietta's Zion Baptist Church. Officially constituted in 1866, a year after the Civil War, Zion was arguably the most important historically black church in the county. The Marietta branch of the NAACP was founded in the mid-1950s, largely due to the leadership of Johnson's predecessor, Rev. Jesse W. Cook. For a number of years, the branch held its membership meetings at the church.[288]

Based on Silver's recommendations, President Siegel invited eighteen people to the first discussion session. Many of them had NAACP ties, including Cobb branch president Oscar Freeman, former Marietta City councilman Hugh Grogan, Deane and Jesse Bonner, James and Jerry Dodd, and Mother Annie Mae Solomon. The group also included Johnson, Marietta physician Dr. James Fisher, businessman Winston Strickland, and one of the first black managers at Lockheed, Charles Ferguson, who also served on the board of Kennestone Hospital. Over time, the advisory board expanded in size. In 1984, a year after the first meeting, President Siegel hosted a dinner for the community leaders.[289]

Along with Siegel and Silver, Ed Rugg attended the early sessions of the advisory board and found them eye-opening. The nearby City of Kennesaw had passed an infamous, unenforceable gun law in 1982, ordering heads of household, with some exceptions, to own a firearm and ammunition. An advisory board member joked about expecting to see lots of people at Kennesaw College carrying pistols. The black leaders made it clear that, up until that moment, they had never been issued an invitation to come on campus and they perceived an uncrossable bridge between their communities and the college. The gun law was merely the latest in a long history of events that made African Americans feel unwelcome in that part of the county.

One of the fortuitous results of those meetings was that Rev. Johnson went back to his church and organized what became an annual Kennesaw College Appreciation Day, where the campus community joined the Zion congregation for a church service and fellowship. On one of the appreciation days, he invited President Siegel to deliver a Sunday morning sermon, where she extended a personal invitation to visit the campus. Johnson became a staunch advocate of the college, encouraging young people in his congregation to consider Kennesaw as they made their college plans.[290] Silver, Rugg, and other campus leaders subsequently delivered Sunday morning sermons at Zion during KC Appreciation Days, helping cement the strong ties of the two communities.

In their effort to recruit black faculty members, Siegel and Rugg decided to set an example for the rest of the campus by placing talented African Americans in major advisory roles in the Administration Building. At about the same time in 1983 that Pete Silver became coordinator of minority affairs, another African American, Arthur N. Dunning, became assistant to the vice president for academic affairs (AVPAA). With the creation of masters' programs in 1985, Dunning moved into a new position as dean of graduate studies and sponsored research, and a new black colleague, Dr. Deborah S. Wallace, replaced him as assistant to the vice president.

Kennesaw was able to hold Dunning for only a few years before he moved to the Board of Regents as senior vice chancellor for human and external resources. After nine years at the board, he became the CEO of the Georgia Partnership for

Excellence in Education, a post he held for several years before working at the University of Georgia from 2000–2010 as vice president for public service and outreach. Currently, he is the vice chancellor for international programs and outreach in the University of Alabama System.[291] Despite his departure from Kennesaw, the Siegel administration continued to recruit and train promising African Americans for senior leadership positions. For example, Dr. Janice Epps was hired as director of Kennesaw's fledgling Center for Excellence in Teaching and Learning. Had black leaders, such as Dunning, Silver, and Epps, not been lured away to positions of greater responsibility elsewhere, Kennesaw's achievement in the employment of black administrators would have been even more impressive. Even so, their subsequent accomplishments are part of the college's success story in advancing diversity.[292]

TABLE 5	Percentage of African American (AA) Students and Faculty, Fall 1983–2000					
YEAR	**Students**			**Faculty**		
	AA	TOTAL	%	AA	TOTAL	%
1983	140	5,383	2.6	7	154	4.5
1984	161	5,821	2.8	13	165	7.9
1985	223	6,866	3.2	19	190	10.0
1986	242	7,296	3.3	21	195	10.8
1987	231	7,946	2.9	21	209	10.0
1988	275	8,614	3.2	23	227	10.1
1989	320	9,140	3.5	27	254	10.6
1990	424	10,030	4.2	25	266	9.4
1991	507	10,913	4.6	20	293	6.8
1992	635	11,670	5.4	29	320	9.1
1993	758	12,273	6.2	28	350	8.0
1994	802	11,915	6.7	32	360	8.9
1995	832	12,100	6.9	34	364	9.3
1996	877	12,537	7.0	31	354	8.8
1997	1,078	13,094	8.2	31	371	8.4
1998	1,121	12,861	8.7	29	370	7.8
1999	1,223	13,158	9.3	30	371	8.1
2000	1,303	13,373	9.7	27	375	7.2

Sources: Kennesaw College 1987 Fact Book; Kennesaw State College Fact Book, years 1988–1996; Kennesaw State University Fact Book, years 1997–2000.

Black community leaders advised President Siegel that increasing the number of African American faculty in the classroom was the key to convincing potential black students and their parents that Kennesaw was sincere in its desire to serve and support them. Table 5 reveals that she took their advice, as the number of black faculty tripled between 1983 and 1986 (from seven to twenty-one). By 1986, African Americans accounted for 10.8 percent of the full-time faculty (at a time when the student body was only 3.3 percent black). After the initial spurt, the percentage growth of minority faculty members slowed until the comparable figures for black students began to catch up. During the late 1980s Kennesaw's top priority seemed to be the recruitment of minority students rather than minority faculty. However, the new black faculty members of the early 1980s would play crucial roles for years to come in building a more diverse campus community.

The twenty-seven African American faculty members in 1989 included four full professors, six associates, thirteen assistants, and four instructors. By 1995, Kennesaw employed thirty-four African American professors and instructors (the high-water mark in the twentieth century), but the percentage of the total faculty had dropped to 9.3 percent. By 2000 the respective numbers were down to twenty-seven faculty members and 7 percent. Unfortunately, as the faculty expanded in the 1990s, the institution seemed temporarily to lose focus on diversity. The main cause of the declining numbers was lack of effort at recruitment, not at retention, because black professors tended to stay once they were hired. As a result, the proportion of black faculty members who had earned tenure exceeded the proportion of whites at the turn of the century (70 percent as opposed to 57 percent). Starting in the Siegel era, Kennesaw's success in building a diverse faculty and student body compared favorably with most of its peer colleges in Georgia.[293]

The Nigerian Student Controversy

With positive change underway, the last thing the campus needed was a divisive racial incident, but that is what happened in the winter and spring of 1984 when a confrontation between two black students and the campus police was played out in the press and the legal system. During the 1983–84 school year, the 154-member faculty included only 3 black men and 4 black women, and African Americans accounted for just 2.6 percent of the student body. In the fall of 1983, KC had fewer than one hundred international students. Fifteen of them were Nigerian, and two of the Nigerians were at the center of the controversy.[294]

It began with an encounter of two Nigerian students and Caucasian mathematics instructor Harriet S. Gustafson, a member of the faculty since 1967. According to Gustafson's handwritten police report, Ehia Emiantor-Akhabue and John I. Sadoh entered her Mathematics 099 classroom on January 12, 1984, around a quarter past ten in the evening, while she was staying late to help a student with a math problem.

They told her they were on her class roll, but could not attend because they were simultaneously registered for English 101.

What they said next became the basis of a serious misunderstanding. Gustafson felt threatened when they remarked that they intended to take the final exam and pass the course. Not wanting to cross them while she was alone in a nearly empty building, she offered to check to see whether one could take a final exam without attending class. The next day, she called Betty J. Youngblood, the assistant dean of the college, who promised to contact the students and arranged for the campus police to escort Gustafson to her car at night until the matter was resolved.[295]

The next week, while walking her to her vehicle, Officer Dennis McSwain spotted the two students. Afterwards, McSwain and another officer patted them down for possible concealed weapons. There were none. The students denied any intention to harm Gustafson and claimed they were near the building waiting for a ride to take them home. Later, the frisking of the students would become a matter of contention, dividing those who saw it as standard operating procedure in investigating potentially violent suspects, and those who thought the students were being harassed because they were black and foreign.[296]

In its 1983 administrative reorganization, Kennesaw created a Department of Safety and Security and appointed a director, Frederick C. Stilson, to head a small force of about six officers. Previously, the college had relied on a private guard service to provide a measure of campus protection. One of the original police officers, Theodore J. (Ted) Cochran, was a Cobb County native who had served in Vietnam, graduated from Kennesaw Junior College, and spent a decade on the Cobb County Police Force. He claimed that the college by 1983 had grown too large and too complex for the private guard service, which consisted largely of men who were "old, crippled, and half-blind." The final straw came when William E. (Bill) Durrett, the Director of Business Services, was working in his office on a Sunday, when one of the guards spotted him, and, with a shaky hand, pointed a gun in his direction. After that, Roger Hopkins, who had supervisory authority over the guards, persuaded the administration to hire properly trained officers.[297]

Fred Stilson's background was as a provost in the United States Marine Corps and a planner for the Georgia Bureau of Investigation (GBI). He, unfortunately, had no experience working for a local police force or public college. Ted Cochran, who replaced Stilson as director in the aftermath of the Nigerian student crisis, remembered the 1980s as a time when "most [police] departments wanted people who could fight, shoot, and drive fast." Little attention was devoted to whether officers were psychologically suited for the job or possessed social skills. Stilson seemed to

(Opposite Page) Theodore (Ted) J. Cochran

lack tact at a time when diplomacy would have been helpful in defining the proper role of an embryonic campus police force. The Nigerian incident would force Kennesaw to grapple with the unique problems of policing at a commuter school.[298]

Unfortunately, the January encounter in the Social Sciences Building was followed by one incident after another. On the morning of February 21, 1984, the campus police arrested the students following a public program in the gymnasium. Two officers drove Emiantor-Akhabue and Sadoh to the Cobb County Police headquarters.[299] In the process, they discovered that Emiantor-Akhabue had two Kennesaw College identification cards with differing social security numbers, an altered birth certificate, and a Georgia driver's license with a date of birth that did not match Kennesaw records.[300]

While the investigation was underway, President Siegel and her staff had not seen the police files and had only partial knowledge of the pertinent details. It is probably true, however, that, even if all the facts had been known, people of goodwill would have drawn different conclusions. The controversy occurred just two decades after the Civil Rights Act of 1964 brought an official end to segregation in Georgia, and, needless to say, Georgia society was still in the beginning stages of making right the injustices of the past. No one involved in the case was color-blind. The administration found itself with an explosive situation that threatened to undo the progress it had made in the previous year in reaching out to African Americans on campus and in Cobb County. Its reactions were shaped to some extent by that reality.

Three days after the arrests, President Siegel received a letter from the Black Student Alliance that undoubtedly expressed the viewpoint of most African Americans on campus and elsewhere. The central beliefs stated in the letter were that the incidents on February 21 were "a continued pattern of harassment" aimed at two of its members, and that "Kennesaw College security didn't handle this matter in a competent, professional manner." The students noted that President Siegel had said many times that she wanted "an open, inviting environment for all minorities." They warned that they would judge her sincerity by her response to the crisis.[301]

President Siegel moved rapidly to reverse the actions of the police officers. Even before the Black Student Alliance sent the memorandum, she ordered Chief Stilson to drop the charges against the two Nigerians. Stilson responded in a memo to executive assistant Rugg on the morning of February 24, 1984 that he had been informed by Cobb District Attorney Tom Charron that only a prosecutor could "drop" a warrant and anyone attempting to influence the dropping of charges would be guilty of compounding a crime. A few days later, however, the college administration and the attorney for the students apparently worked out an agreement in which the college agreed to drop all charges, and the students agreed not to sue the college or the police officers.[302]

If the controversy had ended at this point, it would probably have been quickly forgotten, but during the following month matters became much worse. On March 1 the Clayton County Police Department issued arrest warrants for Emiantor-Akhabue and Sadoh, alleging credit card fraud. The GBI and Atlanta-area police departments had been investigating an alleged Nigerian ring that was suspected of identity theft. Supposedly, it applied for credit cards, using the names of legitimate attorneys and physicians, but giving false addresses and phone numbers. The cards were presumably used to purchase electronic equipment and jewelry that was shipped to Nigeria and sold on the black market to earn profits that went to revolutionaries trying to overthrow the government and put the old regime back in power.[303]

We will probably never know whether the allegations against the students were true. As soon as Chief Stilson learned of the warrants, he sent a handwritten memo to Rugg, saying that he planned to arrest them later that day. Before he could act, however, Siegel and Rugg ordered him not to do so. President Siegel later explained that she was operating under advice from the Board of Regents, based on a April 22, 1970 ruling from Georgia Attorney General Arthur K. Bolton, that "the arrest powers of campus police and security personnel are limited to those instances in which offenses have been committed upon property under the jurisdiction of the Board of Regents."[304]

The campus police did not see the two Nigerian students on campus again until they were spotted on March 13 in Dr. Pete Silver's office in the Social Sciences Building, studying between final exams. Silver made sure that the students were undisturbed while they were with him. When Emiantor-Akhabue and Sadoh left campus at a quarter past five, Officers McSwain and Maloney radioed the Marietta and Cobb Police Departments and followed them onto I-75. After the students saw the police car, they sped down the interstate, reaching speeds of over ninety miles an hour. Officer David Fann of Marietta joined the chase at South Marietta Parkway. He turned on his blue lights and siren, but Emiantor-Akhabue and Sadoh kept going at a high rate of speed until they hit heavy traffic at Delk Road, allowing Fann to force them to the curb, where they were arrested.[305]

The Kennesaw College administration was extremely upset over the involvement of campus police in a high-speed chase. Through executive secretary Henry Neal, the chancellor's office made clear that it backed the president and believed that the officers should be reprimanded for "manifestly and grossly improper conduct." The Cobb County Solicitor's Office and others in the community were equally outraged that Kennesaw College police officers were prohibited from making an arrest on campus that could have prevented the high-speed chase.[306] Solicitor Herb Rivers was running for reelection and portrayed himself as a defender of law and order standing against the soft-on-crime attitudes of President Siegel and her staff.

On Friday, March 16, an angry Chief Stilson concluded that he could not work without the support of the president and her executive assistant and submitted his resignation. In his last action as chief, he went before a Cobb County magistrate judge and swore out warrants against Rugg on the misdemeanor charge of obstructing justice, and Silver on a felony charge of hindering the apprehension of persons wanted on felony charges.[307]

Stilson alleged that Silver knew about the arrest warrants, but still harbored the two suspects in his office. There was no clear evidence, however, to support his assumptions. As President Siegel said at the time,

> It is our understanding that Pete Silver did not know that there were warrants out for their arrests.... They were in his office studying for an exam between exams, and there is nothing unusual about that at all. There was absolutely no attempt to hide them.... In cases involving the arrests of people who have committed offenses outside the jurisdiction of the college, we will assist external law enforcement agencies and in emergency situations, particularly those involving violent crimes, Kennesaw College officers may make arrests as appropriate. Under other circumstances, Kennesaw College will follow its past practice of assisting other law enforcement officers who are invited to serve their warrants on campus.

According to Ed Rugg, an apologetic Cobb County sheriff Bill Hutson, who served the warrants, phoned President Siegel to say, "I know Pete. I've taken classes with him. I know this is outside the bounds of fairness and even appropriateness, but [Stilson] exercised his right as a sworn officer of the court." He recommended that Rugg and Silver turn themselves in the next morning and that the college engage a prominent Marietta lawyer. They chose one of the best, Thomas J. (Tom) Browning, a partner of future governor Roy Barnes. Browning concurred that the warrants were without foundation, but election politics got in the way of resolving the matter quickly. Ultimately, the charges against Rugg and Silver would be dropped.[308]

Now that the controversy had become public, the administration of Kennesaw College encountered more negative publicity than ever before. A common perception was that the campus was coddling criminals, and its leaders were living in a dream world where they thought they were above the law. Rugg recalled hearing from a fellow Kiwanian, "What are you doing defending these guys? These folks don't belong here." Fortunately, the *Marietta Daily Journal* took a middle ground, editorializing that the college had "a right to determine the role of the campus police" and that its only mistake was in not being more aggressive in locating the students and notifying Cobb County Police to come on campus and make an arrest.[309]

The biggest remaining problem was that Solicitor Herb Rivers decided to revisit the February 21 arrest of the Nigerian students for obstructing an officer. He repudiated the deal to drop the charges, and decided to go ahead with their prosecution. As it turned out, however, the students never came to trial in Cobb or Clayton County. Before they had their day in court, the federal government intervened and an Immigration and Naturalization Service judge signed a deportation order, giving the men until July 26, 1984 to leave the country. Thus, the Nigerian crisis came to an end.[310]

Breaking Stereotypes through Faculty and Administrative Leadership

In the long run, the campus police benefited from the events of 1984. After Stilson's departure, Ted Cochran was offered the job as chief, based on the recommendations of a number of people on campus, important courthouse officials, and veteran legislators Joe Mack Wilson and A. L. Burruss. A Kennesaw graduate and veteran Cobb County policeman, Cochran possessed a strong commitment to the college and community. Many of the problems of 1984 may have been avoided if he had been chief from the beginning. Before taking the job, he sat down with his immediate supervisor, Roger Hopkins, and reached an understanding that the department would operate independently, but listen to the concerns of the administration. In time, he won the trust of all the chief administrators and worked closely with them on delicate issues. During Cochran's long tenure, the department recorded a number of firsts for campus police forces, including the first in Georgia to be nationally accredited.[311]

In hindsight, it seems clear that the administration's handling of the crisis paid benefits down the road. If the college had not supported its arrested administrators and had not insisted that the campus police take a low-key posture, the consequences would have been disastrous for race relations, and the progress of the previous year would have been undermined. African Americans on campus generally came out of the crisis believing, perhaps for the first time, that the administration was sympathetic to their concerns.

The arrests of Rugg and Silver did not hurt their careers. After Jim Kolka stepped down in 1986, Rugg became vice president for academic affairs, a position he held for the next sixteen years. In looking back on his career, he saw Kennesaw's efforts at diversity as the initiative in which he took greatest pride. Silver relocated to the Board of Regents in 1985, first on a Regents Administrative Development Fellowship and then as assistant vice chancellor for academic affairs. In 1997, he became the chief academic officer at Savannah State, and then in 2010 the provost of Clark Atlanta University. In 2012 he was elected president of Alabama State University. Even after leaving Kennesaw College, he remained active in the Marietta community, serving for a number of years on the board of Girls Inc., the M. J.

191

and Kathryn Woods Foundation, and other civic groups. He played a vital role in the 1980s in connecting the college to the African American community, and is still remembered fondly throughout the county by those who had the privilege of working with him.[312]

Following the Nigerian incident, the Siegel administration redoubled its efforts to diversify the campus. In his 1985 report to the chancellor, *Accepting the Challenge of Desegregation*, Ed Rugg noted major improvements since 1983 in every Equal Employment Opportunity category and a major shift in campus culture from an attitude of "have to" to "want to" and from "can't do" to "can do." Noting that the number of African Americans at predominantly white schools reflected campus climate more than recruitment strategies, he affirmed Kennesaw's commitment to a climate that "is receptive, inviting, supportive."

Rather than bemoaning the allegedly small pools of qualified black applicants, KC, according to Rugg, chose to capitalize on its competitive advantages in coming up with creative ways to recruit. For example, Rugg and Dean Harry Lasher discussed how Kennesaw's location in metropolitan Atlanta, a hub for black professionals, gave the School of Business an advantage that did not exist in other parts of the

state. If black faculty members preferred not to live in Cobb County, they could find homes in Atlanta and enjoy a quick, morning commute north on I-75 while rush hour traffic backed up in the opposite direction heading downtown.

More importantly, the School of Business, under its founding dean, offered exciting opportunities for growth and development that did not exist at many other universities. Lasher and his team displayed creativity in recruiting by going through Atlanta's Gate City Bar to find two black attorneys who joined the faculty to teach business law. Through this and other innovative strategies, Lasher's school added four new African American faculty members in 1984, more than any of Kennesaw's other schools. Kenneth P. Gilliam, an economics professor with a PhD from Lehigh University, was one who began a long career at Kennesaw, including several years as Associate Dean of the Coles College for Undergraduate Programs.[313]

The African American faculty arriving in the mid-1980s quickly organized an informal Black Faculty Caucus. Among those present by 1985 were Harold L. Wingfield, Oral L. Moses, Rosa Bobia, Rodney J. Dennis, Nataline J. Matthews, Melvis E. Atkinson, Julia M. Collier [Griffith], and Diane W. Wilkerson. Wingfield took Pete Silver's place on the Political Science faculty, and Atkinson, a mathematician, was Silver's replacement as the minority affairs coordinator. A product of segregated schools in Washington, Georgia, Wingfield completed his bachelor's degree at Fisk University in Nashville and then earned a PhD in political science from the University of Oregon in 1982. He recollected:

> What's kept me here [was] a cadre of black faculty; we now call ourselves the Black Faculty Caucus. Pete was also responsible for my staying even after he left because I used to talk to him. Those of us who were here would always talk to him about problems or issues that we had.... Somehow, we coalesced together, and even now we wonder, how did this ever get started? We became a major kind of support system that we developed where we'd get together and talk and share recipes and formulas on how to deal with this problem or that problem. Many times it was always nice to know that somebody else already had these problems that you were now having.... That support, year after year after year, has now led to my being a tenured, full professor.[314]

A central part of the Black Faculty Caucus, Oral Moses, had just earned a DMA from the University of Michigan when Music Department chair Wayne Gibson called and asked him to come to Kennesaw. He also had a job offer from Penn

(Opposite Page) Harold L. Wingfield

State, but liked the fact that Kennesaw was closer to his childhood home in Olive Grove, South Carolina, where his father had once been a sharecropper. He also was attracted to the cultural opportunities of metropolitan Atlanta and the presence of an international airport, making it easy for him to continue an extensive performance schedule in America and abroad. A former Fisk Jubilee Singer with a magnificent bass voice, Moses completed a National Endowment for the Humanities (NEH) summer seminar with Eileen Jackson Southern at Harvard University during his second year at Kennesaw and began a career-long project devoted to writing about and performing the music of Harry T. Burleigh.

Reflecting in 2006 on the reasons for spending more than two decades at Kennesaw, Moses noted:

> I've met a lot of good people here at Kennesaw.... And certainly coming to Kennesaw has opened a lot of doors in a lot of different kinds of ways for me. I think about that; if I'd gone to Penn State, would I have done the NEH? And that NEH grant opened the door for all of these other recordings.... Since I've been here, it's just building and developing and developing, which is always that door—there's a door to be opened to do things. That's what's happened to me here, because I know friends of mine who are at universities like [Penn State], they are there, they are in their position and that's where they've stayed. So it's been fast-paced at Kennesaw, it's been incredibly fast-paced, but I can say that, also, has not allowed me to sit down [laughter].[315]

Moses also stayed at Kennesaw because of the music program's success in recruiting outstanding students, such as Mac Powell, a pioneer in the 1990s in contemporary Christian rock, whose Third Day band would produce more than two dozen number-one singles and win numerous Grammy and Dove awards. After he completed school, Powell asked Moses to put together a group of singers to provide the background for his CD, *Third Day Offerings: A Worship Album.* After it went to the top of the charts, he called and said, "Dr. Moses, I have something for you, I need to drop by your office." When Powell came into the Music Building, Moses recalls that "all the students in the hallway were looking at him with mouths wide open.... He came in with this big box, and he said, 'I just wanted to give this to you.' It was a gold record. The CD had sold more than 500,000 copies." He added, "Mac is still a very good friend, and I've gone down to Philips Arena to see him with about 40,000 other folks.... But he's a Kennesaw student."[316]

(Opposite Page) Mac Powell, music alumnus and lead singer of the Grammy Award-winning Christian rock band Third Day

From 1987 to 1989 Harold Wingfield, French professor Rosa Bobia, and their colleagues organized an annual Georgia Conference for Blacks in Higher Education, which brought national awards for its sessions on recruiting, promoting, and retaining African American faculty members. With no released time and with Kennesaw unable to provide much financial support, they solicited grants to cover the costs, including a $25,000 gift from AT&T. For several years, Wingfield also edited a newsletter for the National Conference of Black Political Scientists. He argued:

> Diversity at Kennesaw for a long time meant that we want a black person to come, but we want them to sound like us, and we want them to think like us. To borrow a phrase from the '60s, what they were looking for and what they seemed to almost insist upon was the "Oreo," a person who was black on the outside, but white on the inside, like the cookie. That's what we used to call that in the '60s. No matter where you were educated, you bring with you your entire culture and your history with you when you walk into the classroom.

Wingfield won Kennesaw's Philip Preston Community Leadership Award in 2003 for outstanding community engagement. Among other accomplishments, he was elected to four terms on the Polk County School Board. President Siegel maintained an open-door policy for black faculty and staff to discuss individual and campus-wide problems. Wingfield and the Black Faculty Caucus, by taking full advantage of that opportunity, played an influential role in shaping short- and long-term policy.[317]

The college's successful recruitment of black professionals was a crucial part of its effort to change the campus culture and become more diverse. The impressive accomplishments, leadership, and initiative demonstrated by Kennesaw's black professors of the 1980s broke stereotypes that historically had separated majority and minority communities. The college took pride in the distinctive ways in which it removed barriers to inclusiveness and diversity at a formative stage of its maturation.

Encouraging Research through a Boyer Model of Scholarship

While the campus was learning to embrace diversity, it struggled with another type of identity problem—defining the role of faculty research at a young college known primarily for teaching and service. By 1990, when Ernest L. Boyer published his trailblazing report, *Scholarship Reconsidered: Priorities of the Professoriate*, Kennesaw had been teaching upper-level undergraduate courses for a little more than a decade

(Opposite Page) Oral L. Moses

197

and graduate courses for five years. The expansion of academic programs helped fuel a faculty debate over the place of scholarship and creativity activity at state colleges.

At the time, the college could provide only limited support for faculty research, and was at a competitive disadvantage in seeking externally funded grants and contracts. Consequently, the path to tenure and promotion for most faculty members was through notable teaching, exemplary service, and a modest amount of scholarship. Kennesaw took pride in the quality of its teaching and the accomplishments of its graduates. Almost no one wanted Kennesaw to become a "publish or perish" institution. Indeed, some faculty members thought the term, "research," had a negative connotation and preferred the use of the broader term, "scholarship." Nonetheless, practically everyone conceded the need for more scholarly productivity and looked to the administration for help in facilitating it.

The fundamental problem for college professors everywhere was that they had been trained in graduate school to do research and produce scholarly papers for professional publication. Those who loved teaching above everything else wanted nothing more than to work in a teaching institution. But most academics enjoyed research and expected to divide their professional time between scholarship and teaching. Of course, the number of PhD holders vastly exceeded the number of jobs at research universities. Most new professors would find jobs at state colleges and universities, small liberal arts colleges, or junior colleges where the preponderance of their time would be taken up with teaching, grading, and mentoring.

Some of Kennesaw's best teachers and scholars chose employment at KSC over offers from research universities precisely because their passion was teaching and professional service. But other professors felt they had been "switched at birth" and ended up at a teaching school when they were supposed to be researchers. The latter tended to have morale problems and found the institution a poor fit for their aspirations. In addition to the problem of limited time, they confronted the reality that Kennesaw provided almost no equipment or facilities for conducting research. While travel money could be found to present papers at professional conferences, there was very little support for research at off-campus sites.

Soon after the start of the Siegel era, Kennesaw followed the recommendations of the View of the Future Committee and developed elaborate guidelines for tenure and promotion, where recommendations were made by elected department, school, and college committees, as well as by administrators. The most important requirement for advancement was evidence of notable teaching, based on student evaluations and other documentation. Each faculty member was expected to demonstrate some achievement in service and scholarship, but could choose which of the two should carry the greater weight. In the 1980s, the majority of faculty members elected service over scholarship. The choice produced angst, however, in those who saw their scholarly expertise slipping away. No matter how good they were as teachers, and no matter how valuable their service, they often felt inferior to colleagues who were more productive scholars.

A promising approach to this dilemma came from Ernest Boyer, the president of the Carnegie Foundation for the Advancement of Teaching (CFAT). In *Scholarship Reconsidered*, he called on colleges and universities "to break out of the tired old teaching versus research debate and define, in more creative ways, what it means to be a scholar." He added that it was "time to recognize the full range of faculty talent and the great diversity of functions higher education must perform."[318]

In a discussion of "Scholarship over Time," Boyer noted the irony of the post–World War II era producing on one hand a few elite, well-funded, "federal grant universities," and on the other, a proliferation of state and community colleges, stimulated by the GI Bill and the Truman Commission's report, *Higher Education for American Democracy*. While the nation developed an array of colleges with diverse missions, Boyer argued, the rewards system for professors narrowed, and the "publish or perish" model of the elite schools came increasingly to apply everywhere. This development was bad, not only for faculty, but also for students and the colleges themselves. Boyer added, "Research *per se* was not the problem. The problem was that the research mission, which was appropriate for *some* institutions, created a shadow over the entire higher learning enterprise."[319]

The CFAT president's solution was an enlarged definition of scholarship that conformed better to the mission statements of different types of colleges and what faculty members did with their time. He proposed four different types: scholarship of discovery (what most academics regard as research), scholarship of integration (drawing connections across disciplines that give meaning to isolated facts), scholarship of application (the use of knowledge to solve societal problems), and scholarship of teaching (the study of what works in the classroom).

Boyer recognized that his four types of scholarship overlapped. The scholarship of application was more than applied research, because the act of application (for example, in shaping public policy) often led to new understanding (discovery). Scholarly service, he claimed, "both applies and contributes to human knowledge." In the final analysis, he admitted, the four categories are inseparably tied together. He argued, however, that it was worthwhile to think of the various types of scholarship as a way of broadening the traditional definition of what the academy means by the term.[320]

Boyer presented a vision of the professoriate that seemed particularly relevant to state colleges such as Kennesaw, and, in fact, articulated themes that President Siegel had advocated for years. His work quickly became the "bible" for the KSC family. Faculty members already engaged in nontraditional types of scholarship — textbook writing or oral history, for example — found affirmation for what they were doing. Those who had stopped publishing in their narrow specialties and needed their creative energies recharged found encouragement in the idea that they could study what worked in their classrooms, do presentations at teaching conferences, and have it count as scholarship of teaching and learning.

Boyer was one of many academic visionaries that President Siegel invited to Kennesaw to share their expertise with the campus community. She later reflected,

> When Ernest Boyer was here on campus he said that we operate very much like a residential liberal arts college—we feel like that, but yet we are the prototype of the college of the nineties. I've never forgotten his quote. I thought that was a strong affirmation of the kind of college that we could be. So pursuant to that goal then came a whole series of endeavors….
>
> I'm proud of the people that I've brought in as advisors. When I brought in Ernest Boyer, I listened to him. I listened to Art Levine [former president of Teachers College, Columbia University]; I listened very carefully to Howard Gardner [developmental psychologist best known for the theory of multiple intelligences]. I listened very carefully to Lee Shulman [a major figure in the scholarship of teaching and learning and Boyer's successor as CFAT president] and Charlie Glassick [former president of Gettysburg College]. These are all people who were my heroes and they've taught me. George Keller taught me about strategic thinking. So I've learned from them.[321]

Part of President Siegel's goal was to "take the campus off campus" through the creation of "centers of excellence that would draw the faculty out into the community, to serve the community." As a result, Kennesaw created a number of institutes and centers, including the Office of International Programs (1988), the Family Enterprise Institute (1986), the Small Business Development Center (1984), the A. L. Burruss Institute of Public Service and Research (1988), and the Econometric Center (1990). Named in memory of a prominent Georgia legislator and KC Foundation trustee, the A. L. Burruss Institute is a good example of a campus entity that provides technical assistance and applied research to a variety of governmental and nonprofit agencies seeking solutions to practical problems. Since July 1988, it has produced numerous reports on topics such as: the quality of life, the economic impact of various policies, Georgia legal needs, and water quality of Lake Allatoona. By 2012, it had brought in about $10 million in sponsored funds.[322]

(Opposite Page) Thomas H. Keene

W. Wray Buchanan, a professor of marketing, was hired in 1984 to direct the Small Business Development Center (SBDC). Later, he would serve as director of the MBA program and interim dean between the administrations of Harry Lasher and Tim Mescon. Following Buchanan, Gary L. Selden would serve briefly as SBDC director, and then Carlotta D. Roberts. The SBDC existed to provide free one-on-one counseling to small companies seeking planning advice or diagnostic assessments of their operations. Among other things, the SBDC helped them improve their business plans, marketing strategies, and record keeping and also advised them on possible new sources of capital.

The concept of such centers began in the 1970s with Dean William C. Flewellen of the University of Georgia who wanted to do for business what the Cooperative Extension Service had long done for farmers. In 1977, the Georgia General Assembly adopted a resolution authorizing the state to support SBDCs and directing the Board of Regents to designate UGA as the coordinating agent for the various local affiliates. In 1980 President Jimmy Carter signed into law a Small Business Development Center Act. Kennesaw's SBDC received funding, in part, through a cooperative agreement with the US Small Business Administration and the University of Georgia.[323]

The Office of International Programs was established in 1988 with political scientist Royce Q. Shaw as director, and historian Thomas H. Keene as assistant director. Keene took charge in 1989 after Shaw accepted a job at another institution.

Nancy E. Zumoff

He was ably assisted from 1995 to 1997 by fellow historian Akanmu G. Adebayo, and after 1997 by Daniel J. Paracka. Since 1986 Keene had headed a major study of the baccalaureate that led to the appointment of a general education coordinator and a greatly revised core curriculum. Among other things, the study called for a greater global emphasis and, for the first time, included as part of the core introductory philosophy, geography, and economics courses. Kennesaw began teaching world history course rather than Western civilization courses in the early 1970s while it was still a junior college. However, the English Department offered little non-Western literature before the study of the baccalaureate. Kennesaw had received a grant to fund the study, and Keene was able to use some of those funds to retrain faculty members to teach non-Western material.

Much of the Office of International Programs' early work was to write Fulbright group project grants and, in general, to encourage study abroad for faculty and students. Keene received his first Fulbright as early as 1980 to study for six weeks in India. In 1986–1987, he spent a year on a faculty exchange teaching at a Chinese university. Even before the office was created, faculty members had begun "Year of" programs that celebrated a different country each year with special academic courses, public programs, and studies abroad. The first, in 1984–85, had been a Year of Japan, followed in 1985–86 by a Year of Mexico. After its founding, the international office coordinated these activities.

Faculty exchanges were greatly enhanced in 2002 when the KSU Foundation bought nine houses along Frey Lake Road (today's Campus Loop Road), across from University Place (the first campus residence halls). The house closest to the main classroom buildings became the International House, where foreign visitors stayed while teaching and studying on campus. Keene returned to the Department of History and Philosophy in the 2002–03 academic year when the international center was replaced by the Institute for Global Initiatives under the direction of fellow historian and former associate director Akanmu Adebayo. For his numerous contributions to KSU, Keene was awarded the Distinguished Service Award in 2007.[324]

While the centers increased Kennesaw's involvement in applied research and public service, a few stellar faculty members, acting largely on their own, were remarkably successful at writing and receiving major national grants. Christopher B. Schaufele and Nancy E. Zumoff were shining examples of the Boyer model of scholarship as they created a nationally recognized Earth Algebra course and textbook in the early 1990s. Schaufele earned a PhD from Florida State University in 1964, taught for a decade at Louisiana State University and the University of Georgia, earned tenure at UGA, but grew tired of campus politics and accepted a job at Kennesaw Junior College in 1974. A long-distance runner, he bought an athletic shoe store and gave up teaching for several years in the late 1970s, but he soon lost interest in the shoe business and resumed his career at Kennesaw in 1980.[325]

Christopher B. Schaufele

203

During his absence, Nancy Zumoff joined the math faculty. A native of Nebraska, Zumoff earned her doctorate in 1973 from the Courant Institute of Mathematical Sciences at New York University. After teaching her first class as a graduate student, she found her calling. A political activist, she opposed elitism in any form and particularly loved teaching people who struggled with mathematics. By 1976 she was on the faculty at the University of Georgia, where she set up the mathematics part of the Developmental Studies Program. UGA, of course, was selective in its admissions standards, and she found that most of her students were athletes or children of alumni that could not meet the regular entrance requirements. Disgusted with the university's exploitation of football players, many of whom had little chance of graduating, Zumoff jumped at an opportunity in 1978 to join the faculty at Kennesaw College just as it was beginning upper-level classes.[326]

Schaufele and Zumoff discovered they had a common interest in algebraic topology and group theory and coauthored a traditional research paper. They were subsequently thrown together on a mission that was classroom related. When Kennesaw first created academic departments in 1983, Schaufele was the founding chair of the Department of Mathematics and Computer Science. Unfortunately, he inherited a morale problem caused by administrative pressures to do something about the high dropout rate in the introductory algebra course. Nonscience majors complained that the class was unreasonably hard. President Siegel empathized with them and suggested that the mathematicians find new ways of teaching that increased student success. Most of the math professors, including Schaufele, griped that the president was asking them to water down their courses. Later, he would come to appreciate Siegel's point of view, but at the time, he resigned his chairmanship, because he disliked being caught in the middle of a raging dispute.[327]

In 1989 or 1990, with Tina Straley serving as chair and with the algebra problem still unresolved, Schaufele stood up in a department meeting and announced that the college algebra class was a nightmare—that the students hated it, the faculty hated it, and he hoped he never had to teach it again. Zumoff immediately responded that she agreed with everything he said. As a result, Straley asked the two of them to head a task force to find a solution. One of the members of the study group that gave them strong support was Marlene R. Sims who offered the "radical" suggestion that if they wanted "the students to be interested, maybe we should teach something of interest." Schaufele and Zumoff remembered that advice later in the year when they went to a meeting of the Mathematics Association of America (MAA) in North Carolina to find out what worked on other campuses.[328]

While there, they attended a session where one of Schaufele's old friends, Harvey Carruth, discussed an introductory course he had developed in which students received data about retirement funds and annuities and used computers to determine the best investments. Schaufele and Zumoff liked the idea of solving real-world problems, but thought the subject matter would bore the average nineteen-year-old student who was not thinking about retirement. As they drove home along the Blue Ridge Parkway, their discussion of the natural beauty around them turned to their concern for the environment. The conference had occurred on the twentieth anniversary of Earth Day, and somewhere during the ride they came up with the idea of a course to be called Earth Algebra.[329]

Back on campus, they gathered some environmental data on matters such as fossil fuel consumption and changes in temperatures and devised a few problems that students could solve that hopefully would generate discussions of issues such as global warming. That summer, Schaufele taught a six-week introductory algebra course. The first four weeks, he lectured and did things the way he had always done. The last two weeks, he asked Nancy to join him in trying out some of their new concepts. According to Schaufele, "The way I like to describe it is the first four weeks, the students looked like their faces were painted on the backs of their chairs. We put this material in and got the students working in groups and trying to solve problems by themselves, and the class just became really alive! It was really exciting, and it was fun again."[330]

The new approach gained the enthusiastic support of the administration. With Tina Straley's help, they applied for a grant from the National Science Foundation (NSF). At the time, Jackie L. Givens was the one-woman Office of Sponsored Programs. She took the NSF proposal, reworked it, and mailed it off to the Department of Education's Fund for the Improvement of Postsecondary Education (FIPSE). To the mathematicians' surprise, both agencies provided one-year grants to initiate the project, and then agreed to extensions for a number of years. Ultimately, Zumoff and Schaufele received about $1 million in federal grants at a time when grantsmanship hardly existed at Kennesaw outside a few centers.[331]

Before long, book publishers found out about the grants and began knocking on their door while they were still developing their materials. Eventually, they signed a contract with HarperCollins Publishers, despite, or perhaps because, the company representatives told them they had come down to see if they were insane and concluded they were just crazy. Apparently, there was nothing like *Earth Algebra: College Algebra with Applications to Environmental Issues* when it went on the market in 1992. Within a year over one hundred colleges had adopted it. Critics complained that the course did not teach enough algebra, but Schaufele and Zumoff saw the Earth Algebra course as a way to teach appreciation for math that nonscience majors might retain long after they forgot everything else. In their minds, the goal was not unlike what the fine arts do when they teach appreciation courses designed to turn out art lovers rather than artists.

During the 1990s they published three texts with environmental themes for algebra, trigonometry, and calculus. After the early editions became out of date, they

began putting new materials into modules and placing them on a website where students and teachers could access them for free. While some of their Kennesaw colleagues preferred to teach in traditional ways, others, such as Marlene Sims, enthusiastically adopted their innovative approach. Schaufele retired in 2000 and Zumoff five years later. Near the end of her career, she reflected that "when I get discouraged…I feel that Chris and I shifted a little bit some of how people look at presenting mathematics to a larger audience." In 1998 they were the recipients of Kennesaw's Distinguished Scholarship Award.[332]

In the 1980s and early 1990s a few other faculty members, operating alone or in small teams, with the support of Jackie Givens in Sponsored Research, had similar success in finding external funding and overcoming the barriers to research on the Kennesaw campus. The best early example was chemistry professor Patricia H. (Patti) Reggio who won the Distinguished Teaching Award in 1987, was the first recipient of Kennesaw's Distinguished Scholarship Award in 1997, and was the Board of Regents' Distinguished Professor for Undergraduate Research in 2000. She joined the Kennesaw faculty in 1979, not long after she completed her PhD at the University of New Orleans.

A theoretical chemist, Reggio was able to continue her research since she needed only a computer rather than a research lab. During the summer of 1980, the college awarded her a small faculty development grant that paid her travel expenses to New York to collaborate with a colleague and mentor, Harel Weinstein. He was working on hallucinogenic compounds, using computer modeling to understand their molecular structure and what made them hallucinogenic. At the end of the summer, he gave her a computer that she could use at home so they could continue their collaboration during the academic year. They published two papers together, and after that, he helped her write an application for a Research Opportunity Grant from the National Institutes of Health (NIH). At Weinstein's suggestion, her project was computational work on the cannabinoids, the compounds in marijuana. After several years of rejections and revisions, she finally received a $60,000 grant in 1985.[333]

Over the years, the grant was renewed several times, and the dollar amount grew. With the first grant, she recruited two undergraduates (Patrick K. Macy and Don H. Sams) to be her assistants. Despite the fact that her grants over the years were regular research grants that did not specifically call for undergraduate research, she always included paid students and helped them write and present their own papers. Over the next twenty years, she brought to Kennesaw about $3 million in grants from a variety of agencies and was much in demand at the NIH to serve

(Opposite Page) Patricia (Patti) H. Reggio

on grant review panels. She planned to spend her entire career at Kennesaw, but, in 2004, when her college diverted the indirect payments from her grant to other initiatives, she saw her secretarial support and equipment and supplies budget cut drastically. Consequently, she took her grants to the University of North Carolina at Greensboro (UNCG), where she was recruited as a senior research professor. Currently, she chairs the UNCG Department of Chemistry and Biochemistry.[334]

While Reggio was bringing in significant grants that combined traditional scholarship with undergraduate research, and while Schaufele and Zumoff were finding national funding for the scholarship of teaching and learning, Sarah R. Robbins started bringing in big dollars, by Kennesaw's 1990s standards, for projects that provided an integrated blend of teaching, scholarship, and service. A veteran high school teacher and administrator, Robbins completed her PhD at the University of Michigan in 1993 in English and English education, with a concentration in American studies.

She was lucky enough to receive six job offers in English education, all but one at a research university. However, she selected Kennesaw, the one school that lacked a doctoral program, primarily because it allowed her to return to her southern roots at a time when Zell Miller was governor and funding for higher education in Georgia was on the upswing. Kennesaw, she claimed, was the one place she visited where the faculty already was engaged in significant collaboration with multiple public school teachers. It also helped that she was able to renew an acquaintance with Kennesaw English professor, Jo Allen Bradham, one of her professors from years earlier when she did undergraduate work at Agnes Scott.

Robbins said later that, "I think Kennesaw has a very strong sense of its professional faculty member as having a public responsibility. I like working at a public institution; I like being accountable to the citizens for what I do." She had hardly arrived on campus before two Cobb County school administrators approached her about applying for a grant from the National Writing Project. Soon, she was one of the most prolific grant writers on campus. To her surprise, they were funded on the first try and held their first Summer Institute for teachers in 1994. Out of that effort, Robbins and her colleagues created the Kennesaw Mountain Writing Project, a local site of the National Writing Project, to continue summer institutes and provide in-service training, contract work with the schools, and similar activities.

The next year, Robbins teamed with her English colleague Dede Yow to apply to the National Endowment for the Humanities (NEH) for a summer institute at Kennesaw on "Domesticating the Secondary Canon," a study of women's literature. That was followed by a three-year NEH project in collaboration with the

(Opposite Page) Sarah R. Robbins

University of Michigan and the University of California, Berkeley, on the history of instruction in American literature titled "Making American Literature." Next, she received about a quarter million dollars in funding from the NEH and the National Writing Project for a project with school teachers on "Keeping and Creating American Communities."

In the early 1990s, Kennesaw provided minimal secretarial support, and, along with her work as English education coordinator, Robbins frequently put in as much as thirty to forty hours a week merely on clerical and bookkeeping requirements. Sarah often commiserated with Nancy Zumoff about how difficult it was to administer their grants when they had to spend so much time monitoring their budgets. According to Robbins,

> At that point, there was absolutely no support for budget management of grants. I used to spend hours and hours and hours not just filling out forms to pay for things but creating records to track the expenditures. There was no support for doing that, and Nancy was doing the same…. So finally we had some extended conversations with [B.] Earle Holley [vice president for business and finance], and they hired Shannon [A.] Kinman to work in the office of Grants and Sponsored Programs. Then after that, they hired two staff administrative accountants to work with her, and that was an absolute sea change.

Afterward, Zumoff and Robbins wrote in their annual reviews, independently of each other, that they considered the employment of the accountants in the Office of Grants and Sponsored Programs as the most significant contribution they had made at Kennesaw, because few others would have the patience to put up with the minutia that became part of their daily existence.[335]

While running workshops and teaching her classes (sometimes up to nine contact hours per week), Robbins managed to write and edit a number of books. A purpose of the Kennesaw Mountain Writing Project and the NEH summer seminars was to help public school teachers see themselves as professional writers. The "Keeping and Creating American Communities" project led to two coedited volumes of workshop-participant scholarship, *Writing America: Classroom Literacy and Public Engagement*, with Mimi Dyer in 2004; and *Writing Our Communities: Local Learning and Public Culture*, with Dave Winter in 2005.

Somehow, Robbins found time to engage in traditional scholarship as well. While at Kennesaw, she published *Managing Literacy, Mothering America: Women's Narratives on Reading and Writing in the Nineteenth Century* in 2004 and *The Cambridge Introduction to Harriet Beecher Stowe* in 2007. In 2004 she won Kennesaw's Distinguished Scholarship Award and was the first recipient of the KSU Foundation's

Distinguished Professor Award. She also received the university system's Research in Education (scholarship of teaching and learning) Award in 2002 and a Governor's Award in the Humanities in 2006.[336]

In reflecting on her professional accomplishments at Kennesaw, she observed that, "Figuring out how to synthesize the teaching and the scholarship in ways that would potentially have a public impact on other people's learning has been really important to me." She added, "I love working in the archives; I love the most traditional kind of scholarship you can do"; but she found her greatest satisfaction in "figuring out ways to connect that to daily life and real people and get other people excited about doing work that will make new knowledge—bringing undergraduates and graduate students into the process of making scholarship, helping them see themselves as scholars, helping them, literally, do the work of scholarship."[337]

Robbins played major service roles at Kennesaw, heading the development of an American Studies Program and serving as President Daniel S. Papp's faculty

executive assistant. Generous with her time, she always seemed thrilled by the accomplishments of others and was the first to offer congratulations for publications and other major achievements. Even after she left Kennesaw in 2009 for an endowed chair at Texas Christian University, she remained in contact and continued to encourage former American studies colleagues, at least by e-mail, and remained a part of the campus community. Clearly, the adoption of the Boyer model expanded the definition of legitimate research at Kennesaw. Scholars such as Robbins, Reggio, Zumoff, and Schaufele pioneered grant-supported scholarship that improved the lives of students and served community needs. Their creative "can-do" spirit overcame the lack of internal resources and helped the college develop a reputation for scholarship as well as teaching.

Masters' Programs and the Rise of Scholarship Expectations

The development of graduate programs was a major factor in the growth of scholarship on the Kennesaw campus. During her first month on the job, in September 1981, President Siegel wrote Vice Chancellor H. Dean Propst to thank him for meeting with her and for being receptive to the expansion of undergraduate and masters' degrees. She told him that the college planned "to give careful consideration this year to the possibility of graduate study—most likely in the areas of Education and Business."[338] In persuading the regents, Siegel recalled:

> I'm certain that community support was helpful to us in those days, but this became an exercise in really amassing very good data and making the arguments very compelling. The board was unresponsive at first, and I could understand why they would be. We were new. We had just been building our four-year program. They thought that for us to take on additional responsibilities of a graduate program while we were still building our upper division courses would be difficult for us. Indeed, it was. By the same token, we knew that it was very important for us to have a graduate program.... We've moved on a very fast timetable.... I would put our faculty up against any faculty anywhere as a model, because rather than foot-dragging, they simply were equal to the task of moving on into a new direction.[339]

Following the approval of the Board of Regents in June 1984, a Southern Association of Colleges and Schools (SACS) committee visited campus in November and awarded Kennesaw candidacy status for its MBA and MEd programs. The SACS committee recommended and received assurances that Kennesaw would hire more personnel, reduce the workload for the graduate faculty, and build a new academic building to handle the anticipated enrollment growth.[340]

The MBA program began in January 1985, with the MEd just a few months behind. The School of Education offered one graduate class in the spring of 1985 and a full slate of courses in the summer. The MBA and MEd were the only two graduate degrees during the 1980s, and the MBA program was by far the larger. By fall 1990, some 445 students were enrolled in graduate business courses, with all but 26 working for a degree. In contrast, the MEd program had just 64 students, although an additional 309 were taking graduate courses to gain, retain, or add on to their teacher certification. In the 1990–91 school year, seventy students earned MBA degrees, compared to eighteen MEd degrees.[341]

For the first six years of the MBA program, the business faculty occupied facilities that were barely adequate in the old Humanities Building (today's Willingham Hall) and some modular buildings behind it. Dean Harry Lasher recollected: "We were all teaching out of trailers…. They were functional, except it did get a little warm in there, or a little cold." Lasher was heavily involved in designing a new one-hundred-thousand-square-foot business building. At the time, Kennesaw's only five-story structure was the Sturgis Library. The business building would be the first five-story classroom structure. Lasher's vision was a facility that would be "number one, functional; number two, as close to a corporate-type building as possible; number three, one that was easy access for students to faculty; and [four] one that would encourage faculty to want to come to work, interact, and be there."

By design, the dean's suite was located on the second floor (the entrance level from the parking lot) to make the dean as available as possible. According to Lasher, "The first bank I worked with, Crandall Melvin was the CEO and essentially owned the bank, and he was a very successful attorney. His desk was right on the main floor of the bank. He saw every customer coming in. People who made commercial loans were all on that first floor. Early in life you get exposed to some things, and that was one that registered with me."[342]

Lasher resigned as dean in December 1990 to return to his real passion for teaching and consulting work. Later, he would be called back into administrative roles from time to time, but he always found a way back to the classroom as quickly as possible. When he announced his decision to step down, President Siegel met with Craig Aronoff, the holder of the chair of private enterprise, and gave him three choices: replace Lasher as dean, serve as interim dean, or chair the search committee to find Lasher's successor. Aronoff chose to head the search committee. Through his efforts, Kennesaw was able to recruit Timothy S. Mescon, the son of Aronoff's former boss at Georgia State, Mike Mescon. The new state-funded building opened in 1991 about the time of Tim Mescon's arrival. It was named for the late representative A. L. Burruss, who had been instrumental in the 1970s in helping Kennesaw gain four-year status.[343]

In January 1993, the Business School added an eighteen-month MBA for experienced professionals. That fall it enrolled the first graduate students in accounting. About the same time, the School of Arts and Behavioral Sciences started its first two masters' programs. In the fall of 1993, the Department of Public Administration and Human Services initiated a graduate public administration degree. Two years later the English Department enrolled the first professional writing (MAPW) students and the School of Business began an MBA for physician executives. The final graduate degree added prior to Kennesaw's conversion to university status was the master of science in nursing (MSN), authorized by the Board of Regents in May 1995 and in operation by January 1996.[344]

By design, all these programs were in applied, professional areas. The struggle that the English Department faced in winning approval for a master's program illustrates the Board of Regents' thinking in that era. The MAPW was a collaborative effort of the English and Communication Departments. Both wanted a degree that would turn out graduates certified as writers. The chair of the English Department, Bob Hill, and representatives from communication placed the term "Professional Writing" in the title to differentiate the program from a fine arts degree. But from the beginning, the MAPW was a hybrid program where the most popular concentration was creative writing, traditionally a fine arts field.[345] As Vice President Ed Rugg recalled:

> We were restricted, if you will, by the Board's decision that in this state, there weren't going to be more than four doctoral granting institutions for a long time, and that the rest of us needed to focus on high-demand programs, which often were in the professional areas. At the graduate level we were often restricted in our thinking to professionally oriented programs. A great example was the MAPW—it took three years to get that proposal approved because initially it went down as an MA in English or in literature with a concentration in writing. It just looked too much like a traditional English master's to them.[346]

The Business School's annual statements of "Key Issues/Opportunities" for the late 1980s are good examples of the focus on teaching and service and relative lack of scholarship. For the 1984–85 and 1985–86 academic years, business included among its primary objectives a "quality implementation" of the MBA, "faculty integration" into the business community, and increased emphasis on students' communication and computer skills. By 1989–90 the Business School began to

(Opposite Page) **Timothy S. Mescon**

215

articulate its perceived issues and opportunities in greater detail, while still focusing primarily on the classroom, service to "external customers" through the creation of centers, and greater leadership roles in professional organizations. Nowhere did the words "research" or "scholarship" appear, although service provided by centers would inevitably include applied research.[347]

Dean Lasher occasionally had problems with faculty members whose talents ran more toward publishing than teaching or service. He maintained that he was never antiresearch, but classroom demands at the time made it impossible for him to award much released time for scholarship. According to Lasher, "The one thing that has always bothered me…is the perceived rewards at Kennesaw for doing research-type things is to be out of the classroom; that's the reward. I don't get it. I thought the reason we were here was to work with students and expand minds."[348]

When Tim Mescon became dean in 1991, the emphasis on scholarship increased for at least some of the faculty. A major reason for the transition in thinking was the campaign in the early 1990s to gain accreditation through the Association to Advance Collegiate Schools of Business (AACSB). Prior to 1994, AACSB had been something of a closed shop, representing the research universities. Kennesaw had trouble attracting top students to its MBA for experienced professionals when schools such as Georgia State were AACSB accredited and Kennesaw was not. Fortunately, in 1994, the association developed new guidelines calling for "mission-driven standards" that moved away from a research-obsessed "one-size-fits-all" mentality and focused instead on each institution's unique mission and how its strengths and values were incorporated into its learning goals. Mescon was quick to realize that the new guidelines represented an opportunity for Kennesaw. Jerry D. Sawyer and other members of the business faculty joined with Mescon in strategic planning and in preparing a self-study that would highlight the Business School's assets. Mescon maintained that,

> Probably the most profound document…as part of this initial accreditation process…was a document around faculty performance guidelines…. It created for us really what has been a paradigm for our faculty—three workload tracks for our business school. We have teaching track, a balanced track, and a research track. That document has continued to really be the heart and soul of our strategic direction…. There's a direct proportionate relationship between the size of your MBA program and the level of research expected by AACSB. So because they had a high research expectation, there was an expectation that we really had to have a lot of productive faculty in terms of scholarship.

The chair of the Marketing and Professional Sales Department, Armen Tashchian, chaired a faculty committee to devise the original faculty performance guidelines. Under the plan, instructors on the teaching track had heavy teaching and service loads, but were not expected to produce much scholarship. Those on the balanced track taught fewer sections, but had higher scholarship expectations. Those on the research track taught about half as many sections as those on the teaching track, but had to justify their released time by being prolific authors of scholarly works. When Kennesaw moved to the semester system, the breakdown was four classes a semester for the teaching, three for the balanced, and two for the scholarship track.

The system allowed the Business School, for the first time, to recruit faculty specifically as researchers and to gain a reputation for scholarship that would not have been possible if everyone had taught the same load. It also gave faculty members the flexibility to negotiate different roles at different stages in their careers, so that one might start on the research track, but later move to a different track. By the early twenty-first century, approximately 40 percent of the business faculty was on the research track, and the business model was increasingly being copied across campus, particularly in professional areas such as nursing.[349]

Gradually, over the first fifteen years of the Siegel era (1981–1996), Kennesaw developed a clearer understanding of its true identity as it moved into what the great psychologist, Erik Erikson, described as the stage of young adulthood. The college had always prided itself on its commitment to students first. By the time it achieved university status in 1996, it had adopted the persona of an institution committed to diversity, to community service, and to a broad definition of scholarship that was both globally and locally focused. Kennesaw in the 1990s endured a series of crises that forced the college community to reevaluate what it believed and who it was. But its responses to those crises were shaped by a self-image developed through the struggles of this era, thus creating a welcoming and supportive educational environment where scholarship would be on a more equal level with teaching and service.

Chapter 7

Weathering the Storms of a Troubled Era

Between 1993 and 1998, the midpoint of the Siegel era, Kennesaw State endured one crisis after another and the largest raft of critical newspaper stories in its history. National publications that had never heard of Kennesaw State suddenly dispatched reporters to Georgia to dig up unflattering details about an upstart college that allegedly had compromised its integrity by supporting the partisan aims of a powerful Republican politician, that almost simultaneously lost accreditation for its supposedly excellent School of Education, and that was being sued by employees and students over charges of racism and anti-Semitism. Kennesaw was repeatedly bombarded by accusations that ran contrary to its reputation and self-image. The mid-1990s proved a tumultuous time when the good sense of key administrators and the institution's commitment to fairness and diversity came under question.

The crises provided vivid lessons in how viciously the game of politics is sometimes played—on and off campus—and how easily an individual or institution can be victimized by a distorted view of reality based on half-truths and preconceived notions. In hindsight, it seems obvious that some of Kennesaw's usually reliable leaders were responsible, on occasion, for alarming lapses in judgment. But it is also clear that many of the charges against the college were without merit. Over the years, President Siegel and her administrative team worked well with elected officials of both major parties and were passionately committed to equal rights. How Kennesaw endured the storms of the 1990s and emerged stronger and more united is the central story of this troubled era.

Newt Gingrich and "Renewing American Civilization"

The greatest mistakes of the Siegel era tended to hinge on personnel decisions. Arguably, the worst error in judgment was to offer Newt Gingrich a part-time contract as an unpaid adjunct professor to teach a course titled, Renewing American Civilization, that was funded in a manner that polarized the campus and the nation. Initially, the proposal seemed to be a legitimate intellectual exercise designed to challenge students to think. Dr. Gingrich claimed the class would draw on his knowledge as a trained historian and practical politician to enable students to analyze, from a conservative point of view, how America had deviated from its founding principles, and how the country could get back on track. In the words of a graduate student who helped Gingrich with background research, opposition to such noble ideas could come only from those who were "small-minded" and enemies of the academic freedom they claimed to protect.[350]

Behind the scenes, Gingrich's congressional staff and political action committee, GOPAC, were deeply involved in fundraising to transmit the course by satellite to a cadre of activists across America. Gingrich thought his lectures would give committed, young right-wingers the intellectual underpinnings they needed to persuade others that the welfare state had to go. In Gingrich's mind, academic and political objectives were not mutually exclusive; rather, they were partners in an audacious vision of citizen scholars uniting to restore the national spirit that once made America great. Of course, left-wing as well as right-wing college activists

have often blurred the lines between academics and politics. But few have been as imaginative, or as powerful, as the future Speaker of the House.

Gingrich possessed the required academic credentials to teach Renewing American Civilization. In 1971 he earned a PhD in history from Tulane University with a dissertation on "Belgian Education Policy in the Congo, 1945–1960." He joined the history faculty at West Georgia College (WGC) in 1970 and then moved in 1974 to the Geography Department, where he helped develop WGC's Environmental Studies Program. However, his passion was politics, and in 1974 he launched his first race for Congress as a Republican against veteran Democratic incumbent Jack Flynt, an old-school, former segregationist, who was so far to the right that he made Gingrich look moderate in comparison.[351]

Even though he lost in 1974, Gingrich received 49 percent of the vote and was encouraged to keep trying. His commitment to public service prevented the concentration on scholarship he needed to earn tenure at West Georgia. But that became irrelevant when he won the seat in Georgia's Sixth Congressional District in 1978. During the next fifteen years, he achieved a national reputation as an intelligent, articulate spokesperson for conservative causes, and in 1989 his Republican colleagues selected him to a top leadership position as minority whip.

Following the 1990 census, Georgia House Speaker Tom Murphy took advantage of the reapportionment process to dismantle Gingrich's Sixth Congressional District. A resident of Bremen, just twelve miles away from Gingrich's home base of Carrollton, Murphy hoped to redraw the congressional boundaries to make it difficult for Gingrich to win reelection, and, at least, to make sure he no longer represented Bremen. Murphy and his fellow Democrats at first placed Gingrich's Carrollton residence in the Third District, and then, at the last moment, moved it to the Fifth District, where civil rights icon John Lewis was firmly entrenched. They relocated the old Sixth District from west Georgia to a new, Republican-rich, suburban district that included east Cobb, south Cherokee, north Fulton, and west Gwinnett. Realizing he could not win if he stayed in Carrollton, Gingrich moved to east Cobb and narrowly won reelection in 1992, besting the popular state senator Herman Clark in the Republican primary.[352]

With his new home base, Gingrich considered Kennesaw State College the logical site for the course he wanted to teach. The School of Arts and Behavioral Sciences might have seemed a natural fit for an examination of American civilization from a historical perspective. However, there was no chance that would happen as long as George Beggs was dean. While the course was being developed, Beggs

Congressman Newt Gingrich teaching the Renewing American Civilization class

communicated his strong opposition to the president and her cabinet, comparing Gingrich to the Tar Baby and suggesting that, like Brer Rabbit, Kennesaw was about to get stuck in a mess from which it would not easily be extracted. That characterization turned out to be prophetic.[353]

The main campus advocate for the course was Dean Timothy S. Mescon of the School of Business Administration. An innovative, entrepreneurial administrator, Mescon had made great strides in building Kennesaw's business programs. He saw Renewing American Civilization as a way of gaining national publicity for Kennesaw State College and the Business School. Gingrich was still a year away from becoming Speaker of the House of Representatives, but he was already the Republicans' most vocal critic of President Clinton and Democratic policies, and was putting together the movement that produced the "Republican Revolution" of 1994. There seemed little doubt that Gingrich would help make the name of the college nationally known. The question at KSC was whether association with Gingrich would bring the institution praise or embarrassment.

It is unclear whether Gingrich or Mescon first came up with the idea to teach the class at Kennesaw, but Gingrich obviously had been thinking about it for some time. On January 25, 1993, he entered into the *Congressional Record* a long speech that began, "Mr. Speaker, I want to talk about renewing American Civilization." The address included all the major points he would develop in his Renewing American Civilization course. The first formal planning meeting with Mescon took place on March 1, 1993. At that time, they agreed they would coteach the special-topics course. The five-credit class would be offered on Saturday mornings starting fall quarter, with Gingrich lecturing for two hours and Mescon leading a seminar for the remainder of the time. Mescon volunteered to work with the House Ethics Committee and the Board of Regents to write a contract that met everyone's requirements. Since the regents had a policy against university system employees running for or holding state or federal office, Gingrich said he would be glad to teach for free "because the intellectual content is so important to our future."[354]

By March 1, Gingrich already had an outline of the topics to be covered each week. Renewing American Civilization was cross-listed as a graduate (GBA 890) and undergraduate (MGT 490) special-topics course. During fall quarter 1993, twenty-six graduate students and sixty-eight undergraduates signed up for elective credit. The management course designation (MGT 490) seemed unusual even for some professors in the Business School. For example, the Accounting Department allowed its majors to substitute Renewing American Civilization for their required upper-level liberal arts elective because it "equates to a sociology or political science course."

Dean Mescon, however, justified the MGT 490 listing on the grounds that the course focused heavily on entrepreneurial free enterprise, the spirit of invention and discovery, and W. Edwards Deming's concept of Quality.[355] Deming was the American statistician who taught Japanese business leaders of the post–World War II era how to build products of quality and precision, thus helping to turn that nation into a major economic force. Mescon and Gingrich saw free enterprise, invention, discovery, and quality as the core principles of American civilization, along with personal strength—especially "integrity, courage, hard work, persistence and discipline." In the course description, they maintained that these core principles were "indispensable to both a free market and a free society."

As the instructor of record, Mescon did all the grading in the Renewing American Civilization course. He gave undergraduates a midterm and final and weighed class contributions as 30 percent of the final grade. For graduate students, the final exam and class participation accounted for half the final grade. The other half came from a research paper due on the last day of class. Students were expected to do their readings ahead of time. For each session, they received an extensive reading list, but were required to master only one article a week from *Readings in American Civilization*, edited by Albert Hanser, Gingrich's former chair in the West Georgia History Department, and Jeffrey Eisenach, a one-time economics professor at the University of Virginia and Virginia Polytechnic Institute.[356]

The articles in the reader were written by such prominent scholars as Barbara Lawton, the president of the Deming Foundation and holder of an endowed chair at the University of Colorado; and Everett Carll Ladd, the director of the Institute for Social Inquiry at the University of Connecticut and president of the Roper Center for Public Opinion Research. At the end of the quarter, Gingrich and Mescon held an all-day Curriculum Review Conference that included breakout sessions headed by the textbook authors and other nationally known scholars. For a registration fee of one hundred dollars, the public was invited to participate in critiquing the course and helping to improve it for the next quarter. As Gingrich later told the Board of Regents when the course became controversial, the intellectual content of Renewing American Civilization compared favorably with similar classes taught in the university system. Mescon added that it was unprecedented "to have this level of cooperation and participation in reviewing and improving the substance of a college course."[357]

It is easy to understand Dean Mescon's enthusiasm when he considered what Kennesaw State might gain from offering an exciting course cotaught by a famous national statesman. One can imagine how intoxicating it was to hear from Gingrich's staff and from GOPAC the names of nationally known business leaders who supported the congressman and this initiative. The School of Business Administration, for the first time, could write to these people with a reasonable expectation that they would read the letter and make a donation to KSC. The possible benefits of such contacts must have tempted the dean to overlook the seamier side of what Gingrich was doing.

In President Siegel's cabinet meetings, Roger Hopkins and a few others raised concerns about potential adverse publicity, but the president endorsed the proposal, arguing that it was a special-topics course that had come up through the proper channels, and that to deny it would make the business faculty think she was micromanaging something that should be their prerogative. Like Mescon, she was intrigued that Gingrich wanted to help Kennesaw raise money for equipment to broadcast the class across the country. They thought it might make Kennesaw a pioneer in the use of new technology and distance learning.[358]

On July 28, 1993 President Siegel wrote to Chancellor H. Dean Propst, requesting administrative approval for the employment of Gingrich, with no compensation, as adjunct professor of management and entrepreneurship in the School of Business Administration. On August 6, Propst granted administrative approval. Soon afterward, the chancellor, started to have serious misgivings, and Vice President Rugg and President Siegel had to travel down to his office to defend the course. Just two weeks after the administrative approval, Rugg sent the Chancellor a note to emphasize that "Dr. Mescon has assured me and his colleagues that our fundamental interests in free speech and academic integrity will be protected."[359]

Propst, Siegel, and Rugg did not know at the time what Gingrich and the course coordinators were saying to potential financial supporters or to College Republican chapters, who were being encouraged to view Gingrich's lectures by satellite link on their respective campuses. Kennesaw's critical mistake was to allow the Renewing American Civilization team, with the help of GOPAC, to raise about $300,000 and deposit it in a KSC Foundation account to fund the production and broadcasting of the course. The operating budget for the fall of 1993 designated about a third of those revenues ($107,250) for program production, including uplinking to a satellite. Another $77,000 paid salaries for six months to the project director and various coordinators. Additional funds went to advertising and office expenses. The total budget through the end of fall quarter was set at $291,775.[360]

For some time, Gingrich had been displaying remarkable fundraising talent for the Republican Party in his attempt to end forty years of Democratic control of Congress. Central to that effort was the political action committee he headed, GOPAC. One of the first questions that Kennesaw should have asked about Renewing American Civilization was why Dr. Jeffrey Eisenach would resign as executive director of GOPAC (while continuing to remain on the payroll) to become project director for the Renewing American Civilization course. Mescon would later admit, "We just didn't ask any questions, or we didn't ask the right questions." The consequences were most unfortunate.[361]

On July 21, 1993, Eisenach sent out a batch of letters on KSC letterhead to potential donors around the nation. To those who had backed Gingrich's conservative causes in the past, the letters were blatantly political. For example, the

Spartanburg, South Carolina, textile magnate Roger Milliken received a "Dear Roger" letter that proclaimed, "The goal of the project is simple: To train by April 1996, 200,000+ citizens into a model for replacing the welfare state and reforming our government." Eisenach predicted that "the current system will not be with us forever—it will be replaced. The question is how quickly that will happen—i.e., how quickly it is possible to get a citizens' movement in place, ready to make the needed changes." Mescon was copied on the letters. In a CNN interview on September 3, 1993, Brian Cabell asked Mescon whether he should have notified Ed Rugg of Eisenach's ties to GOPAC. His reply was exceedingly naive for such a savvy administrator: "Probably," he responded, "I messed up, and I'm sorry about any dilemmas it's caused internally. But I think that everyone involved with this is not at all formally linked to GOPAC."[362]

Gingrich was sending out a host of letters as well. A form letter to over one thousand College Republican chapters stated: "The recent tribulations of the Clinton Administration have made all of us feel a little better about our short-term prospects. But conservatives today face a challenge larger than stopping President Clinton. We must ask ourselves what the future would be like if we were allowed to define it, and learn to explain that future to the American people in a way that captures first their imagination and then their votes." Gingrich went on to say that he was devoting the next four years to teaching the Renewing American Civilization course and that they could be part of it by satellite. The course coordinators pledged to help the various college chapters find an advisor, if necessary, to help them gain college credit at their respective institutions. Gingrich admonished the students to realize the importance of having a thorough grounding in American history if they were "to succeed in replacing the Welfare State with an Opportunity Society." Finally, he gave them a phone number at Kennesaw State that they could call to offer their help in making Renewing American Civilization available on their campus in the fall.[363]

GOPAC and Gingrich's congressional staff fed Mescon a list of possible contributors for him to contact. One memorandum from GOPAC's finance director, Pamla Prochnow, suggested that Mescon or Eisenach contact Richard Berman, the director of the Employment Policies Institute, who promised a large donation if the course included some ideas on entry-level employment that had recently been published in the *Journal of Labor Research*. According to Prochnow, Berman particularly wanted the course to explain that entry-level jobs are not always a dead end. She added that Berman's interest flowed from the fact that his clients included restaurant chains. A couple of months later, Berman sent Gingrich a $25,000 check with a note stating that "I've spoken with Jeff Eisenach (who has been very helpful) about making available to you anecdotes, stories, and general information that you can use for program material. I'm delighted that it will be part of your lecture series."

J. Larry Stevens

In a handwritten note at the bottom, he added, "Newt—Thanks again for the help on today's committee hearing."[364]

J. Larry Stevens, the president of the KSC Foundation at the time, considered his support for Renewing American Civilization the "dumbest thing" he ever did. A Price Waterhouse partner, Stevens began to suspect something was wrong when he discovered that one of his clients, Roger Milliken, "the staunchest of Republicans," had donated $10,000. For the first time he began to think, "This just smells like politics." A decade later, Stevens admitted, "I've thought about this a lot, and to some extent we were all naive. As smart as Tim is and as smart as I think I am, and as smart as we all know Betty is, we were all a bit naive because we got caught up in the notion that this is a great opportunity for KSU."[365]

Most of the KSC faculty first became aware of the course during summer quarter when Laura Ingram wrote a story for the campus newspaper, the *Sentinel*, titled, "Newt Presents Bigwigs at KSC." The article's most controversial assertion was that Gingrich would not allow liberal ideas in the classroom. He was quoted as saying that, "The whole point of this course is that [liberal ideas] failed." He described it as "a cooking course…about a philosophy and a formula for making America healthy again." Presumably, liberal ideas could be entertained during the second half of each session when Mescon conducted a seminar discussion of Gingrich's lectures and the assigned readings. But that part of the course would not be taped or broadcast around the country.[366]

Before long, a host of faculty members, primarily from the arts and sciences, began writing letters to President Siegel to express their dismay. During the break between quarters, a petition circulated and was signed by about forty professors.

One of the petition organizers, Helen Ridley, a political scientist, told the *Chronicle of Higher Education*, that "GOPAC's involvement was evident from the get-go." The head of the English Department, Bob Hill, alluded to GOPAC in a letter to the president and concluded, "I'm past saying it's embarrassing. It's just wrong."

On the other hand, an equal number of faculty members, mainly from the School of Business, signed a counterpetition supporting the course in the name of academic freedom. A series of e-mails from Dorothy E. Brawley, an associate professor of management and entrepreneurship, reflected their opinion. One to Gingrich thanked him for a lecture on entrepreneurship and free enterprise, which she described as "just the right mix of non-partisan integrity, humor, seriousness, sense of urgency and personal accountability to empower change." Another e-mail to President Siegel thanked her for "supporting our judgement, freedom of speech, and academic freedom through all of the conflict surrounding the course." Many people who heard Gingrich's Saturday morning lectures agreed with Brawley that they were interesting and provocative and gave students an opportunity to discuss important issues with a dynamic political leader.[367]

Some of the money deposited in the KSC Foundation account was used to advertise the course in publications such as the *Chronicle of Higher Education*. An ad placed in the July 28, 1993, issue announced that one could view the lectures live via satellite for an enrollment fee of $24.99, or one could purchase the entire video series for $119.95. Interested parties were encouraged to call 1-800-ToRenew and to have their Visa or MasterCard ready. By early September

Christina F. Jeffrey

some 132 sites around the nation had plans to broadcast Gingrich's lectures, including such well-known institutions as Michigan, Vanderbilt, Wisconsin, Auburn, Clemson, the Hoover Institute at Stanford, and the University of California, Berkeley. At Clemson and several other schools, a local professor played the role that Tim Mescon played at KSC, leading a seminar on what Gingrich said, grading the students' work, and awarding college credit.[368]

For the satellite broadcasts, Christina F. Jeffrey, an associate professor of political science and public administration, acted as site host from the KSC library where the satellite feed was located. Her job was to lead an hour-long discussion on Gingrich's lectures for the people taking the course for credit in the Continuing Education Division. She did that by herself only once. Soon after the first class, she made a suggestion to Gingrich that it would be nice if he popped in sometime. Rather than making one cameo appearance, he decided to attend on a regular basis. After Jeffrey talked for about five minutes, Gingrich would take over for the rest of the hour, lecturing and answering questions, much to the delight of the satellite audience.[369]

The problem for the KSC Foundation was its status under section 501(c)(3) of the Internal Revenue Code. It was legally entitled to accept charitable contributions, and donors were allowed to deduct those gifts when they itemized their income taxes. While the foundation existed to support legitimate functions of the college, it was prohibited from spending money for partisan, political causes. If Gingrich's motive was to train a cadre of grassroots organizers for his conservative revolution, then the foundation could be accused of violating its 501(c)(3) IRS authorization. Responding to a public outcry, primarily from Democrats, the Internal Revenue Service launched an investigation.

At about the same time, the Board of Regents decided to close a loophole in its policy prohibiting employees from holding federal or state elected office. On October 13, 1993, it amended the old policy with the added prepositional phrase, "with or without compensation." Gingrich denounced the change as censorship, but Chancellor Propst argued that "we have to be very careful to separate the institutions from the political realm. We're not always successful. But I think we have to make a conscientious effort. That's the motivation." Consequently, Gingrich moved the course for winter quarter to nearby Reinhardt College, a private school, where Jeff Eisenach's Progress and Freedom Foundation financed and handled off-campus distribution. Reinhardt allowed its good name to be used, but assumed no fundraising responsibility for the class.[370]

Renewing American Civilization lasted only a few more quarters. By then, Gingrich was fully occupied with the duties of Speaker and an ethics investigation in Congress. On October 4, 1994, during a heated campaign season, Gingrich's aides filed a report with the House Ethics Committee that accurately, if incompletely, described the soon-to-be Speaker's role in developing Renewing American

Civilization. When the committee asked for more information about GOPAC's involvement, Gingrich's attorneys filed two responses, dated December 8, 1994, and March 27, 1995. Both came while Gingrich was devoting his attention to pushing through Congress a conservative "Contract with America" that was at the heart of the Republican revolution.

Unfortunately for Gingrich, he did not read carefully his lawyers' briefs before he signed them. Those attorneys served him poorly, as the contents were inaccurate and in conflict with the attachments. For example, one of the briefs said that GOPAC had no connection to the course, but the attachments mentioned GOPAC numerous times. In December 1995 the Ethics Committee cleared Gingrich of all charges regarding the course itself, but continued to investigate the lawyers' conflicting statements. Eventually, Gingrich admitted that he had unintentionally filed erroneous reports, accepted a reprimand, and paid the committee $300,000 to cover the costs of the investigation.[371]

The KSU Foundation remained under scrutiny by the Internal Revenue Service until February 2, 1999, after Gingrich had left office. During the investigation, the foundation paid the legal firm of King & Spalding close to $400,000 to protect its interests. With a dark cloud hovering above, the foundation had difficulty persuading benefactors to make large donations and had to postpone plans for a concert hall on the Kennesaw State campus. Eventually, it signed an agreement that, according to foundation trustee Larry Stevens, stated, in essence, "You're not going to do anything like this anymore, and you'll put controls in place to ensure that the foundation is not a rubber stamp of the administration." Stevens recalled,

> So we signed the agreement and commenced to put the appropriate controls in place. Ron [Ronald H.] Francis [was foundation chairman while] all this happened, and I never will forget, I went to Washington, and I think I was with one of these Chamber of Commerce Washington fly-ins that we used to do. I saw Newt. Newt said, "Larry, how's it going at Kennesaw with the IRS?" I said, "Newt, we've hired King & Spalding to help us through this." Newt Gingrich looked at me, and he said, "That's terrific. That's a great law firm. I'll raise the money to help you pay for it." My head was like a wedge because I was hitting my forehead saying, "Newt, you don't get it! We don't need you to raise this money! This is a foundation issue. We'll pay the bill. We don't need any more political money."[372]

The IRS investigation forced the foundation to take seriously its responsibilities as a 501(c)(3) organization. Meanwhile, President Siegel, KSU Foundation CEO James A. Fleming, Larry Stevens, and other trustees were transforming the foundation in another significant way. In the early years, the trustees had practically all come from Cobb County and contained a preponderance of "Old Mariettans" (OMs). While these individuals had served admirably, their vision of what a foundation could do was somewhat limited. So Kennesaw began reaching out to greater Atlanta and recruiting individuals such as Michael Coles, Tommy Holder, and Norman Radow—business leaders who would embark in the next decade on a land acquisition and building campaign that brought dramatic and permanent changes to the face of the university.

Gingrich's election as Speaker had one more negative consequence for the Kennesaw community. Shortly after his 1994 victory, Gingrich fired the historian for the House of Representatives and asked KSC faculty member Christina Jeffrey to assume the post. The main function of the office was to work with the Cable-Satellite Public Affairs Network (C-SPAN) covering House activities and to produce programs about Congress and its history. Unfortunately, the Democrats accused Gingrich of politicizing the position and took out their wrath on Jeffrey. She became an easy target when an official in the Clinton administration apparently leaked a supposedly confidential grant review she prepared for the US Department of Education in 1986.

The grant proposal was for a Holocaust course that, among other things, compared the Nazis in Germany to the Ku Klux Klan in America. One of the questions on the evaluation form was whether the course was balanced. Jeffrey, rather awkwardly, responded that it was not balanced because it made no attempt to explain Nazism or the ideology of the Klan. Jeffrey later admitted that she could have been more careful in her use of language, but her intent was clear, when read in context. She had attempted to argue that no one could grasp what happened in Germany without understanding the Nazis or what happened in the South without knowing what produced the KKK. No one acquainted with Jeffrey believed that she harbored Nazi or Klan views. She, in fact, said some good things about the proposed course and was happy to learn her remarks proved useful to the grant applicant. Nonetheless, Gingrich's enemies took a few sentences out of context to denounce her as a right-wing nut and the Speaker as a dangerous man.

Months later, Congressman John Lewis would apologize to Jeffrey for his harsh words. Ultimately, she gained endorsements from Jewish leaders such as Abraham H. Foxman, director of the Anti-Defamation League of B'nai B'rith, who stood with her at a news conference to denounce accusations of anti-Semitism leveled against her. Jeffrey had to fight her battles alone, however, as Gingrich and his staff disassociated themselves from her as quickly as they could. The Speaker's press secretary, Tony Blankley, advocated her firing and issued a press release indicating she had been fired about three hours before Gingrich even asked for her resignation. When he finally called Jeffrey, Gingrich told her he could not afford the political capital it would take to plead her case. He said he needed to concentrate all his energy on the ethics complaint against him and the battle to enact the "Contract with America."[373]

Jeffrey was forced out without a hearing. At the cost of a damaged professional reputation and some $40,000 in moving expenses, she packed to return to Georgia. Fortunately, Kennesaw State had granted her a leave of absence and reemployed her after her sudden, unexpected return to her scholarly responsibilities. Ten months later, Gingrich offered a partial apology, writing that she was "treated shabbily" by the national press and his political opponents. After she criticized this "lame statement," he met with her in December 1995 and told reporters that his decision to fire her was "totally inappropriate" and motivated not by evidence but by the "media frenzy." Noting her "tremendous courage," the Speaker said that Jeffrey deserved "vindication." She got it when the Associated Press issued a memo to all reporters that if her name was mentioned in connection with Gingrich, the fact that she had been exonerated by all concerned had to be noted.[374]

The NCATE Accreditation Crisis and Strengthened Teacher Education

At the time that the Gingrich controversy was engulfing the Business School, the School of Education received embarrassing news that its application for reaccreditation had been denied by the National Council for the Accreditation of Teacher Education (NCATE). After a reaccreditation committee visit, the school had come up short on a majority of the NCATE standards and was temporarily removed from membership. During the 1992–93 school year Kennesaw had awarded 214 degrees to students in the Education Program (42 masters' and 172 bachelors' degrees), more than double the number of just five years earlier. The program was obviously popular with students. Year after year, the pass-rates for Kennesaw graduates on the Georgia Teacher Certification Test were well over 90 percent.[375] Principals and superintendents in the neighboring school systems repeatedly asserted that KSC graduates were well prepared to teach. So, most people assumed that the School of Education was doing well and perhaps had not taken the reaccreditation process as seriously as it should have. There is no doubt that the self-study report failed to make a compelling case for compliance and did not adequately emphasize the school's many strengths.[376]

Nonetheless, the school had serious problems, which the NCATE review helped to reveal. Some of the faculty saw the self-study as a whitewash, and visited with search committee members at their hotel after hours to express their unhappiness. Notably, the program had become exceedingly traditional, moving away from a collaborative model between the School of Education and faculty in the content disciplines that once had been its strength. As the education faculty grew in size, it tended to hire teaching discipline specialists so that programs such as Secondary English Education could be served by faculty in the School of Education rather than the English Department. This insular approach meant that faculty across campus had less input and held less stake in teacher education. Also, because Kennesaw was perennially underfunded by the regents, it seemed that too many professors were handling responsibilities outside their main teaching area, supervising student teachers in math education, for instance, when their academic specialization was something else.[377]

Fortunately, the Board of Regents and the Georgia Professional Standards Commission gave KSC a year to put its house in order. The response was immediate, beginning with the resignation and reassignment of Dean John A. Beineke to a full-time teaching role in social science education.[378] Vice President Rugg then asked his associate vice president for academic affairs to assume the position of dean of education. The interim dean, Dr. Deborah S. Wallace, had come to Kennesaw some eight years earlier on a Regents Administrative Development Fellowship. At a time when the university system suffered from a lack of African American administrators (outside the historically black colleges) the Regents had established the Fellows Program to prepare promising young professors for administration. Formerly a special education professor at Georgia State, Wallace spent the 1984–85 academic year under the mentorship of President Siegel. Afterwards, she became an assistant vice president for academic affairs and later also dean of graduate studies, before assuming leadership of the School of Education.[379]

In December 1993, just after the conclusion of fall quarter, Wallace and Vice President Rugg gathered together all full-time faculty members involved in the teacher education programs (some seventy professors from ten academic departments) for a four-day retreat, beginning on a Saturday, to start planning how to regain

Deborah S. Wallace

232

accreditation. They initiated a collaborative model like the one that had worked in the past. Taking an NCATE term, they formally established Kennesaw State's Professional Teacher Education Unit (PTEU) consisting of a team of campus-wide faculty members involved in teacher education from both pedagogical and content areas. They also formed the Teacher Education Council that became the curriculum committee for the PTEU. Finally, they housed the secondary education programs for English, social sciences, and math in the respective arts and science departments, rather than the School of Education. The various program coordinators served on the Teacher Education Council and the PTEU, thereby establishing a link to the dean of education for NCATE purposes.

The organizational switch meant major new responsibilities for key professionals in the various disciplines. For example, Sarah Robbins had been hired by the English Department in the spring of 1993 to play a support role in the English Education Program. She arrived for fall quarter about the time the NCATE decision plunged the campus into crisis. With the placement of English education in the English Department, she found herself in charge of that program. Her dean and department chair were also required to take on a greater supervisory role. From this time on, the deans and chairs in the content areas were responsible for the recruitment of secondary education faculty with expertise in both the academic disciplines and teacher education.[380]

Dean Wallace had no time to establish rapport with her PTEU colleagues before telling them that they had to rewrite every syllabus and spend an inordinate amount of time in committee meetings. Over the next nine months they reconstructed the curriculum, added multicultural courses, increased the emphasis on technology, and, in general, met all of NCATE's demands. Beverly Mitchell, the acting head of the Department of Health, Physical Education, and Recreation, and later an associate dean, remembered that "we worked many, many hours, and every day way past quitting time and on holidays. But we came back stronger, and it was evident."

During the summer of 1994, Wallace invited five professionals from around the country to conduct a mock NCATE review. Within a month's time, Kennesaw made all the changes that the mock evaluators recommended and submitted the new self-study to NCATE. In November the NCATE review team announced that the PTEU had met all eighteen standards for reaccreditation and gave Kennesaw a special commendation for its college-wide collaborative effort. In April 1995 NCATE sent Dean Wallace and President Siegel the official notification that the Teacher Education Program was approved for reaccreditation. Rugg recalled that, "Deborah and her team and all of us did three years of work in one year." In the opinion of everyone, the reestablishment of a college-wide collaborative commitment was the main outcome of the reaccreditation process and a strength of the Teacher Education Program ever since.[381]

Claims of Race Discrimination and Allegations
of Anti-Semitism in the Kaspers Case

At about the same time as the Gingrich and NCATE battles, Kennesaw State University went repeatedly to court over matters with civil rights overtones. A serious question of racism emerged in 1993 when two black female athletes, DeWayna Jacobs and Wanda Coleman, filed a complaint with the US Department of Housing and Urban Development against Kennesaw State and College Quarters Associates, a private apartment complex just north of campus that catered to Kennesaw students. At the time, Jacobs was a center on the basketball team. A commuter school, Kennesaw leased fourteen of College Quarters's seventy-six units, primarily to house scholarship athletes.

According to the complaint, the rental application allowed tenants to indicate whether there were any types of people with whom they preferred not to live. Allegedly, the housing manager accommodated those who did not want to live with blacks. The two student athletes complained they were forced to move suddenly to a predominantly black section to make room for a white coach. By the time the matter was settled, the two women had graduated. On October 24, 1996, KSU and College Quarters, without admitting guilt, signed a consent decree to pay $25,000 to each of the former students and to report to the Atlanta United States Attorney's Office the racial composition of the residents and any tenant transfers. KSU, of course, had a long-standing policy not to discriminate on the basis of race and had made progress over the last decade in attracting black students, faculty, and staff. It had no direct control over the actions of College Quarters, but was entangled in the suit nonetheless. The ultimate solution to the problem came a few years later when the KSU Foundation purchased the apartment complex as part of the conversion to a residential campus.[382]

Despite the embarrassment of the College Quarters case, Kennesaw could at least make a plausible argument that it was not directly responsible. Unfortunately, the plaintiffs in another case in federal court pointed directly at administrative actions that they interpreted as anti-Semitic. In the end of a long legal process, a federal jury found KSU and the Board of Regents guilty of retaliating against a former Communication Department chair, Candace B. Kaspers, and awarded her $275,000 in compensatory damages. To avoid the risk that Judge William C. O'Kelley might order Kennesaw to reemploy Kaspers, the State's attorneys negotiated a compromised final settlement of $750,000 that covered the jury award, Kaspers's attorney fees, and all other expenses, but included a stipulation that she relinquish her claims to reinstatement.[383]

While Kennesaw continued to deny the validity of Kaspers's claims, it found itself with a massive public relations problem. Most of the newspaper coverage outside Cobb County downplayed the fact that the court dismissed seven of Kaspers's eight allegations before the case came to trial and ruled only on the narrow ground of retaliation rather than the larger charges of anti-Semitism. The headline in the *Atlanta Journal-Constitution* read, "Kennesaw University Loses Bias Suit: Ex-Department Chair Had Questioned Dismissal of Jewish Faculty Members." The story by Charles Walston began by claiming that Kaspers had been fired one day after she raised concerns about anti-Semitism on campus. Kaspers was quoted as saying, "I was shocked to be asked to resign within 24 hours of raising an objection."[384]

Coverage in the *New York Times* was similar. The story by Kevin Sack, titled, "Teacher Demoted Over Dismissal of Others Is Awarded $275,000," again left the impression that Kaspers was "demoted" because she questioned the "dismissals" of her only two Jewish faculty members. The story made no mention of the fact that Kennesaw offered Kaspers her full administrative salary and faculty rank. Nor did it explain that the "dismissed" faculty members continued to teach for eight months after Kaspers lost her chairmanship. In fact, they taught until their temporary employment contracts ended after which their lines were filled with permanent, tenure-track faculty members. Instead, the distorted story recapped the Gingrich affair and left the impression that Kennesaw State University in suburban Cobb County had suspiciously close ties to right-wing extremists.[385]

The relationship between Candace Kaspers and Kennesaw State, in fact, was nuanced and complicated, revolving as much around personalities as principles. She was originally hired as a tenure-track faculty member and chairperson of a new Department of Communication in 1991, while George Beggs was still dean. At the time, the department had only six faculty members, but was second to psychology in the number of majors (353 in fall 1991) of the nine departments in the School of Arts, Humanities, and Social Sciences.[386]

Kaspers and Beggs got along beautifully and he consistently gave her outstanding annual evaluations. Not least among her strengths was her ability to forge valuable contacts in the worlds of journalism and business. The department chairs in her school asked her to represent them on the college senate for the 1994–95 academic year, and when Beggs retired in June 1994, Kaspers headed the search committee for his replacement. The committee's unanimous choice was Dr. Lois E. Muir, a developmental psychologist. Vice President Ed Rugg would later testify that he had doubts about Muir's lack of experience in an academic supervisory role. Nonetheless, Kaspers was adamant that Muir be appointed. President Siegel was also enthusiastic about the choice. Deborah Wallace was the only woman who had ever served as an academic dean, and she was still in an interim role as dean of the School of Education. So, as a result of a national search, Muir became the first permanent female dean of one of the four schools.[387]

Muir replaced Beggs in July 1994 and almost immediately had problems with the assistant to the dean, Karen M. Thomson, and at least three of the nine department chairs (Kaspers, Willoughby G. Jarrell in political science, and M. Louise Bill in public administration and human services).[388] Muir arrived at a particularly bad time for the college. The NCATE controversy was one of several factors that had a devastating effect on the size of the student body. For only the second time in Kennesaw's history, fall quarter enrollment (1994) dropped from what it had been the previous year, with negative and unexpected consequences for the college budget. Consequently, vice president for academic affairs Ed Rugg asked the department chairs to increase class sizes, eliminate about one hundred sections, and cut back on part-time faculty expenses. The chairs had only two weeks to handle a difficult and distasteful task, and they were not in a good mood at the start of the new school year.[389]

Some faculty in the School of Arts, Humanities, and Social Sciences blamed Muir for not protecting their interests. The situation would have been difficult for an experienced dean and perhaps overwhelming for a novice. Muir would last only two years at Kennesaw. By the spring of 1995 she was having difficulties with practically all nine of the chairs in her school. Eventually, Rugg and Siegel lost confidence in her leadership and reassigned her to be dean of the Graduate Studies Program, where she would have no departments to supervise until her 1995–96 contract ended.[390]

By the time Muir reached Kennesaw, the administration had already decided to convert nine temporary lines in the School of Arts, Humanities, and Social Sciences to permanent tenure-track faculty positions. As it turned out, a number of the temporary full-time people were Jews, including the only two Jewish members of the Communication Department. Since the institution did not ask employees about their religious preferences, the administration had never considered the impact of its reorganization on Jews until Kaspers brought it to their attention. Nothing in the court documents indicated that Siegel or Rugg had ever said or done anything that could remotely be construed as anti-Semitic. Rather, they had expressed many times over the year their strong support for religious, ethnic, and gender diversity.

One of the Jewish faculty members was Alan Schwartz, a professor emeritus from the City University of New York and former director of special projects for Turner Publishing in Atlanta. He was temporarily filling a slot in organizational communication while a national search was conducted for a permanent, tenure-track assistant professor. Although Schwartz did not apply for the permanent position, he seemed to think that Kennesaw planned to keep him in some other capacity. Kaspers may have believed she could work out something to renew his one-year contract, as she had done in the past with the other temporary person, Bari Levingston.[391]

In the meantime, the relationship between Muir and her department chairs went steadily downhill. In an August 11, chairs meeting, Muir asked for anyone to

236

speak up who had a problem with her leadership, but no one did. A month later, on September 22, Kaspers became the first chair to confront Muir directly. Apparently upset over the reduction in sections and part-time positions, she became openly combative in a chairs' meeting, accusing the dean of not standing up for her school. That same day, Muir met with Rugg and first broached the possibility of removing Kaspers as chair. Rugg urged her to try to reconcile their differences.[392]

Matters came to a head on October 27, when Muir called a meeting of the Communication Department, inviting everyone who had a tenure-track position, but excluding the two temporary faculty members, Bari Levingston and Alan Schwartz. Levingston had been teaching on one-year contracts since 1989, was generally regarded as a good teacher, but lacked a PhD, and was unlikely ever to be selected in a national search for a permanent position. Muir used the occasion to announce that both temporary positions would be eliminated, but the department would receive one new tenure-track line in addition to filling the open post in Organizational Communication. She asked department members to express their preferences for the specialty focus of the new position, and after a lengthy discussion, they indicated a strong desire for someone with a PhD in print journalism.[393]

Kaspers would later tell reporters and the US Equal Employment Opportunity Commission (EEOC) that she did not know about the plans to eliminate the two temporary instructor positions prior to the October 27, meeting.[394] She met with Muir on October 31, in an explosive confrontation that apparently exhausted all possibility that the two could work together. At that time, Kaspers first argued that the reorganization would eliminate the Jewish members of the department and expose Kennesaw to potential legal action. She reminded Muir that both Levingston and Schwartz had raised concerns before about religious insensitivity on the campus. Kaspers alleged that Kennesaw had not adequately addressed the concerns of religious minorities and argued that the terminations of Schwartz and Levingston would add to the sense that the campus was hostile to Jews. Muir's counterargument was that the permanent positions gave the department a chance to employ underrepresented minorities and women in tenure-track, rather than temporary, positions.[395]

Following the encounter, Muir met with the president and vice president, but apparently failed to mention Kaspers's charges of religious insensitivity. Still in the dark about the issue that would bring Kennesaw national notoriety, Siegel and Rugg suggested that Muir make one more attempt to resolve the issue harmoniously, possibly suggesting a voluntary resignation with some perks to make the transition to a teaching role more palatable. Muir spent the rest of the evening composing a removal letter, to be issued if necessary, based on Kaspers's alleged "unwillingness to work cooperatively." The next day, when Kaspers refused to resign, Muir handed her the letter.[396]

Kaspers was not interested in staying on the payroll as a full-time teacher, even at a department chair's salary. Instead, she and her husband William, a lawyer, proposed a contract buyout at a little more than two years' salary plus benefits and a campus office for at least one more year. Siegel and Rugg turned down the offer, but if they had anticipated the steep price Kennesaw was about to pay in reputation and legal expense, they may have negotiated a deal and moved on to other pressing priorities.[397]

While Kaspers won her case on the relatively narrow ground of retaliation, four Jewish faculty members in the School of the Arts, Humanities, and Social Sciences were not so fortunate. Their positions had all been eliminated in the upgrading of temporary lines to tenure-track assistant professorships. Nonetheless, when they sued in federal court on grounds of religious discrimination in employment, they all lost. For example, in the case of *Alan Schwartz v. Kennesaw State College*, US magistrate judge John R. Strother Jr. ruled on July 23, 1997, that the facts of the case failed to rebut Kennesaw's reasons for not renewing Schwartz's temporary

contract. Schwartz's failure to apply for either of the permanent communication jobs was a key factor against him. Two months later, William C. O'Kelley, the same senior judge who presided over the Kaspers trial, concurred with Judge Strother and dismissed all of Schwartz's claims.[398]

There is no doubt that Kennesaw's leadership had taken strong stances against racial and religious bigotry on a number of occasions. Several months before Kaspers's removal, when someone posted a racist, neo-Nazi symbol on political scientist Harold Wingfield's office door, Rugg denounced the action as "reprehensible, uncivil, and inhumane" and reported the incident to campus police, the Georgia Bureau of Investigation, and the FBI. President Siegel followed with an open letter to the campus community stating that such acts were repugnant, appalling, and "will not be condoned" at KSC.

Following the distribution of anti-Semitic tracts on campus, Siegel issued another open letter on July 7, 1994, that referred to a "troubling national trend toward anti-Semitism" and called on the campus to rally together to affirm every individual, honor diversity, and combat prejudice. After Kaspers raised concerns in her EEOC complaint about the underrepresentation of Jews on the faculty and staff and in the student body, Siegel called a meeting in the Jolley Lodge of any Jewish personnel who wanted to express their views. At the gathering, several people raised questions about commencement services being scheduled for Friday evenings or Saturday mornings during the Sabbath. In response, President Siegel changed the schedule as soon as she could to hold the ceremonies either on Saturday evenings or during the week.[399]

Siegel, Rugg, and others in the president's cabinet had devoted their careers to battling against racism, sexism, and religious bigotry. So the charges and the jury verdict in the Kaspers case were extremely hurtful and embarrassing. Yet, President Siegel showed remarkable resilience through the crises of the 1990s. In a September 24, 1993, interview, while the Gingrich and NCATE crises were brewing, the president said: "I'm really in a fantastically regenerative mood. I mentioned to the faculty the other day, I'm bloodied but not bowed. I'm really not. Someone was asking me the other day, have I lost sleep? No, I really have not. Now, I've been working long days, long hours and all that, but I really haven't lost sleep about this. It kills me that we have been perceived in the press in a negative way. Can you imagine what it does for us as a college?"[400]

The following month she elaborated on her comment about not losing sleep by explaining, "You have to be an optimist." Placing "optimist" at the top of her list

(Opposite Page) Flora B. Devine

239

of essential attributes, she ran through several more, claiming that one should be a populist ("you really have to be of the people, understand the people"), ethicist ("you have to believe that what you're doing is the right thing to do"), essentialist ("you really need to concentrate on what is important"), and humorist ("don't take yourself so seriously; this, too, will pass").[401] While the Gingrich, NCATE, and Kaspers affairs occupied everyone's attention, the Siegel administration redoubled its efforts at being an inviting college of the future. One of the important steps in doing so was to revisit the old View of the Future and update it for a new generation.

A New View of the Future

Two years in the making, the New View of the Future was completed in May 1995. The three principal authors all served prestigious fellowships in the president's office where they were mentored by Betty Siegel. The lead author, Flora Devine, had an American Council on Education (ACE) Fellowship. Just beginning a long career at Kennesaw, Devine would become the university attorney and special assistant to the president for legal affairs. She was joined by Nancy King and Curtis D. (Kurt) Daw. King was already an associate dean and director of CAPS when she was awarded an American Association of State Colleges and Universities (AASCU) Fellowship. Since she had family responsibilities, she was allowed to complete it on her home campus. A Presidential Fellow, Daw was an associate professor of theatre. The *New View of the Future* report was the principal project of their respective fellowships.[402]

The *New View* study was an attempt to apply to the Kennesaw campus the revised vision for the university system produced by Chancellor Stephen Portch under the title, *Access to Academic Excellence for the New Millennium*. Among other things, the Chancellor's vision called for higher standards, the preparation of students for leadership, learning communities to help students develop ethical principles and intellectual flexibility, and increased partnerships with business, government, and cultural agencies.[403]

In February and March 1995, the three fellows coordinated numerous focus groups with representatives from a wide variety of campus constituencies. Recommendations fell into four major categories: planning and institutional research, delivery of college services, services for diverse and nontraditional student populations, and means of improving the delivery of services. Specific suggestions included a review to ensure that all personnel policies complied with EEOC requirements and the creation of a more inviting campus by providing attractive offices and additional personnel in areas such as CAPS and the Office of Financial Aid. The *New View* report also urged more leadership training, diversity workshops, and CETL mentoring programs for students and new faculty. The focus on leadership seems to be the inspiration for one of Betty Siegel's favorite creations, the Institute for

240

Leadership, Ethics, and Character (later renamed the Siegel Institute following the president's retirement). The student-focused study also recognized the need for graduate research assistants in institutional research and an increased focus on grantsmanship and the Office of Sponsored Programs.[404]

A major strategic emphasis was on student success. As Nancy King recalled, "Why we exist is to help our students be successful—not only in the classroom, but to prepare them to go out and be successful in the real world, successful citizens, all of that." Prior to this point, Kennesaw operated in a traditional manner with a Division of Student Affairs. By the start of the 1995–96 academic year, the former dean of student affairs resigned suddenly, and President Siegel took advantage of the opportunity to reorganize that area with King becoming interim vice president for student success and enrollment services. The latter part of the title was unusual for someone in the field of student affairs. Previously, admissions reported to development, the registrar to academic affairs, and financial aid to student affairs. Under the new plan, the three areas reported to King. When President Siegel wrote the advertisement for a permanent vice president, she stipulated that the successful candidate should have a background in an academic discipline as well as experience in the field of student affairs. With her doctorate in English literature, King fit the job description perfectly, and, following a national search, became the first woman to be a vice president at Kennesaw State.[405]

The concept of student success was a special interest of President Siegel. As she said in an October 1993 interview:

> I think what we try to do is build a sense of student successes. I really want to be known as a president who cared for students. I think what we've tried to do with SOAR orientation, CAPS, SALT students [Student Assistance for Leadership in Teaching], and Ambassadors. Those are all initiated in this watch. The involvement of student organizations has grown—athletics, team spirit, a sense of identity—those are things we've worked hard at. We still have to work hard at it. I had a wonderful meeting with the student services people yesterday talking about new things to do—new exciting things to do. We were all just energized when we left; we were all so excited because we have "miles to go before we sleep."[406]

One of the first changes resulting from the New View was the reorganization of the Learning Support Department, headed by Joanne Fowler. At a time when the campus was completing the process of phasing out traditional developmental studies courses, the department took on expanded KSC 101 and senior-year experience courses, as well as the English as a Second Language (ESL) and Honors

Programs. In July 1995 Vice President Rugg announced that three members of the department were taking on new strategic initiatives: Dr. Patricia E. (Liza) Davis became director of the Honors Programs (including a special honors initiative for joint enrollment high school students); Kathy Matthews was appointed director of KSC 101; and Bobbie Brooke was placed in charge of ESL. Two years later, Joanne Fowler was promoted to a new position as dean of academic services and general education, where she would be instrumental in facilitating KSU's transition, by the fall of 1998, from the quarter to semester system. Under Liza Davis, KSU's distinctive undergraduate Honors Program, which accommodated nontraditional as well as traditional-age undergraduates, received a Regents Award for Excellence.[407]

Kennesaw had always attempted to put students first, and one of the unsung heroes in that effort was Carol J. Pope, a former public school teacher, who began working for Dean Herbert L. Davis in 1983 in the School of Science and Allied Health. Davis was one of the first people on campus to invest heavily in technol-

ogy, and Pope learned programming in his office. After a short time, she went to work for Dean Eleanor T. (Toby) Hopper in the Office of Student Development as the first administrative assistant on campus. They soon developed a positive working relationship. When President Siegel charged Hopper with developing new programs for students, the dean came up with ideas and Pope implemented them.[408]

Their first project was the creation of a Wellness Center, a natural for Hopper who came out of the Physical Education Department. The dean sent Pope to a National Wellness Conference in Wisconsin to come up with ideas for the center. After Pope got it up and running, Hopper found funding to conduct a search for a specialist to serve as permanent coordinator, while Pope went on to her next assignment, working with adult learners.

Jerome Ratchford

Once Pope had established the Adult Learner Program, the campus again hired a permanent director, while Pope developed new initiatives for minority students. Next, she took on the Student Leadership Program and then the Judiciary Program.

In the late 1980s, a student enrolled in Kennesaw with severe cerebral palsy. Although the faculty and staff did all they could to help, there was no consistency in services across campus. Dean Hopper was prodded by this situation to develop an Office of Disability Services and again asked Carol Pope to start it up. Prior to the Americans with Disabilities Act (ADA) in 1990, Kennesaw had not paid much attention to disabled students. As coordinator for the Disabled Student Support Services Program, Pope found her calling. Hopper stepped down from the deanship about this time, and there was never a search for a specialist to become permanent director. Pope continued as coordinator. Within a few years, the areas that Pope helped start were consolidated into the Student Development Center with Jerome Ratchford as director and Pope as assistant director for the disAbled Student Support Services Program. The unusual spelling of disAbled attempted to place the emphasis on student abilities rather than disabilities.

In addition to serving as campus ADA officer to ensure that students received all the services to which they were entitled, Pope worked tirelessly to help faculty accommodate student needs without lowering academic standards. She used her technological skills to acquire the first voice recognition equipment on the market, so that students who had trouble writing could dictate their papers into a computer that typed what they said. Numerous students over the years took supervised exams in her office where they were free of distractions and had more time to answer questions. Her office began wheelchair races and scavenger hunts for able-bodied students to sensitize them to the difficulties of wheelchair-bound people. As of 2011, about 370 students were officially registered for certifiable disabilities, but, thanks to the leadership of her office, the campus had become so accessible that many wheelchair students no longer found it necessary to register.[409]

Pope's longtime boss in the Student Development Center, Jerome Ratchford, came to Kennesaw in October 1988 as coordinator of the Office of Minority Student Retention Services. He was the first full-time professional hired to work with minority students. When he arrived, he found that the old Black Student Alliance was nearly defunct. Through his efforts, it was rebuilt and renamed in 1989 as the African American Student Alliance (AASA). Nearly a quarter century later, it is still an active, viable part of the campus community. Ratchford was also instrumental in bringing to campus the Alpha Kappa Alpha sorority (1992),[410] a branch of the NAACP (1997), and a Black Alumni Society (1999). AASA established the Dr. Jerome Ratchford Award of Excellence in 2002, and bestowed a Lifetime Achievement Award on him in 2008. The Department of Student Life also honored him with a Dr. Jerome Ratchford Student Engagement Award in 2010.[411]

According to Ratchford, the Student Development Center is a unique concept, organized to handle the various student populations that need specialized attention—adult learners, students over the traditional age, minority students, international students, gay and lesbian students, and the disabled. The Volunteer Kennesaw State University Program was also made an integral part of the center. Under Ratchford's leadership, the Student Development Center attempted to make everyone feel welcome in every group's activities. For example, the American-born were encouraged to attend the activities of international student groups and vice versa. Black History Month events were expanded, with majority as well as minority students invited to participate.

After the retirement of Nancy King in 2008, Dr. Ratchford became vice president of student success, while Carol Pope became his replacement as student development director. In a 2011 interview, Ratchford maintained that,

> The Student Development Center is rare and absolutely unique and noteworthy as an example of what can be done.... Whether you're talking about women, or you're talking about any group that's presumed to be out of the mainstream, you've got to have advocacy. You have to have someone that will provide the leadership and the management to enable whatever you desire from a goal oriented inclusive perspective to occur. You can't just leave it to chance. And that's what Student Development does; it does not leave that kind of intervention, that kind of advocacy to chance.[412]

Perhaps, the most notable diversity achievement of the Siegel era was the increased inclusion of women in leadership roles. As table 6 reveals, the creation of academic departments in 1983 was especially significant in the trend toward gender balance. For most of the Siegel era, close to half of the department chairs were women. The same was true of academic deans from the mid-1990s into the first years of the new century. As Kennesaw's chief academic officer from 1986–2002, Ed Rugg played a key role, along with the president, in the advancement of women to leadership positions as department chairs and academic deans.

Rugg was especially pleased with a number of internal promotions, including Deborah Wallace (education dean), Barbara Calhoun (continuing education dean), Joanne Fowler (academic support and general education dean), Tina Straley (graduate dean and associate vice president for academic affairs), Judy Perkins (health and human services dean), and Linda Noble (humanities and social sciences dean). During his tenure, KSU's record in maintaining an approximately 50-50 percent balance of male and female faculty members was substantially higher than that of most other four-year colleges and universities. Throughout most of the Siegel era,

Kennesaw took pride in its exemplary record of advancing women into faculty and administrative roles.[413]

TABLE 6						Faculty and Student Gender Balance		
YEAR	Deans of Schools and Colleges		Instructional Department Chairs		Total Faculty		Students	
	M	F	M	F	%M	%F	%M	%F
1984	4	0	9	8	55	45	42	58
1985	5	0	9	7	57	43	41	59
1986	5	0	9	7	54	46	41	59
1987	5	0	8	8	56	44	40	60
1988	4	1	10	8	56	44	39	61
1989	4	1	12	6	54	46	39	61
1990	4	1	11	7	52	48	38	62
1991	4	1	11	10	51	49	38	62
1992	4	1	11	11	50	50	37	63
1993	4	1	11	12	51	49	38	62
1994	3	2	11	12	51	49	39	61
1995	3	3	11	13	49	51	39	61
1996	3	3	11	13	50	50	39	61
1997	3	3	10	14	51	49	39	61
1998	3	3	11	13	48	52	38	62
1999	3	3	13	13	49	51	38	62
2000	3	4	13	13	48	52	38	62
2001	3	4	14	13	48	52	38	62
2002	5	2	15	11	48	52	38	62
2003	5	3	16	11	—	—	38	62
2004	5	3	18	9	48	52	39	61
2005	5	3	19	9	49	51	38	62

Sources: Kennesaw College Undergraduate Catalog, years 1984–1987; Kennesaw State College Undergraduate Catalog, years 1988–1995; Kennesaw State University Undergraduate Catalog, years 1996–2005; Kennesaw College Fact Book, years 1984–1987; Kennesaw State College Fact Book, years 1988–1995; Kennesaw State University Fact Book, years 1996–2005.

Clarice C. Bagwell

And so, Kennesaw weathered the storms of the 1990s by keeping focused on what mattered most. The KSU Foundation emerged from the Gingrich fiasco as a dynamic force that reshaped the face of the campus in the early twenty-first century. The Bagwell College of Education became one of the largest and best producers of teachers in Georgia, with 427 degrees granted in 1999–2000 (348 undergraduate and 79 graduate), a growth of 99 percent in just five years.[414] Rather than leaving permanent scars, the Kaspers controversy spurred the campus to greater efforts toward diversity and inclusion. And, in 1996, Kennesaw achieved the long-sought goal of university status. This achievement propelled Kennesaw's growth in stature, as it built on the achievements of the past to evolve into a dynamic metropolitan university.

Chapter 8

Becoming a University, 1996–2006

By the end of the 1995–96 academic year, Kennesaw had offered classes for three decades. In that brief time, the institution had gone through the equivalent of a childhood and adolescence and had embarked on its young maturity. Its dynamic, energetic president exemplified the school's youthfulness. When President Siegel was not representing Kennesaw across the nation and the world, she often could be found starting her day before dawn at the Waffle House adjacent to campus, where she prepared for a schedule that would exhaust most anyone. Those who saw her in action back then may have been shocked to learn she was old enough for Medicare. However, she still had ten years to go before relinquishing her presidency. And that last decade from 1996 to 2006 was, in many ways, the most productive and consequential of her career.

Kennesaw reached an important milestone in 1996 when it gained university status. A crowning achievement for Horace Sturgis had been Kennesaw's achievement of four-year status in April 1976, almost eleven years into his presidency. President Siegel spent fifteen years building a wide array of bachelors' and masters' programs before the Board of Regents made Kennesaw a university. The name change to Kennesaw State University facilitated many other transformations, none more significant than a public/private partnership built by the president and the KSU Foundation that resulted in the construction of KSU's first residence halls and parking decks and, later, many other badly needed support facilities.

Throughout its history, Kennesaw's growth in enrollment substantially outstripped state appropriations for capital improvements. Consequently, operational funding and physical square footage per full-time equivalent student fell short of what most other state universities received. Part of the problem was that the campus was so new that it was constantly playing catch-up with the older colleges on infrastructure improvements. Unfortunately, some of Kennesaw's funding

Aerial view of Kennesaw
State University campus

problems were self-inflicted. For a few years in the 1980s the college made a strong case that it could not sustain its growth without more support from the regents. But cries of alarm tend to become counterproductive if continued too long, and gradually Kennesaw abandoned that approach. When Dan Papp became senior vice chancellor for academics and fiscal affairs in 2000, he found that everyone at the Board of Regents thought Kennesaw was "Camelot" because KSU projected an image that everything was fine. If everything was going well, it was hard to persuade the regents to spend more on KSU, despite the fact that it was near the bottom in appropriations per full time equivalent student.[415]

As public funding for higher education contracted over the years, capital expansion often became limited to instructional and student support services buildings. A new major classroom building typically took five years to work its way up the regents' priority list and another two to three years for planning and construction once funding became available. A door opened at the turn of the century for university foundations to step in and provide supplemental funding for new buildings and additional acreage, often at a much quicker pace. The KSU Foundation took advantage of new opportunities and became a leader in securing low-cost public bonds for facility expansion.

New buildings acquired between 1996–2006 as a result of this public/private partnership included the KSU Center (1999), Clendenin Computer Science Building (2003), Bobbie Bailey Athletic Complex (2002), Chastain Pointe (2003), Town Point (2005), Dr. Bobbie Bailey and Family Performance Center (2007), three student apartment complexes with 2,100 beds (2002 and 2004), three parking decks with 3,700 spaces (2002 and 2004), nine residences along Frey Lake (currently, Campus Loop) Road converted to campus use (2002), and a host of property acquisitions stretching in all directions from the original campus.[416] Meanwhile, state funding, supplemented by student fees, led to Kennesaw Hall (1999), a major addition to the Carmichael Student Center (1999), the Visual Arts Building (1999), an addition to the English Building (2004), the Convocation Center (2005), an addition to the Student Recreation and Wellness Center (2004), and the largest classroom building at that time—the Social Sciences Building at 162,600 square feet (2006).

As additional buildings opened, state funds paid to renovate older buildings for new purposes. In the decade between 1996 and 2006, Kennesaw State nearly tripled the total square footage of its physical plant. In the process, the center of campus life shifted from the west side quadrangle where the original one- and two-story buildings were located, to the east side where an expansive new Campus Green

(Opposite Page) Peter (Ed) Bostick in front of the new
Science Building

was flanked by stately, large, new structures. The physical changes fueled a rapid growth in enrollment and amazed people who remembered the smaller college of earlier years.[417]

Residence halls played a crucial role in producing a new identity as a university of choice for prospective undergraduates. They offered a full college experience twenty-four hours a day and seven days a week. Consequently, an institution long known for its focus on commuter and nontraditional students experienced a gradual drop in average age of undergraduates and a growing demand for services that catered to the needs of a younger clientele. Although the number of undergraduate transfer students, many of nontraditional age, remained greater than the number of traditional-aged beginning freshmen, the gap narrowed, thanks in large measure to the expansion of on-campus housing.[418]

A contributing factor in Kennesaw's ability to attract traditional-aged students was a thriving Athletic Department that also appealed to alumni and the general public. During this era, Kennesaw won a number of NCAA Division II national championships and began a transition to Division I. These changes in academics, campus life, and athletics turned Kennesaw State, by 2006, into the third largest university in Georgia.

Achievement of University Status

For decades, a number of state colleges jockeyed for an opportunity to receive university status from the Board of Regents. Up until 1990, the board limited this status to only four of its units (University of Georgia, Georgia Tech, Georgia State University, and the Medical College of Georgia). The door was cracked when Georgia Southern became a regional university in 1990, followed by Valdosta State, in 1993. During those years Kennesaw State College repeatedly argued that its programs, enrollment, and service area (northwest Georgia) compared favorably to the universities in Statesboro and Valdosta.

Chancellor Stephen R. Portch deserves much of the credit for the conversion of KSC into a university. In the summer of 1995, he created a Blue Ribbon Committee to help the various university system institutions revise their mission statements. When the committee presented its report to the Board of Regents in October 1995, it noted that most of the four-year state colleges would be called universities in other states. That observation encouraged Portch to appoint an advisory committee of five external consultants chaired by Dr. Paul Hardin, the chancellor from 1988 to

(Opposite Page) President Siegel cutting a cake at the celbration of university status.

1995 of the University of North Carolina at Chapel Hill. The consultants looked at mission statements and academic programs in determining which colleges deserved to be called universities.

The goal was to bring about nomenclature changes that would help students seeking employment or applying to graduate school and would assist institutions in recruiting superior students and professors. The new universities, however, were expected to retain their old mission statements. Georgia Southern and Valdosta

KENNESAW HALL

Kennesaw Hall

State had received supplemental funding and expanded educational missions upon their elevation to university status. The regents could not afford to do that for other state universities. Consequently, the regents warned schools such as Kennesaw not to expect new programs, increased budgets, or reduced teaching loads solely as a result of the conversion. Expanded missions and programs were to be considered on a case-by-case basis, and only where needs could be documented.[419]

The first state colleges to gain university status were those that offered masters' as well as bachelors' degrees and had names that everyone agreed could be changed merely by substituting "university" for "college." On June 12, 1996, Kennesaw was one of seven state colleges to be given the "university" designation. For another five colleges with more complicated names, the regents took an extra month or more to be sure the new names had alumni and community support and honored traditional missions. For example, Marietta's Southern College of Technology had to wait until July before being renamed Southern Polytechnic State University. The only regent to vote against the nomenclature revisions was John Henry Anderson of Hawkinsville, who argued

LeoDelle L. Jolley

that legislators representing the affected schools would apply pressure to make them "universities in more than letterhead." His negative vote occurred while the board was meeting as a Committee of the Whole. When the regents returned to regular session, however, he apparently realized that opposition was futile and joined his colleagues in making the decision unanimous.[420]

Kennesaw's name change came during the break between spring and summer quarters, so many students and faculty were away at the time. Nonetheless, about three hundred people gathered in the Carmichael Student Center for what President Siegel described as "an instantaneous celebration," complete with a cake and shirts sporting the name "Kennesaw State University." The president told a reporter that Kennesaw had been operating as a university in all but name ever since it established its first masters' programs eleven years earlier. "It's a very long-awaited milestone," she said, that "puts us on par with other institutions around the country as far as nomenclature, which is very important."[421]

By the time the student newspaper, the *Sentinel*, put out its first summer issue several weeks later, the new name was apparently taken for granted, as there was no front-page story, and the only coverage was in the form of student comments. The main student reaction seemed to be one of hopeful anticipation that recognition as a university would lead to "greater opportunities," "more funding," and

improvements in "campus atmosphere." A pragmatic student remarked that the new title was something that "looks better on a resume."[422] Faculty reaction was similar, although perhaps more apprehensive, as professors wondered how the elevated status would affect scholarly expectations, in light of the regents' clear intention not to provide additional funding or altered workloads.

The KSU Foundation and the Advancement of the University

While Kennesaw grew into its altered status as a university, the KSU Foundation played a central role in transforming the campus through public/private partnerships that proved amazingly successful in acquiring buildings and land for future growth. The foundation was incorporated in April 1969, but played a relatively modest role before Kennesaw became a university. Then it matured into a powerful force along with the institution. The Office of Development showed a similar progression. Before James A. Fleming became special assistant to the president

James A. Fleming

in July 1984, private fundraising had not been a high priority at Kennesaw or, for that matter, at any of Georgia's state colleges.

The Kennesaw College Foundation contained some of Cobb County's most prominent local leaders, but they typically did not look beyond the county line and raised less than $1 million during the first decade of operation (1969–1979). With the support of President Siegel and administrators such as Jim Fleming, the foundation trustees became a little more active in the 1980s, raising about $2 million between 1979 and 1989. During the 1990s, fundraising was stagnant, even declining slightly during the Newt Gingrich controversy. By the start of the new century, however, the foundation was playing a truly major role on campus, not so much as a fundraiser, but as a bond holder for the expansion of campus facilities.[423]

Fleming was hired primarily to improve the institution's external contacts and its fundraising ability. After receiving two degrees in marketing from the University of Alabama (BS 1963 and MA 1964), he worked briefly for Georgia Tech and the University of Georgia, and began a doctoral program at UGA. His graduate work led to assignments in Latin America with the US Agency for International Development as a senior marketing advisor, and later for the country of Brazil where he supervised a food distribution system. Upon his return to the United States, he worked for the State of Mississippi as chief of staff for Governor Charles Clifton Finch (1976–1980). When Finch's term ended, Fleming headed the University of Mississippi's first capital campaign with a mandate to raise $25 million. By the time he left in 1984, Ole Miss had raised $42 million.[424]

At the time, Cullene M. Harper served as the director of development and executive secretary to the Kennesaw College Foundation. She and her executive assistant, Ellen Smith, were the only Kennesaw employees, other than the president, whose job description involved fundraising. A staff member since 1967, Harper had been director of community services in the junior-college years and then director of development and public services at the end of the Sturgis and start of the Siegel administrations. Her strengths, however, were in writing and public relations, and Siegel and Fleming persuaded her to relinquish her foundation responsibilities to build the Office of College Relations, where she was the first director.[425]

Fleming also recommended that the president hire Dr. Norman H. McCrummen III as director of development. McCrummen had earned a PhD from the University of Alabama in 1976 with a dissertation on educational programs and community development in the Arab states. A world traveler, McCrummen was a popular lecturer on the modern Middle East and had worked briefly for Fleming at the University of Mississippi. He would serve as director of development for the rest of the 1980s before enrolling in seminary and becoming a Presbyterian minister. In the early 1990s, Ronald P. Hyde served as interim director before Dr. Jack H. Gibson assumed the permanent position. Hyde was a former commander of the

Atlanta Naval Air Station. Gibson had been assistant vice president for development at Georgia State University before coming to Kennesaw.[426]

Fleming worked with all these directors to increase the number of trustees from outside Cobb County. It seemed obvious to him and to President Siegel that the foundation would not become a major fundraiser until it crossed the Chattahoochee River and attracted some of Atlanta's corporate and civic leaders. One of the important early additions was J. Larry Stevens, a Price Waterhouse partner with expertise in investment banking. Stevens lived in Cobb County by the time he became a trustee, but he was originally from Macon. He operated out of a downtown Atlanta office until January, 1983, when he became the first Price Waterhouse partner to move to the Cumberland/Galleria area in Cobb's booming Platinum Triangle near the convergence of I-75, I-285, and US Highway 41. After gaining sixty new clients in the first year, he and several colleagues were able to lease an

entire floor of 200 Galleria. About that time, Stevens responded to an invitation from Ronald E. King to attend a Cobb Chamber of Commerce breakfast. King was president of the Cobb Federal Savings Bank, a KC Foundation trustee, and a member of the chamber's Finance Committee. Soon King and chamber chairman Chester A. (Chet) Austin of Tip Top Poultry invited Stevens to join the Finance Committee. Stevens became increasingly active in Cobb Chamber of Commerce affairs, rising to the chairmanship by 1991.[427]

President Siegel was also involved in the chamber and would serve as its chairperson in 1996. Largely through her influence, many of the people who led the chamber became KC Foundation trustees. Stevens did so in 1985. His mentor at Price Waterhouse, Ed Harris, told him that service on a college or university foundation was the highest volunteer position to which one could aspire. His first few years with the KSC Foundation, however, made him question whether his mentor was correct. He recalled going to an annual fundraising breakfast in the Carmichael Student Center, where pledge cards were distributed around a horseshoe-shaped table:

> The trustees would go around, and you would pick up pledge cards that you would call on, and you would ask them for money. We were asking them for a hundred dollars here, for twenty-five dollars here. To ask someone for a thousand dollars would just be incredible. So we literally raised money for the annual campaign by picking up pledge cards, and everybody would take five or six pledge cards, and then you would make your calls. I was naive, and so I would take doctors and physicians…. I can remember asking doctors for twenty-five dollars for KSU, and being told, "No, I have to give away free medicine, so I can't give fifty dollars." I had surgeons tell me, "I can't give fifty dollars." So I remember thinking, [Ed Harris] is…probably talking about Duke University or someplace else, but he can't be talking about Kennesaw.[428]

For Stevens and other trustees of the late 1980s, the biggest challenge was raising enough money to pay President Siegel's expenses when she hosted events for which state funds could not be spent or when she did outreach for the college and sent the bill to the foundation. According to Stevens, the trustees at the time grumbled about the president obligating funds before asking permission. In retrospect, he realized that they should have spent less time wringing their hands and more time raising revenues to support the president's efforts at promoting the college.[429]

**(Opposite Page) President Siegel
with Hillary Clinton**

A year or two after he joined the foundation, Stevens became chair of the annual campaign. One of the changes he implemented was to use telephone solicitation for the smaller, twenty-five-dollar donations, and to become more aggressive in establishing relationships with people able to give larger amounts. While the annual drives began to exceed the $100,000 level, they remained far below the half million dollars that he saw as a reasonable goal. He gives Jim Fleming much of the credit for helping the trustees to develop a larger vision. As his term as chamber chair came to a close, he assumed leadership of the foundation, serving as chairman from the fall of 1991 to 1994.

As foundation chairman, he was responsible for at least three consequential decisions. In his opinion, his biggest mistake was to let the foundation serve a custodial role in handling the funds collected from political operatives for Newt Gingrich's Renewing American Civilization course. That error was more than balanced by his success in bringing more Atlantans onto the Board of Trustees and in increasing the foundation's assets. One of the Atlanta businessmen was Jack A. Dinos, the former owner of the Southern Tea Company, who was already endowing chairs in the School of Business, as a result of the efforts of Craig Aronoff and Tim Mescon, but Dinos had never been asked to be a trustee. Once Dinos was on board, Stevens appointed him to the Nominating Committee. He recalls telling Dinos, "What I want you to do is to shake this board up because we have to stop this mentality that exists that if it's on the other side of the [Chattahoochee] river it can't be any good."[430]

The Nominating Committee also included Michael J. Coles, the founder of the Great American Chocolate Chip Cookie Company, who, in 1994, made the first million-dollar contribution to Kennesaw State College.[431] Coles, Dinos, and the other committee members identified people with regional and national connections, such as Thomas M. (Tommy) Holder of Holder Construction, a company located in the Cumberland/Galleria area, but doing business throughout America. The committee first approached Tommy Holder's father, Robert M. Holder Jr. who started the family business in 1960, but he asked that the foundation appoint his son instead. Tommy Holder was a Georgia Tech graduate and did not know much about Kennesaw State. He, nonetheless, knew about Betty Siegel and thought that service as a trustee might be interesting.[432]

For the first few years, Holder did little more than attend board meetings. He was thinking about resigning when Michael Coles, the chairman from 1998–2002, announced at an annual meeting that he was naming Holder to the Executive

(Opposite Page) Michael J. Coles

Committee. Coles had not even asked Holder whether he was willing to serve. After recovering from the shock, Holder said to himself that he might enjoy playing an insider role, so he accepted. A few years later in 2002, Coles asked Holder to take his place as chairman. Holder would head the foundation from 2002–2007, during which time construction was completed on three parking decks and two phases of the residence halls, the most important projects undertaken by the foundation to that time.[433]

Another major player in the growth of the foundation was Lawrence D. Wheeler. A commercial banker, he spent many years with the Citizens & Southern Bank system before joining Barnett Bank in 1992 as head of its corporate and real estate operations in Atlanta. After becoming a Cobb County resident, he approached one of the KSC trustees, Fred E. Stillwell, to see if he could become involved at Kennesaw. A subsequent lunch meeting with Jim Fleming led to an invitation in 1994 to join the board. Wheeler saw the foundation as an organization with unrealized potential. While the staff was efficient and energetic, it managed a budget of only a few hundred thousand dollars and had "a very limited endowment."

In 1998 the foundation took the first major step toward building its assets when it acquired the Kinder Outlet Mall, across I-75 from the main campus, for about $16 million. After completing renovations, the foundation leased the new KSU Center to the Board of Regents, starting July 1, 1999, for the Division of Continuing Education and other programs. At the time, the foundation had little experience in managing properties, so it worked through a nonprofit organization called The University Financing Foundation (TUFF) that played the role of a third-party facilitator in making the purchase. According to Larry Wheeler, TUFF "wanted to use our project as their poster child. They would be the vehicle through which the transaction was done. For a fee, TUFF acquired the mall and leased the property. The [foundation] helped in arranging the financing. The [foundation] had not done a bond financing, and TUFF's name was known in the market." In turn, TUFF sold the property to the foundation for a nominal fee.[434]

In addition to recruiting Tommy Holder, Michael Coles played a central role in bringing Clyde C. Tuggle, Michael Russell, and Norman J. Radow into the foundation. Tuggle was the assistant to Roberto C. Goizueta, the Coca-Cola Company chairman and CEO. Michael Russell was the son of Herman J. Russell, the founder of one of the nation's most successful minority-owned construction and real estate companies. A highly successful attorney and entrepreneur, Radow would follow Holder, in 2007, as chairman of the foundation. As a law student, he had bought

(Opposite Page) Fred E. Stillwell

and renovated a downtown Manhattan building to pay for his school expenses. In 1994 he founded RADCO Companies to redevelop the Grand Hotel in Atlanta into a Four Seasons. Over the years, RADCO developed or redeveloped numerous properties across the country. The inclusion of such business leaders with instant name recognition greatly assisted the foundation and the university in gaining access to major donors.[435] The last years of the Siegel era were quite important in "friend-raising," preparing the institution and the foundation for record-shattering fundraising during the presidency of KSU's third president, Daniel S. Papp.

Student Housing and an Expanding Physical Plant

From the early days of her presidency, Betty Siegel dreamed of student housing at Kennesaw. Her long-time assistant and foundation president, Jim Fleming, described her as "the Unsinkable Molly Brown" for her persistent championing of residence halls. For many years she was unsuccessful in convincing the Board of Regents. Fleming recalled: "They would nod and roll their eyes, and explain that UGA had room vacancies. In the community, people were very polite but didn't do much to be supportive. To Betty's credit she kept saying, 'You know, it would be great to have dorms'.... I believe one of the great moments for Kennesaw State was when it was able to add residential students to the mix on campus. It changed the character of Kennesaw State forever.... So Betty trumpeted that. She did it in many circles. She was a great external president."[436]

When he became foundation chairman in 1998, Michael Coles supported the president in her efforts to influence the regents. As it became evident that their best lobbying efforts were going nowhere, Coles devised an alternative plan. His basic concept was that student housing would be built without state money. The KSU Foundation entered into a contract with the Board of Regents to build, own, and operate the residence halls on campus under a ground lease to the state-owned land. With this agreement in hand, the foundation sold bonds to pay the construction cost. Then it contracted with private companies to supervise the construction and administer the properties. A facilities management group collected rents from students to retire the bonds over the next twenty-five to thirty years. Once all debts were paid, the foundation planned to donate the property to Kennesaw State and give up all control.

The same arrangement was employed to build the parking decks, where the regents approved substantial increases in student parking fees that KSU collected and turned over to the foundation for debt retirement. Trustee George Kalafut often heard from KSU night students who worked for him at the Genuine Parts Company (GPC) that parking was their biggest problem. They claimed, "We can't find a parking spot." A former US Navy captain with expertise in logistics and finance, Kalafut became chief financial officer and then executive vice president of the Genuine Parts Company. He joined the KSU Foundation in 1992.[437]

As a member of the Finance Committee, Kalafut assisted in diversifying the investment of foundation assets. He recalled that "Michael Coles had laid a great base in starting to invest our endowments in something other than money market funds. We had relatively few invested dollars at that point, but we began the process

(Opposite Page, L-R) Foundation trustees Norman J. Radow,
Thomas M. Holder, and Thomas E. Clendenin

(Above) Rendering of University Village Phase II
(Opposite Page) The Ann and John Clendenin Computer Science Building

of spreading our investments among a number of equity- and fixed-income managers." Kalafut claims that Coles, Tommy Holder, and Norman Radow deserve the major credit for building the first campus housing. Kalafut recalled:

> In the case of Tommy and Norman, their real estate and construction expertise was particularly important. I don't know what we would have done had we not had folks like them overseeing the construction projects which followed. Michael started it all by getting the first project approved, but then Tommy and Norman took over. But these two guys led us through this growth period. And behind the scenes were Jim Fleming and Wes [Wesley K.] Wicker and their foundation staff working to support these efforts. If this were a small business, it'd be in one of the *Inc.* magazine's fastest growing businesses lists.[438]

The first phase of student housing, the seven-hundred-bed University Place, opened on August 17, 2002, just in time for fall semester. In a story titled, "Welcome Home," *Sentinel* reporter Rachel Brooker focused on the excitement of the occasion, as students and campus administrators reflected on its significance. A number of staff members and volunteers from neighboring churches showed up to serve coffee and donuts and to help the students carry heavy items into their rooms. Courtney Elder of Dalton and two of her roommates arrived long before the eight o'clock starting time so that they could be first in line to move in. A *Sentinel* photograph showed President Siegel, vice president for student success Nancy King, and coordinator of residence life Amy Wrye, all in work clothes, as they helped the day go smoothly.[439]

These were clearly not the dormitories that previous generations of college students had experienced. From the outside, they looked like typical suburban apartment buildings. After all, they had to compete for student rentals with existing garden apartment complexes near the campus. Inside, the seven hundred residents each had a fully furnished private bedroom and bathroom and then shared a common living area and kitchen with one to three other apartment mates. Built and administered by Place Properties, the various buildings were arranged around streets with antiquated street signs, lamp posts, and fountains that, according to the *Sentinel*, projected an image of a small town's Main Street. To help create community spirit, the developers put a Town Hall Building in the center of the complex with meeting rooms, computer labs, a lounge, and recreational facilities.[440]

The Commons Student Dining Hall

In addition to University Place at the southwest corner of the campus, the foundation purchased and renovated 358 units of an older apartment complex, built in 1984, on the northeast end of campus. Altogether, 1,058 students became campus residents in the fall of 2002, living in eighteen separate apartment buildings. The only regret that anyone seemed to have on opening day was that Kennesaw could not accommodate everyone who wanted to live there. According to director of student life Kathy Alday, some 2,200 students had sought residency. The campus housing, along with the West and East Parking Decks, helped boost student enrollment by 12 percent over the previous fall, surpassing the fifteen thousand mark for the first time. The biggest increase was in the freshman class that grew by 829 students over the previous year (jumping from 3,788 in fall 2001 to 4,617 in fall 2002).[441]

A fifth-year senior, Brian Hedrick, editorialized that a "sometimes dull university has come into her own" now that Kennesaw was a place that students "can call home." President Siegel concluded that having students on campus twenty-four hours a day would bring about a cultural "sea change." With one success behind them, the president and the foundation set to work almost immediately on the second phase of student housing. In 2004 University Village Phase I and II, with

270

878 beds, opened on the north side of campus. Next to University Village, the foundation built the North Parking Deck for resident use. To make way for the deck, the university tore down the old Plant Operations Building and moved that department to Chastain Pointe, acquired by the foundation in 2003 at the corner of Chastain and Big Shanty Roads.

Kennesaw would continue to build parking decks and student housing in the Papp era. In 2008 the eight-level Central Parking Deck was completed by the foundation for 2,700 additional cars. Also in 2008, KSU and the foundation added 914 more beds in University Village Phase III and IV. That was followed in 2012 — the tenth anniversary of the start of student housing — with the opening of University Place II on the south side of campus. By this time, University Place was designated specifically for upper classmen while University Village catered to freshmen and sophomores. With the completion of these projects, about 3,500 students lived on campus.[442]

Housing and parking were just two areas where the foundation played a decisive role in the new millennium in innovative public/private partnerships. The residence halls and parking decks illustrated one type of collaboration, where no taxpayer dollars were involved, but where the Board of Regents agreed to retire the foundation's debt with student rents or parking fees. That model of foundation financing continued in later years in the construction of The Commons Student Dining Hall (2009), where most students had to purchase a meal plan, and in the purchase of eighty-eight acres for student recreational activities (the last phases opened in 2012), where a student recreation fee and lease agreements with community soccer associations began to pay off the bonds.

A second type of public/private partnerships involved joint funding. The first example of this arrangement was the building of the John and Ann Clendenin Computer Science Building, with a contribution of $1 million from the Clendenins in 1999 that supplemented $4 million in state expenditures. John Clendenin was a retired president and CEO of BellSouth. Kennesaw broke ground on the thirty-seven-thousand-square-foot Clendenin Building in October 2001. When it opened to students in January 2003, it contained twelve high-technology classrooms and office space for the computer science faculty.[443]

The Clendenin model was followed for projects such as years the Bailey Field House (2002) and the Prillaman Health Sciences Building (2010). The Bailey Field House was constructed between the baseball and softball fields (Stillwell Stadium and Bailey Park, respectively) and made possible by a contribution of $1 million from foundation trustee M. Bobbie Bailey, coupled with matching external gifts and athletic fee reserves. The Prillaman Building was a major project of the 2007–2011 comprehensive capital campaign, where private donations totalling $8 million were added to $47 million from the General Assembly to construct a state-of-the-art

Bailey Park

facility for health science education. At present, it is the largest classroom building at KSU with 192,000 square feet of floor space.[444]

Through the acquisition of properties for the university, the KSU Foundation increased its assets from next to nothing at the start of Betty Siegel's presidency to about $200 million by the time she retired in 2006. Former foundation president Jim Fleming noted that the trustees were, by this point, adding more to the unrestricted budget from interest on investments than they could ever hope to collect through annual solicitations. His successor, Wes Wicker, has similarly argued that during his five years as executive director (2005–2010), the foundation became virtually self-sufficient, no longer relying on state money to pay staff salaries. Even as the foundation needed more people to keep the books and manage assets, it was able to pay for them through investment income. Including the employees of KSU Housing LLC, a foundation subsidiary, the total number of people on the foundation payroll grew from four or five at the start of the new century to about fifty by 2011. So, the KSU Foundation became a powerful, positive force that helped bring about President Siegel's "sea change" of campus culture.[445]

CETL and the Scholarship of Teaching and Learning

Further evidence of the maturation of the university was the expanding role in the first decade of the twenty-first century of the Center for Excellence in Teaching and Learning (CETL). Since its founding in the early 1980s, CETL had operated with part-time directors and without a permanent home. Diane Willey, Joe Kelly, Janis Epps, Richard Welch, Don Forrester, and Lana Wachniak made important contributions to the institution through their service as CETL directors. However, there was only so much they could do in a part-time role with limited funding. Lana J. Wachniak was perhaps the most active director during her tenure in the 1990s. Both Wachniak and Don Forrester spent much of their time organizing the annual Georgia Conference on College and University Teaching, editing CETL's *Reaching through Teaching*, and coordinating Leadership Kennesaw, a year-long faculty development seminar. Wachniak went the extra mile in holding a series of faculty workshops, largely dealing with technology. Still, CETL reached far fewer faculty members than it was created to serve.[446]

The person who played the central role in transforming the center into a major force on campus was G. William (Bill) Hill IV, a psychology professor who joined the faculty in 1979 just after Kennesaw began offering upper-level courses. He was

(Opposite Page) G. William (Bill) Hill IV

a student favorite from the beginning, winning their praise for the excitement and enthusiasm he brought to his lectures and the many hours he spent mentoring them. Even before he received tenure, he became the 1985 recipient of the Distinguished Teaching Award, only the fourth Kennesaw faculty member so honored.

Achieving Kennesaw's highest award so early in his career was sobering for the young professor. He felt that he was a good mentor of students, but he thought distinguished teachers should be senior faculty members who were known as mentors to their colleagues as well as students. That was something for which he did not yet feel prepared. He was still being mentored himself by his department chair, Ruth Hepler, and senior members of the Psychology Department, such as Grace Galliano. About the same time he won the teaching award, he began attending every conference he could find on the teaching of psychology, hoping to gain a better scholarly understanding of what worked best in the classroom. In 1988, when he succeeded Hepler as department chair, he was ready to assume a faculty mentoring role, helping his fellow psychologists find opportunities to reach their full scholarly potential. To assist colleagues throughout the region, he founded in 1989 the Southeastern Conference for the Teaching of Psychology—a highly successful annual event that he coordinated for the rest of his career.[447]

Hill carried his belief that administrators should be good facilitators into the Office of Academic Affairs, where he became assistant, then associate, and finally interim vice president between 1998 and 2002. Much of his time in this role was spent mentoring department chairs. He also worked to resolve misunderstandings that faculty members and review committees had in the tenure and promotion process. Working with Vice President Ed Rugg, he began thinking of ways for CETL to help more faculty members on matters important to their careers. When Don Forrester retired in 2000 and the CETL directorship became vacant, Rugg agreed to let Hill take over the position as part of his duties in academic affairs.

In his two years as interim CETL director, Hill worked with Rugg to make two significant changes. First, they created a larger budget for the center by altering or eliminating some of its outdated functions. Hill and Rugg concluded that Leadership Kennesaw had outlived its usefulness. Fewer and fewer faculty members were applying to participate in the leadership training program, and deans and chairs seemed no longer to consider it important. Since Leadership Kennesaw annually held two off-campus retreats along with field trips to the state legislature and other off-campus sites, it had a large budget. By discontinuing the program, Rugg and Hill were able to transfer those funds to other CETL functions.

Similarly, *Reaching through Teaching* had required a substantial publication budget that paid for printing and distributing paper copies. With the advent of the web, Hill was able to put the journal online, cutting costs to a minimum while making it more accessible. When he took over operating the Georgia Conference on College and University Teaching, he was able to make a modest annual profit of about $2,500 through registration fees, and he received a similar amount annually from the KSU Foundation. Finally, since he was already paid as a full-time assistant vice president, he diverted the part-time director's salary into CETL's general operating budget. Altogether, he created $50,000–$60,000 that could be used to take CETL in new directions.[448]

Working together, Rugg and Hill created a new type of faculty leadership program, based on two central themes: electronic learning (or e-learning) and the Scholarship of Teaching and Learning (SoTL) Program. For each, they recruited a team of about twenty interested faculty members. The e-learning group produced website resources for their colleagues, while the SoTL group came up with the idea of an expanded CETL center with a full-time director and several half-time faculty fellows chosen on a competitive basis. With that proposal in hand, Rugg and Hill met with President Siegel and won her support.[449]

Under the plan, the half-time fellows continued to be paid by their respective departments, but CETL gave the departments $35,000 per fellow to cover the sections they had formerly taught. Department chairs liked that idea because they could hire a full-time lecturer or several adjuncts for that amount. The original fellows were Kimberly S. Loomis (scholarship of teaching and learning), Army Lester III (student success and retention), Mary L. Garner (scholarly discourse across disciplines), Gary B. Roberts (e-learning), Valerie Whittlesey (diversity in the curriculum), and Sandra M. Hillman (reflective practice of teaching).[450]

The idea of a fellow for the reflective practice of teaching grew out of President Siegel's invitation to Parker J. Palmer to share his ideas on teaching with Kennesaw's faculty and students. As the president said in a 2005 interview, "Parker Palmer tells us we must have the courage to teach. It's not just *what* we teach but *how* we teach and what we believe about teaching…. These are the questions that we as academics ought to be asking: When we ask what new program do we need, what's in it for students, not what's in it for faculty? What's in it for the institution?"[451]

Beverly Mitchell, the recipient of Kennesaw's first Distinguished Service Award in 1997, was one of the Kennesaw professors influenced by Parker Palmer. She had already read his book, *The Courage to Teach*, and incorporated his ideas into some of her own work, before he spoke on campus. After hearing Palmer's convocation address, she joined a delegation of a dozen faculty members that President Siegel took to visit Palmer and his wife in their home in Madison, Wisconsin. Along with colleagues such as Christine B. Ziegler (psychology), Army Lester (biology), and Kim Loomis (education), Mitchell spent four days interacting with Palmer and being transformed by his stimulating ideas. The delegation also included Jennifer R. Reno from the Georgia Teacher Center. Reno returned home with a Betty Siegel idea of a continued dialogue between Kennesaw professors and K–12 teachers.

For the next two years, around twenty-five people met quarterly for a weekend retreat in north Georgia to discuss Palmer's ideas. Mitchell recalled: "The themes were based on the seasons. If you have ever read any of his work, you understand that much of his contribution centers around the seasons and what lessons you derive from the seasons.... So we were challenged to bring back to our own classrooms ways that we could help our students listen and nurture, and be nurtured by the inner teacher.... But to have gone and been in Parker Palmer's presence for a weekend and guided through this thought process was quite an extraordinary event."[452]

The 2011 recipient of Kennesaw's Distinguished Teaching Award, Kim Loomis, had a similar reaction to the encounter in Madison with Parker Palmer. She recalled that after a "fabulous" trip, Bill Hill suggested the creation of the CETL Fellows Program. She applied and became the first SoTL Fellow. After the Parker Palmer experience, Army Lester was chosen as the first Student Success and Retention Fellow, but he also collaborated with Sandra Hillman on the area of reflective practice of teaching. Lester had already won Kennesaw's 1999 Distinguished Service Award for his role in bringing to campus several NSF-funded Summer Science Camps and the Young Scholars Program that exposed high school minority students to careers in science. In a 2005 interview, he recalled:

> I started the CETL fellowship with a notion of student success...but I also got involved with the fellowship on reflective practice, where we talked about how cognitive and affective concepts enhance teaching and learning.... I was involved in some Parker Palmer training. We went through experiences of being true to your inner self, letting your inner self come out and connecting with the class.... It's allowed me to look at this affective side of teaching and learning to see how much who I am as a person impacts the experiences that students have in the classroom.... The responses from the students have been absolutely great.[453]

The CETL Fellows were an extraordinary group who began offering a large variety of workshops and seminars for interested faculty members. They were aided by the fact that CETL (along with the Center for Institutional Effectiveness) had an attractive permanent location in a formerly private residence on Frey Lake (Campus Loop) Road. It was one of nine houses purchased by the foundation from unhappy homeowners who did not want to live across the street from University Place when

(Opposite Page) Beverly F. Mitchell

the first student housing opened. The Center for Institutional Effectiveness (CIE) was directed by Ed Rugg following his 2002 resignation from his old post as vice president for academic affairs. For a few months, Hill and Rugg shared space in the KSU Center. Then they moved together in January 2003 to the spacious new facility, on Frey Lake Road, and worked harmoniously for a number of years until CIE relocated to another foundation property across Chastain Road at Town Point, freeing space in House 54 exclusively for CETL operations and activities.[454]

The two-story CETL House contains a large kitchen, a huge conference room (where a master bedroom once was located) that was outfitted with a big-screen monitor and multimedia connections, a classroom/laptop computer lab in the former garage, as well as more than half a dozen faculty and staff offices in the old dining room, living room, bedrooms, and built-out attic space. The facility also included two cozy gas fireplaces and a large deck for outdoor gatherings. New paint, carpeting, furnishings, and upgraded HVAC systems made the CETL House an attractive and comfortable home for the staff and its many daily faculty visitors.

E-learning Fellow Gary Roberts made full use of the CETL House, hosting, with his wife Carlotta, dinner-and-a-movie evenings designed to generate faculty dialogue on a variety of provocative topics. His greatest contribution was to host weekly e-learning drop-in workshops for faculty members trying to fulfill a university mandate to place their syllabi and other teaching materials online through WebCT. To entice his colleagues to the one-on-one sessions, Roberts offered lunch, prepared on site. On occasion, particularly before the beginning of a new semester, as many as thirty people would attend. But, the numbers were usually small enough for Roberts and his helpers to work individually with novices struggling with the new technology, many unhappy about being forced into newfangled ways of instruction. A born teacher, he had the gift of putting his colleagues at ease and bringing them into the century of computer learning.[455]

Since 2003, the CETL House has been continuously booked with workshops organized by the CETL staff and fellows. For example, the Diversity in the Curriculum Fellows held numerous workshops and book as well as movie discussion sessions. Val Whittlesey's programs tended to focus on practical, hands-on issues such as handling diversity-related conflict in the classroom. As Diversity in the Curriculum fellow from 2005–2008, Dede Yow preferred inviting campus personnel to dinner-and-a-movie or book discussions on popular works of fiction to broaden their perspective on how to use diversity topics in their teaching.[456]

Kim Loomis held a number of workshops to introduce faculty to the scholarship of teaching and learning and took advantage of CETL funding to take small groups of her colleagues to SoTL conferences where they had the opportunity to meet the leaders in the field. Similarly, Mary Garner began organizing week-long faculty seminars to promote scholarly discourses across the disciplines. One of her colleagues in the math department, Josip Derado, was already exploring ways to connect mathematics with other fields of study. So they collaborated on designing an initial program for about fifteen faculty members from mathematics, languages, science, political science, literature, art, and music.

Garner put the idea of collaborative teaching into practical effect with an interdisciplinary honors seminar she taught with Spanish professor Judy M. Holzman and Librarian J. Dewi Wilson on Argentinian writer Jorge Luis Borges, whose stories were "subtly inundated with mathematical principles." She later recalled, "We have had so much fun teaching that course. And the students have been really receptive. For a lot of them, their eyes were opened to the possibilities of mathematics that they never considered and to the philosophy of mathematics that they never considered before…. It was a rich experience for us as well as the students because the three of us were in every class and we never knew what was going to happen…. We would get off on a tangent or give-and-take off each other, and it was great!"[457]

The original fellows were a talented group who won numerous faculty awards over the years. Garner was the recipient of Kennesaw's Distinguished Teaching Award in 2006 and the Distinguished Professor Award in 2009. She also won a 2007 University System of Georgia Excellence in Teaching Award. Both Gary Roberts and Army Lester received the KSU Distinguished Service Award and the Philip Preston Community Leadership Award, and Kim Loomis received a Distinguished Teaching Award.[458]

In time, some of the fellow positions evolved into full-time CETL staff positions. Army Lester's Student Success and Retention Fellowship morphed into

Gary B. Roberts

a full-time associate directorship of mentoring for faculty and student success. In 2004, Linda Noble resigned as dean of the College of Humanities and Social Sciences and went to work with Bill Hill in CETL. One of her first tasks was to take Hill's place in mentoring new faculty members by holding a two-day orientation for them prior to fall semester, followed by a series of workshops throughout the year. Individual sessions dealt with expectations for annual review and a host of practical topics. She also took the lead in revising Kennesaw's tenure and promotion guidelines and working with individual faculty members struggling to understand new expectations. Finally, she worked with Val Whittlesey in operating an orientation session and serving as mentor for new department chairs. After Noble left Kennesaw at the end of 2007 for an assistant vice chancellorship at the Board of Regents, Meghan A. Burke became her replacement, taking over these functions and more.[459]

A professor of mathematics, Burke was the recipient of the 2004 Distinguished Teaching Award. From 2006–2008, she was the CETL Learner-Centered Teaching Fellow, a new position that took over some of the functions of the scholarly discourse across disciplines area. As a faculty fellow, Burke initiated a series of book clubs and workshops, trying to introduce faculty to concepts of learner-centered education. When she moved into the associate directorship, Burke continued these activities in collaboration with Brian M. Wooten, the director of the Center for Student Leadership.

Other aspects of scholarly discourse across disciplines were picked up by Bill Hill and, later, Thomas P. Pusateri. For example, Army Lester, while still a CETL Fellow, had participated in a program on Cognitive Affective Learning through the Carnegie Academy on the Scholarship of Teaching and Learning. After Lester's fellowship ended, Hill took his place in this and another Carnegie Foundation for the Advancement of Teaching Institutional Leadership Program, gaining new ideas that could be shared with the KSU faculty.[460]

Tom Pusateri became CETL's second associate director in 2006 when vice president for academic affairs Lendley C. Black approached Hill about hiring an assessment director. Hill was enthusiastic about the new position, but persuaded Black to broaden the title and the mission by hiring the new person to be a CETL associate director for the SoTL. After all, Hill argued, assessment "really is the scholarship of teaching and learning because you're doing research on whether your curriculum and your practices in the classroom produce student learning." A social psychologist, Pusateri most recently had been assessment director for Florida Atlantic University and executive director for the Society for the Teaching of Psychology, a

(Opposite Page) Army Lester III

283

division of the American Psychological Association. In 2012 he became the recipient of the Board of Regents' Scholarship of Teaching and Learning Award for his work on effective teaching and student-learning practices.[461]

Near the end of his career, Bill Hill reflected in a 2009 interview:

> I think I have played a leadership role in having faculty see [CETL] as worthwhile…. They see it as a go-to place to get things done. I'm proud of the fact that I've redefined CETL to cover all the waterfront of faculty development—that we have a role not only in just teaching but also in assessment of teaching and student learning and enhancing research, which is faculty development to help people get involved in research…. I am proud of the recognition that CETL gained as a can-do organization, resulting in increased support and resources. We are the best teaching center in the state of Georgia and one of the best centers in the country.[462]

After Hill's retirement, CETL turned to Dr. Michele DiPietro in 2010 as its new executive director. DiPietro earned his PhD in statistics from Carnegie Mellon University in 2001. He served in 2012 as president of the prestigious Professional and Organizational Development Network (POD), the major association for college and university teaching centers. CETL continued to host a number of teaching conferences and workshops, and coordinated for the university a variety of competitive incentive grants and sabbatical programs.

DiPietro preserved a trend initiated by Hill of increasing the size of the full-time CETL staff while reducing the number of faculty fellows. In 2012, CETL had three associate directors: Pusateri (SoTL), Burke (mentoring for faculty and student success), and Amy M. Buddie (graduate student support and undergraduate research and creative activity). The recipient of the 2010 Distinguished Teaching Award, Buddie had previously been the CETL Fellow in the area of advancing undergraduate research and creative activity. In a major reorganization under DiPietro's leadership, the earlier fellowship fields were either deemed no longer necessary or absorbed under the duties of the full-time staff. In 2012 the three new fellows were Lynn Boettler (community engagement), Stephen W. Braden (adjunct faculty support), and Diana Gregory (creativity and innovation). Thus, CETL continued to evolve in ways designed to enhance its huge impact on effective teaching and faculty development.[463]

National Championships and the Transition to NCAA, Division I

The growth of the athletic program paralleled Kennesaw State's maturation academically. KSU was a full member of NCAA Division II for only a decade (1994–2004) before beginning the transition to Division I. In that time, Kennesaw teams won five national titles in four different sports (men's basketball, baseball, softball, and women's soccer). Under the direction of Coach Scott Whitlock, the softball team won back-to-back Division II championships in 1995 and 1996, and was joined in the latter year by Mike Sansing's national championship baseball team. Coached by Rob King, the soccer team won its national championship in December 2003, and a few months later on March 27, 2004, Tony Ingle's basketball team brought home a championship, defeating Southern Indiana 84-59 in the final game of the national tournament. Kennesaw athletes also won a number of individual titles, most notably Marjo Venalainen of Finland, arguably the best student-athlete in Kennesaw's history, who won the 1999 and 2000 Division II national cross country championship, was second in 2001, and despite an injury did well enough to earn All-American honors for the fourth time in her senior year of 2002. During her best season in 2000–01, she also won both the 1,500 meter and 3,000 meter runs at the Division II outdoor national track meet.[464]

Coach Scott Whitlock

The soccer championship was a remarkable achievement for a program that was only two years old. In the championship game on December 6, 2003, Kennesaw defeated Franklin Pierce University 2-0 on two goals by first-year student Laura Tucker. The other star of the contest for the KSU Owls was sophomore goalkeeper Jessica Marek, who recorded seven saves and set an NCAA record for five consecutive shutouts in national tournament competition. One of the team's All-American players, Jessie Fream of Woodstock, Georgia, remarked, "What's neat about Kennesaw is we always feel like we're the underdogs, and nobody ever expects much from us…. A lot of my friends go to UGA and Georgia Tech and they're like,

Coach Mike Sansing

'Wow, you won a national championship at Kennesaw?' Just winning is really cool."

The coach, Rob King, was hired in 2001 with a mandate to build a championship program. To do so he only needed to take advantage of the recruiting opportunities for talented athletes in the thriving high school and developmental soccer league programs of metropolitan Atlanta. He was successful from the start, achieving a 43-1-1 record in his first two seasons of competition. The only loss in that time was an early season defeat in 2003 to defending national champion Christian Brothers. Athletic director Dave Waples exclaimed over the unprecedented national title, saying that "in your wildest dreams, you don't hire a coach and then two years later they win a national championship. This just does not happen." But King added, "We have a great group of players, a good coaching staff, and the support of an administration that brought us in a year early to recruit."[465]

The 2004 national basketball championship probably created more favorable publicity for the KSU Department of Athletics than any other single event, simply because basketball is a major sport across the country, and the game reached a national television audience. Coach Tony Ingle was a veteran coach who had headed the basketball programs at Gordon College in Georgia and the University of Alabama in Huntsville, before spending eight years at Brigham Young University (BYU), first as an assistant coach to Roger Reid and then, after Reid was let go, as interim head coach for the last nineteen games of the 1996–97 school year. While the BYU program had been highly successful for the first six years of the Reid/Ingle era, the win-loss record declined after that, and the Cougars won only one game in the disastrous final season. Ingle's contract was not renewed, and he was out of coaching, until the KSU position became available.[466]

(Above) KSU's NCAA Division II national basketball champions, 2004

Acting on a recommendation from Bobby Cremins, the former Georgia Tech coach, Kennesaw hired Ingle as its head basketball coach in 2000. He had an excellent record as a recruiter at the Division II level, assembling a highly talented group of student athletes, some from out of state. The team's point guard, Terence Hill, from Fort Payne, Alabama, remarked that, "I didn't even know where [Kennesaw] was. But Coach Ingle just kept calling me and saying he thought we could win a national championship together. When I came on my visit, I was surprised by the campus and how many people went there." He added that the championship "says Kennesaw State is nothing to be messed with. After this year, everybody should know who we are."

President Siegel joined in the celebration. Since the championship game was held far away in Bakersfield, California, few fans from Kennesaw made the trip. However, the president threw a party in the Carmichael Student Center and invited everyone to come watch the Owls on several giant TVs. About three hundred people attended, and, according to Siegel, "We ran out of food three times. First, I ordered hot dogs, then pizza, then hot wings. It was quite a scene."

The 2003–04 season was the last in Kennesaw's outdated Spec Landrum Centre, a facility with only about a thousand seats that was built for physical education classes and intramurals in 1967 before Kennesaw had intercollegiate athletics. Ingle remembered that during the championship run, it was filled to capacity and they had to turn people away because "we had fire marshals everywhere." The following year, the team inaugurated the new four-thousand-seat Convocation Center. In addition to housing the Athletic Department, that $17 million facility was also used for graduations and a host of public events.

In addition to soccer and basketball, Kennesaw won a third national competition during the 2003–04 academic year in a club sport, when competitive cheerleading came home with top honors from the Chick-fil-A Cheer and Dance Collegiate Championship in Daytona Beach, Florida. On April 7, 2004, Kennesaw held a celebration in the Student Center for the three victorious teams. By this time, Tony Ingle had been named the Division II Men's Basketball Coach of the Year. When he was recognized at the ceremony, he gave the credit to his assistants and players, noting that "only the innocent or the ignorant think that they do something by themselves."[467]

After Kennesaw's success in conquering Division II athletics, there seemed little doubt that the university was ready to make the jump to Division I. In May 2003, Siegel and Waples appointed an eighteen-person Feasibility Committee, headed by two former athletic directors, Spec Landrum of Kennesaw and Homer Rice of Georgia Tech. The committee included faculty, staff, and community representatives, a male and female athlete, and the president and vice president of the Student Government Association. Waples and the Department of Athletics provided staff support. Landrum recalled that after about three meetings, the committee gelled into a team, and, in November 2003, produced a detailed report.

The main conclusion was that Kennesaw needed a Division I Athletic Program to keep abreast with the rising national prominence of its academic programs. The report called for fast-tracking women's soccer and men's golf so that they could immediately compete in postseason tournaments under NCAA rules. The NCAA required the other sports to go through a four-year probationary period in which they were ineligible for postseason national tournaments while the university phased in Division I requirements regarding the minimum number of sports teams, the budget size, academic reporting, and the like. The feasibility study noted that Kennesaw needed to gain acceptance into a Division I conference, commit itself to increased spending, and add at least five additional sports teams. While football would not be one of those sports, the Feasibility Committee called upon the administration to continue studying its possible inclusion. President Siegel was pleased with the report and quickly made the decision to implement its recommendations.[468]

In November 2004, KSU made the official announcement that it was moving to Division I. By then, it was talking to various conferences about possible membership. The best fit was the Atlantic Sun Conference (A-Sun), a non-football conference of schools from Tennessee to Florida. On January 5, 2005, the Atlantic Sun held a press conference to announce Kennesaw as its newest member. The A-Sun was a relatively low-level Division I conference that was something of a stepping stone for growing schools. At the time of the announcement, Georgia State, Central Florida, and Troy State University were on their way out, and East Tennessee State and North Florida were on their way in.

At the news conference, the main topic of discussion was when Kennesaw would join some of the departing members in adding football. President Siegel told the reporters that KSU had "an extraordinary interest in football." KSU trustee Dr. Stan Dysart, who had headed a football exploratory committee a couple of years earlier, volunteered that, "The community wants football. Students want it. Trustees want it. The faculty support it. The president wants it." He added that the main obstacles were finding financial supporters and building a stadium on campus.[469]

Kennesaw had one more year in which all but the two fast-tracked sports competed in Division II. Although the sports teams failed to bring home any more national titles, they did very well locally against Division II competition. In that final year of 2004–05, softball, men's

(Opposite Page) Basketball action in January 1996

A postgame celebration for a baseball victory in May 1998

basketball, and men's and women's cross country won Peach Belt championships, and baseball came in second place. Softball came close to bringing home another national championship. It lost 5-3 in the finals to Lynn University of Boca Raton, Florida. Two years later Lynn University had to give up its title and all its 2005 victories after an NCAA investigation concluded that the coach improperly paid tuition and books for two nonscholarship athletes.[470]

Since it moved immediately to Division I, women's soccer in 2004 had no opportunity to defend its Division II championship and, indeed, had no league in which to compete for a conference title. Nonetheless, the team did quite well, having finished the transitional year with a record of 12-4-1, mainly against Division I teams. After Kennesaw joined the Atlantic Sun Conference, the woman's soccer team finished second in the league in 2005, first in 2006 and 2007, second in 2008, and first in 2009. In 2007, it became the first Kennesaw team to compete in an NCAA Division I tournament.[471]

During the 1990s, the Athletic Program consisted of only eight sports, the minimum required in Division II. With limited resources, KSU preferred to fund a few teams relatively well rather than a large number of teams poorly. In those years, the official sports were men's and women's basketball, men's and women's cross country, baseball, softball, men's golf, and women's tennis. The ninth sport in 2002 was women's soccer. Upon its application to Division I, KSU added men's and women's outdoor track in 2005, and women's golf and men's and women's indoor track in 2006, bringing the total number of sports officially to fourteen, the minimum for non-football Division I schools.

In the years when Kennesaw did not have an official track and field program, Coach Stan Sims, a full-time math professor, continued to work with the cross country runners in the off season. Somehow, he found the necessary funds to take athletes such as Marjo Venalainen to a few track competitions, including the Penn Relays and the Division II national championship meet. An unusual NCAA policy recognized their right to participate, despite the fact that Kennesaw lacked an official team.[472]

Not everyone in the Department of Athletics was excited about the move to the next level. Athletic director Waples recalled, "It was a big shock, and we had some resistance." But the transition brought more publicity and a better situation for everyone, "even though you might get hammered for those four [probationary] years." During the transition, recruiting proved to be a problem, especially in basketball. While Kennesaw could compete for the A-Sun championship, it was barred from the NCAA tournament. According to Waples, "Schools that hadn't

(Opposite Page) Future major league baseball star Willie Harris, 1999 been to the NCAA tournament since Lincoln died would say to a recruit, 'Hey, why would you go to Kennesaw? You can't go to the NCAA tournament.'"[473]

Despite the difficulties of the transition, Kennesaw did well, on the whole, in Division I competition. In the first year in the A-Sun (2005–06), the women's cross country team won the conference meet and the men were third, while Kennesaw had second place finishes in men's outdoor track, women's soccer, and softball. The following year, the soccer and softball teams won championships. In 2007–08 the men's indoor and outdoor track teams and the soccer team led the conference, and the baseball and women's cross country teams came in second. During the final year of probation (2008–09), Kennesaw won no conference championships, but had a series of seconds (baseball, men's and women's indoor and outdoor track, and soccer).[474]

During the probationary years, KSU increased the student athletic fee from $79 in 2003–04 to $144 in 2009–10. With fall semester student enrollment jumping in the same period from 17,485 to 22,389, the student fee allowed the Athletic Department to more than double its budget (from just under $3 million in 2003-04 to $6.8 million in 2009–10). For three straight years, Waples and other administrators attended compulsory NCAA Rules Seminars to master the new requirements. As early as 2005, Kennesaw was subject to the association's Academic Percentage Rating (APR) that required the institution to report on the academic progress and retention of student-athletes, with the threat of possible penalties for poor performances. As a result, in 2008, the Department of Athletics leased from the KSU Foundation the Bowen (Student-Athletic Success Services) Building and beefed up the staff that provided academic mentoring. With these improvements, KSU gradually came into compliance with Division I standards.[475]

In June 2009 the NCAA sent Kennesaw a letter accepting the school as a full-fledged Division I member as of August of that year. Soon afterwards, Director Waples began thinking about retirement and made it official at the end of the academic year. For 2010–11 his longtime assistant, Scott Whitlock, served as interim director. In his twenty-three years of leadership, Waples had seen a small athletic program with a tiny budget go from NAIA to NCAA Division II to Division I, with the possibility of football under serious discussion. He had much for which he could take credit. At the end of his career, however, he preferred to emphasize the team effort of supportive presidents, administrators such as Roger Hopkins, Nancy King, and Ted Cochran, and all the coaches and athletes that had come through the program.[476]

Close of the Siegel Era

The achievements of the Athletic Department paralleled those of the university in general. The years between 1996 and 2006 were pivotal in the evolution of a full-fledged university with a transformed campus culture. Toward the end of this critical era, President Siegel took advantage of the spring 2005 commencement exercises to announce her plans to retire. She originally hoped to leave office by January 2006, but served an additional half year while a successor was chosen and completed his obligations elsewhere. The university community paused often in the 2005–06 school year to take note of the fantastic changes during Siegel's presidency. Many regarded Betty Siegel as the ideal president for the era that was ending. The inevitable question was what type of president would be ideal for the next stage in the university's history.

New President, New Era

Betty Siegel's retirement announcement in 2005 was a watershed moment in the history of Kennesaw State University. She had been president for well over half of Kennesaw's history, and the vast majority of faculty and staff had known no other. During her tenure, the fall enrollment had grown from 4,195 in 1981 to 18,556 in 2005, and the number of full-time employees had expanded from about three hundred to almost fourteen hundred. The opportunity to select a new chief executive promised to say much about what Kennesaw had become and where it hoped to go.

The change in leadership, however, was just one measure at middecade of what KSU was, and what it wanted to be. Since its founding, the institution had gone through an exhaustive self-analysis at least once every ten years as it made its case for reaccreditation to the Southern Association of Colleges and Schools (SACS). The search for the next president took place in the midst of the most recent process. Under new SACS guidelines, Kennesaw had to create a Quality Enhancement Plan (QEP) to improve student learning in one central area over the next five years. The outgoing Siegel administration—much to the delight of incoming President Dan Papp, an expert on international relations—chose to focus on "Global Learning for Engaged Citizenship."

While the SACS review process was well underway, in May 2006 the Board of Regents authorized Kennesaw's first doctoral program, a doctor of education (EdD) degree in leadership for learning. The new post-master's program also included KSU's first specialist in education (EdS) Consequently, KSU quickly prepared and three weeks later submitted to SACS' Commission on Colleges an extensive application for an accreditation "level change." The commission met in June and approved the change, allowing Kennesaw to enroll the first doctoral class just a half year later in January 2007.

Fortunately, KSU made a strong case for SACS accreditation at Level V (institutions with limited doctorates), moving up from Level III (masters' degrees as the highest awarded) and skipping over Level IV (specialists' degrees as the highest rewarded). Not long after, KSU reached the highest category, Level VI (institutions with four or more doctoral programs). The university community's attention for the next several years would focus on the transition from the Siegel to the Papp presidency, the challenge of new SACS accreditation requirements, the implementation of a global learning QEP, and the establishment of Kennesaw's initial five doctorates, including the first PhD program in 2010 in international conflict management.

President Siegel's Legacy

Effective leaders are known for their ability to communicate a clear, simple vision that captures the spirit of a time and place. Kennesaw's first president, Horace Sturgis, dreamed of growing a start-up junior college into a four-year school. From the beginning, his administration focused on recruiting a faculty with senior-college credentials. In his last commencement in June 1980, he had the honor of awarding the college's first bachelors' degrees. Having seen his vision come to fruition, he announced his retirement.

Sturgis left behind a college with unlimited potential, yet practically no one outside Cobb County had heard its story. The challenge for the next president was to move a small, cloistered college out to the various communities it was supposed to serve—making it visible locally, regionally, nationally, and globally. Betty Siegel proved to be the ideal leader to introduce Kennesaw to larger audiences. She shared the view of former University of California president Clark Kerr that presidents who have nothing to say off campus have little worthwhile to say on campus. Charismatic and inspirational, she was an extraordinarily gifted public speaker, much in demand throughout metropolitan Atlanta and beyond.[477]

Siegel had been shaped by mentors who taught that colleges that were cloistered were not colleges of the future, and that leaders in higher education have an obligation to help society see "what is the righteous, good thing to do." At the start of her presidency, she created the View of the Future Committee as one means of making Kennesaw less hierarchical and more inclusive. The first female president in the University System of Georgia, she knew firsthand what it felt like to be excluded and had a long history of supporting inclusiveness and diversity. Her scholarly interest in invitational education shaped her desire to make Kennesaw a learner-centered university with initiatives like the First-Year Experience, the unified CAPS Center (Counseling, Advisement, and Placement Services), and CETL (the Center for Excellence in Teaching and Learning). She believed that education should be more than just a collection of courses; and, even prior to student housing in 2002, she wanted KSU to operate as much as possible like a residential college.[478]

Near the end of her presidency, in 2005, she reflected back on Erik Erikson's eight stages of life, and noted that Kennesaw, at a little over forty years old, was moving from the intimacy of young adulthood into the generativity of early middle age. She observed that intimacy was the opposite of isolation and involved relationships both on and off campus. Success in establishing such relationships prepared the way for generativity, the age where healthy individuals and institutions do the most meaningful work for the betterment of society.[479]

The size of the faculty and staff and the number of programs and buildings grew astronomically during the Siegel era. But she claimed little interest in a legacy based on buildings and programs, arguing that universities exist not just to create and convey knowledge, but to assign ethical meaning. She often said, "I drink from a well that I did not dig," and urged faculty members to help Kennesaw be a "university that matters" by teaching students that "the good life is a life of service, not a life of self-aggrandizement, not a life of possessions."[480]

The President was fond of Carl Sandburg's 1948 novel, *Remembrance Rock*, a work of historical fiction that extolled the American spirit from the Puritans to World War II. Siegel often quoted Sandburg's admonition to "sit on a rock once a year and ask the questions: Who am I?

President Emerita Betty Siegel

Where do I come from? Where am I going?" Just before her retirement in 2006, she had KSU's own Thinking Rock placed between Kennesaw Hall and the Convocation Center with a plaque containing Sandburg's questions plus two of her own: "What is the meaning? How do I matter?" By doing so, she hoped to inspire future generations to reflect on the value of living meaningful lives. "That would be a legacy," she said, "that we would give to them that would make them better leaders for tomorrow."[481]

President Siegel's vision of an ethical, service-oriented university took concrete shape on October 31, 2000, when she had announced the creation of a Center for Leadership, Ethics, and Character that would report to her office. Shortly afterward, she appointed Robert C. Varga as the interim director. Varga would later become

Deborah Roebuck

a special assistant to the president. The center grew in visibility in 2002 with the appointment of Judith M. Stillion as the first permanent director and with the decision to give the center a permanent home in one of the residences the KSU Foundation purchased on Campus Loop Road.[482]

When Wesley K. Wicker arrived at KSU in September 2002, his first task as interim vice president for advancement was to raise funds for the center. A KSU Foundation trustee, Dennis E. Cooper, was chairman of the RTM Restaurant Group, an Atlanta-based company that operated well over seven hundred Arby's franchises. Its principal founder, Russ V. Umphenour Jr., had a scholarly and professional interest in leadership studies and kept in his office an extensive library of leadership books. Siegel and Wicker thought that RTM might be supportive of a center devoted to ethical leadership and approached the company with a request for a $1 million gift.

RTM agreed to give $500,000 to fund the Endowed Chair of Leadership, Ethics, and Character, and another $500,000 for an operating endowment. The university made an official announcement of the gift on December 20, 2002 and indicated that the center would henceforth be called the RTM Center for Leadership, Ethics, and Character. On August 1, 2003, the Board of Regents gave its blessings and elevated the center to institute status, a reflection of its broad, university-wide significance, as opposed to the narrower, discipline-focus of most centers.[483]

Between 2002 and 2005, RTM gave an additional $200,000 to cover the institute's day-to-day operations. The RTM funding lasted until the business was purchased in 2005 by Triarc, the parent of the Arby's Franchise Trust. Other contributors included retired Lockheed Martin executive vice president James A. (Micky) Blackwell, his wife Billie, and President Siegel herself. At a 2006 retirement party for the president, trustee Dennis Cooper suggested that the institute be renamed in her honor. In August 2006, a month after she left the presidency, the name change became official. Claiming that she was redirecting and redefining rather than retiring, the president emerita became the holder of the endowed chair at the Siegel Institute.[484]

In 2006, Deborah Britt Roebuck took over as the institute's executive director. She told the Marietta Rotary Club that the institute "sprang from a great need to address a crisis in the lack of ethics in the management of some of our largest companies.... While they juggled the books and squandered billions of precious shareholder dollars, our country was set back economically." She added that the primary goal of the institute was "to develop and promote ethical leadership among individuals and organizations," and that KSU, under Dr. Siegel's leadership, had created a "Model of Ethical Leadership based on core values of trust, respect, optimism, intentionality, and service."[485]

One of Dan Papp's first decisions as president was to transfer the Siegel Institute from his office to the Office of Academic Affairs. In 2009 Dorothy D. Zinsmeister became interim executive

Linda M. Johnston

director. She served until Linda M. Johnston assumed the permanent position at the start of 2011. Over its first decade of operation, the Siegel Institute developed a fifteen-hour graduate certificate program in leadership and ethics, hosted an annual Phenomenal Women's Conference, engaged in a Character Education partnership with the Cobb County School District, sponsored a regular series of guest speakers for Daring Dialogues Luncheons, operated the Lunch and a Book or Movie Series, held ethics workshops for state advisory boards, and sponsored faculty affiliates and visiting scholars who engaged in applied research on questions of ethical leadership.[486]

President Emerita Betty Siegel continued an active schedule. Late in her presidency, she told the American Association of State Colleges and Universities of her desire to engage other universities in questions of ethical leadership. Upon receiving a positive response from a number of presidents, she issued an invitation in 2005 for an Oxford Conclave on Global Ethics and the Changing University Presidency, held at Balliol College. Founded in 1263, Balliol was England's oldest college. It proved an ideal setting for the discussion she led on the role of colleges and universities in producing a new generation of ethical leaders.[487]

The 2005 Oxford Conclave led to a larger gathering the following year and then a third in 2007. According to Frances Hesselbein, the former CEO of Girl Scouts of the USA and founder of Leader to Leader Institute, "Meeting in a medieval college, founded over 700 years ago, where a sense of history permeated our every deliberation, [underscored] the indispensable place of the university in society." In 2007, Siegel also spent three months as a visiting scholar at Stellenbosch University in South Africa, where she worked with the director of academic support in developing a First-Year Academy. The following April she went back for the Stellenbosch Seboka [a gathering of people for a common cause] on Higher Education and Ethical Leadership, where the participants recreated the Oxford Conclaves. The main purpose was to address the role of universities in producing ethically and socially responsible leaders for Africa. The attendees were primarily university presidents and administrators from southern Africa; speakers included Archbishop Emeritus Desmond Tutu.[488]

In her role as President Emerita, Siegel served on the board of directors for the National Character Education Partnership in Washington, DC. She remained active in the International Alliance for Invitational Education, which she had cofounded years earlier with her former University of Florida colleague, William W. Purkey. In the summer of 2008 she began a Wintering into Wisdom Initiative "to promote the idea of remaining positive, productive, and wise into the later years of a successful life." She also worked to create a Higher Education Past Presidents' Association. She once said, "I am psychologically 39. But I'm not chronologically 39…. I never think of my age until it's in the paper. It doesn't mean anything to me, really. I like to think that each age is a dream that is dying or coming to birth…. What I would like to do would be to use this third act of my life in very creative ways." That was certainly the case in the first several years of her postpresidency.[489]

Selection of Daniel S. Papp as Kennesaw's Third President

Chancellor Thomas C. Meredith asked Dean Joseph D. Meeks to head the search committee for Betty Siegel's replacement. A Kennesaw faculty member since 1975 and the dean of the College of the Arts since its founding in 1998, Meeks had made numerous contacts with arts supporters and was a highly successful dean and fundraiser. In 2002, he established a KSU Benefit Gala for the Arts. Over the first five years, those annual galas brought in more than $1 million for arts scholarships, giving Kennesaw a competitive edge in recruiting talented students.[490]

Chancellor Meredith had attended several of the galas and was sufficiently impressed with Meeks's work to ask him to chair the presidential search. Both Meredith and Meeks understood that a modern president has to be a good fundraiser. As Meeks remarked, "We can't expect the state to keep funding everything we have; it's not going to happen. I think we'll get less of that as time goes on. If we don't have private funding, if we don't have an ambassador that can go out there and charm people and convince people that Kennesaw is the place to invest, then we don't have a future."[491]

Meredith gave the committee its charge on August 4, 2005. Compared to the presidential search of 1981, this one was more top-down. The earlier search had been headed by a member of the teaching faculty and resulted in no less than nine semifinalists coming to campus to interact with faculty, staff, and students. The 2005 search was headed by a dean and also included a former interim dean (Ann Smith), an associate dean (Ken Gilliam), and a department chair (Peter Witte). Faculty members on the committee were Jonathan VanGeest (nursing), Sarah Robbins (English), Ben Setzer (computer science), and Christine Ziegler (psychology). Other representatives included Suzy Millwood of the staff, Thomas Cotton of the Student Government Association, Thomas Holder of the foundation, and Stephen A. Prather the Alumni Association. The chancellor chose the executive search firm of Baker-Parker and Associates to assist the committee in finding qualified candidates.[492]

On October 3, 2005, the KSU Faculty Council expressed alarm over what it perceived as a lack of transparency in the presidential search. The council unanimously adopted a resolution expressing its dissatisfaction with the process. Concerned that no on-campus visits of finalists had thus far been scheduled, the Faculty Council resolved that the search committee invite all finalists to open sessions with the faculty. The Staff Council, Student Government Association, and campus chapter of the American Association of University Professors expressed similar concerns. Fortunately, their complaints were heard, and the search committee announced that five finalists would be invited to campus in January to meet with all constituencies of the university.[493]

The search committee worked quickly to whittle down the original list of fifty-two candidates to ten semifinalists who were interviewed over a weekend at Atlanta's Hartsfield-Jackson International Airport. According to Meeks, the interviews were invaluable in revealing which candidates had the psychological and philosophical makeup to handle the pressures of the job and to support the concept of shared

(Opposite Page) Presidents Papp and Siegel

304

governance. Foundation chairman Tommy Holder found the process to be rewarding for a different reason—that it revealed how many "really outstanding individuals across this country…wanted badly to be the president of KSU." After three days of interviews, the committee decided upon five strong finalists.[494]

Utilizing comments from committee discussions and feedback from a campus survey, Meeks and the committee prepared a one-page summary of strengths and

weaknesses for each of the five candidates. Meeks then presented the search committee's findings, unranked, to a Special Regents' Committee consisting of Michael J. Coles, James R. Jolly, and Donald M. Leebern Jr. There seemed little doubt that three candidates stood out above the rest. Two of the candidates were local—senior vice chancellor for academics and fiscal affairs, Daniel S. Papp, a thirty-three-year Cobb County resident; and Timothy S. Mescon, the dean of the Coles College of Business. The third strong candidate was John Dunn, the provost and vice chancellor of Southern Illinois University–Carbondale.

The regents committee made a site visit to Illinois and came away impressed with Dunn's outstanding performance. But the members also thought highly of Mescon and Papp. Michael Coles claimed that the search committee had made the Regents' job easy and difficult at the same time—easy, because the report so clearly spelled out the candidates' strengths and weaknesses, and difficult, because they were all stellar administrators. In the end, one candidate emerged as the favorite. On February 16, 2006, the Board of Regents unanimously selected Dan Papp.[495]

Born in 1947, Papp grew up in a working-class neighborhood in Cleveland, Ohio, where he developed a keen interest in foreign affairs from listening to his father and his buddies talk about their experiences abroad in World War II. Between 1965 and 1969 he attended Dartmouth College on a need-based scholarship, majoring successively in chemistry, mathematics, economics, and international affairs—a valuable experience, he claims, when students come to him with their anxieties about their future and their inability to settle on a major. International affairs appealed to him because the field was interdisciplinary and dealt with life and death issues at the peak of the Cold War when the nuclear arms race threatened the future of humanity.

The young scholar by no means spent all his time in the library worrying about world events. He was recruited to play football, and was a member of the Dartmouth team until being sidelined with a knee injury. Afterwards, he took up rugby, among other sports, and gravitated toward faculty members who valued athletics as well as academics. He also joined a fraternity. At the height of student protests over the Vietnam War, he managed to keep his hair cut short and maintained ties to both sides of the ideological divide. When Students for a Democratic Society (SDS) occupied the Dartmouth administration building, Papp and a couple of fraternity brothers set up a lemonade stand that did business with the New Hampshire State Troopers as well as the SDS and generated enough revenue for a weekend in Boston.[496]

(Opposite Page) President Papp's inauguration in October 2006 with the chairman of the KSU Foundation, Thomas M. Holder, and Provost Lendley C. Black assisting in the robing ceremony.

Having graduated from Dartmouth, Papp spent the 1969–70 school year teaching American government and history and coaching multiple sports at his old high school in Cleveland, Ohio. That experience impressed upon him how exhausting public school teaching is and how little academic freedom teachers have where course content is dictated by state rules. After "burning out" as a public school teacher, Papp moved from frigid Cleveland to sunny Florida, where he enrolled in the International Affairs Doctoral Program at the University of Miami. There, he flew through graduate school, starting in June 1970 and walking away with a PhD three years later in August 1973, with a dissertation on "The Soviet Perception of the Goals of and Constraints on American Policy toward Vietnam, June 1964–December 1965."[497]

The Center for Advanced International Studies at Miami contained a remarkable faculty that brought real-world experience into the classroom. Many were retired from the State Department or the various national think tanks, and, while they had PhDs, relatively few advanced through the traditional academic ranks. Their focus

was on moving promising students through school as rapidly as possible, encouraging them to find term paper topics from their first semester that would eventually be incorporated into their dissertations. In this applied research environment, Papp thrived, studying and writing about big idea topics that seemed relevant and that could conceivably help policymakers dealing with Cold War issues.[498]

Doctorate in hand, Papp joined the faculty of Georgia Tech in the fall of 1973, at a pivotal moment in the school's history when President Joseph M. Pettit was operating under a mandate from the Board of Regents to build a true research university. Perhaps the major drawback for someone in the liberal arts was that Tech, in the 1970s, was an engineering school without a political science undergraduate major or graduate program. On the other hand, the new faculty member discovered that he had freedom to teach what he wanted to teach and research what he wanted to research. He took satisfaction that students shared his excitement when he introduced into the classroom his discoveries about American-Soviet relations.

Each quarter, he taught a general education section of American Government to 225 students and two upper-level sections of American or Soviet Foreign Policy, US Defense Policy, or International Relations. Over a typical three-quarter school year, he taught about nine hundred students, without the help of graduate teaching assistants—no easy task, but one that allowed him (over a three-year period) to teach about a third of all the undergraduates attending Tech. Playing essentially a service function for the engineering schools, the social science faculty put teaching first and operated under the motto that "every student is our student." The system suited Papp well, and by 1976, at the end of his third year, he was selected by the Student Government Association for the annual Outstanding Faculty Member Award.[499]

Papp's philosophy of teaching was first to capture students' interest, and then to confuse them with ideas and information that challenged their beliefs and made them want to do research on their own to decide what was true. His goal was to turn them into critical thinkers. As long as they established a solid intellectual basis for their beliefs, he thought he had achieved his purpose, even if the students, in the end, still adhered to the beliefs they had in the beginning. His love of research came from an understanding that the questions he studied were critically important to the United States and the world—and to the students he taught.

As a junior professor, he threw himself into a variety of service commitments, most notably as faculty advisor to Sigma Alpha Epsilon fraternity and the Georgia Tech Rugby Club (which he founded). His community service activities included

(Opposite Page) President Papp and Jerome Ratchford with an international student

President Papp talking to international students

working with the Buckhead-based Southern Center for International Studies, speaking to high school classes around the state, coaching youth sports, and doing church work in Cobb County, where he established his residence. At the same time, he engaged in extensive traveling, taking a group of students to the Soviet Union in 1975 as director of a Georgia Tech Summer Program, going to Australia in 1977 and Shanghai in 1984 on visiting professorships, and spending a year as a research professor in 1977–78 at the United States Army War College

Strategic Studies Institute in Carlisle, Pennsylvania. As a result of his work at the War College, Papp was awarded an Outstanding Civilian Service Medal by the US Army in 1979.[500]

Seven years into his career at Tech, Papp "wandered into" administration when the director of the School of Social Sciences resigned in 1980. The twenty-four faculty members that made up the school acted sometimes like a dysfunctional family, with historians, political scientists, sociologists, and others engaging in "internecine combat" over matters such as which discipline would receive the next new faculty position. Papp recalled, "I just had a knack to bring people together. So a couple of other faculty members said, 'Gee, we're spending all of our time politicking; why don't you let us nominate you to be chair because you can probably bring everybody together. Then we'll all have more time to do our teaching and our research and our writing because we won't have to worry about politics.' So that's what happened."

While Papp believed in giving everyone a chance to speak, he had a results-oriented approach and insisted on reaching a final decision as expeditiously as possible. His administrative philosophy was that "instead of conniving behind each other's backs, we'd sit down and have meetings and, 'At the end of this hour, we're going to reach consensus. If at the end of this hour we don't reach consensus, we're still going to have a decision, but everybody will have heard everybody else's arguments and we'll be done. Then we can go teach and research and write.'"[501]

Papp headed the School of Social Sciences until it was abolished in 1990. John Patrick Crecine, the Tech president at the time, had a mandate from the Board of Regents to increase the number of majors. Over the years, the social sciences faculty had developed a master's program in technology and science policy that had three tracks (history of technology, technology policy analysis, and international security and development). Crecine decided that each of the tracks was large enough to become a school with its own master's program. Unfortunately, Crecine's authoritarian style riled the social sciences faculty who felt left out of his curriculum planning. As a result, many of them resisted the attempt to divide the multidisciplinary School of Social Sciences.

Papp objected to some of the specifics of the top-down plan, but generally supported what the president was trying to do. He told Crecine at the time, "Pat, your problem is you don't have enough confidence in the value of your own ideas. Instead of trying to do things via force, just go out and explain it, and people are going to sign on like crazy." Crecine's initial resentment of Papp's critique almost ended the administrative career of Kennesaw's future president. But in the end, Crecine conceded the wisdom of Papp's advice and made him the founding director of the School of International Affairs, one of the three new schools to come out of the old School of Social Sciences.[502]

Papp headed that school for three years (1990–93), and then from 1994–1997 served as professor of international affairs and the executive assistant to the next Georgia Tech President, G. Wayne Clough. One of his achievements in that period was helping to persuade retiring US Senator Sam Nunn, in 1996, to let Tech name its School of International Affairs in his honor. Throughout the 1980s and 1990s and into the early 2000s—despite his huge time commitment to administration—Papp continued to research and publish a large number of works on international affairs, including ten books. His first book, *Vietnam: The View from Moscow, Peking, Washington*, came out in 1981. In 1984, Macmillan published his popular textbook, *Contemporary International Relations: Frameworks for Understanding*, which had gone through six editions by 2002. His second and third monographs, *Soviet Perceptions of the Developing World during the 1980s* and *Soviet Policies toward the Developing World in the 1980s* came out in 1985 and 1986, respectively.[503]

Between 1975–2002, he published some sixty-two refereed articles or book chapters. At the same time, he edited or coedited a number of books on international affairs and played a central role in helping former US secretary of state Dean Rusk complete his autobiography, *As I Saw It* (Norton, 1990). After his tenure at the State Department, Rusk, a Georgia native, spent fourteen years teaching international law at the UGA Law School, and then remained in Athens for the rest of his life. In the 1960s, Dean Rusk had become alienated from his son Richard over the Vietnam War, which the father ardently supported and the son strongly opposed. After the former secretary suffered a stroke, Richard, in an effort at reconciliation, attempted to assist his father in writing the autobiography. Unfortunately, the book project stalled, and Dr. Papp was invited to step in to save it. Papp conducted a series of interviews with Rusk (producing about three thousand pages of transcripts), and arranged the relevant material in a coherent order, sometimes rewriting material and running it by Rusk for his approval. In the end, Papp edited 100 percent and wrote 30 percent of *As I Saw It*.[504]

Dan Papp's outstanding accomplishments in teaching, research, service, and administration were recognized in 1993 when the Georgia Tech Honors Committee chose him to receive the university's annual Distinguished Professor Award. Consisting of faculty, students, alumni, and administrators, the Honors Committee had always granted the award to someone from engineering or math and the natural sciences. Papp was the first social scientist to be so honored.[505]

Papp's first experience as a college president came between July 1997 and August 1998 when the chancellor asked him to step into an interim role and help resolve a crisis at Southern Polytechnic State University (SPSU). The previous president, Stephen R. Cheshier, had just retired after a faculty vote of no confidence in his leadership. According to Papp, Cheshier's problem was that he "was too nice a guy" and would not fire administrators who should have been removed. A major source

of contention was the leadership of the vice president for academic affairs, another "nice man," according to Papp, who "had retired on active duty." The chief academic officer had recently demoted several deans and department chairs in retaliation for their vote of no confidence in his leadership.

Arriving on a campus with gaping holes in the administrative team, Papp began by listening to everyone and concluding he had inherited a situation where no one was right. He handled the problem by backing the vice president's decision, but asked him to retire by January, something he, fortunately, was ready to do. Then Papp announced that the empty chair and dean positions would be filled by national searches, and the displaced administrators were free to apply like anyone else and take their chances. Several of them submitted their applications and won their jobs

back. The interim president also had to fire the basketball coach/athletic director who had been illegally cashing his players' Pell Grant checks, doling out the funds as he felt the players needed them, and depositing in the Athletic Department budget whatever remained. While resolving personnel disputes, Papp led the faculty in developing SPSU's first strategic plan in years. As a result, he had a successful thirteen months as interim president and left the campus with a stronger sense of community for his successor, Lisa A. Rossbacher.[506]

In 1999, Governor Roy E. Barnes and Chancellor Stephen A. Portch chose Papp to direct the Yamacraw Broadband Education Programs, a $100 million initiative of the governor to make Georgia a leader in designing and marketing high-speed communications systems. The educational component was to hire seventy to eighty additional faculty members at eight campuses across the state, to develop state-of-the-art computer science and electrical engineering curricula, and to engage in multiuniversity, world-class collaborative research. KSU and Southern Poly were heavily involved in the research effort, along with UGA, Georgia State, and Georgia Tech. The Clendenin Computer Science Building at Kennesaw was one of the beneficiaries of Yamacraw's investment in telecommunications education. Papp's primary role was to develop a strategic plan, decide how to divide the pool of money, and bring together the various university presidents in implementing project objectives.[507]

After a year with the Yamacraw Project, Papp became the university system's senior vice chancellor for academics and fiscal affairs in 2000, a position he held for six years. He almost left Georgia in 2002 to become chancellor of the University System of Florida, but he hastily backed out when it became apparent that the Florida universities were subject to a degree of political control that Georgia had not seen since the days of Eugene Talmadge. Just after his selection, the presidencies of four major Florida universities became vacant; but before he was consulted on any of them, three were filled by politicians with minimal educational qualifications. When Papp discovered that he would not even have control over his staff, he turned down the chancellorship and stayed in Georgia.[508]

In September 2005, about two months after KSU's presidential search committee began its work, Chancellor Meredith left Georgia to become commissioner of higher education in Mississippi. As a result, the search for the next USG chancellor coincided with KSU's presidential search. Dan Papp became a finalist for both positions, but was bypassed for the top post in December 2005, when the regents selected Erroll B. Davis Jr. as the first African American ever to head the University

(Opposite Page) Presidents Papp and Siegel with Michael J. Coles and Governor Ervin (Sonny) Perdue III

System of Georgia. The chairman of the board of Alliant Energy Corporation, Davis was a businessman rather than an academician. He had an electrical engineering degree from Carnegie Mellon and an MBA in finance from the University of Chicago, and also served on the boards of trustees of both institutions. It was unusual in Georgia to choose someone who had not come up through the academic ranks, but Davis had the support of Governor Sonny Perdue, and the regents chose him in an apparent attempt to bring an outside voice from the business world into the management of the university system.[509]

Frustrated in one candidacy, Papp devoted his energies to the Kennesaw search. He was not a stranger to the KSU campus. Over the years he had spent many hours on the weekends in the Sturgis Library, taking advantage of the fact that Kennesaw's library was open longer than Tech's. He had also spoken on campus on occasion. When he came on January 12, 2006, to audition for the job, he told an open campus forum that the next president needed to be a visionary, a collegial leader over a community of learners, a fundraiser, an ambassador, and a creative problem solver. He claimed that, despite Kennesaw's strong record in teaching and service, it needed to increase its graduation and retention rates, develop a new strategic plan, and forge more partnerships with other institutions, especially nearby junior colleges. He added that priorities for the next president should include faculty development, increased diversity, and greater attention to alumni affairs.

Papp concluded that, "I've been a Cobb resident for thirty-three years. I've watched Kennesaw grow from a small college to what it is today…. Where Kennesaw can go is incredible." The search committee

Carol Pope, assistant director for disAbled Student Support Services, listens to President Papp respond to student questions.

and the Board of Regents obviously liked what they heard. And so, on February 16, 2006, in an executive session that included newly elected Chancellor Davis and Interim Chancellor Corlis Cummings, Papp was picked as KSU's third president.[510]

The Start of a New Era

Dan Papp made his first official presidential address at the opening faculty and staff meeting on August 16, 2006. At that time, he identified six goals for the coming year:

1. Become one of the best learning-centered universities in the nation.

2. Improve KSU's retention and graduation rates through, among other things, better advising and mentoring.

3. Be reaccredited for another ten years by the Southern Association of Colleges and Schools (SACS), with the centerpiece a Quality Enhancement Plan concentrating on "Global Learning for Engaged Citizenship."

4. Develop and implement a strategic plan for 2007–2012, devised by a newly created President's Policy and Budget Advisory Committee.

5. Launch a major Comprehensive Capital Campaign under the direction of vice president for advancement Wes Wicker.

6. Expand KSU's traditional emphasis on across-the-board excellence especially by focusing on research and creative activities; by revamping the administrative structure to fit more closely with the university's vision and mission; and by improving accountability through stricter financial auditing and review systems, greater attention to campus safety, and an updated twenty-first-century focus on management by objectives.

This was not the Betty Siegel-type address that the campus had grown accustomed to hearing. The previous president typically spoke with few if any notes and went straight for the hearts of her listeners with a series of personal and inspirational stories and ideas, often focused around one major theme per year. Papp stuck to his prepared remarks, laid out a comprehensive set of important major initiatives, and engaged his audience in a direct and forthright manner. While their styles were quite different, both were effective, and many found Papp's down-to-earth approach refreshing.

A close analysis of Papp's presidential addresses reveals a president who was just as idealistic as his predecessor and just as committed to diversity, inclusiveness, and the centrality of teaching. But his speeches sounded something like a briefing, complete with walking orders and the specific steps by which the many goals for the year would be accomplished. His idealism was perhaps best demonstrated in

Akanmu G. Adebayo

his actions where he took a no-nonsense approach to doing things the right way. For example, he made only a brief reference in his 2006 Opening of the University speech to his decision in the first month on the job to replace the former vice president for business and finance and bring greater accountability to that office. Describing his ambitious agenda as "weighty," Papp quoted Bob Dylan that "the times they are a-changing" and Bachman-Turner Overdrive that "you ain't seen nothing yet!"[511]

The most immediate concern at the start of the 2006–07 school year was finalizing the SACS reaccreditation report, which was due the following month. SACS's new accreditation requirements (as of 2004), detailed in its *Principles for Accreditation, Foundations for Quality Enhancement*, called on Kennesaw to produce a comprehensive compliance audit/certification report in lieu of the old campus self-study. Fortunately, a campus leadership team, headed by Ed Rugg, had been working on it for several years. Rugg, at that time, was the executive director of the Center for Institutional Effectiveness. The Office of Institutional Research (IR), under Deborah J. Head's direction, reported to him as did the director of the Office of Information Management (IM), Erik Bowe. The IR and IM units were heavily engaged with Rugg and his administrative assistant, Luan Sheehan, in producing reports for KSU's accreditation and managing the logistics for the SACS On-Site Visiting Committee.

Rugg was the principal author and editor for KSU's SACS accreditation reports in 2006–07. President Papp, however, was actively involved, reading and occasionally editing the entire 320-page *Compliance Assurance Report*. Papp had stated earlier that achieving continued SACS accreditation was one of his highest priorities in his first year at KSU. He demonstrated how serious he was about keeping that commitment by rolling up his sleeves and becoming personally engaged in final report preparations. On September 8, 2006, KSU submitted the report to SACS's Commission on Colleges. The major part of the ten-year review, covering KSU's compliance with a host of SACS rules and regulations, sailed through the Reaffirmation Committee's review without a single finding of noncompliance or recommendation for improvement.[512]

A Focus on Global Learning for Engaged Citizenship

After finishing the *Compliance Assurance Report*, Papp and the Center for Institutional Effectiveness began preparing the required Quality Enhancement Plan for submission to the SACS On-Site Reaffirmation Committee in February 2007. When that committee visited campus in March, it intended to focus primarily on how Kennesaw planned to implement its QEP topic — "Global Learning for Engaged Citizenship"— in a way that would improve student learning. The global learning topic had been selected over a year prior to Papp's arrival, and faculty committees had done substantial work to clarify its goals and identify action plans for its five-year implementation. But campus administrators were reluctant at the time to commit future budgetary resources to proposed QEP initiatives without the new president's approval. Only a month after taking office, Papp resolved the issues that had stalled progress and gave each cabinet member oversight responsibilities for the successful achievement of one or more of the QEP's ten goals. Everyone's good work reaped rewards when the visiting SACS committee made only two minor recommendations for improvement and cited the project as a potential national model in the facilitation of global learning.[513]

Kennesaw's stated purpose behind its Quality Enhancement Plan was to raise global learning to the forefront as an educational priority. The solid foundation of international programs started in the Siegel administration undergirded a new series of global learning activities. Kennesaw had supported an Office (later Center) of International Programs from 1988 until the early years of the twenty-first century. When the longtime director, Thomas H. Keene, decided to return to full-time teaching, he met with the dean of the College of Humanities and Social Sciences, Linda Noble, with Assistant Director Daniel J. Paracka, and with former associate director Akanmu G. Adebayo. By this time, Adebayo was working for Dr. Noble as assistant dean. From a series of meetings, a plan emerged to propose the elevation of the Center of International Programs to institute status, positioning it to serve the entire university rather than just one college. Their recommended new name was the Institute for Global Initiatives (IGI).

President Siegel liked the idea and the name, and in 2003, IGI was created with Adebayo as its founding executive director. Adebayo led the institute from 2003–2009, when he returned briefly to the classroom before becoming the director of the Center for Conflict Management. A Nigerian native with a PhD from Oba-femi Awolowo University, Adebayo had extensive teaching experience in Nigeria and Canada before coming to Kennesaw in 1992. He envisioned the institute as a "one-stop shop" for everything international from teaching to scholarship. Under his direction, the institute became home to the Center for African and African Diaspora Studies and the Center for Latin American and Iberian Studies.

As had been the case with the International Center, the Study Abroad Program remained a central function of the Institute for Global Initiatives, although now it served the entire university, and not just disciplines in Humanities and Social Sciences. One of the first things that Adebayo did as IGI executive director was to meet with the president of the Student Government Association to gain his support for a five dollar student activities fee to provide scholarships for students who wanted to study abroad. They conducted a student survey that documented widespread student approval. President Siegel supported the idea, but, regrettably, the Board of Regents did not. The idea of a special fee for study abroad, however, had entered into campus discussion and would be revived under Kennesaw's QEP global learning effort.[514]

In 2007, KSU embarked upon an ambitious ten-goal plan to embed global learning in programs across campus. According to a QEP Mid-Point External Evaluation Report, submitted in late 2010 by Susan Buck Sutton, KSU had met or exceeded most of its goals in just three years. Her report's essential findings were that KSU was "emerging as a national leader in international education," that its work in global learning was "exceptional and highly commendable," and that "it would be difficult to find another university where such a broad range of global learning initiatives, across all dimensions of the institution, is occurring."[515]

KSU's first QEP goal was to ensure leadership from the top with everyone from the president through the department heads committing themselves to promote, expand, and improve global learning. To make sure that global thinking was represented in all top-level meetings, President Papp chose Dr. Barry J. Morris to fill a new position of director of cabinet strategic projects. Morris brought a diverse array of experiences to the job. He possessed a PhD in international relations and international political economy from Emory University and a certificate in Russian language and culture from Moscow State University. He also had spent time studying Chinese and economics at Tsinghua University in Beijing. After several years in the business world, he joined academia as a professor at Georgia Tech and Georgia State and dean of the American University of Nigeria, that country's first American-style university.

(Opposite Page) Barry J. Morris

When Adebayo left the Institute for Global Initiatives in 2009, Barry Morris stepped into that slot, while retaining his other responsibilities. Following a suggestion in Sutton's report that the strategic projects post become permanent and be retitled to reflect its global learning focus, Morris became the first vice provost of global engagement and strategic initiatives in 2011. According to President Papp, the appointment was "critical in the evolution of our commitment to expand global

The Museum of History and Holocaust Education exhibit *Parallel Journeys: WWII and the Holocaust through the Eyes of Teens* **tells the stories of forty teenagers and children who were rescuers, victims, bystanders, and even perpetrators during WWII and the Holocaust.**

learning at Kennesaw State." He went on to say that the job entailed "fostering collaboration among the university's deans, department chairs, faculty, and staff to incorporate global learning into teaching, research, and engagement activities."[516]

To implement the QEP, Kennesaw State University created a list of global learning specialists who were experts on different international topics. By 2010, the global learning coordinators for the various colleges had identified 159 global learning specialists (roughly a fourth of the faculty) who could help their colleagues gain international competencies. Another 176 individuals were designated as global learning contributors who had at least some global learning expertise. By the 2009–10 academic year, 343 courses contained at least 30 percent global content and thirty-six majors or minors had an international focus, including seven globally themed degree programs started since 2007.

KSU committed itself to doubling financial support for global learning initiatives to carry out the objectives of the QEP. By 2009–10 almost $2 million of internal and external funds went toward those purposes. A substantial part of that amount resulted from a change of heart at the Board of Regents, with Kennesaw gaining approval for a global learning fee of fourteen dollars to be paid by every student during fall and spring registration. During 2009–10 the fee made possible $730,022 in study abroad student scholarships and $33,994 in faculty awards to develop additional study abroad opportunities. A special Global Learning Fee Committee, consisting half of students and half of faculty, determined the award recipients. As a result, the number of KSU study abroad programs increased from forty-three in 2008 to fifty-eight in 2010, while the number of student participants rose from 596 to 782.[517]

KSU budgeted between $100,000–$200,000 of state funds annually for direct QEP support, while the KSU Foundation provided a supplemental budget for the Institute for Global Initiatives and supported a Presidential Emerging Global Scholars Program to enable first-year students to travel abroad to work on projects at partner international universities. In addition, the campus provided matching funds for the Confucius Institute, set up in 2008 in partnership with Yangzhou University, to promote the study of Chinese language and culture and to serve as a resource for businesses in the Southeast that wanted to develop networks in China. Among other things, the Confucius Institute was the only site in Georgia that administered the Chinese Proficiency Test; in its first two years, it assisted forty-three KSU students who studied in China.[518]

(Opposite Page) The Museum of History and Holocaust Education at Kennesaw State University

Every college produced an annual report documenting its global learning activities. It was expected that the College of Humanities and Social Sciences and the College of the Arts would sponsor an extensive array of global learning programs. Perhaps more surprising was how much the other colleges did. The College of Science and Mathematics, for instance, created study abroad courses such as Belize Marine Biology, Chemistry and Culture in Germany, and China Revealed through Its Culture and Mathematics. Meanwhile, the Coles College maintained a Center for International Business, directed by Sheb True.

The global learning QEP was supported by a number of external grants. KSU's Museum of History and Holocaust Education, for example, received Museums and Community Collaborations Abroad (MCCA) grants, made possible by the US State Department, to send museum staff and public history students to Casablanca, Morocco. There, they collaborated with the Ben M'sik Community Museum at Hassan II University on an online museum exhibit titled *Identities: Understanding*

Islam in a Cross-Cultural Context. The exhibit featured photographs and oral histories from the Ben M'sik community in Casablanca and the Atlanta Muslim community. By 2012 it seemed clear that the Quality Enhancement Plan broadened and deepened global learning across campus and was one of the distinctive strengths of the university.[519]

The Beginning of Doctoral Programs

Kennesaw's 2006–07 SACS review was unique not only because it focused on global learning, but also because it marked the first time that KSU would go up for reaccreditation as a doctoral granting institution. Doctoral studies at Kennesaw State University reflected a change in philosophy at the Board of Regents. Prior to the twenty-first century, only the four research universities offered doctoral degrees, most of them PhDs. While he was still USG senior vice chancellor, Dan Papp directed a statewide assessment of higher education that determined a need in Georgia for Carnegie research intensive universities, according to the terminology of the time. Such institutions might offer an occasional PhD program, but mainly concentrated on professional doctorates (EdDs, DBAs, DSNs, etc.) where dissertations dealt with practical, real-world problems of interest to practicing professionals. Georgia at the time lacked research intensive institutions, and rapidly growing Kennesaw State, along with Georgia Southern, West Georgia, and Valdosta State, seemed logical choices for this new designation.[520]

One of the rationales for doctorates at KSU was its location in the northern Atlanta suburbs. The *Atlanta Journal-Constitution* reported on March 16, 2006, that of the one hundred fastest growing counties in the United States, eighteen were near Atlanta, and four (Cherokee, Douglas, Paulding, and Bartow) were adjacent to Cobb and in KSU's service area. While the population of metropolitan Atlanta grew in numbers, it also became more diverse and seemed destined by the middle of the twenty-first century to contain more ethnic minorities than non-Hispanic whites. Cobb was experiencing a dramatic increase in African Americans, Asians, and Hispanics and seemed likely to be majority minority by as early as 2020. Recognizing these demographic trends, the Board of Regents called on system institutions to develop new programs and increase diversity.

In response, the Bagwell College of Education expanded its graduate programs, increasing graduate enrollment by 400 percent in the five years between 2001–2006. In May 2006, the Board of Regents approved KSU's first doctorate, an EdD in leadership for learning. EdDs had once been common at research universities, but by the opening decades of the twenty-first century, they had all but disappeared, having been displaced by the more academic PhD. By 2012, the University of Georgia offered PhDs in a host of educational fields, but just one EdD—in educational psychology. Similarly, Georgia State University offered a full complement

President Papp and Dean Arlinda Eaton with James Clinton (Clint) Stockton, the first recipient of a KSU doctorate.

of PhDs in educational fields, but no EdDs. So Kennesaw's new degree program appealed to a different type of student than the typical enrollee at the research institutions. Rather than producing future college professors and researchers, the Bagwell College of Education sought to improve the insights and skills of teachers and administrators, who planned to apply their new knowledge where they were already employed.[521]

Following the May 2006 decision of the Board of Regents, Dr. Nita A. Paris and her colleagues in the Bagwell College of Education worked intensively with

327

Ed Rugg on KSU's application to SACS for a change in accreditation status to doctoral-degree-granting Level V. The timing of the 2006–07 SACS review had been set years earlier, forcing Kennesaw to work with unaccustomed speed to meet long-established deadlines in order to include the doctoral program in the process. Paris, Rugg, and the Bagwell faculty accomplished in three weeks what normally might have taken months of work. In its June 2006 meeting, SACS's Commission on Colleges agreed to consider Kennesaw's reaccreditation at Level V and authorized the visit of the Substantive Change Committee as soon as the EdD program was operational. Since SACS already had an on-site visit scheduled for March 2007 to examine the Quality Enhancement Plan, it simply added two individuals to the on-site team and designated them as the Substantive Change Committee. Thus, that combined review committee generated two compliance reports—one on the institution as a whole for reaffirmation of its accreditation and the other on the EdD in particular. Each report contained only two recommendations for follow-up which were relatively easy to satisfy. Consequently, at the annual meeting of the SACS in December 2007, KSU was accreditation for another ten years, this time as a doctoral-level university offering the EdD degree with no further follow-up required.[522]

The curriculum of Kennesaw's professional doctorate included a series of core courses built on a "distributed leadership" model where educators were trained to move beyond an autocratic style of school administration to one that favored democratic, collaborative decision making. Originally, students selected one of four concentrations (elementary and early childhood education, adolescent education-mathematics, inclusive education, or educational technology). Among the requirements for admission were an earned master's degree, a Georgia Teacher Certificate, current full-time school employment, and at least five years' experience as a teacher and/or administrator.

The first cohort enrolled in January 2007, followed by a new class each succeeding January. As they proceeded through the seventy-five-credit program, the students had the opportunity to pick up a specialist in education (EdS) degree after their first thirty-three hours. In addition to the common courses and concentration-area electives, they concluded their work with a dissertation. Under the distributed leadership model, they were expected to support each other collegially and engage in collaborative problem solving, in coursework and on research projects.[523]

The concept of applied, professionally-focused scholarship was illustrated in the accomplishments of the first student to complete the EdD program. James Clinton (Clint) Stockton, a calculus teacher at Kennesaw Mountain High School, was part of the initial cohort. He completed the program in a little less than four years, graduating on July 28, 2010. Using high school calculus students as subjects, Stockton attempted in his dissertation to offer a theory on why adolescent students find it difficult to finish assignments. With regard to his own success in completing tasks, he noted in a campus interview that his youngest daughter was born during his first semester in the doctoral program, and that time management and self-sacrifice were essential for his whole family.[524]

Kennesaw's peer institutions, West Georgia, Valdosta State, and Georgia Southern, all had EdD degree programs by 2012, although each was somewhat unique. While KSU focused on leadership for learning, Georgia Southern established majors in curriculum studies and educational administration. West Georgia and Valdosta State each had three EdDs. The former offered degrees in school improvement, professional counseling and supervision, and an online EdD in nursing education; the latter developed EdDs in adult and career education, curriculum and instruction, and leadership.[525]

By 2012, the number of doctorates at KSU had grown to five. By that time, leadership for learning had been divided into two degree programs, with Clint Stockton and other classroom teachers working on an EdD in teaching leadership for learning, while administrators typically chose the EdD in educational leadership for learning. On March 19, 2008, the Board of Regents approved the first doctorate in the Coles College of Business, a doctor of business administration (DBA) degree that would enroll its first seventeen students later in the year.

While three of the University System of Georgia's research institutions (UGA, Georgia Tech, and Georgia State) and one peer institution (Georgia Southern) offered PhDs in business fields, Kennesaw was fairly unique in offering the DBA, a three-year program tailored to mid-career professionals who wanted to move up the corporate ladder or teach at the college level.[526] The Coles College pointed out on its website that Kennesaw's provost, Ken Harmon, had a DBA, and argued that the most important thing students needed to know was that KSU's doctoral program was accredited by the Association to Advance Collegiate Schools of Business (AACSB). Kennesaw maintained that its DBA curriculum resembled comparable PhD programs in placing a strong emphasis on research, but differed in its sensitivity to the needs of full-time business professionals, who would be able to combine on-the-job experiences with traditional research skills as they solved practical business problems. Kennesaw described this type of scholarship as "applied research that is theoretically grounded."

One of the strengths of the DBA program was its flexible hours of operation, enabling students from all parts of the country to enroll. Classes met only one weekend a month for ten months out of the year. While they were on campus, students were in the classroom for eight hours a day over a two- to four-day weekend. In line with KSU's focus on global learning, the program gave students a chance to interact with outstanding international faculty brought to campus specifically for the weekend sessions. According to Joe F. Hair, one of the founders and senior scholars in the DBA program, "The premium tuition structure[527] of the [DBA] supports a budget that enables KSU to invite scholars from all over the globe to come to KSU to teach courses, share their research, and supervise doctoral dissertations."[528]

The first eight DBA graduates received their degrees during the May 2012 commencement exercises. Reflecting the program's flexible course scheduling, two of the eight (Doug Boyle and Jeananne Nicholls) resided in Pennsylvania and two (Charlie Ragland and Anne Wilkins) in Tennessee. Of the four Georgians, Vijay Patel commuted from the town of Forsyth; Ruben Boling lived in Alpharetta and taught and directed a center at North Georgia College & State University; Debbie Lasher lived in Marietta; and Juanne Greene lived in Austell and was a senior lecturer in the Coles College. With one or two exceptions, the graduates had college teaching appointments lined up for the fall, and all intended to stay in higher education in some capacity.[529]

In February 2009, the regents approved a doctorate for a third professional college at KSU, the WellStar College of Health and Human Services. The first students enrolled in fall, 2009, just before the completion of KSU's state-of-the-art, $56 million health sciences building, Prillaman Hall. The new degree, a doctor of nursing science (DNS), addressed a critical nationwide shortage of nurses and

(Above) **The Central Parking Deck**
(Opposite Page) **A student walking by the Humanities Building
and the sculpture,** *Pathways to Wisdom,* **by Edward J. Garcia in
November 1998.**

nurse educators. According to Dean Richard Sowell, "The DNS degree is listed
by the American Association of Colleges of Nursing (AACN) as a research-based
degree, unlike a practice degree." He pointed out that the nursing shortage was a
result of the lack of qualified nurse educators. The DNS was designed to eliminate
that problem.[530] Like Kennesaw's other professional doctorates, the DNS filled
a niche in the university system. Both Georgia State University and the Georgia
Health Sciences University (renamed Georgia Regents University in 2012 after its
merger with Augusta State) operated PhD programs to prepare people for research-
intensive academic careers.

In addition to a PhD in nursing, Georgia Health Sciences University (GHSU)
offered a doctor of nursing practice (DNP) degree with most courses taught online,
and with instruction at seven different sites around Georgia and in Tennessee.
Unlike Kennesaw's DNS degree, the DNP was not primarily concerned with preparing graduates for academic careers. Rather, it was a program for nurse clinicians
in leadership and clinical roles. The closest comparable programs to Kennesaw's
were a doctor of nursing practice degree at Georgia Southern University, where

331

(Above) Exterior view of the Science Laboratory Building, (Opposite Page) Interior view of Science Laboratory Building

one could take extra educational courses if one wanted to prepare for an academic career, and a DNP Acute Care Advanced Practice Program at GHSU, where those who wanted to teach took two extra semesters of work through the Program for Accelerated Certification Education (PACE).[531]

On March 10, 2010, the Board of Regents approved Kennesaw's first PhD program. Georgia Southern and West Georgia received authorization for new PhDs at about the same time. All were in relatively narrow fields. Georgia Southern's Business College developed a PhD in logistics/supply chain management. West Georgia's Psychology Department started a PhD program in consciousness and society. Kennesaw's new PhD degree was in international conflict management. In each case, the new program drew on faculty strengths at the undergraduate or master's degree levels. All offered something unique in the university system.

Kennesaw had hoped to offer its first PhD in the broader academic discipline of international policy. The original proposal called for four concentrations: international conflict management, building on Kennesaw successful master's program; international environmental policy, based on a growing undergraduate program; homeland and international security, meeting a critical concern in an age of international terrorism; and international development, also responding to an important global need. Since President Papp's scholarly reputation was in international affairs, an International Policy Program seemed a logical choice.

President Papp noted at the time that the biggest overlap was with Georgia Tech, but Tech had no problem with the proposal. The administration at Tech told him, "The more the merrier; you're going to be competing for a different audience." The University of Georgia also raised no objection. However, Georgia State feared competition with its International Development Program. So, bowing to Georgia State, and, according to Papp, to budget realities, KSU cut back its request to the one concentration of international conflict management.[532]

The first PhD class began during fall semester 2010. KSU advertised this unique program as one that would produce scholars, teachers, and practitioners able to shape the way that policymakers resolved global conflicts. The program was limited to fifteen students per year. The original cohort represented thirteen different countries. Of the thirty students that enrolled during the first two years, ten were United States citizens; seven came from sub-Saharan Africa; six from Europe, including the republics of the old Soviet Union; four from Asia; and three from the Middle East.

Typical of the students was Samy S. Gerges of Egypt, a human rights activist involved in the opposition to the Mubarak regime. Following Mubarak's removal, Gerges listened to the advice of Dr. Volker Franke, director of the International Conflict Management Program, and decided to stick with his studies rather than returning home. He was persuaded that he could be of greater help to his country in the long run if he gained the skills and credentials that the program afforded. From almost the beginning of his studies, he made presentations at international academic conferences, and traveled to the Middle East in the summer of 2011 to work with colleagues from other American universities on a collaborative project on forgiveness in the Middle East.[533]

In a 2009 interview, President Papp conceded that for the next decade and a half Kennesaw was not likely to win approval for a large number of additional PhD programs or professional doctorates. Its niche in the university system in the short run would be as a comprehensive university at the bachelor's level, with growing offerings at the master's level and at least five or six doctorates.[534] Still, the beginning of doctoral education had brought Kennesaw to a new stage in its evolution, and the general sense on campus was that the university would continue to evolve and advance.

An Aspiring Metropolitan Research University

In 2008, the president asked Ed Rugg and a small team of faculty members and administrators to produce a report that analyzed the characteristics of peer and aspirational institutions. They concluded that Kennesaw was part of a relatively new breed of metropolitan universities that served a diverse population of traditional and nontraditional undergraduates; focused on professional degree programs as well as those in the arts and sciences; honored applied as well as basic research; and engaged in extensive off-campus service from the local to the global level. Rugg argued that, while Kennesaw's initial doctorates were limited in scope and professionally oriented, KSU was eventually bound to move into a comprehensive array of doctoral offerings to meet the needs of a growing student population.[535]

The report defined Kennesaw's peers as metropolitan universities of similar size that met the Carnegie Classifications of Master's/Large or Doctoral/Research. At most of the peer institutions, fewer than half of the undergraduate programs had graduate counterparts, and fifty or fewer students earned a doctorate annually. Moreover, the doctoral programs tended to be in professional areas (business, education, nursing, and technology). Specific peer institutions included California State University, Fresno; Oakland University in suburban Detroit; Western Kentucky University; and Middle Tennessee State University. Three of these four were created prior to World War I (Western Kentucky, 1906; Middle Tennessee, 1909; Fresno State, 1911), but today have comparable enrollments to KSU: 21,000, 26,000, and 21,500, respectively.

Of the peer universities, Oakland most resembled KSU in background. Located in affluent Oakland County, near I-75, Oakland University is a product of the demand for higher education of the post–World War II generation. It was founded in 1957 and opened in 1959 with 570 students. Originally a branch of Michigan State University, it achieved full independence in 1970. While the 2012 enrollment of just below twenty thousand was significantly less than that of Kennesaw, Oakland was ahead of KSU in the development of doctoral programs and had already achieved a Carnegie rating as a Doctoral/Research University. Like Kennesaw, Oakland placed a major emphasis on learner-centered education and outreach to the metropolitan Detroit area, with partnerships in place with hospitals, Fortune 500 companies, local governments, and schools. Oakland also resembled Kennesaw in its fundraising abilities, having conducted a first-ever comprehensive campaign, reaching the targeted goal of $110 million in 2009, a year ahead of schedule.[536]

KSU's *Peer & Aspirational Comparator Universities* report went on to argue that KSU's destiny was to become more like metropolitan research universities

(Opposite Page) A view of campus between the Old Social Sciences Building and the new English Building.

335

that currently had larger student enrollments and greater research activity. In such institutions more than half of the undergraduate programs had graduate counterparts, and there was a comprehensive array of doctoral degrees with significantly more than fifty graduates a year. Some of the aspirational institutions were George Mason University, Indiana University–Purdue University Indianapolis, Kent State University, University of North Carolina at Greensboro, University of Central Florida, and University of Memphis.[537]

Of the universities on the aspirational list, George Mason University (GMU) seemed closest to Kennesaw in its history and provided perhaps the best road map to KSU's future. The school began in Fairfax in 1957 as a two-year branch of the University of Virginia. In 1966—the same year that Kennesaw enrolled its first junior college students—the Virginia legislature granted Mason four-year status; then, just six years later, made it a regional university. Between 1966 and 1972, Mason grew from 840 students to about four thousand, then reached ten thousand by the end of the 1970s—a figure that Kennesaw would achieve about a decade later in 1990.

In 1979, George Mason University opened a School of Law and branch campus in Arlington, and in 1997 founded another branch campus in neighboring Prince William County. Under the leadership of President George W. Johnson (1979–1996), GMU gained national recognition, grew in size to about twenty-four thousand students, and started eleven doctoral programs. The fastest-growing university in the Virginia system, it reached 33,320 by 2011–12, including slightly more than 20,000 undergraduates and 2,000 doctoral students. By that time, two of its faculty members had won Nobel Laureates in Economic Science (James Buchanan in 1986 and Vernon Smith in 2002).[538]

As KSU approached its fiftieth birthday, it seemed headed in the direction of George Mason University, and the campus community wondered how long it would take to become a metropolitan research university, and what would be the gains and losses when it did so. Perhaps, the greatest certainty was that nothing would stay the same at Kennesaw for long. From its earliest days, the institution had been evolving—for some, at an alarming rate, and for others, with frustrating slowness. At the same time, the institution had experienced the continuity that comes from having only three presidents in its first half century.

In the first decade of the twenty-first century, Kennesaw made a successful transition of presidencies for only the second time in its history. As we shall see in the concluding chapter, the Papp administration dealt with a budget crisis caused by the nation's worst economic recession since the 1930s, yet somehow managed to accelerate the building pace of the late Siegel era. It purchased, through the

(Opposite Page) A nighttime view of the Visual Arts Building

KSU Foundation, a large tract of land across I-75 from the main campus for a new Sports and Recreation Park. It also opened by 2012 a number of new campus facilities, including Prillaman Hall, the Lab Science Building, additional residence halls, the Athletic Department's Bowen Building, The Commons Student Dining Hall, and the Central Parking Deck.

In late 2012, Kennesaw broke ground on the Zuckerman Museum of Art. In early 2013, a new Bagwell Education Building was started while plans were well under way for additional off-campus warehouse space and a major Sturgis Library rehabilitation. The institution also committed itself to improved retention and graduation rates, expanded student services, and Division I football. At the same time, KSU endured a round of public criticism reminiscent in some ways to the storms of the 1990s over the Gingrich course and other issues. Debate over serious issues, however, is at the heart of any college's mission. The fact that the public took the university seriously enough to critique its internal policies could be seen as a good thing, reflecting KSU's importance to the state and community after a half century of remarkable growth.

(Opposite Page) Trees from the original 1960s campus quad
landscape show many years of growth.

Chapter 10

Kennesaw at Age Fifty

At age fifty, Kennesaw State University took pride in its expanding economic and cultural role in metropolitan Atlanta and northwest Georgia. During fiscal year 2011, KSU added nearly $854 million to the state's economy. Within the University System of Georgia, only the four research universities contributed more. KSU employed some 3,427 people in full- or part-time positions. Another 4,897 private-sector employees held their jobs because of the university's presence.[539] Kennesaw occasionally became the center of controversy, as conservative journalists and activists criticized campus actions, most notably over the immigration status of a Mexico-born student. Nonetheless, on balance, the university enjoyed positive press coverage; and the support of local civic leaders made possible a highly successful comprehensive capital campaign between 2007 and 2011.

In August 2012, President Papp announced a new strategic plan that envisioned a university on its way to national prominence in teaching, scholarship, and service. The previous 2007–2012 strategic plan noted that KSU already had achieved national recognition for a number of programs, but the old statement regarded Kennesaw's service area to be primarily northwest Georgia and metro Atlanta. By omitting a specific service area, the 2012–2017 strategic plan seemed subtly to suggest that KSU no longer saw itself confined to a mere region.

KSU had grown into a residential institution with about 3,500 individuals living on campus and several thousand more dwelling in nearby apartment complexes that catered to KSU students. While Kennesaw students came predominantly from metropolitan Atlanta, a growing number officially resided elsewhere. In fall 2011 Kennesaw enrolled students from all but 25 of Georgia's 159 counties and from all but six of the fifty states. In that semester, 428 American students declared a residence outside Georgia, and 1,552 international students represented 132 different countries. Meanwhile, study abroad programs carried KSU students to Europe, Latin America, Africa, and Asia; and a variety of outreach activities built collaborations with universities around the world. The 2012–2017 mission statement called on students, faculty, and staff to "engage with local, state, regional, national, and international communities to enrich those communities and the university." At least implicitly, the strategic plan suggested that terms such as "state and regional university" and "metropolitan university" had become too restrictive for an institution that hoped to play on a larger stage.[540]

Kennesaw's earlier mission statements had always contained a commitment to teaching excellence. The 2012–2017 strategic plan went a step further in its focus

on what excellent teaching should produce: graduates who were "capable, visionary, and ethical leaders" and "engaged citizens with global understanding and a love of learning." To produce such students, the strategic plan contained action steps to decrease student-to-faculty and student-to-staff ratios and provide more support for the scholarship of teaching and learning and professional development.[541]

The new strategic plan had the most forthright statement to date on the central importance of research and creative activity, envisioning a university where basic research expanded knowledge, applied research promoted economic development, and community-based scholarship improved "the quality of life in the local community, Georgia, the nation, and the world." Recognizing that KSU lagged far behind research institutions and even other comprehensive universities in laboratory space and research funds, the strategic plan nonetheless envisioned an increase in the number of professors with national and international reputations for their scholarly productivity. To that end, the plan enumerated two specific action steps for the next five years: one, create at least two new chaired professorships in each degree-granting college; two, develop a support and incentive plan to assist young scholars on the verge of national prominence.[542]

A Commitment to Improve KSU's Retention and
Graduation Rates for All Students

The 2012–2017 strategic plan placed a major emphasis on recruitment, retention, progression, and graduation rates. Issues of this type had been part of President Papp's responsibility when he had been senior vice chancellor for academics and fiscal affairs at the Board of Regents. So, even before arriving on campus, he was aware that Kennesaw's retention and graduation rates needed improvement. From the beginning of his administration, he advocated improved advisement, better scheduling, and changes in the campus climate to improve retention and reverse KSU's historically poor graduation record.[543]

The entire university system was under pressure to improve retention and graduation rates. Following a 2010 report that only 58.9 percent of full-time students in the university system graduated within six years (a figure slightly below the national average), the Board of Regents issued a directive to its member institutions to improve. Board chair Willis Potts described Georgia's record as "an embarrassment." Threatening to tie presidents' salaries and institutional funding to the graduation rates, he added, "If we take students' money we have a moral and ethical obligation to do everything we possibly can to help them graduate."[544]

In February 2012, Governor Nathan Deal announced the Complete College Georgia initiative to increase the number of college graduates. Georgia was the twenty-second state in the nation to join Complete College America, a nonprofit organization founded in 2009 by a former State of Indiana commissioner of higher education, Stan Jones. Backed by the Bill and Melinda Gates Foundation, the Carnegie Corporation of New York, the Ford Foundation, and other philanthropies, Complete College America claimed that the improvement of the graduation rate was its single mission. Jones had become alarmed that the number of degrees awarded by American institutions of higher learning had not grown much in forty years, despite the fact that college enrollment had more than doubled since 1970. He argued that America had made progress in opening college doors to people of all backgrounds, but had not completed the job of helping minorities and the poor finish with a degree.[545]

According to President Papp, all of Georgia's public colleges, universities, and technical schools were expected to improve graduation rates without sacrificing quality. He noted that Complete College Georgia drew a connection between economic development and the state's success in educating its citizens, and argued that the new initiative would be a major factor in higher education for the foreseeable future. Fortunately, the president was able to point out that Kennesaw had already begun making progress. While KSU's graduation rate was below the state average, it had improved significantly since the start of the Papp era. When the president took office in 2006, the six-year graduation rate for full-time first-time freshmen was only 28 percent. By 2011 it had reached 41 percent. According to Papp, the factors behind the improvement included the emphasis that KSU placed on the First-Year Experience Program, a better advisement system, and a better sense of community and identity, stemming in part from the growing number of students who lived on campus. Committing the institution to further progress, he set a short-term goal of a 45 percent graduation rate and a long-term goal of 50 percent.[546]

TABLE 7	Six-Year Graduation Rates in 2011 at Georgia Public Universities, Fall 2005 Cohort First-Time, Full-Time Students		
INSTITUTION	Institutional (% graduated in 6 years)	Within USG (% graduated in 6 years)	Average SAT Score (fall 2005 first-time freshmen)
University of Georgia	82	85	1237
Georgia Tech	79	81	1328
Georgia State University	48	56	1085
Georgia College & State University	55	70	1120
North Georgia College & State University	52	60	1079
Georgia Southern University	47	58	1098
Valdosta State University	43	55	1028
▶ Kennesaw State University	41	50	1067
University of West Georgia	39	47	1021
Albany State University	41	46	915
Southern Polytechnic State University	34	46	1124
Armstrong Atlantic State University	32	42	—
Georgia Southwestern State University	30	42	996
Columbus State University	31	38	—
Savannah State University	30	37	—
Fort Valley State University	34	36	902
Clayton State University	27	35	984
Augusta State University	22	31	—
System Total	52	60	

Note: The "institutional" rate is for students who started and finished at the same university. The "Within USG" rate is for students who began at that particular university, but graduated from another institution in the University System of Georgia.
Sources: Kennesaw State University Fact Book, years 2005 and 2011; "University System of Georgia Graduation Rate Report," 2005.

Despite progress, table 7 reveals that Kennesaw's six-year graduation rate in fiscal year 2011 fell short of universities with more selective admissions standards and a preponderance of traditional-aged students. The KSU rate was fairly typical of the universities that had recently started professional doctorates, and ranked ahead of most of the other state universities. With a few exceptions, a high correlation existed between the average SAT scores for entering first-year students in 2005 and the percentage that had graduated by 2011. The institutional data on six-year graduation rates was standard information that all colleges and universities were expected to submit to the US Office of Education's National Center for Education Statistics (NCES). However, the data best fit traditional students who did not hold down full-time jobs, did not yet have family responsibilities, and did not transfer from one college to another before they finished their degrees.

Schools such as Kennesaw that emerged from the democratic expansion of higher education after World War II catered, historically, to nontraditional students. If the older students took a few courses somewhere else years earlier, they entered KSU as transfer students and did not figure in the six-year graduation data. In fiscal year 2004, only 19 percent of the students receiving a bachelor's degree from KSU had actually matriculated at KSU as first-time freshmen. The opening of residence halls in 2002 gradually changed the campus culture and demographics, and the proportion of graduates who started and finished at KSU went up accordingly. But even in 2010–11, only 44 percent of the undergraduate-degree completers had started and finished their undergraduate experience at KSU.[547]

Despite the relatively low reported graduation rate, Kennesaw could take satisfaction in a remarkable 84 percent rise in the number of bachelors' degrees awarded between fiscal years 2004 and 2011—from 1,801 in the earlier year to 3,319 in the latter. After Kennesaw's transition from a totally commuter to a partially residential university, the typical student and typical graduate became younger. In 2003–04, only 43 percent of KSU's bachelors' degrees went to traditional-aged students (age 24 or younger), but by 2010–11, the proportion had risen to 56 percent.[548]

At the start of his administration, President Papp noted that a strong Career Services Center was vital if KSU was to succeed in helping graduates find employment. In his first two State of the University addresses, he emphasized the importance of students completing internships and co-ops to gain the practical experiences that potential employers sought. Upon the recommendation of Karen B. Andrews, the longtime director of the Career Services Center, Papp supported a plan to house experiential education associates in the various colleges, where they could interact daily with students and faculty. As a result, the number of students completing co-ops or internships increased from 1,095 in 2006–07 (Dan Papp's first year as president) to 1,696 in 2011–12—a 55 percent increase in just five years. Despite the poor economy, the number of employers making use of the Career Services

Center rose as well, with about a thousand job postings on campus in spring semester 2012 alone.[549]

In committing the university to improved recruitment, retention, progression, and graduation rates (RRPG), the new strategic plan called for the following:

1. better data collection to identify factors unique to KSU and specific initiatives based on those data;

2. national recognition for KSU's RRPG programs;

3. an increase in student engagement programs, including more student mentors and teaching assistants and the creation of an Honors College with discipline-specific honors programs;

4. a greater focus on intervention initiatives, including the implementation of early intervention plans for at-risk students in each degree-granting department;

5. an increase in financial aid; and

6. strategies to increase student participation in career services, counseling, and various leadership and residence life programs.[550]

The strategic plan recognized that retention could be improved through the enhancement of the collegiate experience and by fostering "a welcoming, diverse, and inclusive environment." KSU could take pride in the statistical evidence that the campus was becoming increasingly diverse. In 2003–04, 11 percent of the student body and 11 percent of the graduates were African American. Those figures remained in double-digits year after year. In 2010–11, 14 percent of all students and 12 percent of all graduates were African American. Including Hispanics, Asians, and other minority groups, 27 percent of KSU students and 25 percent of graduates in 2010–11 were classified as minorities.

One can measure KSU's progress in diversity by comparing its record in granting degrees to minorities against national norms. Based on US Department of Education data, the number of degrees awarded nationally to African Americans rose by 53 percent in the decade between the academic years of 1998–99 and 2008–09. The comparable percentage increase at KSU was 92 percent. The rise in degrees awarded to Hispanics was even more dramatic — a 224 percent rise at KSU, compared to 85 percent nationally. In every gender and ethnic/racial category, KSU's improvement in graduation rates was significantly greater than the national averages.[551.]

(Opposite Page) Karen B. Andrews

In 2011, *Diverse: Issues in Higher Education* magazine listed KSU for the first time as one of the top one hundred universities in the nation for undergraduate degrees granted to minority students. The magazine broke down the rankings by discipline and minority group. Kennesaw was thirty-third in the nation in degrees in education awarded to African Americans, and thirty-second in degrees in education awarded to all minority groups. The university was twenty-third in the country in degrees in accounting earned by African Americans, twenty-ninth in degrees in finance, and thirty-first in marketing.

Kennesaw's progress in diversity resulted in part from a Targeted Enhancement Program (TEP), created in 2008 to reach out to minority high school students, helping them through the application process, including financial aid and SAT workshops. Similarly, the Office of Multicultural Student Retention Services, headed by Nicole Phillips, provided advisement, mentoring, tutoring, and leadership development services once minority students arrived on campus. In the first three years that TEP was in operation, African American enrollment increased 38 percent and Hispanic enrollment increased by 62 percent, while the number of degrees awarded to minorities rose by 31 percent.[552]

So, while Kennesaw's graduation rates lagged behind more traditional-aged, elite institutions, it had an exemplary record in educating a diverse student body. As President Papp stated in his 2012 State of the University address, "KSU's view of diversity is expansive. We will make this campus as welcoming and inclusive as possible for all who wish to join our community."[553]

Controversies and Commitments to Community Engagement

While KSU enthusiastically welcomed the growth of its Hispanic student population, one of those students became the center of a national firestorm over illegal immigration. Jessica Colotl enrolled at KSU in the fall of 2006 not long after her graduation from Lakeside High School in DeKalb County. Because she submitted a transcript from a Georgia high school, the university did not question her immigration status. However, her parents were undocumented immigrants who had brought her from Mexico more than a decade earlier when she was a child. The year after Colotl enrolled at KSU, the Board of Regents revised its policy on illegal immigrants, requiring them to pay out-of-state tuition. The Registrar's Office did not go back to check the records of students already enrolled, so Colotl continued to pay the in-state rate ($1,357 a semester for in-state, full-time students during the 2007–08 school year, only a fourth of the $5,428 paid by out-of-state students).

Colotl moved quietly through her academic career until the morning of March 29, 2010, during her senior year, when she was searching for a parking space in the West Parking Deck just before the start of eleven o'clock classes. Like many other students, she pulled out of the lane of traffic and sat in her car, waiting for a space to become available. However, when she spotted a campus police car entering the deck, she drove away, and then circled around and came back later to the same spot. When he saw her doing so, Sergeant J. K. (Kevin) Kimsey, turned on his blue lights and made a "traffic stop," charging her with impeding the flow of traffic. When she failed to produce a driver's license, the officer gave her twenty-five hours to bring it to the campus police station.

The next day, Colotl appeared at the police station with an expired Mexican passport and attempted to explain her situation. At that point, Kimsey arrested her and took her to the Cobb County jail on two misdemeanor charges of impeding the flow of traffic and driving without a valid license. The Cobb County Sheriff's Department was the first in Georgia to enter into the 287(g) Program with US Immigration and Customs Enforcement (ICE) that allowed the county to check the immigration status of detainees at the county jail. Confirming her undocumented status, the sheriff turned her over to ICE, and authorities took her to the Etowah County Detention Center in Gadsden, Alabama. There she remained for a month before having an immigration hearing in Atlanta on April 30. At that time, she was denied bond, but granted voluntary departure, giving her twenty days to leave the country in her own vehicle rather than being deported.[554]

President Papp first learned about the case on April 26, four days before the hearing. He asked the university attorney, Flora Devine, to check on Colotl's status. Devine called the Mexican Consulate, a former Mexican consul general, and Colotl's attorney. Upon a request from Colotl's lawyer, Papp submitted an affidavit in which he said, "I write to request that within the letter of the law, Jessica be provided every opportunity to stay at, or return to, Kennesaw State University." As far as KSU was concerned, the case was closed when the Immigration Court ruled against her on April 30. However, ICE decided a few days later on May 5 to give Colotl an extra year in the US to complete her education. Papp indicated his pleasure with the federal government's decision, but stated that KSU would comply with all US and Georgia laws, and, under Board of Regents policy, would begin charging Colotl out-of-state tuition. The vice president for external affairs, Arlethia Perry-Johnson, told a reporter that the administration also supported Sergeant Kimsey, believing he had followed correct protocol and had shown restraint in giving Colotl an extra day to produce a driver's license. She added that "none of that negates the very unfortunate situation that our student is now faced with."[555]

Despite the Papp administration's relatively limited involvement, it found itself under attack from the anti-illegal immigration camp for its support of Colotl and for allowing her to attend college for the last three years as an in-state student.[556] Seemingly, everyone had a strong opinion about the case. Despite her many critics, Colotl was a poster child for those pushing for the DREAM Act, a proposal in Congress to allow permanent residency status to undocumented immigrants who arrived as minors and attended college or served in the military. The argument was that they were here illegally through no fault of their own and had acclimated to the culture of the United States. As Colotl remarked, "I've grown up in this country, I've adopted all of the American values."

On the other hand, many Georgia conservatives asked why they should subsidize the education of someone here illegally and questioned whether she was taking up classroom space that rightfully belonged to a US citizen. Those questions resonated with a number of Georgia legislators. In the midst of a heated gubernatorial election, where the candidates of both major parties supported a proposed ban on illegals attending university system institutions, the Board of Regents engaged in damage control. On October 13, 2010, the Regents voted to bar illegal immigrants from any college that turned away academically qualified applicants due to lack of space or other issues. That included the four research universities and Georgia College & State University, the state's designated liberal arts college, where class sizes were kept

small to simulate the experience at elite private schools. The other thirty colleges in the university system were required to verify that any student seeking in-state tuition was lawfully in the country.

According to Regent Jim Jolly, who chaired the committee making the recommendation, the Board did not want to put the colleges in the position of acting as "immigration authorities." He noted that the university system enrolled very few students who were classified as "undocumented"—only 29 at the five universities that would bar illegals in the future and only 501 altogether (out of 310,361 total students). While an issue involving only 0.16 percent of all students did not sound like a major problem, Jolly thought it was important to address the public's concerns about undocumented students taking seats away from US citizens and receiving a public benefit at taxpayer expense.[557]

About the same time that the Colotl controversy first appeared in the newspapers, KSU's provost, Lendley C. Black, announced his resignation to accept the presidency of the University of Minnesota Duluth. The search for his replacement generated more unwanted publicity when it was discovered that the person first offered the job had coauthored an article that contained passages critical of the United States and that included controversial views categorized by some critics as Marxist (although that categorization was disputed by a number of experts on Marxism). While the university's academic freedom policies protected the rights of tenured faculty members to hold unpopular views, they obviously did not apply to highly visible administrators who represented the university to the public. President Papp continued to offer public support to his controversial choice for provost, but did not seem unhappy when the candidate withdrew before ever accepting the job. After that, the president reopened the search and, upon the recommendation of a new search committee, headed by history professor Thomas H. Keene, offered the job in December 2011 to W. Ken Harmon, the dean of the Coles College of Business, who had been serving for the past year as interim provost.[558]

The fallout from the Colotl affair and the provost search made it clear that Kennesaw needed to do a better job of telling its story and connecting with the public. Perhaps in part for that reason, President Papp made community engagement a major focus of his Opening of the University address on August 10, 2011. The president told the faculty and staff that he was alarmed at a widening gulf in the nation between town and gown, with many critics dismissing academics as elitists who lived a soft life and were out-of-touch with "real world" people. Papp thought

(Opposite Page) Students enjoying time outside of the old Social Sciences Building during construction of the new multi-use facility which will be housed mostly by the College of Humanities and Social Science.

it was imperative that the university make a greater effort to converse with and be part of society. In his Opening of the University speech, he noted that individuals on campus were already deeply engaged in a variety of community endeavors. But the university needed to do better at inventorying its public service activities,[559] explaining them to the larger community, and expanding upon what was already being done. To that end, Papp appointed a small committee of faculty and staff "to explore exactly what an 'engaged university' might look like."[560]

Professional service and community engagement, of course, had long been central to Kennesaw's mission. Former president Siegel made community engagement the institution's yearly theme on a number of occasions. In August 1999, for instance, she announced that the coming school year would be the "Year of Honoring Service." Two years later, the slogan of the year was "Kennesaw State: The Engaged University." In 2002 an American Association of State Colleges and Universities report, *Stepping Forward as Stewards of Place*, listed KSU as third in the country in its commitment to community engagement. On the eve of Kennesaw's fortieth anniversary celebration in 2003, President Siegel said that civic engagement was central to Kennesaw's goal of becoming the prototype "people's college." So, President Papp's call for community engagement reinforced and expanded upon a longtime commitment.[561]

His Engage KSU Committee launched Kennesaw's most comprehensive community engagement initiative in its history. During the 2011–12 academic year, it met with various campus constituencies; held a town hall meeting on January 25, 2012, to solicit input and participation from students, faculty, and staff; and created five teams to define what the institution should be doing in teaching, research, and service, what infrastructure changes were needed, and what partnerships the institution should forge. At least one goal was to work for a Carnegie Community Engagement Classification.[562]

The 2012–2017 strategic plan suggested ways to carry out the objectives of the Engage KSU Committee. One of the strategic plan's five major goals was to "become more engaged and prominent in the local community, Georgia, the nation, and the world." The action plans to accomplish this goal included efforts to increase financial support, recognition, and rewards for those participating in community engagement activities. Among other things, the plan called upon each degree-granting college to appoint three individuals (one each from the faculty, the staff, and the student body) as Community Engagement Fellows. By 2012, the Center for Excellence in Teaching and Learning was already moving in this direction through its creation of a CETL Community Engagement Faculty Fellowship. The first to hold

(Opposite Page) Provost W. Ken Harmon

the fellowship was Lynn Boettler, assistant professor of First-Year Programs, who for some time had involved her first-year students in community-based learning projects. Her publications included a coauthored monograph, *Serving the Common Good: Ethical Leadership through Building Relationships*. So, while KSU evolved in numerous directions, it made a major commitment at the end of its first fifty years to see that campus initiatives in teaching, scholarship, and service were integrated in ways that promoted community engagement.[563]

The Launching of a $75 Million Comprehensive Campaign

Throughout its fifty-year history, Kennesaw has struggled to find sufficient resources to support an expanding student body and a growing array of academic and community outreach programs. Even in the twenty-first century, KSU remained near the bottom of comprehensive universities in the university system in state funds per full-time student. Tight budgets made it imperative that Kennesaw look to external sources to carry out its more innovative and entrepreneurial ideas. By 2005 Betty Siegel and her vice president for university advancement, Wes Wicker, began discussing the largest comprehensive fundraising campaign in KSU's history. But her decision to retire put the campaign on hold until a new president could take office. In the meantime, the university launched a marketing campaign designed to create a new campus image.

After a quarter century as president, Betty Siegel was the "face" of the university. If the general public knew anything about KSU, they recognized her. The marketing campaign was designed to present the "New Faces of Kennesaw State." Each advertisement featured a photo of a student or faculty member with accompanying text explaining that individual's remarkable accomplishments. The Office of Development placed the ads on billboards along I-75 and in magazines such as *Georgia Trend* and the *Atlanta Business Chronicle*, where they were likely to be seen by business and community leaders.

The image campaign proved highly effective and won a number of awards, but to Wes Wicker's surprise, the advertisements were best remembered for a tag line that read, "Georgia's third largest, fastest growing university." It was not anyone's intent to make size the main selling point, but when Wicker ran into Atlanta business leaders, he heard constantly that they had no idea Kennesaw was so large. They seemed to think that Kennesaw was somewhere south of Chattanooga, far away from the rest of metropolitan Atlanta. Wicker noted it was as though Kennesaw had become Avis competing against Hertz—not the largest, but "we try harder."[564]

Meanwhile, KSU contracted with John O'Kane of Coxe Curry & Associates, a fundraising consulting firm, to do a feasibility study. After conducting approximately thirty interviews with potential donors and holding further discussions with chief administrators and alumni, O'Kane concluded that KSU could probably raise a

President Papp and Wesley K. Wicker, the vice president for university advancement

maximum of about $65–$67 million. Many of the staff suspected that the campaign was liable to fall short of that amount and advocated a more modest goal to make sure the university was not embarrassed.

When President Papp officially took office in July 2006, he thought Kennesaw should think big, going for as high as $100 million. Ultimately, the administration settled on a figure of $75 million. The KSU Foundation endorsed that amount at its annual meeting in the fall of 2007. By that time, the Office of Development had received gifts or pledges of $28 million (about 37 percent of the campaign goal) and was negotiating other major gifts. After a successful silent phase, KSU publicly announced the start of the five-year comprehensive campaign on October 25, 2007.[565]

The fund drive was remarkably successful, reaching its goal more than a year ahead of schedule, despite the almost simultaneous collapse of the American housing market and beginning of a worldwide recession. The cochairs, Bob Prillaman and Chet Austin, were successful Cobb County businessmen with deep roots in the community and long records of service to Kennesaw State. A retired senior vice president of Caraustar Industries, Prillaman had been a KSU Foundation trustee for a quarter century and was a former chairman of the WellStar Health System's board of trustees. In the early century, he played a central role, along with Foundation trustee Dr. Robert A. Lipson, in bringing those two boards together and in persuading WellStar to make a $3 million gift to Kennesaw in 2003 for the naming rights to the WellStar College of Health and Human Services and WellStar School of Nursing.

Dr. Lipson not only was president and CEO of WellStar Health Systems, he was also a KSU alumnus, having worked with Dean Tim Mescon to initiate an MBA program for physician executives. Along with more than a dozen WellStar physicians, he was part of the first graduating class. Unfortunately, he was killed in a motorcycle accident on November 10, 2006. His death delayed, by about two years, the process of gaining WellStar backing for Kennesaw's proposed $56 million Health Sciences Building. The Board of Regents appropriated about $47 million of

(Above) The ribbon cutting ceremony for Prillaman Hall, on August 5, 2010, with (L-R) Dean Richard Sowell, Gregory Simone, Norman Radow, Bob Prillaman, President Papp, Lil Prillaman, Georgia Lt. Governor Casey Cagle, Regent Kessel Stelling Jr., and Connie L. Engel. (Opposite Page) Bob M. and Lillias (Lil) B. Prillaman

taxpayer funds to construct the new building, but Kennesaw had to raise the rest. Thanks to the efforts of WellStar's new CEO, Dr. Gregory Seimone, and of Bob Prillaman and fellow WellStar board member Tom Phillips, the hospital system agreed, in late 2007, to a gift of $5 million.[566]

The rest of the money for the 192,000-square-foot Health Sciences Building came from a $300,000 federal grant, $1.9 million diverted from the 1903 WellStar gift, and an additional $1.1 million raised privately. When it opened in August 2010, Kennesaw named the state-of-the-art facility for Bob Prillaman and his wife Lil, in recognition of their years of service to KSU, the hospital system, and many other worthy causes. Prillaman Hall made it possible for the WellStar School of Nursing to increase the number of nursing graduates from about 185 to 250 a year and to operate a first-rate doctoral nursing program.[567]

That technologically-advanced facility supported the most sophisticated laboratory research in Kennesaw's history. Led by KSU Distinguished Professor of

Prillaman Hall

Health and Human Services Svetlana Dambinova, a team of neuroscientists and neurologists made use of Prillaman Hall's new Brain Biomarkers Research Lab to study the chemical reactions that occur following strokes and concussions. The most important discovery to date has been a molecule that travels from the brain into the bloodstream after a stroke or head trauma that can be useful in making early diagnoses. The team presented their findings in July 2011 at the annual meeting of the American Association for Clinical Chemistry. In collaboration with colleagues at the medical schools of Pennsylvania State University and the University of Pittsburgh, Dambinova and her associates helped to develop a blood test that could be administered in emergency rooms or on battlefields. A $2.38 million grant from the Department of Defense supported this promising line of research.[568]

By October 2011, when the comprehensive campaign officially ended, some 5,062 contributors had made a total of 17,201 separate gifts. These included fourteen donations of at least $1 million each. Some $6.3 million went to scholarships, including the creation of the Clendenin Fellows, Kennesaw's first graduate fellowship program. Supported by a $1 million gift in 2008 by former BellSouth CEO John Clendenin and his son Tom, the program provided annual fellowships of up to $15,000 to students working on masters' or doctoral degrees at any accredited institution, with a preference given to applicants currently enrolled or on the faculty at KSU.

At a time of tight state budgets, Kennesaw relied on lower-paid young instructors and adjuncts to teach a majority of the general education courses. Many of them were still working on doctorates, and the program gave them a chance to complete their graduate courses and dissertations while they were gaining teaching experience at KSU. John Clendenin noted that work and family responsibilities prevented him from attending graduate school, and that the Clendenin Fellowships fulfilled a lifetime desire to help others with their graduate education. The first six fellowships were awarded in June 2009, from a pool of sixty applicants; by the summer of 2011 the total number of fellowship recipients had risen to twenty-one.[569]

Support for the Arts

Like John Clendenin, a number of major donors lacked the opportunity in their younger days to go as far in school as they would have liked. One of the most remarkable stories is that of Bobbie Bailey, a self-made Atlanta businesswoman. Her older brother Leon was a gifted mechanic, and as a child she held tools for him while he

(Opposite Page) John L. Clendenin with his daughter, Mary Kathryn (Kay) Clendenin, and his son, Thomas E. Clendenin

worked on cars. In the process, she developed mechanical skills that few other girls possessed. She earned her high school diploma from Central Night School while working full-time at Orr Refrigeration in the Virginia-Highlands neighborhood.

For the Orr brothers, Bailey ran the parts counter, worked as a mechanic, handled the books, and moved into management. When they sold the business, she joined one of the brothers in 1948 in a new company called Our-Way Machine Shop, and became the CEO in 1952. Eight years later, while continuing to run the machine shop, she started Our-Way Inc., which ultimately became the world's largest remanufacturer of commercial refrigeration and air conditioning compressors. By 1978, after outgrowing her downtown location, she moved the 350-person work force to seventeen acres she owned in Tucker.[570]

In the meantime, Bailey became the manager of the Lorelei Ladies, a women's semipro fast pitch softball team that won several national championships. The team was supported in part by a generous backer named Hollie Lough, who left a trust fund for the team after his death. When the team disbanded in the1980s, Bailey began looking for an appropriate way to dispense the remaining funds. After hearing about Betty Siegel and Kennesaw's softball program, she made an appointment.

The two women became close friends, and Bailey became a key contributor to the women's athletic program, setting up a scholarship fund for female athletes in 1991 and donating about half of the $3 million needed in 2002 for athletic facilities. The funds helped to build an attractive softball stadium, Bailey Park, and a modern Bailey Field House, located between the softball and baseball fields, with locker rooms and offices for both sports. In appreciation of her contributions and her lifetime of service, Kennesaw recognized Bailey in 1998 with an honorary doctorate.[571]

In addition to backing athletics, Bailey became a major donor to the arts. She recalled that her mother played by ear, but never could afford her own piano. As early as 1972, Bailey went into business to help aspiring musicians, eventually producing records on her RX-Melody and Southernaire labels. For advice, she turned to Atlanta entertainment attorney Joel A. Katz, who numbered among his clients James Brown and Willie Nelson. In time, Bailey and Katz formed a partnership under the name of Oryx Music Publishers. A member of the National Academy of Recording Arts & Sciences (NARAS) since 1972, she served twice as president of the Atlanta chapter, three terms as a national trustee, and over a decade on the NARAS' Finance Committee. In 1989, she became president of the Friends of Georgia Music Festival and executive producer of the *Georgia Music Hall of Fame Awards Show*, televised on Georgia Public Broadcasting.[572]

(Opposite Page) M. Bobbie Bailey

Through the encouragement of President Siegel, Dean Joe Meeks, and others, Bobbie Bailey began attending musical events on campus and was impressed with the talent of KSU students. Her connection to the comprehensive capital campaign came when President Siegel approached her with a brochure, prepared by Stacie Barrow and Cheryl A. Brown of the development staff, for a new performing arts building. At the time, Kennesaw was still about $1 million short of what it needed to fund the project. Bailey agreed to provide the $1.5 million asking price for naming rights to the facility. Bailey also donated a Steinway piano. Then, at the October 2007 opening of the Dr. Bobbie Bailey and Family Performance Center, she surprised everyone by announcing plans to give KSU an additional twenty-six Steinways, making Kennesaw the third All-Steinway School in Georgia (along with UGA and Spelman College).[573]

The Bailey Performance Center contained an art gallery dedicated to the works of Georgia artist Athos Menaboni, thanks to the Robert W. Woodruff Foundation and a unique gift from Kennesaw alumnus Don Russell Clayton. Menaboni was one of the Georgia's most important twentieth-century artists, best remembered for his remarkably accurate paintings of birds in their natural habitats. Starting in the 1940s, Coca-Cola Company president Robert W. Woodruff commissioned Menaboni to do the artwork for his annual Christmas cards. That partnership lasted for forty-four years until Woodruff's death in 1985. The Woodruff connection led Russ Clayton to Menaboni. While he was a teenager, Clayton began collecting Coca-Cola memorabilia. When a family friend gave him a share of Coca-Cola stock as a high school graduation present, Clayton wrote to Woodruff and, surprisingly, Woodruff wrote back. They became pen pals throughout Clayton's four years as a student at Kennesaw College. He graduated in 1981 in the first class to go all the way through after "junior" had been dropped from the school's name.[574]

During his career as a social science teacher in Cobb County, Clayton got up the nerve to call Menaboni, and they established a relationship that lasted until Menaboni's death in 1990. Over the years, Clayton collected whatever he could afford of Menaboni's works and eventually possessed forty of the forty-four Woodruff Christmas cards along with thirty-seven paintings. In the early twenty-first century, Clayton began planning to give his collection someday to an institution or institutions that would honor Menaboni's memory. Several delegations from Kennesaw visited his home around 2004 to view the collection. According to Wes Wicker, "I've never seen anything like this. It's one of those days you remember of your working career.... He literally had Menaboni paintings from floor to ceiling in every room in the house. Even the bathroom had a Menaboni painting in it. Literally, every wall space was covered with a Menaboni painting. It was unbelievable."[575]

Clayton's main concern was that the paintings be permanently displayed and not locked up in a closet where no one could see them. Fortunately, Kennesaw was able to tell him about the plans to build an art gallery in conjunction with the performance center and promised a special gallery devoted primarily to Menaboni. In December 2004 KSU displayed the forty Woodruff Christmas cards in the Art Gallery at the Sturgis Library. That was followed in April 2005 with a well-attended exhibit in the Wilson Building Fine Arts Gallery of Clayton's thirty-seven Menaboni paintings, along with some lithographs and a few Menabonis on loan from other owners.[576]

In the meantime, Wicker approached the Robert W. Woodruff Foundation about a contribution to the comprehensive campaign for the performance hall. Until this time, the Woodruff Foundation had never made a gift to a nonresearch university and did not fund performance halls. But when Wicker mentioned the almost complete collection of Christmas cards, the Foundation executives were intrigued. Not even the Woodruff Foundation had a complete set of the Woodruff cards. So, they came out to the KSU campus a few months later and agreed to $1 million donation to build an art museum and atrium inside the Bailey Performance Center.[577]

According to Wicker, the Woodruff gift was like the Good Housekeeping Seal of approval. It opened up other pocketbooks and helped Kennesaw receive grants from the J. M. Tull, the Rich, and the Price Gilbert Foundations. In the Anna F. Henriquez Atrium, KSU displayed sculptures of Ruth V. Zuckerman from the collection that her husband, Bernard A. Zuckerman, donated in 1996 following her death. Inspired by the opening of the Bailey Center and a desire to honor his late wife's memory, Zuckerman made a $2 million pledge in August 2010 for a Phase II of the art museum. That pledge led to other gifts, including an additional $300,000 from the Woodruff Foundation. In April 2012, the Board of Regents approved the naming of the Bernard A. Zuckerman Museum of Art, a $3 million, 9,200-square-foot project. Scheduled to be completed in 2013, the Zuckerman Museum was designed to connect with the Anna F. Henriquez Atrium and to contain three exhibition galleries and a pavilion.[578]

Gifts from Unexpected Donors

One of the reasons why the comprehensive campaign met its goal a year ahead of time was that a number of major gifts came unexpectedly from donors who were not targeted in the early planning. A prime example was the support of Bernard Osher for the Osher Lifelong Learning Institute. Before the campaign, the staff in the Office of Development had never heard of Bernard Osher or that his foundation funded lifelong learning centers for senior citizens at over one hundred colleges and universities. Fortunately, retired banker Richard J. Harp, began working with the seniors' programs for KSU's College of Continuing and Professional Education. He learned about Osher, and contacted him.

By the early years of the new century, the College of Continuing and Professional Education, under the direction of Dean Barbara S. Calhoun, was offering

(Opposite Page) Richard J. Harp

several thousand classes and programs a year to more than twenty thousand students. Following Dick Harp's application for support, the Bernard Osher Foundation donated $1 million to KSU early in 2006, and then later in the year made an unsolicited donation of another $1 million. As a result of these contributions, the Osher Lifelong Learning Institute was able to offer more than one hundred noncredit courses annually, along with social activities and other special events. In addition to his belief in continuing education, Osher wanted to help nontraditional students return to the classroom to finish their academic degrees. An additional gift from the Osher Foundation of well over $1 million set up an endowment to provide reentry scholarships annually to about forty to fifty students between the ages of twenty-five and fifty. Altogether, Osher contributed about $3.5 million to the comprehensive campaign.[579]

Another unexpected gift came from a remarkable local businessman named Jodie Leon Hill, the owner of a beautiful fifty-six-acre farm in Bartow County. Hill grew up in near poverty in Bartow County, and never finished high school. While working in local factories and foundries, he developed an artistic talent and, even as a teenager, had his own country band (Jodie Hill and His Midnight Ramblers) and a local radio show. After serving in the 293rd Combat Engineer Battalion in Europe during World War II, he returned home to a job with the Life and Casualty Insurance Company, opening offices in Marietta and Cartersville in 1946. In the late 1950s and early 1960s he worked in a supervisory capacity at the company headquarters in Nashville where he met and sold insurance policies to such Grand Ole Opry stars as Minnie Pearl, Porter Wagner, Roy Acuff, and Eddy Arnold. Then he returned to Marietta where he retired in 1985.[580]

In his retirement, Hill's artistic talents were perhaps best revealed in his woodworking projects, including beautifully restored violins and antique furniture, and a collection of practically every woodworking tool imaginable. In 1996 he purchased a historic, but run-down farm in northern Bartow County to prevent another potential buyer from tearing down most of the buildings and putting up chicken houses. Over the next decade, he devoted a considerable amount of time and money to its restoration. The most historic structure was a Native American cabin built before the Cherokee removal of the 1830s. After the Cherokees were driven westward, the property had many owners. The owner from 1913–1935 was the Georgia novelist Corra Harris. She built a house around the cabin and a freestanding library, chapel, and Delco battery building to provide electricity in pre-Rural Electrification Administration days. Harris named the farm, "In the Valley."

For several years, Hill, by now in his 80s, searched for someone with an appreciation of historic preservation who would protect the farm from developers. Retired KSU history professor J. B. Tate lived in Cartersville and had visited the farm and talked to Hill on a number of occasions. Tate was an advisory board member of KSU's Center for Regional History and Culture. At one of the meetings, he mentioned that Hill might be willing to donate In the Valley to the university. The center then informed Dr. Wicker, who contacted Hill and persuaded him to give the farm to Kennesaw in the fall of 2008.

"In the Valley"

"In the Valley"

Appraised at over $1 million, In the Valley had obvious educational possibilities for KSU's Public History Program as well as a variety of other disciplines. The use perhaps most in keeping with its original purposes was to provide food for The Commons, the main dining hall for KSU's students and employees. Starting in 2008, the farm provided The Commons with large supplies of beans, tomatoes, cucumbers, and spinach, along with other types of fresh produce. Kennesaw's culinary workers have also maintained eighteen bee colonies with about a half million honey producers, and a three-thousand-square-foot organic herb garden that supplies the campus with all the rosemary, oregano, thyme, and basil it needs. According to culinary services director Gary Coltek, Kennesaw harvested enough basil in the fall of 2009 to last through the winner, saving KSU $12,500 on herbs alone.[581] As Wes Wicker noted,

> One of the things, in my opinion, that all great universities have is some unusual aspect of the university. A working farm, for example, a historic site you're closely affiliated with. I would daresay Gettysburg College would not have the luster that it has had not it been located next to a famous battlefield.... [In the Valley] is a historic site [where] our students can go and learn and touch history.... I really felt good about this gift when students say, "It's one thing to sit in the classroom and hear about history, but it's something else when you actually go see it and touch it."[582]

A $1.5 million gift from the Harnisch Foundation in 2009 established Kennesaw's Center for Sustainable Journalism. According to Leonard Witt, the holder of the Robert D. Fowler Distinguished Chair in Communication, a column on his Public Journalism Network blog attracted the attention of Ruth Ann Harnisch. Witt had advocated a concept called representative journalism as a way to increase investigative reporting on environmental issues or other special interest topics. Harnisch responded to the blog, saying, "Len, we can make this happen." At the time, he did not know who Harnisch was. With a little research, he discovered that she was a veteran journalist and she, along with her husband William, ran a multimillion dollar foundation. With her support, Witt became founding executive director of the Center for Sustainable Journalism, which had as its mission the research and development of ethical and sustainable ways to produce news. Among its initiatives was the Juvenile Justice Information Exchange, a website covering juvenile justice issues. It also produced *Youth Today*, a print and online newspaper for professionals dealing with young people.[583]

Conclusion of a Successful Comprehensive Campaign

Bernard (Bernie) Marcus and the Marcus Foundation made a $590,000 gift to the Museum of History and Holocaust Education (MHHE) in 2010, matching a previous $590,000 grant from five years earlier. Located in the KSU Center, the museum opened in 2003 as the Holocaust Education Program with a traveling exhibition, *Anne Frank in the World, 1929–1945*. Vice president for advancement Wes Wicker and President Siegel recruited Catherine M. Lewis to teach in the Department of History and Philosophy and work with the new program. At the time, she was a faculty member at Brenau University and a consulting curator with the Atlanta History Center. Along with Siegel and Wicker, she helped persuade the Marcus Foundation that KSU could play a unique role in serving audiences that may not be familiar with the Holocaust and its importance in modern history. As a result of the Marcus Foundation contributions and continued support from the university, the MHHE grew in its first decade of operation to become one of the most vibrant and effective university-based Holocaust programs in the nation.

The mission of the Museum of History and Holocaust Education was to present public events, exhibits, and educational resources focused on World War II and the Holocaust in an effort to promote education and dialogue about the past and its significance today. In 2012, the MHHE served more than 140,000 people through onsite and traveling exhibitions, public programs, summer institutes for teachers and high school students, traveling trunks, and outreach into schools. Its exhibits have included *Parallel Journeys: World War II and the Holocaust through the Eyes of Teens*; *V for Victory: Georgia Remembers World War II*; and *The Tuskegee Airmen: The Segregated Skies of World War II* which was a project of one of KSU's public history classes under the direction of Jennifer Dickey. A unique exhibition was *The Butterfly Project*, created to assist the Holocaust Museum Houston in collecting 1.5 million butterflies to memorialize the children killed in World War II. Schools and community groups created butterflies for this revolving exhibition. The MHHE also produced traveling exhibitions for schools, libraries, and other cultural institutions on topics such as women in the Holocaust and women in World War II.

In 2011 President Papp and Vice President Randy Hinds brought the university's outreach resources under one umbrella, creating the Department of Museums, Archives, and Rare Books (MARB) under the leadership of Dr. Lewis as executive director and Dr. Tamara Livingston as associate director. The department housed the MHHE, the Bernard A. Zuckerman Museum of Art, the Bentley Rare Book Gallery, the KSU Archives, and the Office of Records Management.[584]

As the comprehensive campaign proceeded, other major gifts came in. Tommy and Beth Holder continued their support of KSU with a $1 million endowment of the Holder Awards for Professional Development. These annual competitive grants of up to $5,500 provided seed or supplemental funds for professional travel and other

expenses related to course or curriculum improvements, research, or creative activity.[585] Kennesaw State University counted, as part of the comprehensive campaign, any competitive national grant designed to increase the number of scholarships at KSU. In September 2010, the university announced that it had received a $2.85 million grant from the National Science Foundation's Robert Noyce Teacher Scholarship Program to recruit and retain outstanding physics and chemistry teachers.

One of the goals of the Noyce Program was to enable veteran science teachers from local school districts to become master teachers. The Master Teaching Fellows were offered a $10,000 stipend each year for five years for professional development. A second goal was to help science professionals make a midcareer transition into the teaching field. They received a $10,000 Teaching Fellowship while they were enrolled in a fourteen-month curriculum leading to a master of arts in teaching and completion of teacher certification. Then, they were required to teach in a Georgia high-needs school district for four additional years. During that time, their teacher salary was supplemented with an annual stipend of $10,000 plus an additional $5,000 for travel and supplies. The program was a partnership with Georgia Tech, the American Chemical Society, and the Metropolitan Regional Educational Service Agency, and was one of only eight such programs throughout the nation.[586]

The value of some gifts to the comprehensive campaign could not be measured primarily in dollars and cents. During the planning stage, KSU learned of a sculpture titled *Spaceship Earth* by a renowned Finnish American artist named Eino. The massive quartize sculpture had been commissioned by PowerBar owners Brian and Jennifer Maxwell to honor environmental activist David Brower. His statute was placed prominently on top of the globe-like structure. The Maxwells originally offered the work to the University of California Berkeley, but changed their minds when they did not like the site that Berkeley chose to display it. Kennesaw learned about the sculpture because Eino had a home in the mountains of North Georgia near Laurence I. Peterson, the dean of the College of Science and Mathematics.

Kennesaw agreed to display the work in a prominent location outside the new Social Sciences Building, where the Environmental Studies Program would be located. By the time the Maxwells gave it to KSU, Eino had cut the pieces of the massive sculpture on location in Brazil and had loaded them on a ship destined for San Francisco. Kennesaw was able to reroute it to the port of Savannah. The work was dedicated on the KSU campus in the fall of 2006. Unfortunately, Eino had used a new epoxy to hold the pieces together, rather than the rebar system that had originally been planned. In the Georgia sun, the epoxy expanded. Then, during

(Opposite Page) *The Butterfly Project*, initiated by the Holocaust Museum Houston in 2001, honors the 1.5 million children who perished in the Holocaust.

(**Above and Opposite Page**) *Spaceship Earth* **with the Social Sciences Building in the background**

December weather, it contracted and cracked. Water seeped into the inner cement core and during the first freeze, the ice expanded, causing the sculpture to collapse into a number of pieces. KSU had received a small amount of national publicity when it first gained title to the sculpture, with San Francisco papers particularly interested in how an upstart college in Georgia "stole" Berkeley's artwork. But the earlier publicity was nothing compared to that of *Spaceship Earth* crashing to the ground. One story indicated that we now had proof that the earth was flat, at least at KSU. Once campus experts determined the cause of the explosion, the institution negotiated with Eino to return and connect the pieces together properly. As of 2013, the restored *Spaceship Earth* was still standing.[587]

On the opposite side of the Social Sciences Building, Kennesaw placed another gift to the university, a large slab of the Berlin Wall about the size of a large door. It was donated by local attorney Chuck Clay, the grandson of General Lucius Clay of Berlin Airlift fame. After the collapse of communism in Eastern Europe, the German nation gave the piece of the wall to the Clay family in gratitude for General Clay's role in keeping West Berlin free in the late 1940s. Chuck Clay first loaned the wall to Kennesaw to be placed outside the KSU Center while the *Anne Frank in the World* exhibit was on campus. Later, he made it a permanent gift. Wes Wicker recalled,

> When I look back on my career here, that's one of the things I'm really proud I was involved in.... I'd like to think it's one of the significant things on our campus. I was particularly touched one day this fall [2011], when I was walking past the Social Sciences Building. Someone had place a bouquet of flowers at the base of the wall on the anniversary of its fall. There was a note attached to the bouquet, honoring all the people who suffered and died because of that wall. It was written by one of our faculty members, who is of German origin.

The aspect of the comprehensive campaign that promised to have the largest impact on student life was the purchase of eighty-eight acres for recreational use, east of the main campus between the KSU Center and I-575. In early 2008, President Papp asked W. R. (Bob) Heflin Jr., the director of real estate on the foundation

KSU Sports and Recreation Park

staff, to find undeveloped land near campus that could be used for intramural and athletic fields. At the time, KSU had more than twenty thousand students and only a 1.7-acre field for student recreation. Despite all the development in recent years in the I-75/I-575 corridor, Heflin, surprisingly, found a forty-five-acre farm site along Big Shanty Road only about a mile from the main campus. Near it were seven smaller, separately-owned, undeveloped tracts, totaling another forty-three acres. The only occupied building on any of the properties was a Gold's Gym, and the tenants were planning to downsize and relocate. So, all eight parcels were potentially on the market, if the price was right.[588]

The forty-five-acre Nelson-Cobb farm had not been cultivated in some time. An old, abandoned farmhouse still remained. One of the three heirs was Kappy Ackerman, wife of BellSouth CEO F. Duane Ackerman, a close friend of KSU benefactor John Clendenin. A developer had recently made an offer of a little over $15 million, but could not close the deal after the 2008 real estate market crash. None of the heirs desired to reside there, so they hoped to sell it for a profit. Their main problem from a tax standpoint was the enormous capital gains tax they would have to pay, since they had no money invested in this inherited property. Kennesaw's challenge was to show them how to reduce their tax burden. The KSU Foundation offered $13 million, with the heirs writing off as a charitable contribution the $2.1 million difference between Kennesaw's bid and the previous offer.[589]

With the Nelson-Cobb property in hand, the KSU Foundation was able to close deals on the other tracts as well. The former Gold's Gym was renovated into the Owls Nest, a sixteen-thousand-square-foot indoor training facility. To guarantee that the foundation recovered its costs, President Papp persuaded the Student Government Association and the senate to support a student recreation fee. Approved by the Board of Regents in January 2010, this thirty-five dollar fee was designed gradually to retire the bonds on the foundation's purchase and pay to construct a soccer stadium, an NCAA-regulation running track, a nine-thousand-square-foot amenities building, numerous athletic fields (the majority with synthetic turf), and a 0.92-mile walking/jogging trail around a nine-acre lake. All phases of the KSU Sports and Recreation Park, a $50 million project, were opened by April 30, 2012.[590]

The soccer stadium was built with the support of Fitz Johnson, the owner of the Atlanta Beat, a professional women's soccer team. To house the customary crowds at KSU soccer games, the university wanted only about a 2,500-seat stadium. Johnson needed over eight thousand seats to make a profit. After Johnson donated $875,000 to the comprehensive campaign, Kennesaw agreed to build an 8,300-seat stadium. It opened in May 2010 and was so attractive and so perfect for soccer that the NCAA held its 2011 Division I Women's College Cup at KSU, with Stanford defeating Duke 1-0 in the championship game.[591]

Wes Wicker left Kennesaw shortly after the successful completion of the comprehensive campaign. The $75 million fundraising had greatly enhanced the quality of life for Kennesaw's faculty and students while generating a large amount of favorable publicity. He noted in parting that,

> In the evolution of every college or university, there are milestones that the institution must pass as it grows toward its aspirations. One such milestone is the standard set in fund raising. Michael Coles' gift to the College of Business set a standard. KSU had never before received a million dollar gift. Within fifteen years, we've received seventeen more gifts at that level or higher.... I would like to think that the legacy I left as Vice President of University Advancement is that we set a new standard—a new expectation—for fund raising at Kennesaw State University.[592]

Wicker credited Presidents Siegel and Papp for much of the success of the comprehensive campaign—Siegel for her many years of friend-raising, and Papp for challenging the Office of University Advancement and personally leading the $75 million fundraising effort. Without Papp's leadership, the campaign would no doubt have fallen far short of its goals. He was able to take advantage of KSU's past friend-raising successes to establish a remarkable record of fundraising at the start of his presidency.

Vince Dooley and a Football Exploratory Committee

Kennesaw's beautiful new soccer stadium was built with the thought in the back of top administrators' minds that, with modifications, it could suffice for football at least until the program was well established. As far back as 1999, President Siegel, athletic director Dave Waples, and a study committee had discussed the feasibility of intercollegiate football. The sport had the potential of solving a host of problems. One of those was figuring out ways to bring students on campus for something other than classes. Kennesaw badly needed to generate student pride, loyalty, and traditions. Another was to build brand recognition for an institution that was not well known outside Cobb County and the surrounding counties. A great many southerners follow football passionately and see it as an essential part of a complete college experience. So, Betty Siegel wanted a football team, although she admitted to being neither a participant nor a fan of any sport.

When KSU announced it was joining the NCAA Division I in November 2004, it decided that the time was not yet right for football. The main stumbling block was money. As Athletic Director Waples recalled in a 2011 interview, "If T. Boone Pickens had given us $168 million like he did Oklahoma State, we would

The Fifth Third Bank Stadium at night

have football right now." Siegel had always hoped to announce the start of football before she retired, but reluctantly gave in to top advisors who thought the decision should be left to the next president.[593]

Dan Papp was a former college football player who identified with student-athletes and recognized the value of intercollegiate and club sports in producing well-rounded, fully educated individuals. His love of athletics was on a level with his love of academics. Yet, he at first described himself as an "agnostic" on the football question until the university had done its homework in demonstrating widespread student, faculty, and community support and identifying adequate funding sources—not only for football, but, in the age of Title IX, for new women's sports that would have the same total number of scholarship athletes as football.

The first step was to set up the Football Exploratory Committee, headed by a well-known, highly-respected football expert, Vince Dooley, the legendary former coach and athletic director at the University of Georgia. His thirty-two-member committee contained faculty, staff, student, and community representatives. Dooley submitted his report on September 14, 2010. According to Dooley, the committee overwhelmingly favored the start of football. However, the Positive Alternatives Subcommittee did so with several reservations, most importantly that football not be funded at the expense of the other sports and that future student polling go beyond a mere "yes" or "no" vote to provide a third option of financing first-class intramurals and club sports.[594]

The vision of KSU athletics presented by the Positive Alternatives Subcommittee was the most articulate, passionately argued part of the final exploratory committee report. The subcommittee, headed by Tom Keene, suggested that if Kennesaw did not pursue football, it could make use of its new Sports and Recreation Park to involve a high percentage of residential students in participation sports, thus turning KSU into a national leader in providing recreational opportunities for all students. By doing so, the subcommittee maintained, Kennesaw had the potential to transform its identity in the minds of students in ways that would be "a point of pride…, a positive boost to the quality of campus life, and a superb recruiting tool for students eager to sustain an active life-style." It further argued that by rejecting football in tough economic times, KSU might win praise in the community for doing the "fiscally responsible thing" and for placing academics over athletics. The subcommittee proposed a slogan, "Be a Player, not a Spectator," and at a fraction of the price of football.

The Positive Alternatives Subcommittee provided evidence that KSU under-funded several sports, compared to other Division I nonfootball schools. The biggest

Kennesaw State University's Kelsey Barr attempts to keep the ball from two Samford University players on September 2, 2011.

gap was in basketball. According to the latest KSU figures, the men's team spent $768,000 annually on operating costs (not counting scholarships) and the women's team $616,000. The comparable numbers for all Division I-AΛA (nonfootball) schools were $1,449,000 and $1,015,000, respectively. If football was not started, the subcommittee argued, the operational budgets of the existing intercollegiate sports should be bolstered to reach the averages of peer institutions.

In his summary of the full committee's recommendations, Vince Dooley conceded that finances would be the central challenge in creating a successful football program, particularly since less than 20 percent of current American football programs turned a profit. Nonetheless, he maintained that the benefits of football outweighed the liabilities. He claimed that football would help attract good students, energize the alumni, appeal to potential new donors, and bring state legislators and community leaders to campus, making them more favorably disposed toward the university. He also pointed out that Georgia produced the fourth largest number of college football players in the union. So Kennesaw would have no problem recruiting talented athletes from its own backyard.[595]

With the committee report in hand, President Papp's next step was to determine whether students were willing to pay for football with an increased student fee. The matter was determined in an online survey, shaped by the Student Government Association, during the week of November 8, 2010. Students were asked to vote "yes" or "no" on a one-hundred-dollar per semester fee to begin no sooner than fall 2012. Some 7,358 students participated in the poll, and 55.5 percent gave their support to the fee increase. With a minimum two-year lag between the time of the vote and the date of implementation, upperclassmen were clearly voting for a tax that would not take effect before they graduated. So, some question lingered as to the degree of support among students who would actually be around long enough to pay the fee. Nonetheless, the pro-football advocates had passed a major test and were able to proclaim broad-based student enthusiasm.[596]

Dave Waples retired in August 2010 after twenty-three years as athletic director. Softball coach Scott Whitlock filled in as interim director while a committee of students, faculty, and administrators, headed by Tom Keene, conducted a national search. In April 2011, President Papp announced the selection of University of Connecticut (UConn) Associate Athletic Director Vaughn Williams. At UConn, Williams's major responsibilities were strategic planning, facility master planning, and policy and procedure improvement.[597]

Having filled the top position in the Athletic Department, the administration turned its attention to finding potential donors. By the fall of 2012 Kennesaw reached a tentative agreement with Fifth Third Bank. The bank had long been a major financial institution in the Midwest, dating back to the Bank of the Ohio Valley in 1858. That bank was acquired a few years after the Civil War by the Third

Bank, which merged in 1908 with the Fifth Bank, thus producing an institution named the Fifth Third National Bank of Cincinnati. It entered Georgia in 2008 through the purchase of the nine branches of First Horizon, all in the Atlanta area.[598] In time, the bank expanded to new locations in Atlanta and throughout the state. One of the branches was on Chastain Road, little more than a stone's throw from KSU's stadium. In an agreement that was kept confidential until the Board of Regents approved the deal, Fifth Third pledged to contribute a half million dollars annually for ten years, providing a total of $5 million. In exchange for this investment, KSU agreed to make Fifth Third Bank the official bank of the KSU Athletics Program; to rename the soccer/lacrosse/football facility the Fifth Third Bank Stadium; and to give the bank sponsorship recognition at the Convocation Center, at the baseball and softball fields, and in media advertising.[599]

On October 10, 2012, the administration gained approval from the KSU Student Fee Committee for a one-hundred-dollar increase per semester, starting in the fall of 2013. The fees would support football and the additional women's sports needed to meet Title IX requirements. In November, President Papp and Athletic Director Williams went to the Board of Regents with a detailed business plan that included projected expenses and revenues for six years into the future. The regents considered the matter for several months, giving final approval on February 13, 2013. At a press conference the following day, Papp and Williams unveiled the deal with Fifth Third Bank and announced the opening of a search for a football coach. Once that person was hired, the Athletic Department expected to begin recruiting players and searching for a football conference in which to compete at the Football Championship Subdivision (formerly Division I-AA) level. If all went well, Vaughn Williams predicted that KSU should field its first team in the fall of 2015. As President Papp said at the time, "This is an exciting day for Kennesaw State University and a milestone that is the culmination of the hard work and support from many individuals on and off campus."[600]

Epilogue

As KSU approached its fiftieth birthday, no one could say for certain what its future would be. To improve service and efficiency, the Board of Regents on January 10, 2012, approved a plan submitted by Chancellor Hank Huckaby to consolidate eight of the university system's thirty-five units into four larger institutions. In May, the board announced the names of two of the new schools: the University of North Georgia, created through the merger of North Georgia College & State University and Gainesville State College; and Middle Georgia State College, resulting from the linking of Macon State to Middle Georgia College in Cochran. The regents also approved a mission statement for Middle Georgia State College that included a plan for its elevation to university status by June 2014. In August, the university system approved name changes for the other consolidated institutions: South Georgia State College, formed from the merger of Waycross College and South Georgia College (Douglas); and Georgia Regents University, created from two institutions in the City of Augusta—Georgia Health Sciences University and Augusta State University. In December 2012, the Southern Association of Colleges and Schools approved prospectuses submitted by the four new institutions, and on January 8, 2013, the Board of Regents gave its final approval to the mergers.[601]

It was not certain at the time whether these mergers were the conclusion or merely the start of a process. It seemed possible that the Board of Regents might someday consolidate two or more institutions in northwest Georgia. KSU and Southern Polytechnic State University, for instance, maintained campuses only about ten miles apart, while KSU and Georgia Highlands College (headquartered in Rome) were already working cooperatively to offer courses at a campus in Dallas. With about twenty-five thousand students, Kennesaw would be by far the largest institution if such mergers should occur; but any consolidation would no doubt have far-reaching consequences for the way future generations viewed Kennesaw and its history.

Despite such questions, one thing seemed certain. In fifty short years, Kennesaw had far exceeded the expectations of its founders. Decade after decade, the dreams of campus visionaries reached fruition and became the foundation stones for the plans of new generations of builders. The first eight yellow-brick structures still stood in 2012, but not one retained its original name or function. Kennesaw operated as a junior college for only one decade before the Board of Regents approved four-year status in April 1976. Charter president, Horace Sturgis, retired in 1980, after presiding over the first senior-class graduation and the growth of the student body to about four thousand. He was replaced by Betty Siegel, the first woman ever to head a University System of Georgia institution. That watershed moment in 1981 brought the college national publicity and a dynamic new vision of what it could become. As Kennesaw aspired to be a prototypical college of the future, it passed many landmarks, including the start of graduate programs in 1985, the achievement of university status in 1996, the opening of the first residence halls in 2002, and a quadrupling of the student body during the twenty-five years of the Siegel era.

By the time Dan Papp became Kennesaw's third president in 2006, the university was already the third largest in the university system. Yet, the first six years of the Papp presidency witnessed accelerated student growth and some of the most significant transformations in KSU's history. The enrollment of the first cohort of doctoral students in January 2007 was a major event in Kennesaw's evolution, as were the successful completion of a $75 million comprehensive capital campaign, the gaining of full NCAA Division I status, and the first steps toward a football program. Meanwhile, the eighty-eight-acre Sports and Recreation Park provided students with the finest facility in the university system for intramurals and club sports, and in October 2012 President Papp announced the Board of Regents' approval for a new $38.7 million Dr. Betty L. Siegel Student Recreation and Activities Center to be built next to the current Student Recreation Center and to contain indoor and outdoor pools, an indoor track, multiple basketball courts, and many other modern features.[602]

Throughout the early twenty-first century new buildings sprang up on campus at a remarkable rate. In the Papp years, additional classroom facilities included a new Social Sciences Building, Prillaman Hall, and the Lab Science Building. In early 2013, construction began on the $20 million extension of the Bagwell College of Education. The new Bailey Performance Center and art galleries provided unprecedented opportunities for students as well as outreach to the community, and in 2012, Kennesaw began work on the Zuckerman Museum of Art. In addition, new residence halls opened every few years, including University Place Phase II in time for the start of the 2012–13 school year. The Commons won awards as one of the best food service facilities in the nation. The opening of the eight-story Central Parking Deck and initiation of a shuttle bus service helped with transportation problems for commuter students. As soon as one building project was completed, another seemed always ready to begin to keep pace with the constant expansion of the student population.

Kennesaw was blessed throughout its history with visionary leadership, an excellent faculty and staff, and a foundation of extraordinarily talented individuals who donated their time, creativity, and financial resources to the betterment of the university. Kennesaw was always blessed with outstanding students and alumni. Like many modern colleges created in the aftermath of World War II, Kennesaw's average SAT scores did not begin to measure the true quality of nontraditional students who brought commitment, maturity, and life experiences to the enrichment of their academic careers.

On August 14, 2013, the Board of Regents recognized Kennesaw State's extraordinary progress by reclassifying it as one of the university system's four "comprehensive universities." Such institutions offer numerous undergraduate and master's level programs and some doctoral programs, and are expected to engage in basic and applied research at a level above the state colleges and universities, but just below the research universities. They operate on a mandate from the Board of Regents to be world-class academic institutions. President Papp said that the change in status was "a defining moment in the university's 50-year history" and "appropriately timed as we begin the university's next chapter." The designation as a "comprehensive university" gave KSU much to celebrate as it turned fifty. In its first half century, it grew from a small college to a large university with an entrepreneurial spirit that promised to keep it from ever being satisfied with past accomplishments. One suspects that KSU will continue to surprise generations to come with its exemplary commitment to students, scholarship, and public engagement. As it looks to the future with optimism and confidence, the university envisions the next fifty years to be full of exciting opportunities for service to students and its many local, national, and worldwide publics. That is Kennesaw's plan and its promise.

Endnotes

Chapter 1

1   "Cobb County Gets New Junior College," *Marietta Daily Journal*, October 9, 1963, 1; Harold Paulk Henderson, "Howard Hollis (Bo) Callaway," *New Georgia Encyclopedia*, September 12, 2002; Kate Lanning Minchew, "Callaway Family," *New Georgia Encyclopedia*, August 17, 2009, www.georgiaencyclopedia.org; Weather Forecast *Marietta Daily Journal*, October 9, 1963; and Weather Forecast, *Atlanta Constitution*, October 10, 1963.

2   Minutes, Board of Regents of University System of Georgia, October 9, 1963, 194, "Board of Regents Meeting Minutes, 1963–1968," Box 1, KSU/01/04, Kennesaw State University Archives, Kennesaw, Georgia; Myron Wade House, "University of West Georgia," *New Georgia Encyclopedia*, May 1, 2006.

3   Boyd had a long personal history in the university system. From 1935–61, he was a physics professor at Georgia Tech, where he did groundbreaking work in microwave propagation through grants from the Office of Naval Research. In the post–World War II era, he played a major role in making Tech's Engineering Experiment Station (EES) a national leader in radar-related research and headed the EES for four years before assuming the presidency of West Georgia College in 1961. Robert C. McMath Jr., Ronald H. Bayor, James E. Brittain, Lawrence Foster, August W. Giebelhaus, and Germaine M. Reed, *Engineering the New South: Georgia Tech, 1885–1985* (Athens: University of Georgia Press, 1985), 400.

4   Minutes, Board of Regents, October 9, 1963, 199; Harold Stephens Willingham Jr., interview by Beverly D. Hale, July 11, 1987, and Mary B. Cawley, September 28, 1988, no. 11, transcript, Cobb County Oral History Series, Kennesaw State University Archives; "Cobb County Gets New Junior College" The Adlai Stevenson quotation came from his concession speech after he lost the presidency to Dwight D. Eisenhower in 1952. Actually, Stevenson was quoting a humorous remark from Abraham Lincoln after Lincoln was asked for his reaction to a loss by his political party. Charles Cowan's sister, Sue, was married to Horace W. Sturgis, the first president of the junior college.

5   Founded in 1948, Southern Tech was a branch of Georgia Tech until 1980. Georgia Perimeter (originally DeKalb College) opened in 1964, but was under local control until it joined the university system in 1986.

6   John R. Thelin, *A History of American Higher Education* (Baltimore: Johns Hopkins University Press, 2004), 271–74, 277–78.

7   Cameron Fincher, *Historical Development of the University System of Georgia, 1932–2002*, 2nd ed. (Athens: Institute of Higher Education, University of Georgia, 2003), 35.

8   Thomas G. Dyer, *The University of Georgia: A Bicentennial History, 1785–1985* (Athens: University of Georgia Press, 1985), 296–301, 358.

9   Daniel S. Papp, interview by Thomas A. Scott and Dede Yow, August 3, 2006, no. 50, Kennesaw State University Oral History Project, Kennesaw State University Archives.

10 This is the James Boyd who served as president of West Georgia College throughout the 1960s. He was serving as vice chancellor of the university system when he was called upon to become acting president of Georgia Tech in 1971–72, between the presidencies of Arthur G. Hansen and Joseph M. Pettit. McMath et al., *Engineering the New South*, 212, 214, 400; August W. Giebelhaus, *Reader's Report*, September 19, 2012, copy in Kennesaw State University Archives.

11 McMath et al., *Engineering the New South*, 409–15.

12 McMath et al., *Engineering the New South*, 414–15, 432–33; Papp interview, no. 10; Georgia Tech website: http://www.gatech.edu/about/factsandfigures.html.

13 James T. Patterson, *Grand Expectations: The United States, 1945–1974* (Oxford: Oxford University Press, 1996), vii–ix, 312, 450–51.

14 Kenneth Coleman, ed., *A History of Georgia*, 2nd ed., (Athens: University of Georgia Press, 1991), 341.

15 See the author's *Cobb County, Georgia, and the Origins of the Suburban South: A Twentieth-Century History* (Marietta: Cobb Landmarks and Historical Society, 2003), especially chapters 5–7 for the story of the Bell plant and chapters 8 and 13 for Lockheed's first decade in Marietta. Jeffrey L. Holland, *Under One Roof: The Story of Air Force Plant 6* (Wright-Patterson Air Force Base, Ohio: Aeronautical Systems Center, Acquisition Environmental, Safety and Health Division, 2006) is a fine illustrated history of the Marietta plant that was written as part of the remediation agreement by which the Georgia Historic Preservation Division signed off on the demolition of the World War II-era B-2 (administration) building.

16 Patterson, *Grand Expectations*, 68–69; Thelin, *History of American Higher Education*, 262–64; Dyer, *University of Georgia*, 250–51.

17 Dyer, *University of Georgia*, 251–64; McMath et al., *Engineering the New South*, 242–43.

18 Merl E. Reed, *Educating the Urban New South: Atlanta and the Rise of Georgia State University, 1913–1969* (Macon, Georgia: Mercer University Press, 2009), particularly chapters 8–14; for the questionable GI Bill payments, see 128–29.

19 See Gail Kennedy, ed., *Education for Democracy: The Debate over the Report of the President's Commission on Higher Education*, vol.15, Problems in American Civilization (Boston: D. C. Heath and Company, 1952) for an excellent contemporary discussion of the commission report.

20 Janet D. Stone, *From the Mansion to the University: A History of Armstrong Atlantic State University, 1935–2010* (Savannah: Armstrong Atlantic State University, 2010), 91–99; Fincher, *Historical Development of the University System of Georgia*, 49–50; Edward J. Cashin, "Augusta State University," *New Georgia Encyclopedia*, June 3, 2005; Craig Lloyd, "Columbus State University," *New Georgia Encyclopedia*, January 2, 2004.

21 Paul Stephen Hudson, "Georgia Perimeter College," *New Georgia Encyclopedia*, updated June 28, 2012.

22 Hugh T. Atkinson, David B. Kelley, Joel H. Paul, and Bowling C. Yates Jr., *Higher Education in Cobb County* (Marietta: Cox Printing Company, 1966), 55–61; "University Division To Be Located Here Soon," *Cobb County Times*, June 14, 1951, 1.

23 Atkinson, *Higher Education in Cobb*, 42–43; Willingham interview, 53–55; "Green Light Given Center by Griffin," *Marietta Daily Journal*, January 29, 1958; Minutes, Cobb County Advisory Board, May 7, 1957, and March 4, 1958, Cobb County Courthouse, Marietta, Georgia.

24 Atkinson, *Higher Education in Cobb*, 42–43; Willingham interview, 53–54.

25 Willingham interview, 54–55; Fred D. Bentley Sr., interview by Thomas A. Scott and Mary Boswell Cawley, July 11, 1987, no. 8, 33–34, transcript, Cobb County Oral History Series, Kennesaw State University Archives; "Vandiver Forces Celebrate Defeat of Griffin's Rural Road Measure," *Marietta Daily Journal*, January 29, 1958.

26 Robert W. Dubay, "Marvin Griffin and the Politics of the Stump," in *Georgia Governors in an Age of Change: From Ellis Arnall to George Busbee*, eds. Harold P. Henderson and Gary L. Roberts (Athens: University of Georgia Press, 1988), 101–12; Richard A. Bennett, *Southern Polytechnic State University: The History* (Marietta: Southern Polytechnic State University Foundation, 1998), 51–52; Willingham interview, 55–56.

27 Atkinson, *Higher Education in Cobb*, 39–41; Bennett, *Southern Polytechnic State University*, 4–54.

28 Bennett, *Southern Polytechnic State University*, 45; Willingham interview, 56–58; Minutes, Cobb County Advisory Board, May 6, 1958.

29 In the following legislative session Willingham pushed through a bill allowing the Marietta Housing Authority to issue revenue bonds to build dormitories. The bonds would be retired through rentals. "Bill Authorizes Southern Tech Dormitory Work," *Marietta Daily Journal*, February 4, 1959; "Governor Signs STI, Absentee Ballot Bill," photograph caption, *Marietta Daily Journal*, February 19, 1959; Willingham interview, 58; Bennett, *Southern Polytechnic State University*, 51–53; Minutes, Cobb County Advisory Board, November 5, 1958.

30 William R. Tapp Jr., interview by J. Denise Lockaby, March 14, 1985, vol. xi, 8, transcript, Collected Interviews, Kennesaw College Oral History Project, Kennesaw State University Archives; "Marietta Architect to Plan Institute," *Marietta Daily Journal*, July 9, 1958; Willingham interview, 57; L. V. Johnson, "The History and Development of Southern Tech," report to Academic Advisory Council, November 18, 1966, History: General File, Rare Book Room, Southern Polytechnic State University; Bart Parker, "McClure Headed Southern Tech during School's Move to Marietta," *Marietta Daily Journal*, April 20, 1988.

31 Rachel Nichols, "History of Chattahoochee Technical College," *Institutional Self-Study*, (2002); Minutes, Marietta Board of Education, April 20, 1961; Scott, *Cobb County, Georgia, and the Origins of the Suburban South*, 314–17.

32 Atkinson, *Higher Education in Cobb*, 78–79.

33 Bentley interview, 25; Fred D. Bentley Sr., telephone conversation with the author, September 8, 2011, notes in author's possession; "Cobb Wins Junior College," *Atlanta Constitution*, October 10, 1963.

34 Commissioner Herbert McCollum headed the list of office holders on the steering committee. Former and present mayors included J. B. "Jake" Ables (Smyrna), James "Johnny" Adams (Kennesaw), L. Howard Atherton (Marietta), Dr. Luke G. Garrett (Austell), George Kreeger (Smyrna), Mary B. McCall (Acworth), and Sam J. Welsch (Marietta). Current and past legislators included Cy Chapman, Robert E. Flournoy, Edward S. Kendrick, E. W. (Bill) Teague, Joe Mack Wilson, Harold Willingham, and Kyle Yancey. Ex-ordinary (probate judge) J. J. Daniell concluded the list of office holders. Representing the educational community were Marietta Center director Dr. Archie Rushton; Marietta school board chairman Dempsey Medford and superintendent Henry Kemp; and Cobb school board chairman Dr. W. C. Mitchell, superintendent Jasper M. Griffin, deputy superintendent T. C. Cantrell, and former Cobb superintendent W. P. Sprayberry. Other community representatives included R. H. Lindley, A. D. Little, Richard L. Sims, and Elizabeth Tomlinson. College committee listed in "Ground Breaking Ceremonies, Cobb County, University of Georgia System, College," November 18, 1964. Xerox copy of program in Thomas Scott Collection, Kennesaw State University Archives.

Robert Dobbs Fowler left the *Marietta Daily Journal* shortly after leading the junior college steering committee to become the owner of a newspaper in Gwinnett County. KSU's Robert D. Fowler Distinguished Chair in Communication is named in his memory thanks to a generous gift from his family, http://communication.hss.kennesaw.edu/about/fowler-chair/. "Fowler Resigns as Editor, Buys Gwinnett Newspaper," *Cobb County Times*, June 18, 1964, 5.

[35] Willingham interview, 59–61; Application from the Cobb County and Marietta Governmental Agencies to the regents of the university system for the Establishment and Operation of a Junior College, April 3, 1963.

[36] Fincher, *Historical Development of the University System of Georgia*, 57.

[37] Minutes, Board of Regents, October 9, 1963; J. H. Dewberry, Memorandum for the Record, February 20, 1964, included in Minutes of a Special Meeting of the Board of Regents, March 3, 1964; "County Wins Fight to Get Junior College," *Cobb County Times*, October 10, 1963.

[38] Dewberry, Memorandum, Special Meeting of Board of Regents, March 3, 1964.

[39] McCollum interview, 31; Willingham interview, 61–63; Jim Wynn, "Site Selected in North Cobb," *Marietta Daily Journal*, March 3, 1964.

[40] Willingham claimed that Governor Sanders asked him, as a favor, to place the campus as far north as possible. The Cobb legislator replied, "Well, that won't be any favor; we were planning to do that anyway—get as far from your constituents in Atlanta as possible." Willingham interview, 61; Dewberry, Memorandum, Special Meeting of Board of Regents, March 3, 1964.

[41] The two that Tapp suspected were Willingham and Bozeman. Fred Bentley reached the same conclusion. He was critical from the beginning of what he calls Cobb County's "Yazoo Fraud." The *Atlanta Journal*'s John Pennington engaged in investigative reporting that exposed some of the sordidness of the transaction. Even Willingham's critics conceded that he deserves much credit for the growth of modern Cobb County. What they questioned was the ethics of using inside knowledge for a speculative advantage. One of the members who wrote the critical Grand Jury report, Howard Ector, was a Trust Company of Georgia executive, a former Georgia Tech football star, and, in later years, a trustee of the Kennesaw State Foundation. He once remarked that "Harold had more ability and more brains and more know-how than anybody I've ever known, but I'm sorry to say I don't think he used them for the best interests of the county." Willingham interview, 40–41; William R. Tapp Jr., to fellow members of Cobb County Recreation Authority, November 6, 1962, attachment to Grand Jury presentments, January–February 1963 term, Cobb County Courthouse, Marietta, Georgia, 571–73; Tapp interview, 13; Bentley interview, 26; W. Howard Ector, interview by Thomas A. Scott, June 16, 1995, no. 38, 5, 18–22, transcripts, Cobb County Oral History Series, Kennesaw State University Archives. See the author's *Cobb County, Georgia, and the Origins of the Suburban South*, 298–305, for more detail and documentation of the Pinetree scandal.

[42] Pinetree had already staked out lots along the east side of Frey Lake Road (on the campus site) that were worth more than the regents wanted to pay. But Willingham claims he told his friends in the corporation that they were going to have to give in, and they reluctantly did so. Willingham interview, 62–63; Pennington, "Controversial Cobb Tract"; Minutes of a Special Meeting of the Board of Regents, March 3, 1964; Harold S. Willingham to Honorable Hubert Dewberry, July 31, 1964, KSU-Correspondence 1964 file, Box 6/9, Thomas Scott Collection, Kennesaw State University Archives.

[43] On July 31, 1964, Harold Willingham, in his capacity as Cobb School Board attorney, mailed a letter to Hubert Dewberry with a check for $2 million, copies of the Georgia Highway Department's plans to extend McCollum Parkway and improve Big Shanty Road, and a copy of the revised plat for the college site deeding one hundred feet of right-of-way to the Highway

Department along Steve Frey Road. He added that the state was "incidentally letting a contract for the paving of this road on August 7th next." The told bonded indebtedness was $2.35 million. After giving $2 million to the Board of Regents and spending quarter million dollars to purchase the 152-acre campus, Cobb County spent the remaining $0.25 million on grading, paving, and utilities. "Junior College Gets Okay from Voters: Bonds Approved by 8-1 Margin," *Marietta Daily Journal*, April 23, 1964; "College Bonds Win in Lopsided Vote," *Cobb County Times*, April 23, 1964; Harold S. Willingham to Honorable Hubert Dewberry, July 31, 1964.

[44]   The author is grateful to Fred Bentley Sr. for confirmation that the ground breaking took place on or near the site of the future Administration Building (currently Campus Safety Building). Fred Bentley Sr. telephone conversation with author, February 18, 2013. Both Bentley and Malinda Jolley Mortin, who attended with her father, Lex Jolley, recall a cocktail reception afterwards at the Pinetree Country Club. Malinda Jolley Mortin, converstaion with author, February 14, 2013. Also see the *Marietta Daily Journal*, November 19, 1964, and the Atlanta Constitution, November 19, 1964, for an account of Governor Sanders's speech. The program of the event, including the names of the twenty-eight-member steering committee, can be found in the KSU Ground Breaking Ceremonies file, Box 6/9, Thomas Scott Collection, Kennesaw State University Archives.

Chapter 2

[45]   Horace W. Sturgis, interview by Thomas A. Scott, November 13, 1986–February 19, 1987, no. 1, 31, transcripts, KSU Oral History Series, Kennesaw State University Archives.

[46]   Sturgis interview, 1–3.

[47]   Sturgis interview, 3–6; James Davis (Spec) Landrum, interview by Thomas A. Scott, February 12, 2004, no. 5, 4, 15–18, transcripts, KSU Oral History Series, Kennesaw State University Archives.

[48]   A distinguished educator, Cocking is best remembered as a target in 1941 of Governor Eugene Talmadge, who accused him of attempting to integrate a demonstration school for teachers at the University of Georgia and, basically, of being too liberal for Georgia. After the Board of Regents fired Cocking, a large number of colleagues came to his defense, including UGA president Harmon Caldwell, who threatened to resign if he was not reinstated. When the board voted to give Cocking a hearing, Talmadge forced out three regents and replaced them with political cronies. The hearing was little more than a kangaroo court, and Cocking was fired again. Talmadge then turned his wrath on the entire university system, purging ten more prominent educators and thoroughly demoralizing college faculties. For these infringements of academic freedom, the Southern Association of Colleges and Schools took accreditation away from all of Georgia's public colleges. The political consequence was Talmadge's defeat in the election in 1942 by a much more liberal Ellis Arnall, who managed to restore accreditation by giving the Board of Regents greater freedom from political interference. See James F. Cook, "Cocking Affair," *New Georgia Encyclopedia*, August 12, 2002, www.georgiaencyclopedia.org.

[49]   Sturgis interview, 9–22.

[50]   Sturgis interview, 22–29.

[51]   Minutes, Board of Regents, May 12, 1965, 593–94; Sturgis interview, 30–42. The statement that it was "inconceivable that I would be hired today with the credentials I had then" is on page 38. The discussion of Simpson's role in hiring Sturgis is on pages 34–35.

52 Sturgis interview, 45–49, 55; Minutes, Board of Regents, July 21, 1965, 42; "It's the Talk Around Town," *Marietta Daily Journal*, August 9, 1965. Also see the university scrapbooks in the KSU Archives for the various early names.

53 Sturgis interview, 46–49; John S. Frey Jr. and Nina Chinault Frey, interview by Jennifer L. Ramsey [Biddy], July 3, 1984, 4, transcript, copy in possession of author; Kelly Mahar, "Mary McCall: Her Vision for a Small Town," May 2002, term paper, HIST 2275, Box 6, Local History Term Papers, Kennesaw State University Archives; *Marietta Daily Journal*, July 23, 1965, July 29, 1965, and August 9, 1965; *North Cobb News*, July 29, 1965 (a copy of the *North Cobb News* editorial, "What's In a Name?," can be located in the university scrapbooks in the Kennesaw State University Archives).

54 Minutes, Board of Regents of the University System of Georgia, August 11, 1965, 75.

55 Minutes, Board of Regents, June 10, 1964, 615 and February 10, 1965, 421–22. These plans were for a project to cost no more than $2 million. In April 1965 the board gave the Marietta architectural firm an additional contract to draw up final plans and specifications for physical education facilities at a projected cost of $510,615. Minutes, Board of Regents, April 14, 1965, 515.

56 Minutes, Board of Regents, September 15, 1965, 142; "Atlanta Firm Gets JC Bid," *Marietta Daily Journal*, September 19, 1965.

57 Of the $2,350,000 approved in the April 1964 bond referendum, $2 million went to the Board of Regents for campus construction, $100,000 was used to buy the land, and $250,000 was designated for grading and utilities. For Barrett's meeting with the Board of Regents, see Becky Smith and Jim Mathis, "Union Fight, Money Threatening College," *Marietta Daily Journal*, March 3, 1966, and "Workers Are Back at Kennesaw JC," *Marietta Daily Journal*, March 16, 1966. Also see Sturgis interview, 44.

58 Phil Hudgins, "Strike Delaying Work on College," *Marietta Daily Journal*, October 22, 1965.

59 For newspaper accounts of labor unrest at the campus worksite, see the *Marietta Daily Journal*, October 22, 1965, November 8, 1965, March 3, 1966, August 12, 1966, and November 24, 1966. Also see the *Atlanta Journal*, August 1, 1966. The editorials can be found in the *Marietta Daily Journal*, March 13, 1966 and the *Smyrna Herald*, March 17, 1966. All the above are also in the university scrapbooks in the Kennesaw State University Archives.

60 Horace W. Sturgis to J. H. Dewberry, May 16, 1966; Dewberry to Sturgis, May 17, 1966; the author read this letter in a file labeled "History of College" that formerly was located in the office of KSU's vice president for business and finance, Roger E. Hopkins; unfortunately, the file disappeared after his retirement. Also please see Robert J. Greene, interview by Thomas A. Scott, August 3, 2007, no. 68, 8, transcript, KSU Oral History Series, Kennesaw State University Archives; and Roger E. Hopkins, interview by Thomas A. Scott, August 15, 1988, transcript in possession of author. Dr. Greene was the first head librarian, and Mr. Hopkins was the second controller, arriving in 1967. More details can be found in "Kennesaw Junior College Opens in Piecemeal Status," *Atlanta Journal*, August 1, 1966.

61 Sturgis interview, 59; Minutes, Board of Regents, December 13, 1967, 321.

62 Sturgis interview, 58.

63 The problem with Banberry was that the city-county line was just to its east, so school children in unincorporated east Cobb had to attend county schools and could not go to Banberry, even if it was closer. On the other hand, US 41 was just to its west, and Marietta parents on the other side of the busy Four Lane Highway (US 41) had no intentions of letting their children cross such a busy road. So its service area was severely restricted.

64 Derrell C. Roberts, interview by Thomas A. Scott, November 20, 1998, for "A Celebration of Service to the Institution: Interviews with Longtime Faculty and Administrators at Kennesaw State University," no. 66, 22, transcript, Cobb County Oral History Series, Kennesaw State University Archives.

65 Roberts interview, 23; Minutes, Board of Regents, September 15, 1965, 114; "Dr. Roberts Named Dean at Kennesaw," *Marietta Daily Journal*, December 29, 1965. Roberts's revised dissertation was published in 1973 by the University of Alabama Press under the title of *Joseph E. Brown and the Politics of Reconstruction*.

66 Roberts interview, 22–24; *The Kennesaw Junior College 1966–68 Catalog*, copy in the Kennesaw State University Archives. The catalog lists everyone who served on the faculty in the first two years. Of the forty-two members of the full-time teaching faculty, five taught only the first year, nine only the second year, and twenty-eight both years. The three nonadministrators with doctorates were Virginia Hinton with a PhD in English, Jere W. Roberson with a PhD in history, and assistant professor of biology Mary L. Lance who held an EdD All three received their doctorates from the University of Georgia.

67 Roberts interview, 23.

68 Sturgis interview, 44.

69 Minutes, Board of Regents, February 9, 1966, 355; April 19–20, 1966, 494; George H. Beggs, interview by Thomas A. Scott, November 20, 1998, for "A Celebration of Service to the Institution," 26–27, transcript.

70 All the original top administrative positions went to white males, but President Sturgis was proud of the fact that he initially offered the chairmanship of the Division of Natural Sciences and Mathematics to a woman, Vera B. Zalkow, who had a PhD from Wayne State University and was teaching at the time at Oglethorpe University. Zalkow would join the Kennesaw faculty in 1976 as a chemistry professor, but, at the time she was hesitant to move to a new two-year school about which she knew very little. Beggs interview, 26; *Sentinel*, July 20, 1967; Sturgis interview, 63–64; Virginia Cooksey Hinton, interview by Thomas A. Scott, June 4, 1987 and July 9, 1987, no. 17, 25, transcript, Cobb County Oral History Series, Kennesaw State University Archives.

71 Bowman O. Davis Jr., interview by Thomas A. Scott, June 4, 2004, no. 2, 5–6, 9, 18, 20, transcript, KSU Oral History Series, Kennesaw State University Archives.

72 Horace W. Sturgis, *The President's Report for the Year, 1975–1976*, 39–40, "Annual Reports, 1966–1991," KSU/03/02/001, Kennesaw State University Archives; Beggs interview, 27–28.

73 *Sentinel*, October 3, 1966, 4; Greene interview, 2–5, 8, 10.

74 In introducing the Developmental Program, the initial catalog claimed that, "Some students show evidence that they can profit from a college education; yet, for various reasons, they do not meet all the standards required for admission. The Developmental Program is designed to serve such students by providing a learning situation in which they can sharpen their basic skills in reading, communications, and mathematics." *Kennesaw Junior College 1966–68 Catalog*, 18.

75 *Marietta Daily Journal*, September 14, 1966; Madeline M. Miles, interview by Thomas A. Scott, May 28, 1992, transcript in possession of author; David M. Jones Jr., interview by Thomas A. Scott, November 20, 1998, for "A Celebration of Service to the Institution," no. 32, transcriptw.

76 Sturgis interview, 59–61; *Sentinel*, October 3, 1966, 4.

77 *Sentinel*, October 3, 1966, October 31, 1966, December 1, 1966, and February 2, 1967.

78 *Sentinel*, December 1, 1966; Roy Blount Jr., "Kennesaw Junior College Opens at Campus on Hill," *Atlanta Journal-Constitution*, January 8, 1967.

79 Minutes, Board of Regents, January 11, 1967; Mary H. Swain, interview by H. G. Pennington, April 27, 1979, Kennesaw College Oral History Project, vol. 1, 6, transcript, Collected Interviews, Kennesaw State University Archives.

80 *Sentinel*, February 2, 1967; Madeline M. Miles, interview by Thomas A. Scott, May 28, 1992, transcript in possession of author; C. Grady Palmer, interview by Kurt Roenitz, April 9, 2011, 4, transcript, class project, HIST 4425; C. Grady Palmer, interview by Thomas A. Scott, August 17, 1988, transcript in possession of author; Ralph E. Slay (Architect, Bothwell and Associates) to Frank C. Dunham (Associate Director, Construction, and Physical Plants), regents of the university system, September 28, 1967, "History of the College," Building Notes file, Roger E. Hopkins (file now missing, please see endnote 60).

81 Miles interview.

82 J. B. Tate, interview by Kristin Dalton and Brenda Eubanks, April 19, 2011, no. 101, 3, 15, transcript, KSU Oral History Series, Kennesaw State University Archives.

83 *Institutional Self-Study for Kennesaw Junior College* (Spring 1972): 148–49, Kennesaw State University Archives.

84 Tate interview, 10.

85 Stephen E. Scherer, interview by Thomas A. Scott, November 7, 2006, no. 59, 8–9, 14, transcripts, KSU Oral History Series, Kennesaw State University Archives.

86 Scherer interview, 13; Elaine M. Hubbard, interview by Thomas A. Scott, June 24, 2004, no. 7, 6–9, transcript, KSU Oral History Series, Kennesaw State University Archives.

87 "Campus Personalties—Faculty Member of the Month," *Sentinel*, February 2, 1967, 3.

88 Kathleen Sherlock Scott, Conversation with the author; Minutes, Board of Regents, March 12–13, 1974, 413–14.

89 "Who's Whoo—Lynnda Bernard, Student of the Month," *Sentinel*, December 1, 1966, 3; "Lynnda Eagle—Post 1," Cobb County Board of Education, http://www.cobbk12.org/board/; "Lynnda Eagle Not Seeking School Board Re-election," May 25, 2012, *Acworth Patch*, http://acworth.patch.com/articles/lynnda-eagle-not-seeking-school-board-re-election.

90 Stevan H. Crew, interview by Thomas A. Scott, September 16, 2009, no. 91, 6–9, 17–24, transcript, KSU Oral History Series, Kennesaw State University Archives.

91 Ralph W. Walker III, interview by Thomas A. Scott, May 9, 2007, no. 74, 3–5, transcript, KSU Oral History Series, Kennesaw State University Archives.

92 Melonie J. Wallace, interview by Thomas A. Scott, June 29, 2009, no. 98, 1–2, 6, 15, transcript, KSU Oral History Series, Kennesaw State University Archives.

93 Tate interview, 11.

94 Annual Report, Kennesaw Junior College, 1967–68, 38; *The President's Report for the Year, 1975–1976*, 27; *Kennesaw Junior College 1975–1976 Catalog*.

95 "Cobb County Symposium Inc. Collection, 1966–1993, Box 1, Kennesaw State University Archives. For a brief history of the symposium and the quotations from President Sturgis, please see a newsletter in folder 5 titled *Symposium Synopsis '78*, a publication of the Cobb County Symposium Inc., March 1978.

Chapter 3

[96]   In time, Kennesaw would add bachelors', masters', and doctoral degrees in nursing.

[97]   Minutes, Board of Regents, March 12–13, 1974, 399–400. Details of the secretarial science curriculum can be found in the catalogs of the era; one example is *Kennesaw Junior College 1973–1974 Catalog*, 72. Another cooperative program was the business administration-accounting career option.

[98]   Sturgis interview, 98–100; "The System First," editorial, *Atlanta Constitution*, November 22, 1974.

[99]   Nancy Lewis, "Junior Grows Up: Kennesaw College Conversion Causing Stir," *Atlanta Journal-Constitution*, August 1, 1976, 10-A; Bradley R. Rice, John A. Shiffert Jr., and Gina Finocchiaro, "Clayton State University," *New Georgia Encyclopedia*, updated October 22, 2009.

[100] President Horace W. Sturgis to Chancellor George L. Simpson Jr., "Statement on Affirmative Action and Statement on Policy," May 30, 1973, Board of Regents General Correspondence, Box 2, 1/71–5/74 folder, Board of Regents Correspondence, 1974–1991, Kennesaw State University Archives; Belita Kuzmits, ed., *Annual Report, July 1, 1971 through June 30, 1972, Higher Education Achievement Program, Kennesaw Junior College, Marietta, Georgia 30061* July 1972, 149.

[101] Sturgis to Simpson, "Statement on Affirmative Action."

[102] Roberts assumed the presidency of Dalton Junior College in the fall of 1970. John A. Hutcheson Jr., "Dalton State College," *New Georgia Encyclopedia*, updated September 21, 2009.

[103] Minutes, Board of Regents, September 15–16, 1970, 125–26; Horace W. Sturgis, *The President's Report for the Year, 1973–1974*, 3, "Annual Reports, 1966–1991," KSU/03/02/001, Kennesaw State University Archives.

[104] The other colleges accepted into the HEAP consortium in 1971 were S. D. Bishop State Junior College (Mobile, Alabama); Kittrell College (Kittrel, North Carolina); Brunswick Junior College (Brunswick, Georgia); Florida Keys Junior College (Key West, Florida); Meridian Junior College (Meridian, Mississippi); Coahoma Junior College (Clarksdale, Mississippi); Delgado Junior College (New Orleans, Louisiana); and Laredo Junior College (Laredo, Texas). Texas Southmost College (Brownsville, Texas) joined the consortium in 1972. Jefferson Community College (Louisville, Kentucky) and St. Philip's College (San Antonio, Texas) joined in 1973, while Florida Keys Junior College dropped out.

[105] Kuzmits, *Annual Report, 1971–72*, v–vi; Stewart Phillips, ed., *Annual Report, July 1, 1972 through June 30, 1973, Higher Education Achievement Program, Kennesaw Junior College, Marietta, Georgia 30061*, June 1973, v–vi; Ronald D. Carlisle, ed., *Annual Report, July 1, 1973 through June 30, 1974, Higher Education Achievement Program, Kennesaw Junior College, Marietta, Georgia 30061*, June, 1974, 4.

[106] Sturgis interview, 113; Sturgis, *The President's Report for the Year, 1970–1971*, 12–13.

[107] Kuzmits, *Annual Report, 1971–72*, 47–52, 89.

[108] Kuzmits, *Annual Report, 1971–72*, 47–52; Sturgis to Simpson, "Statement on Affirmative Action"; Carlisle, *Annual Report, 1973–1974*, 13–14.

[109] Kuzmits, *Annual Report, 1971–72*, 71–78.

110 Carlisle, *Annual Report, 1973–1974*, 10, 65; Sturgis interview, 114. M. J. Woods served thirty-one years (1929–1960) as principal of Lemon Street High School, Marietta's black high school in the age of segregation. Kathryn Woods was the most influential civil rights leader in Cobb County at the time. For a more complete description please see the author's *Cobb County, Georgia, and the Origins of the Suburban South*, 76, 376–80.

111 Horace W. Sturgis, *The President's Report for the Year, 1972–1973*, 1. Under the original statutes, KJC's faculty governance included three main advisory councils: the Administrative Council, chaired by the president and containing the principal administrators plus two elected faculty members and the SGA president; the Academic Council, chaired by the dean of the college, and including the dean of student affairs, the registrar and director of admissions, the division chairs, the librarian, the chair of the Physical Education Department, eight elected faculty members, and two students elected from the Student Affairs Council; and the Student Affairs Council, chaired by the dean of student affairs, and including the dean of the college, the controller, the registrar, the director of counseling and placement, the director of student financial aid, the coordinator of student activities, eight elected faculty members, and four executive officers and ten senators from the Student Government Association.

112 Kuzmits, *Annual Report, 1971–72*, 36–37, 40–41; Carlisle, *Annual Report, 1973–1974*, 8, 65; Minutes, Board of Regents, March 12–13, 1974, 413–14. Jackson addressed the Board at the March 1974 meeting with a request from his Junior College Committee for greater transferability of physical education credits within the system.

113 Kuzmits, *Annual Report, 1971–72*, vii–viii.

114 President Horace W. Sturgis to Vice Chancellor John O. Eidson, July 25, 1973, Board of Regents General Correspondence, 1/71–5/74 folder, Box 2, Board of Regents Correspondence, 1974–1991, Kennesaw State University Archives; Carlisle, *Annual Report, 1973–1974*, i–ii, 1–3, 11.

115 Carlisle, *Annual Report, 1973–1974*, 151–52.

116 Carlisle, *Annual Report, 1973–1974*, 178, 198–204.

117 John W. Hooper to Horace W. Sturgis, January 5, 1978, Box 2, Board of Regents Correspondence, 1974–1991, Kennesaw State University Archives.

118 Mary Zoghby, e-mail to Thomas A. Scott, December 8, 2011, "KSU Book correspondence," electronic file, Kennesaw State University Archives.

119 The data in table 4 is public information provided by the University System of Georgia. The author is grateful to former vice president for academic affairs Edwin A. Rugg for much of the analysis of the last two paragraphs. Ed Rugg, e-mail to Thomas Scott, September 28, 2012, "KSU Book correspondence," electronic file, Kennesaw State University Archives.

120 "Impact Study of Proposed Conversion of KJC to 4-Year Status Minority Enrollment Data" folder, Box 1, Conversion to Senior College Status; Sturgis to Simpson, "Statement on Affirmative Action"; McMath et al. *Engineering the New South*, 389. Kennesaw State University Archives.

121 Sturgis to Simpson, "Statement on Affirmative Action"; Terri Arnold, interview by Ruthie Yow, March 11, 2009, transcript in possession of author; Charles Ferguson, interview by Brent L. Ragsdale, November 17, 2007, transcript, HIST 4425, Bell/Lockheed Oral History Series, Kennesaw State University Archives. The family friend, Marie Bryson, was a nurse in a doctor's office where one of the patients, Betty Robertson, was the secretary to KJC's academic dean. Robertson told Bryson that Kennesaw was trying to recruit a black secretary for the HEAP program.

122 Arnold interview.

123 Sturgis to Simpson, "Statement on Affirmative Action."

124 Michael Bennett, "Pell Grant History," http://pellgranteligibility.net/pell-grant-history/.

125 Thelin, *History of American Higher Education*, 323–26; Clark Kerr, *The Great Transformation in Higher Education, 1960–1980* (Albany: State University of New York Press, 1991), xvii–xix.

126 Tuition by 1976–78 had risen to $106 per quarter for in-state students. The existing data do not allow an exact calculation of the percentage of students receiving financial aid in fiscal year 1977, as some students received more than one type of assistance. *Kennesaw Junior College 1974–1975 Catalog and 1976–1978*; Horace W. Sturgis, *The President's Report for the Year, 1974–1975*, 50; Sturgis, *The President's Report for the Year, 1976–1977*, 43.

127 *Kennesaw Junior College 1974–1975 Catalog*, 22, 136–42; "Federal Student Loan Programs — History," Federal Education Budget Project, http://febp.newamerica.net/background-analysis/federal-student-loan-programs-history; "Who We Are," Georgia Student Finance Commission, www.gsfc.org/gsfcnew/about.CFM.

128 There is some disagreement as to where the first meeting took place. Both Sturgis and Garrison remembered it taking place at Reed's home. Ingram, however, maintains that the first meeting he attended was in Steve Tumlin's living room, and that the meeting at Glenn Reed's house came later. George Conley Ingram III, telephone conversations with the author, June 28, 2010 and October 15, 2012; Sturgis interview, 74; Robert T. Garrison, interview by Thomas A. Scott and Mary Boswell Cawley, June 12, 1987, no. 5, 39, transcript, Cobb County Oral History Series, Kennesaw State University Archives.

129 The other charter members of the foundation included James T. Anderson Jr., Ernest Barrett, Otis A. Brumby Jr., Jasper N. Dorsey, J. Robert Fowler Jr., Wilder G. Little, J. E. Massey Jr., Dr. Henry D. Meaders, William H. Nichols Jr., W. Wyman Pilcher, Gardner A. Potter, and General George H. Wilson. Ingram telephone conversation with author, June 28, 2010; "KSU Foundation History," http://www.kennesaw.edu/foundation/history.shtml; Sturgis, *The President's Report for the Year, 1968–1969*, 30.

130 In his annual reports, Sturgis reported the fundraising totals for the first five years as follows: in 1969–70, 145 donors gave $21,255.50; in 1970–71, 228 donors gave $25,435.50; in 1971–72, 143 donors gave $21,045; in 1972–73, 196 donors gave $25,020; and in 1973–74, an unreported number of donors gave $30,645. Sturgis, *The President's Report for the Year, 1969–1970*, 28; *1970–1971*, 35; *1971–1972*, 25; *1972–1973*, 28; *1973–1974*, 21.

131 Tate interview, 9–10.

132 The Georgia median family income in 1970 was $8,167. Cobb's was $11,247, but Bartow ($8,046), Cherokee ($7,902), and Paulding ($7,563) were below the state average. Horace W. Sturgis, *An Impact Study on the Proposed Conversion of Kennesaw Junior College to Senior College Status*, October 27, 1976, 12, "Desegregation Impact Study and Regular Impact Study" folder, Box 1, Conversion to Senior College Status, Kennesaw State University Archives.

133 Sturgis, *Impact Study*, 7–12.

134 Sturgis interview, 98–101; Horace W. Sturgis to Chancellor George L. Simpson Jr., August 7, 1975, "KJC Four Year Status (Nov. '70 thru Aug. 1975)" folder, Box 1, Conversion to Senior College Status, Kennesaw State University Archives. All the following give insights into the opposition to KJC's conversion; they can be found in the "Newspaper Clippings — Four Year Status" folder, Box 2, Conversion to Senior College Status: "The System First," editorial, *Atlanta Constitution*, November 22, 1974; Frederick Burger, "Busbee Renews KJC Status Vow,"

Marietta Daily Journal, February 19, 1975; Brent Gilroy, "Atlanta Business Group Asks Kennesaw Reversal," Georgia State University *Signal*, June 28, 1976; Mike Faass, "Double Dealing," *Signal*, April 26, 1976; Lewis, "Junior Grows Up," *Atlanta Journal-Constitution*, August 1, 1976.

135   Sturgis interview, 97, 115. The correspondence with civic leaders was especially heavy during 1975. It can be found in a folder titled "KJC Four Year Status (Nov.'70 thru Aug. 1975)", Box 1, Conversion to Senior College Status, Kennesaw State University Archives.

136   Minutes, Board of, January 12–13, 1971, 379.

137   Minutes, Board of Regents, October 10, 1973, 133.

138   Copies of the resolutions may be found in Sturgis, *Impact Study*, 25–28.

139   Joe Mack Wilson, interview by Thomas A. Scott, April 1, 1988, no. 19, 54–55, transcript, Cobb County Oral History Series, Kennesaw State University Archives; Willingham interview, 65–66; "Busbee: He's The Best Man for Governor," *Marietta Daily Journal*, October 30, 1974.

140   Roy E. Barnes, telephone conversation with author, November 14, 2011; Bill Kinney, "Behind the KJC Move," *Marietta Daily Journal*, April 15, 1976.

141   Rick Beene, "Al Burruss—Cobb's Legislative Ace," *Marietta Daily Journal*, March 7, 1976; Frederick Burger, "Busbee Vows KJC Tops List for Conversion," and "Busbee Renews KJC Status Vow," *Marietta Daily Journal*, December 9, 1974 and February 19, 1975; "The System First," editorial, *Atlanta Constitution*, November 22, 1974.

142   Horace W. Sturgis, information furnished to Bob Garrison, January 31, 1975; Robert T. Garrison to the Board of Regents of the University System of Georgia, March 10, 1975, KJC Four Year Status (Nov.'70 thru Aug. 1975) folder, Box 1, Conversion to Senior College Status, Kennesaw State University Archives.

143   "Chamber Group Pushing Four Year Status at KJC," Cobb County Chamber of Commerce *Impact*, April 1975, "KJC Four Year Status" folder; Minutes, Board of Regents, March 12, 1975, 349.

144   Tom Crawford, "Cobb Legislators Vow to Protect KJC Funds," *Marietta Daily Journal*, June 22, 1975.

145   Horace W. Sturgis to Chancellor George L. Simpson Jr., August 7, 1975, "KJC Four Year Status" (Nov.'70 thru Aug. 1975) folder, Box 1, Conversion to Senior College Status, Kennesaw State University Archives.

146   Bill Kinney, "You'll Have to Learn," and "Jimmie Launched Career," *Marietta Daily Journal*, October 1–2, 1975; Thomas A. Scott, "James V. Carmichael (1910–1972), *New Georgia Encyclopedia*, May 14, 2003.

147   "Gov. Busbee to Speak at KJC October 2, 1775," *Dallas New Era*, September 25, 1975; Alexis Scott Reeves, "Busbee Favors 4-Year Status for Kennesaw," *Atlanta Constitution*, October 3, 1975, 8-P.

148   Sturgis interview, 106–07; June R. Krise, interview by Thomas A. Scott, April 24, 2009, no. 103, 11–12, transcript, KSU Oral History Series, Kennesaw State University Archives.

149   Susan Parker, "Aiken Takes Chamber Helm," *Marietta Daily Journal*, January 18, 1976.

150   Rick Beene, "Busbee Promises New KJC Push," *Marietta Daily Journal*, February 12, 1976.

151   Rick Beene, "KJC Funds Stay in Budget Bill," and "Busbee Again Gets KJC Plea," *Marietta Daily Journal*, February 17, 1976 and March 2, 1976.

152 Rick Beene, "Odd Coalition Won for KJC," *Marietta Daily Journal*, April 18, 1976.

153 Garrison merely says that his contact was in the clothing industry, and since he was still alive at the time of the interview, he chose not to name him. Garrison interview, 39–40; Charles T. Oxford to Dr. Horace W. Sturgis, March 24, 1975, "KJC Four Year Status (Nov. '70 thru Aug. 1975)" folder, Box 1, Conversion to Senior College Status, Kennesaw State University Archives. See also a fine term paper by Lynn Keller, "The Kennesaw Cause: Achieving Four Year Status, from Northwest Georgia Junior College to Metro Atlanta Urban University," April 9, 2002, HIST 4499, Kennesaw State University Archives.

154 The 1988 interview with Joe Mack Wilson does not actually name Williams, but the longtime legislator identified the contact as a regent in the newspaper business from Mrs. Kinney's home town. The closest fit is Williams. Wilson interview, 51–52; Dr. Alfred Colquitt to Dr. John H. Robinson III, M.D., June 3, 1975, "KJC Four Year Status (Nov. '70 thru Aug. 1975)" folder, Box 1, Conversion to Senior College Status, Kennesaw State University Archives.

155 Sturgis interview, 109.

156 Minutes, Board of Regents, April 14, 1976, 348; Rick Beene, "Regents OK 4-Year Status for Kennesaw Jr. College," *Marietta Daily Journal*, April 14, 1976.

157 Central Atlanta Progress is a nonprofit organization that has existed since 1941 to promote the economic vitality of the downtown area. Its board of directors includes representatives from most of the main central Atlanta businesses. Central Atlanta Progress, Atlanta Downtown Improvement District, "Who We Are and What We Do," http://www.atlantadowntown.com/about.

158 Georgia State would have to wait until 1982 before the School of Law became a reality. Merl Reed, "Georgia State University," *New Georgia Encyclopedia*, January 7, 2010; Mike Faass, "Double Dealing," Georgia State University *Signal*, April 26, 1976; Brent Gilroy, "Atlanta Business Group Asks Kennesaw Reversal," *Signal*, June 28, 1976; Alexis Scott Reeves, "NAACP Fights Making Kennesaw 4-Year School," *Atlanta Constitution*, July 8, 1977.

159 Minutes, Board of Regents, November 9–10, 1976, Reeves, "NAACP Fights Making Kennesaw 4-Year School"; Lewis, "Junior Grows Up," *Atlanta Journal-Constitution*, August 1, 1976.

160 Sturgis interview, 111. For the majors, see *Kennesaw College 1978–1979 Catalog*, 40 and, *Kennesaw College 1979–1980 Catalog*, 40.

161 Sturgis interview, 120–21.

162 Sturgis interview, 116–17. The author can offer a personal testimony. The author received a pay raise in 1978 not only because of the conversion, but because he earned his PhD in March 1978. Further, salaries were rising everywhere through cost-of-living adjustments to compensate for double-digit inflation. So the author received, for the 1978–79 year, a magnificent 34 percent increase in wages.

163 Sturgis interview, 120–21; *Atlanta Journal-Constitution, Cobb Extra*, September 4, 1980.

Chapter 4

164 S. Frederick Roach Jr., interview by Thomas A. Scott, September 17 and October 1, 2004, no. 11, 19, transcript, KSU Oral History Series; Betty Lentz Siegel, interviews by Thomas A. Scott, Ann Ellis Pullen, and Dede Yow, 1992–2005, no. 25, 21–22, transcript, KSU Oral History Series, Kennesaw State University Archives.

165   Roach interview, 22–24.

166   Krise interview, 23; Roach interview, 26–27.

167   Helen S. Ridley, interview by Thomas A. Scott and Dede Yow, October 19, 2005, no. 39, 15, transcript, KSU Oral History Series, Kennesaw State University Archives.

168   The search process is discussed in detail in the Roach interview, 18–44. The number of semifinalists was greater than the number of candidates who came for campus visits, as several original semifinalists removed their names from the search either before or after their campus visits, and a few others were added to take their place.

169   Siegel interview, 20.

170   James D. (Spec) Landrum, interview by Thomas A. Scott, February 12, 2004, no. 5, 16, transcript, KSU Oral History Series, Kennesaw State University Archives.

171   Mary B. Thompson, interview by Thomas A. Scott, September 17, 2010, no. 96, 19, transcript, KSU Oral History Series, Kennesaw State University Archives.

172   Roach interview, 39.

173   Siegel interview, 20–21.

174   Roach interview, 35–36.

175   Donna Espy, "Woman to be Named Kennesaw President," *Marietta Daily Journal*, August 18, 1981, 1; Roach interview, 36.

176   Dean of the college Eugene R. Huck served as interim president during the interregnum between the Sturgis and Siegel administrations. In the board minutes Chancellor Crawford expressed his appreciation to Huck for his excellent service in this role. Minutes, Board of Regents, August 18–19, 1981, 3–4; Donna Espy, "President: North Carolina Woman Named Kennesaw Head," *Marietta Daily Journal*, August 19, 1981.

177   Siegel interview, 1–5.

178   Siegel interview, 7, 10, 12, 97–98; Minutes, Board of Regents, August 18–19, 1981, 4. The title of her dissertation is "The Interrelationships of the Concepts of Self and Others, Social Acceptability, and Curriculum Patterns."

179   Siegel interview, 12–14; "Betty Siegel: A Conversation," by Susan Hoffman, GPB Television, July 19, 2005. The interview can be accessed through the GPB (Georgia Public Broadcasting) website or through the President Emeritus website at Kennesaw State, www.kennesaw.edu/presidentemeritus/archives.html. A transcript accompanies the video. The information referenced is on page 4 of the transcript.

180   Siegel interview, 16, 103.

181   Siegel interview, 17–18; Espy, "Woman to be Named Kennesaw President."

182   Siegel interview, 18–19.

183   "Betty Siegel: A Conversation," 5.

184   Siegel interview, 18, 22.

185   Siegel interview, 22–25.

186   *Sentinel*, October 1981, 5.

187 Ridley interview, 9–14.

188 The *Kennesaw College 1980–82 Catalog*, lists only five full professors who taught full time (P. Edward Bostick in biology, I. David Harris in physical education, Virginia C. Hinton in English, S. Frederick Roach in history, and Frank W. Walker in chemistry). All were respected members of the faculty: Harris was a former department chair; Roach and Walker would become department chairs; Hinton cochaired President Siegel's inauguration committee; and Bostick would be the 1997 recipient of KSU's Distinguished Teaching Award. However, all were passed over for membership on the View of the Future Committee, perhaps in an attempt to make it a truly "bottom-up" committee.

189 The associate professors on the View of the Future Committee were Helen S. Ridley (political science), Pamela J. Rhyne (biology), M. Thomson Salter (art), and Duane E. Shuttlesworth (psychology). The assistant professors were Hugh C. Hunt (philosophy), Judith Ann Mitchell (education), Jerry D. Sawyer (management), and Mary Zoghby (English). Zoghby was also coordinator of the developmental studies. The three staff persons were Martha A. Giles (associate librarian), Inez P. Morgan (director of the Counseling and Testing Center), and Ross E. Young (director of personnel services).

190 The seven subcategories under the topic of quality of professional life were scheduling; faculty development: skills and techniques; faculty development: research; academic freedom; advisement and registration; support services; and evaluation. The three subcategories under the publics served topic were recruitment, facilities and services, and curriculum.

191 Helen S. Ridley, *Report of the View of the Future Committee*, Kennesaw College, May 26, 1982, 1–4, "View of the Future Committee Records, 1981–1982," Box 2, KSU/59, Kennesaw State University Archives.

192 The complete text of the proposed mission statement was the following: "I) to promote the type of environment which encourages intellectual inquiry and provides an educational foundation which, through mutual respect and trust, increases and enhances awareness and understanding; II) to promote instruction in career and professional areas to prepare students for their life work; III) to promote a collegial environment that encourages a sense of community; IV) to provide programs in Continuing Education and public service."

193 Ridley, *Report of the View of the Future Committee*, 9–16. The official Kennesaw statement of Purpose did not change significantly until the *Kennesaw College 1985–1986 Undergraduate Catalog*, when the new statement described Kennesaw College as "a dynamic, developing senior college in the University System of Georgia, responding to the needs of the northwest region of the state for accessible, relevant, and high-quality undergraduate, graduate, and public service programs." After describing the types of programs that the college offered, the Purpose statement asserted a commitment to providing an "inviting and supportive learning environment" and claimed that the institution "aspires to be a model senior college, respected for its contributions to excellence in education, the realization of personal potential, and the improvement of the quality of life in the communities it serves."

194 Ridley, *Report of the View of the Future Committee*, 75–95.

195 Ridley, *Report of the View of the Future Committee*, 96–102.

196 Ridley, *Report of the View of the Future Committee*, 103–07.

197 Ridley, *Report of the View of the Future Committee*, 55–57.

198 Ridley, *Report of the View of the Future Committee*, 45–50; Siegel interview, 17, 62. The International Alliance for Invitational Education is still active in 2012. Its website is the following: http://www.invitationaleducation.net/.

199   Fincher, *Historical Development of the University System of Georgia*, 84–85; Board of Regents, University System of Georgia, *The Eighties and Beyond: A Commitment to Excellence*, Atlanta: February 1983; Betty L. Siegel, *Kennesaw College Institutional Needs Assessment* (June 1982).

200   Siegel, *Kennesaw College Institutional Needs Assessment*, A-6–A-13.

201   Board of Regents, *The Eighties and Beyond*, 43; Siegel interview, 91.

202   Siegel interview, 39.

203   Siegel interview, 22, 24.

204   Judy Mitchell, correspondence to president's staff, dean's staff, division chairs, and View of the Future Committee, June 2, 1982, "re: Summary of Meeting—May 26th–27th," "View of the Future Committee, Correspondence, Memoranda, Member Lists, 1981–82" folder, "View of the Future Committee Records, 1981–1982," Box 1, KSU/59, Kennesaw State University Archives.

205   Mitchell, "re: Summary of Meeting."

206   George Beggs to President Siegel, August 11, 1982, "re: Implementation of View of the Future Committee Recommendations," "View of the Future Committee, Correspondence, Memoranda, Member Lists, 1981–82" folder, View of the Future Committee Records, 1981–1982, Box 1, KSU/59, Kennesaw State University Archives.

207   The letters can all be found in "View of the Future Committee, Correspondence, Memoranda, Member Lists, 1981–82" folder, View of the Future Committee Records, 1981–1982" Box 1, KSU/59, Kennesaw State University Archives.

208   Betty Siegel to Ed Rugg, September 20, 1982, "re: Recommendations Involving Computer Services," "View of the Future Committee, Correspondence, Memoranda, Member Lists, 1981–82" folder, "View of the Future Committee Records, 1981–1982," Box 1, KSU/59, Kennesaw State University Archives.

209   Edwin A. Rugg, interview by Thomas A. Scott, November 5 and November 7, 2008, no. 100, 8–13, transcript, KSU Oral History Series, Kennesaw State University Archives.

210   Rugg interview, 13–16.

211   Ridley interview, 21.

212   *Kennesaw College Self Study Report*, vol. 1, March 1986, 252–53, Kennesaw State University Archives.

213   *Kennesaw State College Policies and Procedures*, rev. September 1989, 1–17–1.18, 1–31, "Faculty Handbook Policies and Procedures, 1989" folder, "Faculty Handbooks, Policies and Procedures, 1989–2010," Box 1, KSU/14/02/002, Kennesaw State University Archives; University Council website: www.kennesaw.edu/universitycouncil/.

214   Siegel interview, 33.

215   J. Wade Gilley, Kenneth A. Fulmer, and Sally J. Reithlingshoefer, *Searching for Academic Excellence: Twenty Colleges and Universities on the Move and Their Leaders* (New York: American Council on Education/Macmillan Publishing Co., 1986), 140–42.

Chapter 5

[216]   *Kennesaw College Self Study Report*, vol. 2, March 1986, 105, Kennesaw State University Archives; *Kennesaw State College 1990–91 Fact Book*, 12, 31; Betty L. Siegel, *Critical Needs for Additional Funding at Kennesaw College*, February 12, 1983, 1–3, in a bound volume titled *Funding and Faculty Needs, 1983–1986*, Kennesaw State University Archives.

[217]   Betty L. Siegel, *Critical Needs for Additional Funding at Kennesaw College*, February 22, 1984, introduction; Betty L. Siegel, *Unparalleled Growth at Kennesaw Requires Additional Funding*, July 29, 1985, 3; Betty L. Siegel, *Another Year of Unparalleled Growth at Kennesaw Requires Additional Funding*, June 20, 1986, 4–5. She made similar appeals to the regents in September and November 1984, and March 6, 1985.

[218]   Rugg interview, 52.

[219]   Ridley interview, 23; Mark W. Patterson, interview by Thomas A. Scott, August 17, 2007, no. 82, 9–10, transcript, KSU Oral History Series, Kennesaw State University Archives.

[220]   E. Howard Shealy, interview by Thomas A. Scott, July 22, 2004, no. 6, 21, transcript, KSU Oral History Series, Kennesaw State University Archives.

[221]   Jo Allen Bradham, interview by Dede Yow and Thomas A. Scott, June 10, 2004, no. 15, 19–21, transcript, KSU Oral History Series, Kennesaw State University Archives.

[222]   *Kennesaw College Self Study Report*, vol. 1, March 1986, 31, 253–55. According to the *Kennesaw College 1984–1985 Catalog*, 220, the original chairpersons were Faye H. Rodgers (accounting), Randall B. Goodwin (acting chair, economics and finance), Mildred W. Landrum (acting chair, management), S. Alan Schlact (acting chair, marketing and business law), Judith Ann Mitchell (curriculum and instruction), Mary Zoghby (developmental studies), C. Grady Palmer (health, physical education and recreation), John C. Greider (English), S. Frederick Roach Jr. (history), David M. Jones Jr. (liberal studies), R. Wayne Gibson (music), Willoughby G. Jarrell (political science), G. Ruth Hepler (psychology), Dorothy D. Zinsmeister (biology), Frank W. Walker (chemistry and physics), Christopher B. Schaufele (mathematics and computer dcience), and Julia L. Perkins (nursing).

[223]   Huck interview, 9–10.

[224]   S. Alan Schlact, interview by Dede Yow and Thomas A. Scott, October 20, 2004, no. 21, 30, transcript, KSU Oral History Series; Harry J. Lasher, interview by Thomas A. Scott, April 2, 2007, no. 55, 5–6, 10–15, transcript, KSU Oral History Series, Kennesaw State University Archives.

[225]   *Kennesaw College 1984–1985 Catalog*, 220.

[226]   Linda M. Noble, interview by Thomas A. Scott, December 5, 2007, no. 79, 9, transcript, KSU Oral History Series, Kennesaw State University Archives.

[227]   Joseph D. Meeks, interview by Thomas A. Scott and Dede Yow, April 6, 2006, no. 54, 13, transcript, KSU Oral History Series, Kennesaw State University Archives; Wayne R. Gibson, interview by Stephen Watson, HIST 4425, KSU 50th Anniversary Series, still being edited at time of publication.

[228]   Gibson interview; *Kennesaw College Self Study Report*, vol. 1, March 1986, 18–19.

[229]   Roberta T. Griffin, interview by Dede Yow and Thomas A. Scott, March 1, 2005, no. 30, 14, transcript, KSU Oral History Series; Patrick L. Taylor, interview by Stephen Watson, June 27, 2011, no. 108, 12, transcript, KSU Oral History Series, 12, Kennesaw State University Archives.

230   Taylor interview, 9–12.

231   Taylor interview, 15; Griffin interview, 14.

232   Taylor interview, 18; Cheryl Anderson Brown, "Creativity on the Fly," *Flourish*, Summer 2006, http://www.kennesaw.edu/arts/flourish/flourish_4-1/flourish_4-1-andy_azula.htm; Kennesaw State University College of the Arts website: http://www.kennesaw.edu/arts/COTA_News/in_the_news/archives_2009.shtml.

233   Taylor interview, 16; Griffin interview, 9, 18, 21.

234   *Kennesaw College 1987–1988 Fact Book*, 37, 43, 45, 58; *Kennesaw College 1984–1985 Catalog*, 225–33; Lasher interview, 9; Rugg interview, 23.

235   Craig E. Aronoff, interview by Thomas A. Scott, December 15, 2004, no. 23, 8, 13–15, transcript, KSU Oral History Series, Kennesaw State University Archives.

236   Aronoff interview, 2, 6.

237   Aronoff interview, 16–17.

238   Aronoff interview, 18, 25; Scott, *Cobb County, Georgia, and the Origins of the Suburban South*, 595–96.

239   Aronoff interview, 32–36; www.coles.kennesaw.edu/centers/cox-family-enterprise/; http://coles.kennesaw.edu/tetley-event/history.htm.

240   *Kennesaw College 1988–1989 Fact Book*, 55.

241   *Kennesaw College 1988–1989 Fact Book*, 56.

242   *Kennesaw College 1988–1989 Fact Book*, 57.

243   *Kennesaw College 1988–1989 Fact Book*, 54.

244   *Kennesaw College 1988–1989 Fact Book*, 12.

245   *Kennesaw College Self Study Report*, vol. 1, March 1986, 168–69, 253–54; *Kennesaw College 1984–85 Catalog*, 188; Nancy S. King, interview by Dede Yow and Thomas A. Scott, February 13, 2006, no. 42, 5, transcript, KSU Oral History Series, Kennesaw State University Archives.

246   Megan Sexton, "University 101 Leader to Speak at August Commencement," University of South Carolina, August 4, 2012, http://www.sc.edu/news/newsarticle.php?nid=4196#.UAoXBjFH3KZ.

247   *Kennesaw College Self Study Report*, vol. I, March 1986, 23; King interview, 8, 11.

248   Davis interview, 9–10; *Kennesaw College Self Study Report*, vol. 1, March 1986, 179; Bowman Davis, "KC 101 and the New Student Experience Program," *Reaching through Teaching*, (Fall 1987): 9.

249   First-Year Programs website: www.kennesaw.edu/fyp/; Keisha L. Hoerrner, interview by Thomas A. Scott, August 26, 2009, no. 89, 3, 16–20, transcript, KSU Oral History Series, Kennesaw State University Archives.

250   King interview, 5–10, 14–15.

251   King interview, 12–13.

252   King interview, 5–7; *Kennesaw State College 1996–1997 Undergraduate Catalog*.

253 *Kennesaw College Self Study Report*, vol. 1, March 1986, 18–19.

254 *Kennesaw College 1984–1985 Catalog*, 220; *Kennesaw College Self Study Report*, vol. 1, 23.

255 The book by Ernest L. Boyer is *College: The Undergraduate Experience in America* (New York: Harper & Row, 1987). Siegel's comments were from a speech she originally gave for the Luce Lecture Series at Wake Forest University and later appearing in *Vital Speeches*, April 15, 1984. Ed Rugg, "Why Focus on Teaching in CETL"; and Betty L. Siegel, "The Centrality of Teaching in the University," *Reaching through Teaching*, (Fall 1987): 3, 12, www.kennesaw.edu/cetl/resources/publications/reaching_through_teaching.html.

256 CETL website: http://www.kennesaw.edu/cetl/conferences/gaconf/2012.html; Bill Hill, "Sharing Teaching: The 13th Georgia Conference on College and University Teaching," *Reaching through Teaching*, (Fall 2006): 4; G. William (Bill) Hill IV, interview by Thomas A. Scott and Dede Yow, June 17, 2004, no. 4, 34–36, transcript, KSU Oral History Series, Kennesaw State University Archives.

257 Rugg interview, 19; *Kennesaw College Self Study Report*, vol. 1, March 1986, 227.

258 *Kennesaw College Self Study Report*, vol. 1, March 1986, 225.

259 *Kennesaw College Self Study Report*, vol. 1, March 1986, 225–29.

260 Scherer interview, 7–8.

261 Scherer interview, 20–21; King interview, 3–5.

262 *Kennesaw College Self Study Report*, vol. 1, March 1986, 226–30.

263 Scherer interview, 22–24.

264 Rugg interview, 53–54; Scherer interview, 25–26.

265 Rugg interview, 54; Robert B. Williams, interview by Thomas A. Scott, December 2, 2010, no. 94, 13–14, transcript, KSU Oral History Series, Kennesaw State University Archives.

266 At the time, Kennesaw required students to pay relatively little in fees. A full-time resident student in 1997–98 paid, per quarter, a $560 matriculation fee (tuition), an $86 student services fee, $20 for vehicle registration (parking fee), and a $25 technology fee. *Kennesaw State University 1997–1998 Undergraduate Catalog*, 22–23.

267 Rugg interview, 19–20, 54.

268 Sturgis interview, 12; http://www.ghsbp.com/state/boyschamps.html.

269 Sturgis interview, 81–82. The first diploma fee (ten dollars) appears in the *Kennesaw College 1982–83 Catalog*, 28.

270 Landrum interview, 18.

271 Landrum interview, 17.

272 Landrum interview, 17; Siegel interview, 26

273 Siegel interview, 26; Landrum interview, 17–18.

274 David L. Waples, "The Athletic Associations and Conferences," "KSU Athletic History Timeline," "KSU Numbers, re: Athletic Budgets, Fees, Costs and Sports," "Kennesaw State Owls [Coaches'] Records," and "All-time KSU Athletic Employees, 1982–2011," Kennesaw State University Archives.

275   Landrum interview, 20; Waples, "Athletic Associations and Conferences."

276   Landrum interview, 21–23.

277   Landrum interview, 19.

278   Waples, "KSU Athletic History Timeline"; Siegel interview, 26; David L. Waples, interview by Thomas A. Scott, June 17, 2011, no. 106, 14, transcript, KSU Oral History Series, Kennesaw State University Archives.

279   Waples interview, 9–12.

280   Waples, "KSU Athletic History Timeline"; Waples interview, 21.

281   Waples, "The Athletic Associations and Conferences," "KSU Athletic History Timeline," and "KSU Year-by-Year Athletic Records"; Landrum interview, 20; Siegel interview, 27.

282   *Kennesaw State University 1996–97 Fact Book*, 4–5; Siegel interview, 25; Betty L. Siegel to Chancellor Dean Propst, Board of Regents, April 16, 1988.

Chapter 6

283   Purpose statement, *Kennesaw College 1985–1986 Undergraduate Catalog*, 3. In previous catalogs, Kennesaw committed itself to public service and continuing education only "to the extent that resources are available."

284   *Kennesaw College 1987–1988 Fact Book*, 21; *Kennesaw State College 1990–1991 Fact Book*, 31; *Kennesaw State College 1995–1996 Fact Book*, 34; *Kennesaw State University 2000–2001 Fact Book*, 37.

285   Jerome Ratchford, interview by Mia Riccio and Shantina Starks, March 24, 2011, 8, transcript, HIST 4425, KSU 50th Anniversary Series. Tape in Kennesaw State University Archives, transcript still being edited at time of publication.

286   Office of the President, *Accepting the Challenge of Desegregation: A Success Story at Kennesaw College*, a Summary Report for 1983–85 Submitted to the chancellor of the University System of Georgia, July 19, 1985, "Diversity Planning Council 2000" folder, Box 1, Academic Affairs, Vice President's Office, Kennesaw State University Archives. Also see the *Kennesaw College Self Study Report*, vol.1, March 1986, 25, and the Rugg interview, 27.

287   Rugg interview, 27–28; Office of the President, *Accepting the Challenge of Desegregation*. Unfortunately, the pages are not numbered in the desegregation report.

288   For Cook's and Zion's role in civil rights activities, see the author's *Cobb County, Georgia, and the Origins of the Suburban South*, 280, 282, 349; and Felecca Wilson Taylor, interview by Jessica Renee Drysdale, September 25, 2009, no. 2, 12–13, transcript, Cobb NAACP/Civil Rights Series, Kennesaw State University Archives. The earliest reference to the Marietta branch of the NAACP that the author has found is the May 10, 1956 minutes of the Marietta School Board, where a NAACP delegation of Rev. Jesse W. Cook, Paul Brown, and David E. McAfee brought to the board's attention the urgent need for improvements to the Lemon Street High School building. The minutes can be found on microfilm at the Marietta City Schools headquarters.

289   Other attendees of the early discussion sessions were Rev. Collins of Kennesaw Avenue Baptist Church, Donald Killingsworth, Ira Deloach, Jimmy Williams, Henry Shelton, Wanda Stokes, and Eleanor Collins. Office of the President, *Accepting the Challenge of Desegregation*, appendix I.

290 Jeff Racel, "The Right Not to Bare Arms: Richard Butler's Struggle against Kennesaw, Ga.," November 1994, term paper, HIST 275, Local History Term Papers, Kennesaw State University Archives; Rugg interview, 27–28; Office of the President, *Accepting the Challenge of Desegregation*.

291 "International Programs and Outreach," The University of Alabama System, http://www.uasystem.ua.edu/Administration/International%20Programs.html.

292 Office of the President, *Accepting the Challenge of Desegregation*; "A Look Back," Office of the Vice President for Public Service and Outreach, University of Georgia, http://outreach.uga.edu/index.php/about_pso/history/.

293 *Kennesaw State College 1989–1990 Fact Book*, 86; *Kennesaw State College 1995–1996 Fact Book*, 926; *Kennesaw State University 2000–2001 Fact Book*, 97, 101. The comment that Kennesaw seemed to lose focus on diversity for part of the 1990s is based on the author's conversation on April 4, 2012 with Ed Rugg, who was vice president for academic affairs throughout the decade. The administration's commitment to diversity never changed, but its focus tended to be on other problems.

294 *Kennesaw College Self Study Report*, vol. 2, March 1986, 95, 105, 107.

295 Statement of Harriet S. Gustafson, January 25, 1984, Campus Police Report, Kennesaw College, Nigerian Incident file, Kennesaw State University Archives.

296 Officer L. [Dennis] McSwain, Possible Threats/Suspicious Persons, January 19, 1984, Police Report, Kennesaw College, Nigerian Incident file.

297 Theodore (Ted) J. Cochran, interview by Nicholas Harford and Taylor McAllister, April 28, 2011, no. 107, 2, transcript, KSU Oral History Series, Kennesaw State University Archives.

298 Ted Cochran, e-mail to Thomas Scott, November 17, 2011, "KSU Book correspondence," electronic file, Kennesaw State University Archives.

299 One of the incidents between campus police and the Nigerian students took place on February 16, 1984, when Emiantor-Akhabue and Sadoh shouted obscenities at Officer Maloney in front of their red Volvo, which was parked in a handicapped spot in a faculty and staff reserve lot. Two witnesses filed reports corroborating Maloney's story. Sergeant John M. Woodham of the US Army ROTC Program was in the parking lot at the time talking to Maloney. Woodham stated that Maloney responded professionally, but had little success in calming down the two students. An almost identical account was contained in a memorandum from Dean George H. Beggs to Roger Hopkins. Beggs was in his office in the new Humanities Building, overlooking the parking lot, and heard everything. He reported that the students' "extreme verbal abuse of the officer lasted for about 10 minutes" and that "the officer never raised his voice, never demonstrated impatience, and never seemed to treat them in a discourteous manner." After Maloney left the scene, he apparently thought further about the encounter and swore out arrest warrants, alleging obstruction of an officer. Officer Adrian Havens, February 16, 1984, Police Report; Officer Randy Willard, February 21, 1984, Police Report; Officer T. A. Maloney, February 21, 1984, Police Report; Statement of John M. Woodham, February 22, 1984, Police Report; George H. Beggs to Roger Hopkins, February 27, 1984, "Memo for record on observance of a Security and Student Parking Incident," Nigerian Incident file.

300 Officer Maxine Price, February 21, 1984, Police Report; Officer T. A. Maloney, February 21, 1984, Police Report, Nigerian Incident file.

301 Black Student Alliance to Dr. Betty Siegel, February 24, 1984, "Memorandum." Nigerian Incident file. The Black Student Alliance's goals for 1983–84 can be found in an open letter from President Harold Craig to prospective members, October 11, 1983, attachment to an e-mail from Jerome Ratchford, vice president for student success, to Thomas Scott, October 26, 2012,

"KSU Book correspondence," electronic file, Kennesaw State University Archives. At the time, Dr. Ratchford was in the process of gathering relevant documents from his years as coordinator of minority student retention services to donate to the KSU Archives. The earliest date that the author has found for the existence of the Black Student Alliance is 1980, when the members are pictured in the *Montage*, the student yearbook, with their advisor, Diane Wilkerson.

[302] In the days after the charges were dropped, Stilson sent two memoranda to his immediate superior, Roger Hopkins, the vice president for business and finance, providing Hopkins with some of the police reports explaining why the officers frisked the two suspects and countering the charge that there was a pattern of harassment against any black student. State of Georgia vs. Ehia Emiantor Akhabue, Case Number 84M805, Release and Covenant Not to Sue; State of Georgia vs. John Igbosoria Sadoh, Case Number 84M843, Affidavit, February 28, 1984, Nigerian Incident file; Fred Stilson to Ed Rugg, February 24, 1984, "Memorandum," Nigerian Incident file; Fred Stilson to Roger Hopkins, "Subject: Alleged harassment of two African students, investigation of"; February 29, 1984; Fred Stilson to Roger Hopkins, February 29, 1984, "Subject: Internal investigation," Nigerian Incident file.

[303] Merritt Cowart, "GBI Investigating Credit Fraud Ring," *Marietta Daily Journal*, March 18, 1984, 1A; Merritt Cowart, "Police Role at College Raises Furor," *Marietta Daily Journal*, March 18, 1984, 1A; Cochran interview, 2–3.

[304] Fred Stilson to Dr. Rugg, March 1, 1984, "Memorandum"; Arthur K. Bolton to Hon. Henry G. Neal, April 22, 1970, Nigerian Incident file.

[305] Dennis McSwain, Assist Marietta Police Department, March 13, 1984, Police Report, Nigerian Incident file.

[306] Conversation, Henry Neal and Ed Rugg, March 15, 1984, Nigerian Incident file; Bill Carbine and Merritt Cowart, "College Officials to the Arrested," *Marietta Daily Journal*, March 23, 1984, 1A.

[307] Carbine and Cowart, "College Officials to Be Arrested."

[308] Rugg interview, 28–29.

[309] Rugg interview, 29; "Campus Arrest: Incident Is No Reflection," editorial, *Marietta Daily Journal*, March 21, 1984, 4A.

[310] Merritt Cowart, "Nigerian Students Ordered Deported," *Marietta Daily Journal*, no date, Nigerian Incident file.

[311] Ted Cochran, e-mail to Thomas Scott, November 17, 2011; Cochran interview, 4.

[312] Rugg interview, 26, 34, 67; "Board of Regents Appoints President and Vice President at Savannah State," March 12, 1997, Newsroom, University System of Georgia website; Laura Diamond, "New Provost Starts at Clark Atlanta University," *Atlanta Journal-Constitution*, January 11, 2010; "Clark Atlanta's Joseph H. Silver Sr., PhD, Named President of Alabama State University," Press Release, June 22, 2012, http://www.cau.edu/CMFiles/docs/News/SILVER%20PresidentASU.062212.pdf.

[313] Office of the President, *Accepting the Challenge of Desegregation*; Rugg interview, 30; Coles College website: http://coles.kennesaw.edu/departments_faculty/faculty-pages/Gilliam-Kenneth.htm.

[314] Harold L. Wingfield, interview by Thomas A. Scott and Dede Yow, July 20, 2006, no. 57, 1, 18, transcript, KSU Oral History Series, Kennesaw State University Archives.

315 Oral L. Moses, interview by Thomas A. Scott and Dede Yow, March 1 and August 2, 2006, no. 72, 1, 14, 17–19, 43–44, transcript, KSU Oral History Series, Kennesaw State University Archives.

316 Moses interview, 35–36; "Biography," Third Day, http://thirdday.com/content/biography.

317 Wingfield interview, 20, 22–23, 28; *Kennesaw State College 1994–1996 SACS Self Study Report*, xiii, "Accreditation Self-Study Report, Kennesaw State College, 1995–1996," folder 1, Box 1, Academic Affairs, Vice President's Office; Office of the President, *Accepting the Challenge of Desegregation*.

318 Ernest L. Boyer, *Scholarship Reconsidered: Priorities of the Professoriate*, (The Carnegie Foundation for the Advancement of Teaching, 1990), xii.

319 Boyer, *Scholarship Reconsidered*, 10–12.

320 Boyer, "Enlarging the Perspective," in *Scholarship Reconsidered*, 15–25.

321 Siegel interview, 91, 105.

322 Siegel interview, 91; Burruss Institute website: https://burruss.kennesaw.edu/content/about-burruss-institute; Christy Storey, e-mail to Thomas Scott, August 27, 2012, "KSU Book correspondence," electronic file, Kennesaw State University Archives.

323 "About Us," Small Business Development Center, Coles College of Business, Kennesaw State University, http://coles.kennesaw.edu/centers/small-business-development/client-consulting.htm; "Origin," Georgia Small Business Development Center Network, http://www.georgiasbdc.org/subpage.aspx?cart=d8323ce5-9869-46b2-a06e-52b1257aa4c0&page_name=Mission; Gary Roberts e-mail to Thomas Scott, June 22, 2012, "KSU Book correspondence," electronic file, Kennesaw State University Archives.

324 The recommendations of the Study of the Baccalaureate were approved by the faculty during the 1990–91 academic year. *Kennesaw State College 1994–1996 SACS Self Study Report*, 3–16; Thomas H. Keene, interview by Thomas A. Scott and Dede Yow, April 12, 2006, no. 47, 16–23, 29–30, transcript, KSU Oral History Series, Kennesaw State University Archives.

325 Christopher B. Schaufele, phone interview by Thomas A. Scott, May 10, 2006, no. 48, 3–4, transcript, KSU Oral History Series, Kennesaw State University Archives.

326 Nancy E. Zumoff, interview by Dede Yow and Thomas A. Scott, June 13, 2005, no. 29, 7–14, transcript, KSU Oral History Series, Kennesaw State University Archives.

327 Schaufele interview, 8.

328 Schaufele interview, 9; Zumoff interview, 19–22.

329 Schaufele interview, 9–10; Zumoff interview, 19–20.

330 Schaufele interview, 10; Zumoff interview, 21.

331 Schaufele interview, 10–11; Zumoff interview, 22–23, 28.

332 Schaufele interview, 11–17; Zumoff interview, 28.

333 Patricia H. (Patti) Reggio, interview by Thomas A. Scott, July 13, 2004, no. 10, 7–8, transcript, KSU Oral History Series, Kennesaw State University Archives.

334 Reggio interview, 11–12, 17, 19, 21–22; University of North Carolina at Greensboro website: http://www.uncg.edu/che/.

335 Robbins interview, 13, 15–19.

336 Sarah Robbins, e-mail to Thomas Scott, October 19, 2012, "KSU Book correspondence," electronic file, Kennesaw State University Archives; Robbins interview, 25; Sarah Robbins website, Texas Christian University, http://www.eng.tcu.edu/profiles/srobbins.htm.

337 Robbins interview, 21.

338 Betty L. Siegel to H. Dean Propst, September 22, 1981, Board of Regents General Correspondence, Box 2, 6/76–1/82, Board of Regents Correspondence, 1974–1991, KSU/03/02/002, Kennesaw State University Archives.

339 Siegel interview, 28–29.

340 *Kennesaw College Self Study Report*, vol. 1, March 1986, 89–92.

341 *Kennesaw College Self Study Report*, vol. 1, March 1986, 83, 87; *Kennesaw State College 1990–1991 Fact Book*, 18; *Kennesaw State College 1991–1992 Fact Book*, 60.

342 Lasher interview, 15–17.

343 Lasher interview, 15, 22; Aronoff interview, 36–37.

344 *Kennesaw State College 1995–1996 Fact Book*, 6.

345 Dede Yow, e-mail to Thomas Scott, August 11, 2012, "KSU Book correspondence," electronic file, Kennesaw State University Archives.

346 Rugg interview, 40–41.

347 *Kennesaw College Self Study Report*, vol.1, March 1986, 83, 87; School of Business Administration, Kennesaw State College, AACSB Accreditation Self-Study Report, vol. I, 1993, M-4-7, School of Business Accreditation 1993, Box 04/01/001, Kennesaw State University Archives.

348 Lasher interview, 14, 34.

349 Timothy S. Mescon, interview by Thomas A. Scott, May 8, 2006, no. 51, 10–13, transcript, KSU Oral History Series, Kennesaw State University Archives. The College of Business Administration at Georgia State University had a similar model of flexible career paths that undoubtedly influenced what Kennesaw developed. The professional tracks at GSU earned the praise of Ernest L. Boyer in *Scholarship Reconsidered*, 51.

Chapter 7

350 Lois Kubal, to H. Dean Propst, October 16, 1993, Correspondence, folder 1, Box 1, Newt Gingrich Controversy, Kennesaw State University Archives.

351 For an account of Gingrich's career from the perspective of a close friend and West Georgia colleague, see Mel Steely, *The Gentleman from Georgia: The Biography of Newt Gingrich* (Macon: Mercer University Press, 2000). Also see the author's *Cobb County, Georgia, and the Origins of the Suburban South*, 741–45.

352 Scott, *Cobb County, Georgia, and the Origins of the Suburban South*, 745–47.

353 Rugg interview, 67. Also, see Minutes of the KSC Senate Executive Committee, August 18, 1993, Correspondence (Electronic Mail) Gingrich Controversy, folder 13, Box 1, Newt Gingrich Controversy. The executive committee held an extended discussion of the "implications of

endorsing a political figure" and the "appropriateness of offering a course with obvious political intent." Afterwards, it voted nine to one to place a discussion of the course on the agenda for the next senate meeting. The minutes reflect that Beggs praised his fellow committee members for their leadership on the issue.

354   Newt Gingrich to Tim Mescon, March 1, 1993, Course Finding, folder 11, Box 2; *Congressional Record*, January 25, 1993, Xeroxed pages of Gingrich speech, Course Planning Materials, folder 16, Box 2, Newt Gingrich Controversy.

355   Syllabus for GBA 890 and MGT 490, Course Materials, Correspondence, folder 14, Box 2; Undergraduate Course Substitution Form, completed by Paula Morris, approved by Accounting Department Chair Ralph Frey, Correspondence (Electronic Mail) Gingrich Controversy, folder 13, Box 1, Newt Gingrich Controversy.

356   Syllabus for GBA 890 and MGT 490, folder 14, Box 2; Newt Gingrich to Barry Phillips, September 7, 1993, folder 14, Box 2, Newt Gingrich Controversy.

357   First Annual Curriculum Review Conference, December 4, 1993, folder 14, Box 2; Gingrich to Phillips, September 7, 1993, folder 14, Box 2; "Top Scholars Assist Gingrich in Fine-tuning New Course on 'Renewing American Civilization,'" KSU Press Release, July 29, 1993, Course Planning Materials, folder 15, Box 2, Newt Gingrich Controversy.

358   Siegel interview, 35, 70. In a private conversation years ago, Hopkins told the author that he opposed the Gingrich course when it was discussed in the president's cabinet for the reason stated in the text.

359   Rugg interview, 68; Betty Siegel to Chancellor H. Dean Propst, July 28, 1993, folder 1. Correspondence; Meeting Minutes; Petitions; and Open Records Act Requests and Responses, Box 3, Newt Gingrich Controversy.

360   Renewing American Civilization Fall 1993 Operating Budget, Course Budget, folder 15, Box 1, Newt Gingrich Controversy.

361   Peter Schmidt, "2 Georgia Colleges Find Themselves Caught Up in Newt Gingrich's Problems," *Chronicle of Higher Education*, January 24, 1997, A21.

362   Interview with Newt Gingrich and Tim Mescon, CNN, September 3, 1993, transcript, Correspondence, Course Facilities, Notes, and News Releases, folder 9, Box 1; Jeffery A. Eisenach to Roger Milliken, July 21, 1993, Course Financial Information, folder 4, Box 2, Newt Gingrich Controversy.

363   Form letter, Course Budget, folder 15, Box 1, Newt Gingrich Controversy

364   Schmidt, "2 Georgia Colleges," A21; Pamla Prochnow to Joe, Tim, and Jeff, May 10, 1993, Course Financial Information, folder 4, Box 2; Richard B. Berman to Newt Gingrich, July 1, 1993, Box 5; and Course Financial Information, Box 2, Newt Gingrich Controversy.

365   J. Larry Stevens, interview by Thomas A. Scott, April 9, 2007, no. 70, 15–18, transcript, KSU Oral History Series. Also see James A. Fleming, interview by Thomas A. Scott, September 27, 2006, no. 49, 15, transcript, KSU Oral History Series, Kennesaw State University Archives.

366   Laura A. Ingram, "Newt Presents Bigwigs at KSC," *Sentinel*, July 7, 1993, 1. Copy in folder 9, Box 1, Newt Gingrich Controversy.

367   Peter Schmidt, "2 Georgia Colleges," A20; Robert W. Hill to Betty L. Siegel, September 2, 1993; Dorothy E. Brawley to Newt Gingrich, October 5, 1993, and to Betty Siegel, October 9, 1993, Correspondence, folder 1, Box 1, Newt Gingrich Controversy.

368 Charles Watson and Jeanne Cummings, "Gingrich College Class Raises Questions," *Atlanta Journal-Constitution*, September 2, 1993, A1; a copy of the advertisement can be found in Course Materials, Correspondence, folder 14, Box 2. Also see, "Top Scholars Assist Gingrich in Fine-tuning New Course on 'Renewing American Civilization,'" KSC News Release, Course Planning Materials, folder 15, Box 2; and Site Hosts for Renewing American Civilization as of August 2, Course Planning Materials, folder 16, Box 2, Newt Gingrich Controversy.

369 Chris Jeffrey, e-mail to Thomas Scott, March 27, 2012, "KSU Book correspondence," electronic file, Kennesaw State University Archives.

370 Steely, *Gentleman from Georgia*, 250–53; Robert J. Vickers, "New Regents Policy Would Bar Gingrich from Teaching Class," *Atlanta Journal-Constitution*, October 14, 1993, B3; M. Elizabeth Neal, "Regents Pull Plug on Newt," *Marietta Daily Journal*, October 14, 1993, 1; Reinhardt College Press Release, November 5, 1993, Correspondence, folder 1, Box 1, Newt Gingrich Controvery.

371 Steely, *Gentleman from Georgia*, 331–42; *Atlanta Constitution*, January 18, 1997, A-1 and A-9; January 22, 1997, A-4; Stevens interview, 17.

372 Stevens interview, 17.

373 "Her Story: Rise and Fall of the House Historian," *Atlanta Journal*, January 11, 1995, A10; Christina Jeffrey, "Fallout: Former US House Historian Christina Jeffrey: In Washington, It's Hard to Distinguish Between Friends and Foes," *Atlanta Journal*, February 9, 1995, A19; Steely, *Gentleman from Georgia*, 284–85.

374 Kathey Alexander, "Fired Scholar Gets an Apology," *Atlanta Constitution*, October 26, 1995, A6; Jeanne Cummings, "Gingrich Publicly Makes Amends to Historian He Fired," *Atlanta Constitution*, December 1, 1995, B1; Christina Jeffrey e-mail to Thomas Scott, April 4, 2012, "KSU Book correspondence," Kennesaw State University Archives.

375 According to the Georgia Professional Standards Commission, Kennesaw State's pass rates on the Teacher Certification Test for the years 1989–94 were the following: 1989–90, 97.15 percent; 1990–91, 92.3 percent; 1991–92, 91.6 percent; 1992–93, 94.7 percent; 1993–94, 91.9 percent. *Kennesaw State College 1994–1996 SACS Self Study Report*, 3–77, Accreditation Self-Study Report, Kennesaw State College, 1995–1996, folder 1, Box 1, Academic Affairs, Vice President's Office, KSU/14/04, Kennesaw State University Archives.

376 Beverly F. Mitchell, interview by Thomas A. Scott and Dede Yow, October 17, 2005, no. 37, 16–17, transcripts, KSU Oral History Series, Kennesaw State University Archives; *Kennesaw State College 1993–1994 Fact Book*, 62.

377 Rugg interview, 57–58; Mitchell interview, 16–17; Siegel interview, 71.

378 The college's acceptance of the resignation and reassignment can be found with the papers for the Candace Kaspers case as evidence that there were precedents at Kennesaw for full-time administrators to return to the full-time teaching faculty. See Ed Rugg to John Beineke, November 19, 1993, Appendix 2, Kennesaw State College Position Statement Regarding Candace B. Kasper v. Board of Regents/Kennesaw State College/Dean Lois Muir, submitted to the Equal Employment Opportunity Commission (EEOC), December 21, 1994, 5, unprocessed box, 10–047, titled Candace Kaspers v. Board of Regents of the University System of Georgia, 1995–1997, Kennesaw State University Archives.

379 Deborah S. Wallace, interview by Thomas A. Scott and Dede Yow, July 19, 2006, no. 56, 7, transcript, KSU Oral History Series, Kennesaw State University Archives.

380   Rugg interview, 59–60; Robbins interview, 15; *Kennesaw State College 1994–1996 SACS Self Study Report*, 3–58.

381   Wallace interview, 17–18; Mitchell interview, 16; Rugg interview, 61.

382   Bill Torpy, "Two Students to Collect for Forced Move," *Atlanta Journal-Constitution*, October 26, 1996, C-3. For the Foundation's role in purchasing the apartment complex and developing student housing, see Thomas M. Holder, interview by Thomas A. Scott, April 17, 2007, 15, transcript, KSU Oral History Series, Kennesaw State University Archives.

383   Susan L. Rutherford to Chancellor Stephen R. Portch, September 12, 1997, letter with enclosure of Settlement Agreement with Candace Kaspers v. Board of Regents of the University System of Georgia, US District Court, Northern District of Georgia, Atlanta Division, unprocessed box, 10–047, titled Candace Kaspers v. Board of Regents of the University System of Georgia, 1995–1997, Kennesaw State University Archives.

384   The reporter failed to make clear that firing meant only that Kennesaw removed Kaspers as department chair, while allowing her to keep her entire administrative salary as a full-time teacher. Instead, the story focused on the bias charge and concluded with a statement that the Anti-Defamation League hailed the victory. Charles Walston, "Kennesaw University Loses Bias Suit: Ex-department Chair Had Questioned the Dismissal of Jewish Faculty Members," *Atlanta Journal-Constitution*, August 22, 1997, C-1.

385   The *New York Times* also reminded readers that Christina Jeffrey was on the KSU faculty. After remarking that Jeffrey had been dismissed as House historian for allegedly anti-Semitic remarks, Sack correctly conceded, as he was required to do, that "she was eventually defended by religious and academic groups, including the national director of the Anti-Defamation League of B'nai B'rith." Kevin Sack, "Teacher Demoted Over Dismissal of Others Is Awarded $275,000," *New York Times*, August 24, 1997. Sack had worked previously for the *Atlanta Journal-Constitution*.

386   *Kennesaw State College 1991-1992 Fact Book*, 67. Her dissertation was titled, "Symbolism in the Film Adaptations and Novels of D.H. Lawrence's *Sons and Lovers*, *Women in Love*, and the *Virgin and the Gipsy*."

387   Wallace had been a permanent dean of graduate studies, but the graduate dean supervised no faculty and played no direct role in annual reviews or tenure and promotion decisions. For Rugg's opinions, please see Edwin A. Rugg, August 11, 1995, Deposition in the Matter of Candace B. Kaspers v. Kennesaw State College, US District Court for the Northern District of Georgia, Atlanta Division, 17-18, 39. For Kaspers's positive evaluations, see both Candace Kaspers to the EEOC District Office, Atlanta district, November 4, 1994, and Kennesaw State College Position Statement Regarding Candace B. Kasper v. Board of Regents/Kennesaw State College/Dean Lois Muir, submitted to the Equal Employment Opportunity Commission (EEOC), December 21, 1994, 5, unprocessed box, 10–047, Kaspers v. Board of Regents, 1995–97, Kennesaw State University Archives.

388   KSC Position Statement, EEOC, 6 and Appendix 1 (Ed Rugg to Candace Kaspers, November 15, 1994, letter); Rugg deposition, 45, 52.

389   Ed Rugg cited the economy and the institution of HOPE scholarships as other reasons for the decline. The economy of the 1970s was the most sluggish of the postwar era with problems of unemployment and inflation. Rugg claims that when the economy is bad, more people enroll in college; when it is good, more people enter the workforce. By the fall of 1994 the job picture was slightly better than it had been a year earlier and more people were working rather than going to school. With regard to HOPE, Rugg's reasoning was that the state scholarship aid to students who maintained a 3.0 GPA allowed some people to afford more prestigious (and expensive) schools who otherwise would have chosen Kennesaw. Rugg deposition, 45–48.

390   After leaving Kennesaw, Muir had notable administrative successes, eventually becoming pro-
       vost and vice president of academic affairs at the University of Montana and currently serving
       as a professor of psychology at the same institution. Her later achievements suggest that she
       had talent as an administrator. However, she may have learned valuable leadership lessons at
       Kennesaw's expense. Rugg deposition, 52, 62–63. Lois Muir's current listing in the Psychology
       Department of the University of Montana can be found at http://psychweb.psy.umt.edu/www/
       facultyDetails.aspx?id=1102.

391   Rugg deposition, 13; KSC Position Statement, EEOC, 8, and Alan Schwartz resume, Appendix
       4.

392   Rugg deposition, 33–34; KSC Position Statement, EEOC, 6–7; Ed Rugg to Candace Kaspers,
       November 15, 1994, KSC Position Statement, EEOC, Appendix 1.

393   In response to a question from Kaspers whether the department would receive any more new
       positions for 1995–96, Muir seemed sympathetic, but responded that no one could say until the
       fiscal year 1996 budget was prepared toward the end of the academic year. Kaspers also asked
       whether it would be possible to advertise for a higher rank than assistant professor, and Muir
       responded in the negative, in part for financial reasons, and in part because the department
       already had four associate professors, but only one assistant, and needed more balance. Options
       for continuing the employment of Levingston and Schwartz on a temporary or permanent basis
       appeared slim under those circumstances, Levingston because she lacked a PhD, and Schwartz,
       because he was too experienced for an entry-level assistant professorship. Candace Kaspers
       to the EEOC District Office, Atlanta district, November 4, 1994; KSC Position Statement,
       EEOC, 9–11.

394   Erica Weaver, "Department Chair Relieved of Duties," *Sentinel*, November 2, 1994, 1; Kaspers
       to EEOC, November 4, 1994.

395   Rugg deposition, 41; Candace Kaspers to the EEOC District Office, Atlanta district, November
       4, 1994; KSC Position Statement, EEOC, 16.

396   KSC Position Statement, EEOC, 12–13, 16.

397   Ed Rugg to Candace Kaspers, November 15, 1994; KSC Position Statement, EEOC, 14,
       Appendix 1.

398   Alan Swartz v. Kennesaw State College, July 23, 1997, Summary Judgment; Ed Rugg to deans
       and department chairs, October 6, 1997, unprocessed box, 10–047, Kaspers v. Board of Regents,
       1995–97, Kennesaw State University Archives.

399   KSC Position Statement, EEOC, Appendix 8; Betty L. Siegel, August 14, 1995, Deposition
       in the Matter of Candace B. Kaspers v. Kennesaw State College, US District Court for the
       Northern District of Georgia, Atlanta Division, 296–97.

400   Siegel interview, September 24, 1993, 34.

401   Siegel interview, October 27, 1993, 59–60.

402   King interview, 16; Flora Devine, Nancy King, Curtis Daw, and New View of the Future
       focus groups, *New View of the Future: A Report*, presented to Dr. Betty L. Siegel, Spring 1995,
       unprocessed box, 06–024, President's Office, Kennesaw State University Archives.

403   *Access to Academic Excellence for the New Millennium: A Vision for the University System of Georgia*,
       unprocessed box, 06–024, President's Office, Kennesaw State University Archives.

404   Devine, King, and Daw, "Summary Recommendations of New View Focus Groups," *New View*,
       13–18, 27–28; King interview, 17.

405   King interview, 18–19.

406   Siegel interview, October 27, 1993, 74.

407   Ed Rugg to Joanne Fowler and faculty in Learning Support Department, July 17, 1995, unprocessed box, 06–024, President's Office, Kennesaw State University Archives.

408   Carol J. Pope, interview by Mia Riccio and Shantina Starks, April 20, 2011, audiotape, no transcript, HIST 4425, KSU 50th Anniversary Series, Kennesaw State University Archives.

409   Pope interview.

410   Alpha Kappa Alpha began in 1908 at Howard University and is the oldest sorority founded by African American women.

411   Jerome Ratchford, e-mail to Thomas Scott, October 26, 2012, "KSU Book correspondence," electronic file, Kennesaw State University Archives.

412   Jerome Ratchford, interview by Mia Riccio and Shantina Starks, March 24, 2011, 5–7, transcript, HIST 4425, 50th Anniversary Series, Kennesaw State University Archives. Student Development Center website: http://www.kennesaw.edu/stu_dev/index.shtml.

413   According to the 2002 *Digest of Educational Statistics* of the US Department of Education's National Center for Educational Statistics, women made up only 34 percent of all full-time faculty members at public, four-year, degree-granting institutions in fall 1999. The comparable number for KSU was 51 percent. Ed Rugg e-mail to Thomas Scott, May 3, 2012, "KSU Book correspondence," electronic file, Kennesaw State University Archives.

414   *Kennesaw State University 2000–2001 Fact Book*, 69, http://vic.kennesaw.edu/EIMWebApps/vic/fact_books/documents/pdf/FB2000_2001.pdf.

Chapter 8

415   Papp interview, 35–36.

416   Acquisition dates can be found in "Physical Facilities," *Kennesaw State University 2006–2007 Fact Book*.

417   Acquisition dates are often a year or two before the buildings actually opened for use. "Physical Facilities," *Kennesaw State University 2006–2007 Fact Book*.

418   For enrollment and graduation data, please see Erik Bowe, *Complete College Georgia Plan Data Analysis and Goals for Kennesaw State University*, June 9, 2012, http://vic.kennesaw.edu/EIMWebApps/vic/analytic_studies/documents/pdf/ccga_part1.pdf.

419   Minutes, Board of Regents, June 11–12, 1996, 57–59, "Board of Regents Meeting Minutes and Agendas, 1995–1996," Box 10, KSU/01/04, Kennesaw State University Archives, Kennesaw, Georgia.

420   Minutes, Board of Regents, June 11–12, 1996, 63–64; Jamie Floer, "KSC Officially Becomes KSU: Regents' OK Spurs 'Instantaneous Celebration on Campus,'" *Marietta Daily Journal*, June 13, 1996, 1B; AP byline, "Regents OK Name Changes, Tougher Admissions Standards," *Marietta Daily Journal*, June 13, 1996, 2B.

421   Floer, "KSC Officially Becomes KSU."

422   *Sentinel*, July 3, 1996, 3.

423   James A. Fleming, interview by Thomas A. Scott, September 27, 2006, no. 49, 3–5, transcript, KSU Oral History Series; Wesley K. Wicker, interview by Thomas A. Scott, September 13 and 29, 2011, October 4, 2011, no. 102, 22–23, transcript, KSU Oral History Series, Kennesaw State University Archives.

424   Fleming interview, 1–3, 7–8.

425   Fleming interview, 4–5.

426   Fleming interview, 6; Roy Hoffman, "Rev. Norman H. McCrummen III, Looks Back on a Career Touched by Grace, Filled with Gratitude," *Mobile (AL) Press-Register*, June 18, 2011, http://blog.al.com/living-press-register/2011/06/touched_by_grace_and_filled_wi.html.

427   Fleming interview, 8–10; Stevens interview, 1, 4–6, 11.

428   Stevens interview, 8, 12.

429   Stevens interview, 13.

430   Stevens interview, 14–15, 22.

431   The Michael J. Coles College of Business at KSU is named in his honor as a result of this gift. Coles was also an activist in the Democratic Party, running unsuccessfully for Congress against Newt Gingrich in 1996 and for the US Senate against Johnny Isakson in 1998. In 2001, Governor Roy Barnes appointed Coles to the Board of Regents of the University System of Georgia. "Michael Coles Named CEO of Caribou Coffee, Expansion Planned," *Atlanta Business Chronicle*, June 3, 2003, http://www.bizjournals.com/atlanta/stories/2003/06/02/daily14.html; Joanna Soto Carabello, "Michael J. Coles College of Business," *New Georgia Encyclopedia*, July 14, 2006.

432   Holder officially became a foundation trustee in 1995. Thomas M. Holder, interview by Thomas A. Scott, April 17, 2007, no. 66, 1–5, transcript, KSU Oral History Series, Kennesaw State University Archives.

433   Holder interview, 1–5.

434   Lawrence D. Wheeler, interview by Thomas A. Scott, September 15, 2008, no. 84, 1–7, transcript, KSU Oral History Series, Kennesaw State University Archives; Fleming interview, 20.

435   Stevens interview, 22; Wesley Chenault, "Herman J. Russell (b. 1930)," *New Georgia Encyclopedia*, December 18, 2009; "Biography—Norman J. Radow, President/CEO, the RADCO Companies," http://www.imn.org/pages/biography.cfm?personid=NRRG957BMEK8.

436   Fleming interview, 12–13.

437   George W. Kalafut, interview by Thomas A. Scott and Randall L. Patton, May 3, 2007, no. 53, 1–8, 10, transcript, KSU Oral History Series, Kennesaw State University Archives.

438   Kalafut interview, 9.

439   Rachel Brooker, "Welcome Home," *Sentinel*, August 28, 2002, 1.

440   Brooker, "Welcome Home."

441   "List of Facilities," *Kennesaw State University 2011–2012 Fact Book*; Ian Johnston, "Parking Decks, Housing, Boost Enrollment," *Sentinel*, August 28, 2002, 1; "Fall Enrollment Highlights," *Kennesaw State University 2002–2003 Fact Book*.

442 "KSU: The Next Party School?" and Brian Hedrick, "Future Alums of KSU Worthy of Envy," *Sentinel*, August 28, 2002, 3; "List of Facilities," *Kennesaw State University 2011–2012 Fact Book*; Geoff Folsom, "KSU Breaks Ground on New 'High-End' Dorms," *Marietta Daily Journal*, October 7, 2011.

443 Wesley K. Wicker, *The New Faces of Kennesaw State: The Campaign for Our Future, A Case Study*, January 2012, 3, Kennesaw State University Archives; "About the Clendenin Family," The Clendenin Graduate Fellows Program, https://web.kennesaw.edu/clendenin/about-clendenin-family; "Kennesaw State Breaks Ground on New Science Building," KSU Press Release, October 22, 2001, http://access.kennesaw.edu/news_site/news_releases/news_release_139.html; Rick Woodall, "Kennesaw State Celebrates New Additions to Campus," KSU Press Release, January 17, 2003, http://web.kennesaw.edu/news/stories/kennesaw-state-celebrates-new-additions-campus.

444 Wicker, *New Faces*, 3, 9.

445 Fleming interview, 18, 22–23; Wicker interview, 50–51, 78.

446 G. William (Bill) Hill IV, interview by Thomas A. Scott and Dede Yow, June 17, 2004 and January 23, 2009, no. 4, 40, transcript, KSU Oral History Series, Kennesaw State University Archives.

447 Hill interview, 18–21, 38–39; Dr. Bill Hill website: http://ksuweb.kennesaw.edu/~bhill/.

448 Hill interview, 38–42, 48.

449 Hill interview, 44–46.

450 Hill interview, 46; "About Us: Past Fellows," CETL, http://www.kennesaw.edu/cetl/aboutus/pastfellows.html.

451 Siegel interview, 110.

452 Mitchell interview, 18–19.

453 Kimberly S. Loomis, interview by Thomas A. Scott, August 16, 2011, no. 105, 16–17, 21, transcript, KSU Oral History Series; Army Lester III, interview by Thomas A. Scott and Dede Yow, February 10, 2005, no. 34, 28–29, transcript, KSU Oral History Series, Kennesaw State University Archives.

454 Hill interview, 49.

455 After earning his PhD from Georgia State in 1982, Roberts joined the faculty at the University of Tennessee, but was not happy there. After being counseled by his department chair that he was spending too much time with students and not enough on his scholarship, he decided to look for an institution with a greater focus on teaching. Dean Harry Lasher tells the following story of how Roberts became a faculty member in 1985 at Kennesaw's School of Business Administration: "He contacted me, and he said, 'I'd like to come down and talk to you.' This was in February…so I'm in the office working, and it was snowing that day. The college was closed, and I thought, 'He'll never show up.' Well, I'll be darned, he did. I thought anybody that would drive down in this weather to want to come here with his commitment to teaching, there must be something special. Gary was probably one of the best hires that I ever made. To this day, what he contributes to students and to the university is just amazing. I'm really proud of Gary." Lasher interview, 13; Hill interview, 53; Gary B. Roberts, interview by Thomas A. Scott and Dede Yow, January 31 and February 2, 2005, no. 28, 27–29, 48–49, transcript, KSU Oral History Series, Kennesaw State University Archives.

456 Hill interview, 61–62.

457   Hill interview, 56; Mary L. Garner, interview by Thomas A. Scott, September 12, 2006, no. 65, 26–28, transcript, KSU Oral History Series, Kennesaw State University Archives; Mary Garner, "The Vending Machine Model of Undergraduate Education Vs. Interdisciplinary Team-Taught Courses," *Reaching through Teaching*, 15 (Spring 2003): 5–8.

458   Val Whittlesey perhaps would have won her share of awards as well, except for the fact that she was already an assistant vice president and ineligible; and Sandra Hillman left Kennesaw shortly after her fellowship ended. "Faculty Awards," Center for Excellence in Teaching and Learning (CETL), www.kennesaw.edu/cetl.

459   Noble interview, 29–30, Hill interview, 54–55.

460   Meghan A. Burke, interview by Thomas A. Scott and Dede Yow, March 19, 2007, no. 64, 21, 23, transcript, KSU Oral History Series, Kennesaw State University Archives; Hill interview, 57–58, 60.

461   Hill interview, 56–57; "Staff," CETL, www.kennesaw.edu/cetl; "KSU Professor, Administrator Earns Board of Regents' Teaching Award," News Release, October 12, 2011, http://web.kennesaw.edu/news/category/tags/pusateri.

462   Hill interview, 63–65.

463   In addition to the original fellows and those mentioned in the text, the following faculty members have held fellowships through 2012: Robert Hill (scholarly discourse across disciplines, 2004–2005), Tom Kolenko (reflective practice of teaching, 2004–2006), Lewis VanBrackle (scholarship of teaching and learning, 2004–2006), Marina Koether (advancing undergraduate research, 2006–2008), Dede Yow (diversity in the curriculum, 2005–2008), Jorge Perez (e-learning, 2006–2009), and Carlton Usher (diversity in the curriculum, 2010–2012). "Past Fellows," Center for Excellence in Teaching and Learning (CETL), www.kennesaw.edu/cetl.

464   Waples interview, 17; "Men's Basketball," "KSU Athletic History Timeline," and "Cross Country Timeline," Kennesaw State University Archives; KSU Sports Information, "Kennesaw Celebrates 30 Years of Athletics History," Kennesaw State University Athletics, http://www.ksuowls.com/news/2012/6/12/FAN_0612124440.aspx.

465   Rick Woodall, "Soccer Team Wins National Championship," http://web.kennesaw.edu/news/stories/soccer-team-wins-national-championship; Chip Towers, "KSU Muscles Its Way into Athletics Elite: Championships Give School Cause to Cheer," *Atlanta Journal-Constitution*, May 24, 2004, A1.

466   "History: All-Time Season Results," Brigham Young University Cougars Basketball, http://byucougars.com/m-basketball/all-time-season-results; "Kennesaw State's Athletic Department Overhauls University's Men's Basketball Program," Press Release, March 7, 2011, https://web.kennesaw.edu/news/stories/kennesaw-state%E2%80%99s-athletic-department-overhauls-university%E2%80%99s-men%E2%80%99s-basketball-program.

467   Waples interview, 23; "Kennesaw State's Athletic Department Overhauls University's Men's Basketball Program," Press Release; Towers, "KSU Muscles Its Way into Athletics Elite"; Rick Woodall, "KSU Honors Champions," Press Release, April 7, 2004, http://web.kennesaw.edu/news/stories/ksu-honors-champions.

468   Landrum interview, 23–24; "KSU Athletic History Timeline"; "Kennesaw State University Football Timeline"; Waples interview, 30.

469   Charles Odum, "Kennesaw State Moves Up to Atlantic Sun, May Add Football," Associated Press, January 5, 2005, http://www.kennesaw.edu/presidentemeritus/pdf/2005.pdf; "Kennesaw State University Football Timeline."

470   "Sports Briefing, Softball: Division II Title Vacated," *New York Times*, July 18, 2007; "KSU Athletic History Timeline."

471   "KSU Year-by-Year Athletic Records," Kennesaw State University Archives.

472   "KSU Athletic History Timeline"; "Athletics Women's Track"; and "Athletics Men's Track," Kennesaw State University Archives.

473   "KSU Year-by-Year Athletic Records," Kennesaw State University Archives; Waples interview, 19–20, 25.

474   "KSU Year-by-Year Athletic Records," Kennesaw State University Archives.

475   "KSU Athletic History Timeline"; "KSU NUMBERS re: Athletic Budgets, Fees, Costs and Sports," Kennesaw State University Archives; John A. Anderson, e-mail to Charles Bowen and Thomas Scott, October 24, 2012, "KSU Book correspondence," electronic file, Kennesaw State University Archives.

476   "KSU Athletic History Timeline"; Waples interview, 33–35.

Chapter 9

477   Siegel interview, 18, 58.

478   Siegel interview, 91–93, 103–05.

479   Siegel interview, 121–22.

480   Siegel interview, 107, 110.

481   Siegel interview, 93; Kennesaw State University Office of the President Emeritus website: http://www.kennesaw.edu/presidentemeritus/.

482   Linda M. Johnston, e-mail to Thomas Scott, June 27, 2012, "KSU Book correspondence," electronic file, Kennesaw State University Archives.

483   Wicker interview, 14, 17; Johnson to Scott, June 27, 2012; Jon Gillooly, "Putting Ethics in Leadership," *Marietta Daily Journal*, October 1, 2006.

484   Wicker interview, 17–18; Johnston to Scott, June 27, 2012; Jon Gillooly, "Putting Ethics in Leadership," *Marietta Daily Journal*, October 1, 2006; "Retired? Siegel Making Globe Her Playground," *Marietta Daily Journal*, January, RTM,17, 2008; Bill Kinney, "Ethics Are Key…to Moral Development," *Marietta Daily Journal*, April 10, 2006; "RTM Restaurant Group History," http://www.fundinguniverse.com/company-histories/rtm-restaurant-group-history/; "Triarc Will Acquire RTM; Arby's H.Q. Moving to Atlanta," *Atlanta Business Chronicle*, May 31, 2005, http://www.bizjournals.com/atlanta/stories/2005/05/30/daily2.html.

485   Kinney, "Ethics Are Key."

486   Siegel Institute for Leadership, Ethics, and Character website; Johnston to Scott, June 27, 2012; Kinney, "Ethics Are Key"; Gillooly, "Putting Ethics in Leadership."

487   Gillooly, "Putting Ethics in Leadership"; "Briefs," *Marietta Daily Journal Online*, October 4, 2005.

488   Gillooly, Putting Ethics in Leadership"; "Retired? Siegel Making Globe Her Playground"; KSU Office of the President Emeritus website; "A Conversation with Dr. Betty Siegel," *Diverse*

Online, August 9, 2007, copy in "Archives"; KSU Office of the President Emeritus website: http://www.kennesaw.edu/presidentemeritus/archives.html.

489   KSU Office of the President Emeritus website; Aixa M. Pascual, "Q&A/Betty Siegel: KSU's Woman of Vision," *Atlanta Journal-Constitution*, February 2, 2006, Cobb Edition, JF1.

490   Meeks interview, 1, 16, 32.

491   Meeks interview, 25, 30.

492   Karen Kennedy, "Arts Dean Named Chair of Presidential Search Committee," News Release, July 14, 2005, www.kennesaw.edu/news; Chancellor's Report, Minutes, Board of Regents, August 2–3, 2005.

493   Resolution of the Kennesaw State University Faculty Council, October 3, 2005, to the Chancellor and the Board of Regents, Minutes of the Faculty Council, October 3, 2005 (as amended, November 7, 2005), http://ksuweb.kennesaw.edu/~rhill/fc100305.htm.

494   Meeks interview, 29; Holder interview, 21.

495   Meeks interview, 28–29; Minutes, Special Meeting of the Board of Regents, February 16, 2006.

496   Daniel S. Papp, interview by Thomas A. Scott and Dede Yow, August 3, 2006, September 5 and 28, 2006, January 9, 2009, no. 50, 1–2, 4–5, transcript, KSU Oral History Series, Kennesaw State University Archives.

497   Papp interview, 2–3, 12.

498   Papp interview, 3, 8–9.

499   Papp interview, 9–10, 14–15.

500   Papp interview, 15–16; Daniel S. Papp Curriculum Vita, September 2005, copy in possession of author.

501   Papp interview, 16–17.

502   Papp interview, 21–22; Papp Curriculum Vita.

503   Papp Curriculum Vita; Papp interview, 23; Letter from the Interim Chair, Sam Nunn School of International Affairs, Georgia Tech, http://www.inta.gatech.edu/mission/the-sam-nunn-school.

504   Papp interview, 12–13; Papp Curriculum Vita.

505   Papp interview, 14–15; Papp Curriculum Vita.

506   Papp interview, 27–29; "History," Southern Polytechnic State University, http://www.spsu.edu/aboutus/history.htm.

507   Papp interview, 33–34; Raymond Greenlaw, "Yamacraw Initiative Overview," 2003, PowerPoint, cs.armstrong.edu/greenlaw/presentations/yamacraw_initiative_overview.ppt.

508   After Papp's September 2002 selection as chancellor of the University System of Florida, he spent the fall dividing his time between several days a week at the regents' office in Atlanta, and several days in Tallahassee transitioning into his new job. During that period, the presidencies suddenly became open at the University of Florida, Florida State, Florida Atlantic, and North Florida. In most other systems, including Georgia, the chancellor would be expected to conduct searches and make recommendations to the boards of trustees. However, Papp learned from the Florida commissioner of education that the Florida State presidency was going to the former Speaker of the House. Then he learned that the lieutenant governor would become

the president of Florida Atlantic. Finally, he found out just after Thanksgiving that the North Florida presidency was going to the mayor of Jacksonville. None of these individuals had strong academic qualifications. About the same time, without consulting Papp, Governor Jeb Bush's transition team fired about a third of the staff of the University System of Florida. The final straw came on a Friday morning, when he learned that the governor was putting together the strategic plan for his second term and needed by Monday afternoon a report on the needs of the university system for the next five years. Papp recalled that, "I went down to my office and told my secretary to call up Delta and make an airplane reservation home to Atlanta." Thus, his tenure as chancellor of the Florida system ended before he fully moved into the office. Papp interview, 37–39.

[509]   "Regents Name Davis as Chancellor-Designate of the University System of Georgia," December 9, 2005, News Release Archives, University System of Georgia, http://www.usg.edu/news/release/regents_name_davis_as_chancellor-designate_of_the_university_system_of_geor.

[510]   Jennifer Hafer, "USG Vice Chancellor Becomes KSU's Third President," KSU Press Release, February 16, 2006, https://web.kennesaw.edu/news/stories/usg-vice-chancellor-becomes-ksu%E2%80%99s-third-president.

[511]   Dr. Randy C. Hinds had been functioning as vice president for information technology since 1998. In July 2006 he also took on the duties of interim vice president for business and finance. President Papp announced, nine months later, in his first State of the University address that the combination had worked so well that he was making it permanent with Hinds as the vice president for operations. Daniel S. Papp, "Opening of School," August 16, 2006, and "2007 State of the University Address," March 28–29, 2007, electronic versions, Kennesaw State University Archives.

[512]   Ed Rugg to Thomas Scott, July 24, 2012, "critique of Chapter 9," "KSU book correspondence," electronic file, Kennesaw State University Archives; Betty L. Siegel to KSU's Leadership Team for SACS Reaccreditation, May 21, 2003, http://sacs.kennesaw.edu/page_background_information_on_sacs_accreditation/pres_lead_team%5B1%5D.pdf; Daniel S. Papp, "2007 State of the University Address," March 28–29, 2007, electronic copy, Kennesaw State University Archives; Ed Rugg, *Compliance Certification Report*, September 8, 2006, http://sacs.kennesaw.edu/page_compliance_certification_report.html.

[513]   Rugg to Scott, July 24, 2012.

[514]   Akanmu G. Adebayo, interview by Christopher Harris and Cody Bishop, April 1, 2011, digital audio recording, HIST 4425, KSU 50th Anniversary Series, Kennesaw State University Archives.

[515]   Sutton was associate vice chancellor of international affairs at Indiana University–Purdue University Indianapolis. The president-elect of the Association of International Education Administrators seemed well qualified to serve as a SACS external evaluator. She had a good baseline from which to judge KSU's progress since she had previously served as the QEP Lead Evaluator on the SACS On-Site Review Committee in 2007. Susan Buck Sutton, *QEP Mid-Point External Evaluation Report*, Kennesaw State University, November 2, 2010, http://sacs.kennesaw.edu/documents/pdf/sacs/QEP/External_QEP_Mid-Point_Evaluation%20_Report.pdf.

[516]   Sutton, *QEP Mid-Point External Evaluation Report*; Sabbaye McGriff, "KSU Elevates Barry Morris to Vice Provost for Global Engagement," News Release, March 1, 2011, http://web.kennesaw.edu/news/stories/ksu-elevates-barry-morris-vice-provost-global-engagement.

[517]   Sutton, *QEP Mid-Point External Evaluation Report*.

[518]   Sutton, *QEP Mid-Point External Evaluation Report*; Confucius Institute at KSU website: http://www.kennesaw.edu/confuciusinstitute/. Chinese is one of the many languages offered

at KSU. In fall 2012, the Foreign Language Department offered four sections of Chinese 1001 (Introduction to Chinese Language and Culture), two sections of Chinese 1002, and one section each of Chinese 2001, 2002, 3302 (Chinese Conversation), and 3390 (China Study Abroad). KSU Class Schedule Listing website: https://owlexpress.kennesaw.edu/prodban/bwckschd.p_get_crse_unsec.

519   College of Science and Mathematics website: http://science.kennesaw.edu/resources/global.html; Center for International Business website: http://coles.kennesaw.edu/centers/international/; Museum of History and Holocaust Education website: http://marb.kennesaw.edu/identities/.

520   Papp interview, 35; Chancellor Thomas C. Meredith, memorandum to presidents of Georgia Southern University, Kennesaw State University, Valdosta State University, and University of West Georgia, April 7, 2005, "Mission Review: Possible Change from State/Regional University Sector to Carnegie Research Intensive Status, Application for Member Institutions Seeking Accreditation at a More Advanced Degree Level," http://sacs.kennesaw.edu/PAGE_DOCU-MENT_DIRECTORY/A1/A_LINKS/EDD_SACS_SUBSTANTIVE_CHANGE_SMALL.pdf.

521   Dr. Ed Rugg, Application for [SACS] Member Institutions Seeking Accreditation at a More Advanced Degree Level, June 5, 2006, http://sacs.kennesaw.edu/PAGE_DOCUMENT_DIRECTORY/A1/A_LINKS/EDD_SACS_SUBSTANTIVE_CHANGE_SMALL.pdf; College of Education, University of Georgia, http://www.coe.uga.edu/; College of Education, Georgia State University, http://education.gsu.edu/main/225.html.

522   Dr. Wilsie Bishop, *Report of the Reaffirmation Committee*, March 19–21, 2007, http://sacs.kennesaw.edu/PAGE_SACS_REAFFIRMATION_LINKS/SACSReaffirmationReport4.pdf; Dr. Marilyn A. Sheerer, *Report of the Substantive Change Committee*, March 19–21, 2007, http://sacs.kennesaw.edu/PAGE_SACS_REAFFIRMATION_LINKS/SACSSubstantiveChange-CommitteeReport.pdf; Belle S. Wheelan to Dr. Daniel S. Papp, January 9, 2008, http://sacs.kennesaw.edu/PAGE_SACS_REAFFIRMATION_LINKS/ActionsCOC.pdf.

523   Rugg, Application for SACS Member Institutions.

524   Natalie Godwin, "KSU Awards Clint Stockton First Doctoral Degree," *Access: A Publication of Kennesaw State University*, September/October 2010, 1; "KSU Awards First Doctoral Degree," Press Release, July 28, 2010, http://web.kennesaw.edu/news/stories/ksu-awards-first-doctoral-degree; "Choices in Graduate Programs," *Focus Change Innovate: Bagwell College of Education 2010–2011 Annual Report*, 5, Bagwell College of Education, http://mydigimag.rrd.com/publication/?i=96655&pre=1.

525   University of West Georgia website: http://www.westga.edu/index_acad.php; Valdosta State University website: http://www.valdosta.edu/coe/edd/COE_Doctoral_Programs/COEDoctoralPrograms.shtml; Georgia Southern University website: http://coe.georgiasouthern.edu/.

526   The business PhD at Georgia Southern University was in a relatively narrow field of logistics/supply chain management, building on a strong undergraduate program in logistics and materials management. Georgia Southern University website: http://cogs.georgiasouthern.edu/admission/GraduatePrograms/phdlogistics.php.

527   The DBA consisted of forty-eight credit hours of courses stretched over three years (three semesters in residence the first year, two the second, and two the third). While the college did not provide a specific tuition schedule prior to acceptance, it estimated tuition and costs for the DBA 2012 cohort at approximately $90,000. Coles College website: http://coles.kennesaw.edu/graduate/dba/schedules-tuition.htm. In contrast, the *Kennesaw State University 2012–2013 Graduate Catalog* published an in-state graduate tuition rate of $259 per credit hour plus $817 in student activities fees. The credit hour rate multiplied by 48 credit hours comes to $12,432.

Adding the $817 activities fees over seven semesters ($5,719), the total cost of three graduate years would come to $18,151. *Kennesaw State University 2012–2013 Graduate Catalog*, http://catalog.kennesaw.edu/index.php?catoid=13. So the premium tuition structure, indeed, could be expected to support the globalization of the program and much more.

528 Along with a number of PhD in different disciplines, the J. Mack Robinson College of Business at Georgia State, as of 2012, had one non-PhD business doctorate, an executive doctorate in business for senior executives. Georgia State advertised the program as one that would allow executives to improve their research skills and knowledge in addressing practical business problems. In contrast, Kennesaw advertised its DBA as one that prepared individuals either to advance their current business careers or to apply for tenure-track positions at AACSB-accredited colleges. Aixa Pascual, "University Adds New Doctorate of Business Administration and Dance Major," Press Release, March 19, 2008, https://web.kennesaw.edu/news/stories/university-adds-new-doctorate-business-administration-and-dance-major; Aixa Pascual, "Doctor of Business Administration: KSU's Doctorate for Executives in League of Its Own," *Kennesaw State University Magazine*, Fall 2011, 26; J. Mack Robinson College of Business, Georgia State University, http://robinson.gsu.edu; Coles College website: http://coles.kennesaw.edu/graduate/dba/FAQs.htm#vs.

529 "Kennesaw State University Coles College of Business Inaugural Class Doctor of Business Administration Graduates, May 2012," https://web.kennesaw.edu/news/sites/web.kennesaw.edu.news/files/DBA.pdf.

530 Jennifer Hafer, "New Doctorate of Nursing Science Approved by Board of Regents," Press Release, February 10, 2009, http://web.kennesaw.edu/nes/stories/new-doctorate-nursing-science-approved-board-regents; Prillaman Hall Health Sciences Building Fact Sheet website: http://www.kennesaw.edu/prillamanhall/health_sciences_building_fact_sheet.pdf.

531 College of Nursing, Georgia Health Sciences University, http://www.georgiahealth.edu/nursing/dnp.html and http://www.georgiahealth.edu/nursing/acnp_cns.html; Georgia Southern University Doctor of Public Health website: http://jphcoph.georgiasouthern.edu/degrees/doctorate/overview.

532 Papp interview, 59–60.

533 "Board of Regents Approves Kennesaw's First PhD program," News Release, March 10, 2010, https://web.kennesaw.edu/news/stories/board-regents-approves-kennesaw-state%E2%80%99s-first-phd-program; Sabbaye McGriff, "PhD in International Conflict Management: KSU's First PhD Program Outstrips Expectations and Demand," *Kennesaw State University Magazine*, Fall 2011, 27; PhD Program in International Conflict Management website: http://www.kennesaw.edu/incm/docs/cohort-2011.pdf. Gerges was not alone in producing path-breaking applied scholarship. For a number of published articles by international conflict management students, please see the program website.

534 Papp interview, 59–60.

535 Ed Rugg, *Kennesaw State University's Peer and Aspirational Comparator Universities*, October 27, 2008, http://vic.kennesaw.edu/EIMWebApps/vic/analytic_studies/documents/pdf/KSU_comparators_2008.pdf.

536 "Our History" and "Fast Facts," Oakland University, http://www.oakland.edu/?id=15&sid=19.

537 Ed Rugg, *Kennesaw State University's Peer and Aspirational Comparator Universities*, October 27, 2008, http://vic.kennesaw.edu/EIMWebApps/vic/analytic_studies/documents/pdf/KSU_comparators_2008.pdf.

538 "A Brief History of George Mason University" and "Mason's Presidents," George Mason University, http://www.gmu.edu/resources/visitors/history.html and http://president.gmu.edu/masons-presidents/.

Chapter 10

539 The study was conducted for the Board of Regents by the Selig Center for Economic Growth at UGA's Terry College of Business. "Economic Impact of University System Reaches $13.2 Billion," University System of Georgia, http://www.usg.edu/news/release/economic_impact_of_university_system_reaches_13.2_billion; "Kennesaw State University's Economic Impact Reaches $854 Million in Fiscal Year 2011," Press Release, http://web.kennesaw.edu/news/stories/kennesaw-state-university%E2%80%99s-economic-impact-reaches-854-million-fiscal-year-2011.

540 *Kennesaw State University's 2007–2012 Strategic Plan*; *Kennesaw State University 2012–2017 Strategic Plan*, Kennesaw State University Archives; Erik R. Bowe, e-mail to Thomas Scott, September 4, 2012, "KSU Book correspondence," electronic file, Kennesaw State University Archives.

541 *Kennesaw State University 2012–2017 Strategic Plan*, Kennesaw State University Archives.

542 *Kennesaw State University 2012–2017 Strategic Plan*.

543 *Kennesaw State University's 2007–2012 Strategic Plan*; *Kennesaw State University 2012–2017 Strategic Plan*; Papp interview, 49–50.

544 The figures tracked full-time students who entered in fall 2003 and graduated by summer 2009. Laura Diamond, "Georgia Colleges' Graduation Rates Unsatisfactory," *Atlanta Journal-Constitution*, October 27, 2010, http://www.ajc.com/news/georgia-colleges-graduation-rates-694688.html.

545 Papp, State of the University Address, March 29–30, 2012, 19–20; Complete College America website: http://completecollege.org/.

546 Papp, State of the University Address, March 29–30, 2012, 20–21; Papp, Opening of the University Address, August 10, 2011, 3.

547 Erik Bowe, *Complete Georgia Plan Data Analysis and Goals for Kennesaw State University*, June 9, 2012, https://vic33.kennesaw.edu/EIMWebApps/vic/analytic_studies/documents/pdf/ccga_part1.pdf.

548 Bowe, *Complete Georgia Plan Data Analysis*.

549 Karen Andrews became director of the Career Services Center in 1988. At that time, it was housed with CAPS under the direction of Nancy King. While counseling and placement services had some things in common, they also had significantly different missions. For the first four years, the two offices shared a common waiting room. Andrews claims that she knew she had to break away from counseling when a recruiter from Wachovia Bank asked her whether it was normal for students to be sobbing in the waiting room and for a student to be breast-feeding her baby next to an accounting student in a business suit awaiting a job interview. In 1992 the Career Services Center was given its own office space in the Pilcher Building. When Andrews started in 1988, the entire career services staff was two professionals and two support staff. Gradually, she was able to hire professionals for each of the colleges, beginning with Lori Trahan in 1998 who was assigned to the Coles College of Business. Daniel S. Papp, State of the

University Address, March 28–29, 2007, 16; Papp, State of the University Address, February 27–28, 2008, 25–26, electronic files, Kennesaw State University Archives; Karen B. Andrews e-mail to Thomas Scott, August 22, 2012, "KSU Book correspondence," electronic file, Kennesaw State University Archives.

550   *Kennesaw State University's 2007–2012 Strategic Plan.*

551   Bowe, *Complete Georgia Plan Data Analysis.*

552   The Office of Multicultural Student Retention Services was a unit of the Student Development Center, directed by Jerome Ratchford, and later, after Ratchford became vice president for student success, by Carol Pope. "KSU Ranks among Top 100 Producers of Undergraduate Degrees Conferred to Minority Students," Press Release, July 1, 2011, http://web.kennesaw.edu/news/stories/ksu-ranks-among-top-100-producers-undergraduate-degrees-conferred-minority-students.

553   Papp, State of the University Address, March 29–30, 2012, 23–24.

554   Kathryn Dobies, "Traffic Stop Puts KSU Student in Jail as an Illegal Immigrant," *Marietta Daily Journal*, May 1, 2010; Kathryn Dobies Malone, "Illegal KSU Student Found Guilty," *Marietta Daily Journal*, November 12, 2010.

555   Daniel S. Papp, Letter to the Editor, *Marietta Daily Journal*, May 12, 2010; Dobies, "Traffic Stop."

556   See, for example, editorial page editor Joe Kirby's column, "Bad Week for School Brass," *Marietta Daily Journal*, May 16, 2010.

557   Malone, "Illegal KSU Student Found Guilty"; Kirby, "Bad Week for School Brass"; Laura Diamond, "Regents Ban Illegal Immigrants from Some Ga. Colleges," *Atlanta Journal-Constitution*, October 13, 2010. In a jury trial on November 11, 2010 Jessica Colotl was found guilty of driving without a license, but innocent of the charge of impeding traffic. She was sentenced a few days later to pay $1,400 in fines and fees, do twenty hours of community service, and spend three days in jail and a year on probation. Her attorneys appealed but lost before the Georgia Court of Appeals. After the Georgia Supreme Court refused to hear the case, she had a final hearing before Cobb County State Court with Judge Kathryn Tanksley on the morning of June 25, 2012. By that time, all but ten hours of her sentence had been served, so she spent the rest of the day at the Cobb County jail until her release at 8:20 p.m. In addition to the misdemeanor charges against her, she was charged with a felony for false swearing to the Sheriff's Department about her home address. That charge was dismissed in Cobb Superior Court on Wednesday, January 9, 2013. Meanwhile, ICE twice extended her stay in the United States, the last deferment coming in May 2012. By that time, she had graduated from Kennesaw State and was working as a paralegal in Atlanta. Laura Diamond, "Colotl Allowed to Stay for Another Year," *Atlanta Journal-Constitution*, May 7, 2012; Lindsay Field, "Colotl Spends Day in Jail," *Marietta Daily Journal*, June 25, 2012, www.mdjonline.com/bookmark/19099039; Associated Press and Lindsay Field, *Marietta Daily Journal*, January 11, 2013.

558   Sabbaye McGriff, "New Appointments Announced at KSU as Administrators Make Career Moves," Press Release, June 30, 2012, https://web.kennesaw.edu/news/stories/new-appointments-announced-ksu-administrators-make-career-moves-0; Jon Gillooly, "KSU Chief Gives Provost Uproar Silent Treatment," *Marietta Daily Journal*, March 9, 2011; "Kennesaw State Announces New Provost, Vice President for Academic Affairs," December 5, 2011, https://web.kennesaw.edu/news/stories/kennesaw-state-announces-new-provost-vice-president-academic-affairs-0; Daniel Papp e-mail to Thomas Scott, September 6, 2012, "KSU Book correspondence," electronic file, Kennesaw State University Archives.

559   For purposes of tenure and promotion, Kennesaw credits both institutional service (leadership on committees, advising student organizations, etc.) and professional public service related to

one's field of expertise (serving as an officer of a professional organization, making speeches to community groups, etc.) Kennesaw honors other types of service (such as coaching a little league team or working on humanitarian causes), but such activities are regarded as the normal obligations of citizenship and are generally not considered in tenure and promotion deliberations. *Kennesaw State University 2012-2013 Faculty Handbook*, 96–97, https://web.kennesaw. edu/academicaffairs/handbooks. For President Papp's observations on the various types of service, please see the Papp interview, 20.

[560] The "engaged university" committee members were Lora Howard (administrative specialist, Office of the President), Sylvia Inman (assistant director, Volunteer Kennesaw [VKSU] and community service coordinator), LeeAnn Lands (associate professor of history), Jorge Perez (associate professor of information systems and faculty executive assistant to the president), Ivan Pulinkala (department chair, Dance Program) Adriane Randolph (assistant professor of business information systems), Sabine Smith (associate professor of German and 2009 recipient of the KSU Foundation Distinguished Teaching Award), and Rajaram Veliyath (professor of management and entrepreneurship and faculty executive assistant to the provost). Daniel S. Papp, Opening of the University address, August 10, 2011, 27–28, digital copy, Kennesaw State University Archives.

[561] Betty L. Siegel, "Year of Engagement," August 1, 2001, http://web.kennesaw.edu/news/stories/ year-engagement; Betty L. Siegel, "40 Years of Excellence: Daring to Dream and Do," January 1, 2003, https://web.kennesaw.edu/news/stories/40-years-excellence-daring-dream-and-do.

[562] Daniel S. Papp, State of the University Address, March 29–30, 2012, 28–30, digital copy, Kennesaw State University Archives; President Daniel S. Papp to KSU students, faculty, and staff, January 25, 2012.

[563] *Kennesaw State University 2012–2017 Strategic Plan*; "Faculty Fellows," Center for Excellence in Teaching and Learning, http://www.kennesaw.edu/cetl/aboutus/fellows.html.

[564] Wicker interview, 40–45; Wesley K. Wicker, *The New Faces of Kennesaw State: The Campaign for Our Future*, 1–2, Kennesaw State University Archives.

[565] Wicker, *The New Faces of Kennesaw State*, 5–7.

[566] Wicker interview, 73–74; "Robert A. Lipson: 'A Gifted CEO, a Brilliant Physician,'" *Atlanta Business Chronicle*, February 12, 2007, http://www.bizjournals.com/atlanta/stories/2007/02/12/ focus3.html?page=all.

[567] The recession that began in 2008 forced Prillaman's former company, Caraustar Industries, into temporary bankruptcy, undermining its Carolina Foundation that had offered an additional $5 million for the construction of the Health Sciences Building. This was the largest of several losses to the comprehensive campaign that resulted from the sick national economy. Wicker, *The New Faces of Kennesaw State*, 7–9; Brandon Wilson, "New KSU Building Named Prillaman Hall," *Cherokee Tribune*, December 20, 2009; "Prillaman Hall Health Sciences Building Gives Students New Opportunities," The New Faces of Kennesaw State, http://www.kennesaw. edu/newfaces/about.shtml; "Kennesaw State University's New $56 Million Health Sciences Building Opens," Press Release, August 5, 2010, https://web.kennesaw.edu/news/stories/ kennesaw-state-university%E2%80%99s-new-56-million-health-sciences-building-opens.

[568] "Kennesaw State Showcases State-of-the-Art Brain Injury Research Lab," Press Release, July 25, 2011, http://web.kennesaw.edu/news/stories/kennesaw-state-showcases-state-art-brain-injury-research-lab; "Department of Defense Grant Funds Brain Injury Research," The New Faces of Kennesaw State, http://www.kennesaw.edu/newfaces/grants01.shtml.

[569] "Clendenin Scholarships Make Grad School Possible," The New Faces of Kennesaw State, http://www.kennesaw.edu/newfaces/scholarships01.shtml.

570 M. Bobbie Bailey, interview by Thomas A. Scott, May 9, 2008, no. 69, 1–4, 18, transcript, KSU Oral History Series, Kennesaw State University Archives.

571 Bailey interview, 6–7, 19–20; Wicker interview, 65.

572 Bailey interview, 12–14, 18–19; Kathryn Malone, "Biz Lawyer to KSU: Harness Technology," *Marietta Daily Journal*, February 3, 2011.

573 Bailey's contributions to the university did not stop with her own gifts. Along with President Papp, she helped to persuade her partner and friend, Joel Katz, to become involved in the comprehensive campaign. The result was a gift for an undisclosed amount to fund the Joel A. Katz Music and Entertainment Business Program, where students from the College of the Arts and the Coles College of Business could take twenty-four credit hours beyond their degree program to earn a certificate in entertainment and music management. Malone, "Biz Lawyer to KSU"; Wicker interview, 65–55; "Kennesaw State Earns All-Steinway Designation," The New Faces of Kennesaw State, http://www.kennesaw.edu/newfaces/majorgifts01.shtml.

574 Don Russell Clayton, interview by Stephen Watson, June 22, 2011, no.104, 3–6, 18–20, transcript, KSU Oral History Series, Kennesaw State University Archives; Karen Towers Klacsmann, "Athos Menaboni (1895–1990)," *New Georgia Encyclopedia*, July 3, 2010.

575 In addition to Wicker, President Siegel and Dean Meeks were among the top administrators to visit Clayton's home. Art professor Roberta Griffin and art gallery curator Suzanne Talbott also joined Wicker on a visit to see Clayton's Menaboni paintings. According to Griffin, Talbott was the first to write Clayton asking for the entire collection on the grounds that it would be more valuable for study if it was not broken up. Clayton interview, 2–4; Wicker interview, 62; Griffin interview, 17.

576 Clayton interview, 17.

577 Clayton interview, 17; Wicker interview, 62–63.

578 Wicker interview, 62–64; "Board of Regents Approves Name for Kennesaw State University Art Museum," KSU Press Release, April 18, 2012, http://web.kennesaw.edu/news/stories/board-regents-approves-name-kennesaw-state-university-art-museum. Mr. Zuckerman died on February 22, 2013, while the art museum was under construction. "KSU Mourns the Loss of Philanthropist and University Benefactor Bernard A. Zuckerman," KSU Press Release, February 24, 2013, http://web.kennesaw.edu/news/stories/ksu-mourns-loss-philanthropist-and-university-benefactor-bernard-zuckerman.

579 Wicker interview, 93–94; "Get the Facts — Continuing Education at Kennesaw State University," College of Continuing and Professional Education, www.kennesaw.edu/coned/about/fact-sheet.html; Frances Weyand, "Osher Lifelong Learning Institute Receives Second $1 Million Endowment," October 24, 2006, https://web.kennesaw.edu/news/stories/osher-lifelong-learning-institute-receives-second-1-million-endowment; "Osher Institute Offers a Lifetime of Learning," The New Faces of Kennesaw State, http://www.kennesaw.edu/newfaces/scholarships02.shtml.

580 Jodie Leon Hill, interview by Thomas A. Scott, November 11, 20, 25, 2008, no. 80, 9–10, 17–22, 26, transcript, KSU Oral History Series, Kennesaw State University Archives.

581 Hill interview, 42–46, 50–57; Wicker interview, 94; "Campus Dining Features Farm-Fresh Food," The New Faces of Kennesaw State, http://www.kennesaw.edu/newfaces/majorgifts02.shtml.

582 Wicker interview, 94–95.

583 Leonard Witt, interview by Thomas A. Scott, August 21, 2008, no. 75, 22, transcript, KSU Oral History Series, Kennesaw State University Archives; Lindsay Oberst, "Kennesaw State University Awards Ruth Ann Harnisch an Honorary Doctorate," May 10, 2012, https://web.kennesaw.edu/news/category/tags/commencement-2012.

584 Sabbaye McGriff, "Marcus Foundation Renews History and Holocaust Museum Grant," *Access*, July/August 2010, 3, http://www.kennesaw.edu/ur/downloads/Access_0710.pdf; Catherine Lewis, e-mail to Thomas Scott, March 5, 2012, "KSU Book correspondence," electronic file, Kennesaw State University Archives.

585 Wicker, *The New Faces of Kennesaw State*, 8; "2012 Holder Professional Development Awards," CETL, http://www.kennesaw.edu/cetl/faculty_funds/holder.html.

586 Wicker interview, 92; "Kennesaw State University Conducts I-Impact Robert Noyce Induction Ceremony," News Release, February 16, 2012, http://web.kennesaw.edu/news/stories/kennesaw-state-university-conducts-i-impact-robert-noyce-induction-ceremony-0; "KSU Receives $2.85 Million NSF Grant: Grant Will Fund Scholarships to Recruit, Train, Chemistry and Physics Teachers," Press Release, September 2, 2010, http://web.kennesaw.edu/news/stories/ksu-receives-285-million-grant-national-science-foundation.

587 Wicker interview, 54–58.

588 Wicker interview, 68.

589 Wicker interview, 69–70.

590 "Kennesaw State Celebrates Opening of Third Phase of 88-Acre Sports and Recreation Park," Press Release, April 30, 2012, http://web.kennesaw.edu/news/stories/kennesaw-state-celebrates-opening-88-acre-sports-and-recreation-park-0; "Board of Regents Approves Fee for Continued Development of KSU's Sports Park," Press Release, January 13, 2010, http://web.kennesaw.edu/news/stories/board-regents-approve-fee-continued-development-ksu%E2%80%99s-sports-park.

591 Wicker, *The New Faces of Kennesaw State*, 9; "2011 D1 Women's Soccer Championship," NCAA Photo Gallery, http://galleries.ncaa.com/gallery/1323114316627.

592 Wicker, *The New Faces of Kennesaw State*, 15.

593 Waples interview, 30; Wicker interview, 41, 71–72; "Kennesaw State University Football Timeline," Kennesaw State University Archives.

594 Vince Dooley, "A Summary and Recommendation," *Kennesaw State University Football Exploratory Committee Report, 2010*, http://www.kennesaw.edu/football/docs/full_report.pdf.

595 Dooley, "A Summary and Recommendation."

596 "Kennesaw State University Students Say 'Yes' to Football," KSU Press Release, November 16, 2010, https://web.kennesaw.edu/news/stories/kennesaw-state-university-students-say-yes-football-0.

597 "Kennesaw State University Names UConn's Vaughn Williams as Athletic Director," Press Release, April 5, 2011, https://web.kennesaw.edu/news/stories/kennesaw-state-university-names-uconn%E2%80%99s-vaughn-williams-athletic-director-0.

598 Fifth Third Bank, "History and Expansion," www.53.com/doc/pe/pe-about53-history-032609.pdf.

599 Jon Gillooly, "KSU Stadium to Be Named for Fifth Third," *Marietta Daily Journal*, February 15, 2013, 1A.

[600] "TOUCHDOWN! Kennesaw State University to Start Football Program in 2015," KSU Press Release, February 14, 2013, http://web.kennesaw.edu/news/stories/touchdown-kennesaw-state-university-start-football-program-2015; "Kennesaw State University Football Timeline," Kennesaw State University Archives.

[601] "Regents Approve Campus Consolidation Plan," January 10, 2012; "Regents Approve Names for Two Institutions and Mission Statements for Four," May 8, 2012; "Regents Approve New Names for Two Remaining Consolidated Institutions," August 7, 2012; and "Board of Regents Finalizes Consolidations, Appoints Presidents," January 8, 2013; University System of Georgia website: www.usg.edu/news/release/.

[602] "Board of Regents OKs new student recreation center for Kennesaw State," News Release, October 10, 2012, http://web.kennesaw.edu/news/stories/board-regents-oks-new-student-recreation-center-kennesaw-state.

Index

Adebayo, Akanmu G.   202, 318-319, 425
Aiken, V. Fred   92
Akerman, Robert H.   68
Amerson, Elaine M.   70
Andrews, Karen B.   345, 347, 429
Arnold, Terri Ferguson   76
Aronoff, Craig E.   152, 408
Ashcraft, Pat   92
Austin, Chester A. (Chet)   261
Azula, Andres (Andy)   151

Bailey, M. Bobbie   271, 362, 431
Barrett, Ernest   30, 85, 401
Beggs, George Henry   34
Bennett, David N.   139
Bennett, Ronnie   41
Bentley, Fred D. Sr.   15, 393
Black, Lendley C.   283, 306, 351
Blackwell, Barbara L.   76
Bobia, Rosa   193, 197
Boettler, Lynn   284, 354
Boyd, James E.   1
Bradham, Jo Allen   136, 139, 208, 407
Brawley, Dorothy E.   227, 415
Brumby, Otis A. Jr.   107, 401
Buchanan, W. Wray   201
Buddie, Amy M.   284
Burke, Meghan A.   283, 422
Burruss, A. L.   83, 85-86, 92, 94, 141, 191, 200, 213
Busbee, George D.   84-85, 89-93, 393
Bush, Vannevar   4

Caldwell, Harmon   8, 16, 395
Calhoun, Barbara S.   365
Carlisle, Ronald D.   70, 399
Carmichael, James V.   88-89, 92, 402

Carter, Wayne	89
Chan, Micah Y.	52
Chapman, Cy	83-84, 393
Clayton, Don Russell	364, 431
Clendenin, John and Ann	271
Clendenin, Thomas	361
Cochran, Theodore J. (Ted)	186
Coles, Michael J.	262, 306, 315, 420
Colotl, Jessica	348, 429
Cooper, Dennis E.	300
Cowan, Charles	2, 391
Crawford, Vernon	100
Crew, Stevan H.	398
Croft, Larry	92
Dambinova, Svetlana	361
Davis, Bowman O.	37, 397
Davis, Erroll B. Jr.	315
Davis, Herbert L. Jr.	52, 142
Davis, Patricia E. (Liza)	242
Daw, Curtis D. (Kurt)	240
Derado, Josip	281
Devine, Flora B.	239
Dewberry, Hubert	11, 14, 16-17, 19-20, 31, 394-395
Dinos, Jack A.	262
Dinos, Tony	153
DiPietro, Michele	284
Dobson, Charley G. Jr.	52
Dooley, Vince	379, 382, 384, 432
Downs, Harry S.	25
Driscoll, Robert L.	95, 142
Dunaway, William H.	78
Dunlap, James A.	16, 25
Dunning, Arthur N.	182
Durrett, William E. (Bill)	186
Dysart, Stanley H. (Stan)	289
Eagle, Lynnda Bernard	57
Economopoulos, Vassilis C.	117
Eisenach, Jeffrey	223-224
Epps, Janis Coombs	159
Fleming, James A.	229, 258, 415, 420
Forrester, Donald W.	159
Foster, William A. (Bud)	79
Fowler, Joanne E.	241-242, 244, 407

Fowler, Robert Dobbs	15, 394
Francis, Ronald H.	229
Fream, Jessie	285
Frick, Herman	108
Galliano, Grace	276
Gardner, John N.	156
Garner, Mary L.	277, 422
Garrison, Robert T.	78, 83, 85, 401-402
Gerges, Samy S.	334
Gibson, R. Wayne	146, 407
Giles, Martha M. (Marty)	116, 189
Gilliam, Kenneth P.	193
Gingrich, Newt	219, 221, 229, 259, 262, 414-416, 420
Givens, Jackie L.	205
Goltz, Randall C.	160
Goodrum, Charles L. (Chuck)	158
Greene, Robert J.	38-39, 164, 396
Greider, John C.	37, 142, 407
Griffin, Marvin	10, 14-15, 393
Griffin, Roberta T.	146-147, 407
Gustafson, Harriet S.	185, 411
Harmon, W. Ken	351, 353
Harp, Richard J.	365-366
Harnisch, Ruth Ann	370, 432
Harper, Cullene M.	125, 259
Harris, Charles A.	85
Harris, David I.	172
Harris, Joe Frank	79, 83, 86, 92, 94, 135
Henderson, Jack	83
Henderson, James E. (Mack)	153
Hepler, G. Ruth	156, 407
Hill, G. William IV	vii, 279, 283-284, 409
Hill, Jodie Leon	366, 431
Hill, Robert W. (Bob)	215, 227, 463
Hill, Terence	287
Hillman, Sandra M.	277
Hinds, Randy C.	166, 425
Hinton, Virginia C.	37, 405
Hoerrner, Keisha L.	157, 408
Holder, Thomas M.	267, 306, 417, 420
Holley, B. Earle	76
Hopkins, Roger E.	52, 76, 125, 396, 398
Hopper, Eleanor T. (Toby)	242
Hubbard, Elaine M.	52, 398

Huck, Eugene R.	73, 103, 140, 404
Ingle, Tony	285-286, 288
Ingram, G. Conley	78
Jackson, Eddie	71
Jeffrey, Christina F.	227-228
Johnson, Lawrence V.	13, 24
Johnson, Robert L.	181
Johnston, Linda M.	423
Jolly, James R.	306
Jones, David M. Jr.	39, 147, 397, 407
Kalafut, George W.	420
Kaspers, Candace B.	234, 417-418
Keene, Thomas H.	200-201, 319, 351, 413
King, Nancy S.	156-157, 408
King, Rob	285-286
King, Ronald E.	261
Kinney, Alberta	93
Kinney, Bill	12, 83-84, 93, 402, 423
Kolka, James W.	140, 155
Krise, June Rowland	86, 88-89, 92
Krise, Randy	88-89
Krise, Richard	92
Landrum, James D. (Spec)	104, 404
Landrum, Mildred W.	407
Lasher, Harry J.	141, 407
Lester, Army III	277, 283, 421
Levingston, Bari	236-237
Lewis, Catherine M.	371
Lipson, Robert A.	356, 430
Loomis, Kimberly S.	277, 421
Loyd, Pat	86
Maddox, James D.	93
Maples, Karen P.	76
Marcus, Bernard (Bernie)	371
Marek, Jessica	285
Martin, Carol L.	38, 76
Martin, S. Walter	20, 26
Matthews, Kathy L.	242
McCall, Mary B.	27, 393
McClure, Hoyt L.	14
McCollum, Herbert	11-12, 17, 19-20, 393

McCrummen, Norman H. III	259, 420
McDearmid, Robert	41
Meadows, Mark E. (Gene)	38, 40
Meeks, Joseph D.	145-146, 302, 407
Meredith, Thomas C.	302, 426
Mescon, Michael H.	152, 213
Mescon, Timothy S.	153, 213, 215, 222, 306, 414
Miles, Madeline M.	397-398
Mitchell, Beverly F.	279, 416
Morgan, Inez P.	38, 405
Morris, Barry J.	320
Moses, Oral L.	193, 197, 413
Muir, Lois E.	235
Noble, Linda M.	143, 407
Olive, Bobby L.	70
Osher, Bernard	365-366
Palmer, C. Grady	46, 398, 407
Papageorge, Linda M.	117
Papp, Daniel S.	vii, x, 4, 211, 266, 302, 306, 392, 424-426, 428-430
Paracka, Daniel J.	202, 319
Paris, Nita A.	327
Patterson, Mark W.	135, 407
Perkins, Julia L. (Judy)	244, 407
Peterson, Laurence I.	373
Pettit, Joseph M.	4, 309, 392
Pope, Carol J.	242, 419
Portch, Stephen	240
Powell, Mac	194
Prillaman, Bob M.	357, 430
Propst, H. Dean	212, 224, 414-415
Pusateri, Thomas P.	283
Radow, Norman J.	265, 267, 420
Ratchford, Jerome	180, 242-243, 309, 410-411, 419, 429
Reed, Glenn R. Jr.	78, 401
Reggio, Patricia H. (Patti)	207, 413
Ridley, Helen S.	103, 113, 404-405
Roach, S. Frederick Jr.	100, 403, 407
Robbins, Sarah R.	208
Roberts, Derrell Clayton	33
Roberts, Gary B.	277, 281, 421
Roebuck, Deborah Britt	301
Roper, Thomas B. Jr.	155

Rugg, Edwin A.	vii, 125-126, 400, 406, 417
Rundles, Ruth	76
Rushton, Archie S.	12
Sachs, Charlotte S.	—
Salter, M. Thomson III	41
Sanders, Carl	ix, 1, 15, 19, 89
Sanford, Steadman V.	8
Sansing, Mike	174, 285-286
Sawyer, Jerry D.	216, 405
Schaufele, Christopher B.	203, 407, 413
Scherer, Stephen E.	50, 155, 398
Schwartz, Alan	236-238, 418
Scott, Kathy Sherlock	53, 398
Shaw, Royce Q.	201
Shealy, E. Howard Jr.	136
Shuttlesworth, Duane E.	405
Siegel, Betty L.	x, 99, 104, 110, 388, 406-407, 409-410, 414, 418, 425, 430
Siegel, Joel	106, 109
Silver, Joseph H. (Pete)	180
Simpson, George L. Jr.	26, 399, 401-402
Sims, Marlene R.	204
Sims, Stanley G.	174, 293
Stapleton, Morgan L.	72
Stevens, Larry J.	226, 229, 260, 415
Stillwell, Fred E.	265
Stilson, Frederick C.	186
Stockton, James Clinton (Clint)	327-328
Straley, Tina H.	164
Sturgis, Horace Wilbur	23
Sturgis, Sue Cowan	23, 32
Swain, Howell	86
Swain, Mary H.	40, 398
Swindell, Barbara J.	147
Tapp, William R. Jr.	19, 393-394
Tashchian, Armen	217
Tate. James B. (J.B.)	48-50, 61-62, 81
Taylor, Patrick L.	147-148, 407
Terman, Frederick E.	5
Thompson, Mary B.	404
Thompson, William P.	95, 100
Tucker, Laura	285
Tumlin, R. Steve	78
Turner, Carol L. (Cary)	157
Turner, Jennifer	172

Venalainen, Marjo	285, 293
Wachniak, Lana J.	274
Walker, Ralph W. III	60, 398
Wallace, Deborah T.	244, 416
Wallace, Melonie J.	61, 398
Walraven, Wesley C.	37
Waples, David L.	172, 409-410
Wheeler, Lawrence D.	265, 420
Whittlesey, Valerie W.	277, 280, 283, 422
Wicker, Wesley K.	300, 355, 420-421, 430
Willey, Diane L.	159
Williams, Charles	76
Williams, Robert B.	164, 409
Williams, Vaughn	384-385, 432
Willingham, Harold S.	394-395
Wilson, Joe Mack	83-84, 86, 89, 92-93, 128, 151, 191, 393, 402-403
Wingfield, Harold L.	193, 412
Witt, Leonard	370, 432
York, E.T.	109
Youngblood, Betty J.	73, 186
Yow, Dede	vii, 208, 280, 392, 403, 407-409, 412-414, 416, 421-422, 424
Zinsmeister, Dorothy D.	301, 407
Zoghby, Mary	73, 400, 405, 407
Zumoff, Nancy E.	202-203, 413